Communications
in Computer and Information Science 992

Commenced Publication in 2007
Founding and Former Series Editors:
Phoebe Chen, Alfredo Cuzzocrea, Xiaoyong Du, Orhun Kara, Ting Liu,
Krishna M. Sivalingam, Dominik Ślęzak, Takashi Washio, and Xiaokang Yang

More information about this series at http://www.springer.com/series/7899

Brian Donnellan · Cornel Klein ·
Markus Helfert · Oleg Gusikhin (Eds.)

Smart Cities, Green Technologies and Intelligent Transport Systems

7th International Conference, SMARTGREENS
and 4th International Conference, VEHITS 2018
Funchal-Madeira, Portugal, March 16–18, 2018
Revised Selected Papers

 Springer

Editors
Brian Donnellan
School of Business
Maynooth University
Maynooth, Ireland

Cornel Klein
CT RDA SSI
Siemens AG
Munich, Bayern, Germany

Markus Helfert
Dublin City University
Dublin, Ireland

Oleg Gusikhin
Ford Research and Advanced Engineer
Dearborn, MI, USA

ISSN 1865-0929   ISSN 1865-0937 (electronic)
Communications in Computer and Information Science
ISBN 978-3-030-26632-5   ISBN 978-3-030-26633-2 (eBook)
https://doi.org/10.1007/978-3-030-26633-2

This Springer imprint is published by the registered company Springer Nature Switzerland AG
The registered company address is: Gewerbestrasse 11, 6330 Cham, Switzerland

Preface

This book includes extended and revised versions of a set of selected papers from SMARTGREENS 2018 (7th International Conference on Smart Cities and Green ICT Systems) and VEHITS 2018 (4th International Conference on Vehicle Technology and Intelligent Transport Systems), held in Funchal, Madeira, Portugal, during March 16–18.

SMARTGREENS 2018 received 56 paper submissions from 23 countries, of which 11% are included in this book. VEHITS 2018 received 108 paper submissions from 31 countries, of which 11% are included in this book.

The papers were selected by the event chairs and their selection is based on a number of criteria that include the classifications and comments provided by the Program Committee members, the session chairs' assessment, and also the program chairs' global view of all papers included in the technical program. The authors of selected papers were then invited to submit a revised and extended version of their papers having at least 30% innovative material.

The purpose of the 7th International Conference on Smart Cities and Green ICT Systems (SMARTGREENS) was to bring together researchers, designers, developers, and practitioners interested in the advances and applications in the field of smart cities, green information and communication technologies, sustainability, energy-aware systems and technologies.

The purpose of the 4th International Conference on Vehicle Technology and Intelligent Transport Systems (VEHITS) was to bring together engineers, researchers and practitioners interested in the advances and applications in the field of vehicle technology and intelligent transport systems. This conference focuses on innovative applications, tools, and platforms in all areas of technology such as signal processing, wireless communications, informatics and electronics, related to different kinds of vehicles, including cars, off-road vehicles, trains, ships, underwater vehicles, or flying machines, and the intelligent transportation systems that connect and manage large numbers of vehicles, not only in the context of smart cities but in many other application domains.

The papers selected to be included in this book contribute to the understanding of relevant trends of current research on smart cities, green ICT systems, vehicle technology and intelligent transport systems including: smart grids, monitoring data, Internet of Things, electric vehicles, intelligent transportation systems, transportation planning and traffic operation.

With the advances of new and innovative technologies, the field of smart and connected cities is expected to grow even further. Topics such as data privacy, Internet of Things, and architecture or business models for smart cities are becoming increasingly important for both researchers and practitioners. At the same time sustainability and energy are two crucial aspects to consider for the advances and applications in the field of vehicle technology and intelligent transport systems as well as smart cities. In the next few years, we can expect a range of innovative technologies and research results for these topics within the field of smart cities and intelligent transportation systems such as energy and vehicle analytics and autonomous and connected vehicles.

We would like to thank all the authors for their contributions and also the reviewers who helped ensure the quality of this publication.

March 2018

Brian Donnellan
Cornel Klein
Markus Helfert
Oleg Gusikhin

Organization

SMARTGREENS Conference Chair

Markus Helfert   Dublin City University, Ireland

VEHITS Conference Chair

Oleg Gusikhin   Ford Motor Company, USA

SMARTGREENS Program Co-chairs

Cornel Klein   Siemens AG, Germany
Brian Donnellan   Maynooth University, Ireland

VEHITS Program Chair

Markus Helfert   Dublin City University, Ireland

SMARTGREENS Program Committee

Javier M. Aguiar	Universidad de Valladolid, Spain
Carlos Antunes	University of Coimbra/INESC Coimbra, Portugal
Tanvi Banerjee	Wright State University, USA
Ahcene Bendjoudi	DTISI, CERIST Research Center, Algiers, Algeria
Simona Bernardi	Universidad de Zaragoza, Spain
Nik Bessis	Edge Hill University, UK
Riccardo Bettati	Texas A&M University, USA
Blanca Caminero	Universidad de Castilla-La Mancha, Spain
Ken Christensen	University of South Florida, USA
Calin Ciufudean	Stefan cel Mare University, Romania
Cléver Ricardo de Farias	University of São Paulo, Brazil
Paloma Díaz	Universidad Carlos III de Madrid, Spain
Yong Ding	Karlsruhe Institute of Technology, Germany
Venizelos Efthymiou	University of Cyprus, Cyprus
Rania El-Gazzar	University College of Southeast Norway, Norway
Tullio Facchinetti	University of Pavia, Italy
Miguel Garcia Pineda	Universitat de Valencia, Spain
Bela Genge	University of Targu Mures, Romania
Giovanni Giuliani	HPE Italy, Italy
Andre Gradvohl	State University of Campinas, Brazil
Tahir Hanif	Simplex Project Management Limited, UK
Piyush Harsh	Zurich University of Applied Sciences, Switzerland

Muhammad Hasan	Texas A&M University, USA
Kerry Hinton	Centre for Energy Efficient Telecommunications University of Melbourne, Australia
Hartmut Hinz	University of Applied Sciences Frankfurt, Germany
Seongsoo Hong	Seoul National University, Korea, Republic of
Filip Idzikowski	Poznan University of Technology, Poland
Iskandar Ishak	Universiti Putra Malaysia, Malaysia
Bo Jørgensen	University of Southern Denmark, Denmark
Jai Kang	Rochester Institute of Technology, USA
Stamatis Karnouskos	SAP, Germany
Essam Khalil	Cairo University, Egypt
Cornel Klein	Siemens AG, Germany
Sesil Koutra	UMONS, Belgium
Mani Krishna	University of Massachusetts Amherst, USA
Sanja Lazarova-Molnar	University of Southern Denmark, Denmark
Christopher Lee	Massachusetts Institute of Technology, USA
Yann-Hang Lee	Arizona State University, USA
Michela Longo	Politecnico di Milano, Italy
Marcin Luckner	Warsaw University of Technology, Poland
Marco Lützenberger	Technische Universität Berlin, Germany
Zheng Ma	University of Southern Denmark, Denmark
Prabhat Mahanti	University of New Brunswick, Canada
Daisuke Mashima	Advanced Digital Sciences Center, Singapore
Ningfang Mi	Northeastern University, USA
Sumita Mishra	Rochester Institute of Technology, USA
Elsa Negre	Paris-Dauphine University, France
Edoardo Patti	Politecnico di Torino, Italy
Marco Pau	E.ON Energy Research Center - RWTH Aachen University, Germany
Cathryn Peoples	Ulster University, UK
Philip Pong	The University of Hong Kong, SAR China
Evangelos Pournaras	ETH Zurich, Switzerland
Manuel Prieto-Matias	Complutense University of Madrid, Spain
Gang Qu	University of Maryland, USA
Gang Quan	Florida International University, USA
Iván Razo-Zapata	Luxembourg Institute of Science and Technology, Luxembourg
Ana Carolina Riekstin	École de Technologie Supérieure, Montréal, Quebec, Canada
Eva González Romera	University of Extremadura, Spain
Enrique Romero-Cadaval	University of Extremadura, Spain
Javad Sardroud	Azad University Central Tehran Branch, Iran, Islamic Republic of
Gerard Smit	University of Twente, The Netherlands
Jignesh Solanki	West Virginia University, USA
Norvald Stol	NTNU, Norway

Vaibhav Sundriyal	ODU Research Foundation, USA
Paolo Tenti	University of Padua, Italy
Dimitrios Tsoumakos	Ionian University, Greece
Athina Vakali	Aristotle University, Greece
Alexandr Vasenev	TNO, The Netherlands
Silvano Vergura	Polytechnic University of Bari, Italy
Igor Wojnicki	AGH University of Science and Technology, Poland
Yinlong Xu	University of Science and Technology of China, China
Ramin Yahyapour	University Göttingen, Germany
Chau Yuen	Singapore University of Technology and Design, Singapore
Sherali Zeadally	University of Kentucky, USA
Yayun Zhou	Siemens AG, Germany
Sotirios Ziavras	New Jersey Institute of Technology, USA
Imran Zualkernan	American University of Sharjah, UAE

VEHITS Program Committee

Konstantinos Ampountolas	University of Glasgow, UK
Constantinos Antoniou	Technical University of Munich, Germany
Ramachandran Balakrishna	Caliper Corporation, USA
B. Bhandari	JNTUH, India
Neila Bhouri	IFSTTAR, France
Catalin Buiu	Universitatea Politehnica din Bucuresti, Romania
Rodrigo Carlson	Federal University of Santa Catarina, Brazil
Sandra Cespedes	Universidad de Chile, Chile
Gihwan Cho	Chonbuk University, Korea, Republic of
Thomas Christaller	Fraunhofer, Germany
Baldomero Coll-Perales	Universidad Miguel Hernandez de Elche, Spain
Thanh-Son Dao	General Motors, USA
Michel Devy	LAAS CNRS, France
Mariagrazia Dotoli	Politecnico di Bari, Italy
Bertrand Ducourthial	Université de Technologie de Compiegne, France
César Ducruet	CNRS, France
Mehmet Efe	Hacettepe University, Turkey
Nicola Epicoco	Politecnico di Bari, Italy
Peppino Fazio	University of Calabria, Italy
Lino Figueiredo	Instituto Superior de Engenharia do Porto, Portugal
Paul Green	University of Michigan Transportation Research Institute, USA
Yi Guo	The University of Texas at Dallas, USA
Oleg Gusikhin	Ford Motor Company, USA
Andreas Hegyi	Delft University of Technology, The Netherlands
Markus Helfert	Dublin City University, Ireland
Yoichi Hori	University of Tokyo, Japan
Zhongsheng Hou	Beijing Jiaotong University, China

Zechun Hu	Tsinghua University, China
Hocine Imine	IFSTTAR, France
Chul-Goo Kang	Konkuk University, Korea, Republic of
Fu-Chien Kao	Da-Yeh University, Taiwan
Hakil Kim	Inha University, Korea, Republic of
Xiangjie Kong	Dalian University of Technology, China
Anastasios Kouvelas	ETH Zurich, Switzerland
Zdzislaw Kowalczuk	Gdansk University of Technology, Poland
Milan Krbálek	Czech Technical University, Czech Republic
Karl-Heinz Krempels	RWTH Aachen University, Germany
Wei Liu	University of Glasgow, UK
Johann Marquez-Barja	University of Antwerpen - imec, Belgium
Zeljko Medenica	Altran, Germany
Lyudmila Mihaylova	University of Sheffield, UK
Jânio Monteiro	Universidade do Algarve, Portugal
Pedro Moura	Institute of Systems and Robotics, University of Coimbra, Portugal
Pamela Murray-Tuite	Virginia Tech, USA
Mirco Nanni	Italian National Research Council, Italy
Jennie Oxley	Monash University, Australia
Dario Pacciarelli	Roma Tre University, Italy
Sara Paiva	Instituto Politécnico de Viana do Castelo, Portugal
Markos Papageorgiou	Technical University of Crete, Greece
Ioannis Papamichail	Technical University of Crete, Greece
Brian Park	University of Virginia, USA
Alexander Paz	University of Nevada Las Vegas, USA
Paulo Pereirinha	Polytechnic of Coimbra, Portugal
Fernando Pereñiguez	University Centre of Defence, Spanish Air Force Academy, Spain
Hesham Rakha	Virginia Polytechnic Institute and State University, USA
Claudio Roncoli	Aalto University, Finland
José Santa Lozano	University of Murcia, Spain
Oleg Saprykin	Samara State Aerospace University, Russian Federation
Sanjay Sharma	Plymouth University, UK
Shih-Lung Shaw	University of Tennessee, USA
Silvia Siri	University of Genoa, Italy
Uwe Stilla	Technische Universität München, Germany
Wencong Su	University of Michigan-Dearborn, USA
Tatsuya Suzuki	Nagoya University, Japan
Wai Yuen Szeto	The University of Hong Kong, SAR China
Richard Tay	RMIT University, Australia
Helena Titheridge	University College London, UK
Tomer Toledo	Technion - Israel Institute of Technology, Israel
Esko Turunen	Tampere University of Technology, Department of Mathematics, Finland

Emil Vassev	Lero - The Irish Software Research Centre, Ireland
Francesco Viti	University of Luxembourg, Luxembourg
Peter Vortisch	Karlsruhe Institute of Technology, Germany
Mengqi Wang	University of Michigan-Dearborn, USA
Xiubin Wang	Texas A&M University, USA
Kyongsu Yi	Seoul National University, Korea, Republic of
Peng Zhang	Shangai University, China

SMARTGREENS Additional Reviewers

Tobias Küster	DAI-Labor, TU Berlin, Germany
Ioannis Mytilinis	National Technical University of Athens, Greece

VEHITS Additional Reviewers

Claudia Bongiovanni	EPFL, Switzerland
Graziana Cavone	University of Cagliari, Italy
Duc-Tien Dang-Nguyen	Dublin City University, Ireland
Alexander Hanel	Technische Universität München, Germany
Zaher Hinbarji	Dublin City University, Ireland
Teemu Itkonen	Aalto University, Finland
Antti Knutas	Lero, Irish Software Research Centre, Ireland
Konstantinos Makantasis	Technical University of Crete, Greece
Aleksas Mamkaitis	Dublin City University (DCU), Ireland
Francisco Martinez	University of Zaragoza, Spain
Antonio Meireles	ISEP, Portugal
Hermes Moraes	Universite de Technologie de Compiegne, France
Kyriakos Mountakis	Technical University of Crete, Greece
Fabian Ohler	Fraunhofer FIT, Germany
Christian Samsel	Valtech Mobility GmbH, Germany

Invited Speakers

Miguel A. Sotelo	Universidad de Alcalá, Spain
Karl-Heinz Krempels	RWTH Aachen University, Germany
David Prendergast	Human in the Loop, Ireland
Uwe Plank-Wiedenbeck	Bauhaus-Universität Weimar, Germany

Contents

xiv   Contents

Smart Cities and Green ICT Systems

Non-linear Autoregressive Neural Networks to Forecast Short-Term Solar Radiation for Photovoltaic Energy Predictions

Alessandro Aliberti[1], Lorenzo Bottaccioli[1], Giansalvo Cirrincione[3],
Enrico Macii[2], Andrea Acquaviva[4], and Edoardo Patti[1(✉)]

[1] Department of Control and Computer Engineering,
Politecnico di Torino, Torino, Italy
{alessandro.aliberti,lorenzo.bottaccioli,edoardo.patti}@polito.it
[2] Interuniversity Department of Regional and Urban Studies and Planning,
Politecnico di Torino, Torino, Italy
enrico.macii@polito.it
[3] Universite de Picardie Jules Verne, Amiens, France
giansalvo.cirrincione@u-picardie.fr
[4] Department of Electrical, Electronic, and Information Engineering "Guglielmo
Marconi", Università di Bologna, Bologna, Italy
andrea.acquaviva@unibo.it

Abstract. Nowadays, green energy is considered as a viable solution to hinder CO_2 emissions and greenhouse effects. Indeed, it is expected that Renewable Energy Sources (RES) will cover 40% of the total energy request by 2040. This will move forward decentralized and cooperative power distribution systems also called smart grids. Among RES, solar energy will play a crucial role. However, reliable models and tools are needed to forecast and estimate with a good accuracy the renewable energy production in short-term time periods. These tools will unlock new services for smart grid management.

In this paper, we propose an innovative methodology for implementing two different non-linear autoregressive neural networks to forecast Global Horizontal Solar Irradiance (GHI) in short-term time periods (i.e. from future 15 to 120 min). Both neural networks have been implemented, trained and validated exploiting a dataset consisting of four years of solar radiation values collected by a real weather station. We also present the experimental results discussing and comparing the accuracy of both neural networks. Then, the resulting GHI forecast is given as input to a Photovoltaic simulator to predict energy production in short-term time periods. Finally, we present the results of this Photovoltaic energy estimation discussing also their accuracy.

This work was partially supported by the Italian project "Edifici a Zero Consumo Energetico in Distretti Urbani Intelligenti".

B. Donnellan et al. (Eds.): SMARTGREENS 2018/VEHITS 2018, CCIS 992, pp. 3–22, 2019.
https://doi.org/10.1007/978-3-030-26633-2_1

Keywords: Solar radiation forecast · Artificial neural networks · AR · ARMA · Dynamic system · Photovoltaic system · Energy forecast · Renewable energy

1   Introduction

Nowadays, to contrast negative effects of pollution, global warming and waste of energy, green energy represents a very attractive solution, especially solar energy [13]. Indeed, applications like Photovoltaic (PV) systems are changing the electrical energy production, consumption and distribution in our cities [21]. We are witnessing the transaction of our society from centralized and hierarchical power distribution systems to distributed and cooperative ones, generally called Smart Grids. The technology introduced by this new philosophy is opening the electrical marketplace to new actors (e.g. prosumers and energy aggregators). In classic power grids, the stability is achieved by consolidated generation plants using primary and secondary reserve at large-scale [14]. Whilst, in a Smart Grid scenario, new actors can actively contribute to load-balancing by fostering novel services for network management and stability. Demand/Response [39] is an example of such applications for Smart Grid management. It permits to achieve a temporary virtual power plant [44] by changing the energy consumption patterns of consumers (i) to match energy produced by renewable energy systems or (ii) to fulfil grid operation requirements. This process is generally done every 15 min. In these applications, the amount of available energy must be known in advance to optimize the production of power plants [1] and to match energy production with consumption. Thus, we need tools to forecast with a good accuracy of solar radiation and, consequently, solar energy.

Several studies were proposed in the literature to find mathematical and physical models to estimate and forecast solar radiation, such as stochastic models based on time-series [3, 22, 45]. Moreover, classical linear time-series models have been widely used [8]. However, these studies have proven that these methodologies often are not sufficient in the analysis and prediction of solar radiation. This is due to the non-stationary and non-linearity of solar radiation time-series data [25, 30]. Furthermore, stochastic models are based on the probability estimation. This leads to a difficult forecast of the solar radiation time-series. To overcome these limits, non-linear approaches, such as Artificial Neural Networks (ANNs), were considered by many researchers as powerful tools to predict such phenomenons [46]. Generally, ANNs do not require knowledge of internal system parameters and they offer a compact solution for multiple variable problems [34]. However, also the use of an ANN to forecast a phenomenon introduces an error, the so-called *prediction error* [52]. As a result, these models need optimizations to reduce this error. With respect to presented literature solutions to forecast solar radiation, the scientific novelty of our methodology consists of using Multilayer Perceptron, which is the artificial neural network most used for this kind of applications [12]. Generally, most literature methodologies rely on the single past value to perform the forecast [7]. Whilst, the proposed solutions allow to reduce significantly the *prediction error* by using a set of regressors to perform predictions, as discussed in our previous work [2]. However, differently from [2], our goal is to better optimize the neural architecture by adding further levels of difficulty. In particular, we used a more complex and larger dataset to better forecast the solar radiation in short-term, i.e. from future 15 min up to next 2 h.

In this paper, we present and compare two Nonlinear Autoregressive neural networks to forecast short-term solar radiation that is then applied to estimate PV energy production. We trained and validated both neural networks with a dataset consisting of four years of Global Horizontal Solar Irradiance (GHI) samples collected by a real weather station. Both neural networks are Multilayer Perceptron based and they exploit a certain number of regressors to predict GHI in a range of next 15 min up to 2 h. Then, GHI forecast is given as input to our PV simulator [6] that exploits GIS (Geographic Information System) tools to simulate energy production. We also provide an exhaustive comparison of this work with our previous paper [2], highlighting differences and improvements. Finally, we discuss advantages and disadvantages of choosing a neural network rather than another, among those developed and analyzed.

The rest of the paper is organized as follows. Section 2 discusses the followed methodology to define our neural networks for short-term solar radiation forecast. Section 3 details all the steps performed to initialize, train and validate both our neural networks. Section 4 presents the results of solar radiation forecast given by the proposed ANNs. Section 5 briefly introduce our PV simulator [6] and, then, presents the estimation results on PV energy simulations that exploit foretasted solar radiation output of the proposed neural networks. Finally, Sect. 6 discusses our concluding remarks.

2 Methodology

Predicting the energy producuction of a PV system means being able to forecast the level of GHI to which the PV system is exposed to. In turn, predicting the values of GHI means working with time-series information. This kind of information identifies a sequence of values chronologically ordered [16]. The study and manipulation of time-series models brings different benefits. Mainly, it allows: (i) in understanding the underlying forces and structures that produced the observed data and (ii) in fiting a model and in proceeding to forecast and monitor or even feedback and feed-forward control [33].

2.1 The Multilayer Perceptron

Nowadays, one of the most effective methods for prediction is based on neural networks [29]. This is due to their versatility and their ability to model a wide range of systems reducing development time and offering better performances [48]. In the study of systems based on time-series, the most powerful and performing family of ANNs is the Multilayer Perceptron (MLP) [12]. These types of neural networks are composed of units, called nodes or neurons, and organized in a layer of inputs, one or more hidden layers and an output layer. The MLP is a feed-forward architecture with fully connected layers. Connections between units are characterized by adjustable parameters called weights. This refers to the strength of a connection between two nodes [23]. Each neuron computes a function of the sum of the weighted inputs. This function is also called *activation function.*

In this work, we used two different MLP-network architectures. Both are characterized by (i) an hidden layer of neurons with the hyperbolic tangent activation function f and (ii) an output layer with a linear activation function F. The functional model is given by:

$$\hat{y}_i(w, W) = F_i(\sum_{j=1}^{q} W_{ij}h_j + W_{i0}) = F_i(\sum_{j=0}^{q} W_{ij}f_j(\sum_{l=1}^{m} w_{jl}u_l + w_{j0}) + W_{i0}) \quad (1)$$

Weights are specified by the matrices $W = [W_{ij}]$ and $w = [w_{jl}]$; where W_{ij} scales the connection between the hidden unit j and the output unit i and w_{jl} instead the connection between the hidden unit j and the input unit l. The corresponding biases are W_{i0} and w_{j0}. These weights are vectorized in a vector θ. The input units are represented by the vector $u(t)$ while the vector h represents the hidden neuron outputs. The outputs of the network, $\hat{y}_i$, are estimated by Eq. 1. The parameters are determined during the *training process*, which requires a *training set* Z^N, composed of a set of inputs, $u(t)$, and corresponding desired outputs, $y(t)$, specified by:

$$Z^N = [u(t), y(t)], \ t = 1, ..., N \quad (2)$$

The training phase allows to determine a mapping from the set of training data to the set of possible weights:

$$Z^N \rightarrow \hat{\theta} \quad (3)$$

the network can predict $\hat{y}(t)$ that can be compared to the true output $y(t)$. The *prediction error approach* is instead based on the introduction of a measure of closeness in terms of a mean square error criterion, as specified by:

$$V_N(\theta, Z^N) = \frac{1}{2N} \sum_{t=1}^{N} [y(t) - \hat{y}(t|\theta)]^T [y(t) - \hat{y}(t|\theta)] \quad (4)$$

Weights are then found as:

$$\hat{\theta} = arg_\theta min V_N(\theta, Z^N) \quad (5)$$

by some kind of iterative minimization scheme:

$$\theta^{i+1} = \theta^i + \mu^i + f^i \quad (6)$$

where θ^i specifies the current iteration, f^i the search direction and μ^i the step size.

2.2   System Identification

This section details the adopted methodology to use an ANN to predict solar radiation in short-term. Based on the methodology presented in [32] and as widely detailed in [2], the procedure to identify a dynamical system consists of four steps: (i) *Experiment*, (ii) *Model Structure Selection*, (iii) *Model Estimation* and (iv) *Model Validation* (see Fig. 1).

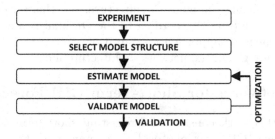

Fig. 1. System identification procedure [2].

The *Experiment* represents the problem analysis, data sampling and collection phase. This phase is the keystone of the whole process. Some of the main issues in this stage consist on: (i) choosing the sampling frequency, (ii) designing suitable input signals, and (iii) pre-processing the dataset. Data pre-processing may include some non-linearity tests and disturbances removal. If the dataset is well organized, all the next steps in Fig. 1 will have less chance to fail. Generally, a big and relevant amount of data is needed to train and validate a neural network. Moreover, an higher number of data allows better forecasting performance [41]. However, it is necessary to avoid overfitting. This means to avoid unknowingly extract some of the residual variation (i.e. the noise) as if that variation represented underlying model structure. [50]. Then, the collected data must be divided into two datasets: training-set and validation-set [19]. Both datasets are used in training and validation phases of the neural network that are *Estimate Model* and *Validate Model* in Fig. 1, respectively. The *Model Structure Selection* phase identifies the correct architecture model and the number of regressors [32]. Generally, this selection is more difficult in nonlinear cases than in linear [9]. In time-series, the regressors represent the previous samplings with respect to the predicted ones [29]. Once the best network model and the appropriate number of regressors are identified, in the *Model Estimation* phase, the network is first implemented and then trained. In time-series scenario, training a neural network is needed to provide: (i) the vector containing desired output data; (ii) the number of regressors to define the prediction; (iii) the vector containing the weights of both input-to-hidden and hidden-to-output layers and lastly (iv) the data structure containing the parameters associated with the selected training algorithm. The training process produces a training error, which represents the network performance index [41]. The *Model Validation* allows validating the trained network in order to evaluate its capabilities [28]. In time-series predictions, the most common validation method consists of analyzing the residuals (i.e. prediction errors) by cross-validating the validation-set [38]. This analysis provides the *test error* [41], that is an index considered as a generalization of the error estimation. This index should not be too high compared to training error, if this happens the network could over-fit the training-set. This means that the selected model structure contains too many weights. In this case, it is required to return in the *Estimate Model* step to change and redefine some structural parameters by optimizing the whole architecture. For this purpose, the superfluous weights must be pruned according to the Optimal Brain Surgeon, which represents one of the most important optimization strategies [17]. Consequently, once new weights are given, the network architecture must be re-validated.

3 Neural Networks for Short-Term GHI Forecast

The purpose of this work consists of forecasting short-term Global Horizontal Solar Irradiance (GHI) for photovoltaic energy predictions. To deal with these time-series data, we adopted, and then compared, two ANNs: (i) Nonlinear Autoregressive neural network (NAR) and (ii) Nonlinear Autoregressive Moving Average neural network (NARMA). NAR belongs to the family of Nonlinear Autoregressive Exogenous Model (NARX) [40]. It is generally considered as one of the best tools for time-series analysis and does not suffer of stability problems [42]. This is due to its nonlinear autoregressive model which has exogenous inputs. This neural network model bases its prediction on (i) a variable range of past values and also on (ii) the current and past values of the driving exogenous inputs of the time-series in analysis. However, this process produces a prediction error that is the knowledge of the past. Indeed, the presence of this error as result of prediction means that the future values of the time-series cannot be predicted exactly. This family of ANNs is characterized by the following equation:

$$y_t = F(y_{t-1}, y_{t-2}, y_{t-3}, ..., u_t, u_{t-1}, u_{t-2}, u_{t-3}, ...) + \varepsilon_t \tag{7}$$

where y_t is the variable of interest; while u_t represents the externally determined variable at time t in Eq. 7. Information about u_t and previous values of u and y helps on predicting y_t with a prediction error ε_t.

On the other hand, NARMA belongs to the family of Nonlinear Autoregressive Moving Average Exogenous Model (NARMAX) [11]. It represents a generalization of the NAR model. However, this model realizes a feed-forward network where a predictor will have a feedback when the regressors are selected. This family is characterized by the following equation:

$$y_t = F(y_{t-1}, y_{t-2}, y_{t-3}, ..., u_t, u_{t-1}, u_{t-2}, u_{t-3}, ...) + C(q^{-1}) + \varepsilon_t \tag{8}$$

where y_t and u_t are the variable of interest and the externally determined variable at time t, respectively; ε_t is the prediction error; C is a polynomial in the backward shift operator expressed as:

$$C(q^{-1}) = 1 + c_1 q^{-1} + ... + c_{nc} q^{-nc} \tag{9}$$

Consequently, the past prediction errors depend on the model output and they are able to establish a feedback.

Comparing the two proposed models, the major difference is that NARMA is a *Recurrent Neural Network* [27], while NAR is not. Thus, NAR has a predictor without feedback while NARMA has feedback through the choice of regressors. Hence, future network inputs will depend on present and past network outputs. This might lead to instability of the ANN itself and it can be very difficult to determine whether or how the predictor is stable. To avoid instability, NARMA architecture uses a linear MA-filter to filter past residuals. This is a Low Pass FIR (Finite Impulse Response) filter, commonly used for smoothing an array of sampled data/signal. It takes a set of inputs at the time, it computes the average of those samples and produces a single output [26].

To implement both NAR and NARMA, we exploit a dataset composed of four years of real GHI values (from 2010 to 2013). These values are 15 min time sampled by the weather station in our University Campus. Differently to the dataset that we used in our previous work [2], this is more complete and much bigger because it also includes the GHI values in the time period between 6 p.m. and 8 a.m., i.e. all evening and night values. In our previous work, we ignored these values because they are less relevant in the GHI prediction procedure leading to a simpler ANN architecture and avoiding over-fitting. However, in this work we demonstrate that if ANN ignores the whole daily period, that is the succession of night and day, the values of GHI predicted in the early hours of the morning are significantly incorrect (i.e. oversized or undersized). A further difference is the use of data to initialize both training set and validation-set. In our previous work, we split the dataset symmetrically according to [32]. Whilst in this paper, we divided the dataset asymmetrically into three years for the training-set (2010–2012) and one year for the validation-set (2013), according to the more recent approach described in [50]. This allows an even more accurate training phase.

Progressively, we started analyzing the number of past signals used as regressors for the prediction. Specifically, we used *Lipschiz* [37] to determinate the *lag-space*. This methodology allows identifying the order of Input-Output Models for Nonlinear Dynamic Systems. Given corresponding input and output sequences, it calculates a matrix of indices that can be helpful for determining a proper lag-space structure. However, as detailed in [20], this methodology is not always effective but it represents a good starting point to define the more suitable number of regressors, which will characterize the future neural networks architectures. Consequently, we started the design of both our ANNs considering a number of regressors in the range between 1 and 10. This arbitrary choice derives from our previous work [2] that exploits 10 regressors. On the other hand, ANNs proposed in this work aim at improving previous performances. Moreover as previously described, we modified the pre-process of the input dataset, this allows designing an ANN with no more than 10 regressors. Figure 2 details the result of the applied lag-space investigation methodology.

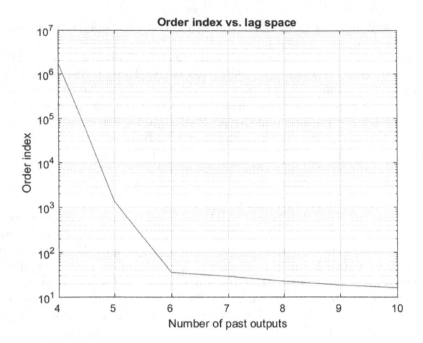

Fig. 2. Evaluation of order index criterion for different lag-space.

Figure 2 suggests that good performance can be achieved with 6 regressors (i.e. 6 previous values for y and u in Eq. 7, respectively). All previous values are not computationally advantageous. Even, between 1 and 4, the result diverges to infinity and therefore they are not displayed in the plot. On the other hand, all values above 6, even if advantageous, would risk transforming ANN architecture into a more complex and less performing structure. Thus, the best configuration in the computation/performance ratio is achieved with 6 regressors (see the knee-point of the plot in Fig. 2). Differently to what we did in [2], in this work we adopted also a design space exploration approach [10]. As a result, we decide to validate (or refute) the results given by Lipschitz. For this purpose, we implemented all the possible network combinations (of both NAR and NARMA models) from 1 to 10 regressors. This allows to evaluate and compare all the obtained architectures' performance and then find the best solutions for both NAR and NARMA. Figure 3 shows the NSSE error trends of the two ANNs based on the number of regressors for each implemented architecture. NSSE error is a network performance index. The lower NSSE the better ANN's performance.

As shown in Fig. 3, NAR and NARMA give the best performance with 4 and 2 regressors, respectively. This also represents the best compromise between ANN's computation and performance. It is worth noting that these NSSE results improve the indication given by Lipschitz methodology that suggested 6 as the best number of regressors (see Fig. 2).

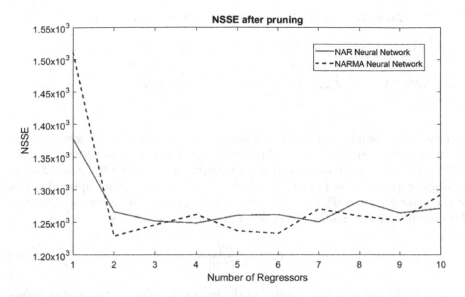

Fig. 3. Evaluation of NSSE after pruning with regard to number of regressors.

Once we found the optimal regressors for both NAR and NARMA, we implemented the two final ANNs starting from two fully connected architectures with one hidden layer of 30 hyperbolic tangent units. This large number of units could be redundant, but it is justified by the pruning technique [43], which is used in the next phases to optimize the network architecture themselves.

Before training, weights of both ANNs are initialized randomly. This allows also to initialize (i) weights, (ii) their decay threshold and (iii) the maximum number of iterations. However, these parameters are overestimated during the very first training iteration. Then, we proceeded with training phase for both NAR and NARMA networks. Training is a minimizing technique to compute the best weights. For both architectures, we used the *Levenberg-Marquardt* algorithm, which interpolates between the Gauss-Newton algorithm and the method of gradient descent using a *trust region* approach [32]. Progressively, we used the methodology illustrated in [31] for validating both ANNs. This methodology performs a set of tests including autocorrelation function of residuals and cross-correlation function between controls and residuals to validate system outputs. The result of this process gives the NSSE error. By definition, this error should not be too large compared to training error. If NSSE is greater than the training error, the predicted results are over-fitting the training-set. Table 1 illustrates the obtained results for both NAR and NARMA.

A shown in Table 1, the validation process yields these indexes as detailed in the column *NSSE after first validation*. The NSSE is equal to $1.25 \times 10^{+3}$ and $1.23 \times 10^{+3}$ for NAR and NARMA, respectively. These indexes will have to be compared with those obtained after the optimization of the architectures. Then, we proceeded to the optimization phase of both networks. Our purpose was to

Table 1. NSSE comparison after the first and final validation.

Neural network	NSSE after first validation	NSSE after final validation
NAR	$1.25 \times 10^{+3}$	$1.24 \times 10^{+3}$
NARMA	$1.23 \times 10^{+3}$	$1.22 \times 10^{+3}$

remove excess weights and obtain a smaller error than the one given during the first validation. To achieve this, we adopted the *Optimal Brain Surgeon* (OBS) [18], which is a technique to prune superfluous weights. OBS computes the Hessian matrix weights iteratively, which leads to a more exact approximation of the error function. The inverse Hessian is calculated by means of recursion. This method allows finding the smallest saliency S_i as follows:

$$S_i = \frac{w_i^2}{2[H^{-1}]_{i,i}} \qquad (10)$$

where $[H^{-1}]_{i,i}$ is the $(i,i)th$ element of the inverse Hessian matrix and w_i represent the ith element of the vector θ containing the network weights. The saliency identifies the quality of the connection between the various network units. This methodology allows verifying the state of the saliency iteratively. If the saliency S_i is much smaller than the mean-square error, then some synaptic weights are deleted and the remaining ones are updated. The computation stops when no more weights can be removed from the network without a large increase of the mean-square error. Once the new weights are given, we re-validated both resulting pruned NAR and NARMA.

Through the same methodology used in the first validation phase, we proceeded to the final networks validation using the new weights. The resulting NSSE error indexes for both ANNs are illustrated in the column *NSSE after final validation* in Table 1. NSSE error indexes are $1.24 \times 10^{+3}$ and $1.22 \times 10^{+3}$ for NAR and NARMA, respectively. In both cases, the new NSSE values are lower than the ones given after the first network validation. Thus, the optimization for both ANNs succeeded. The resulting NAR with 4 regressors and NARMA with 2 regressors are trained and validated. Hence, they are ready to forecast GHI values in short-term time-periods and their results will be discussed in next Sect. 4.

4   Results on GHI Forecast

The purpose of our work is to predict GHI in short time windows, i.e. 15 min. This is the minimum time interval on which many services for smart grid management work (e.g. Demand/Response [39]). However, we moved further predicting also GHI up to next two hours (again with 15 min time intervals). As described in Sect. 3, we implemented two Non-linear Autoregressive Neural Networks, (i) NAR with 4 regressors and (ii) NARMA with 2 regressors, that exploit

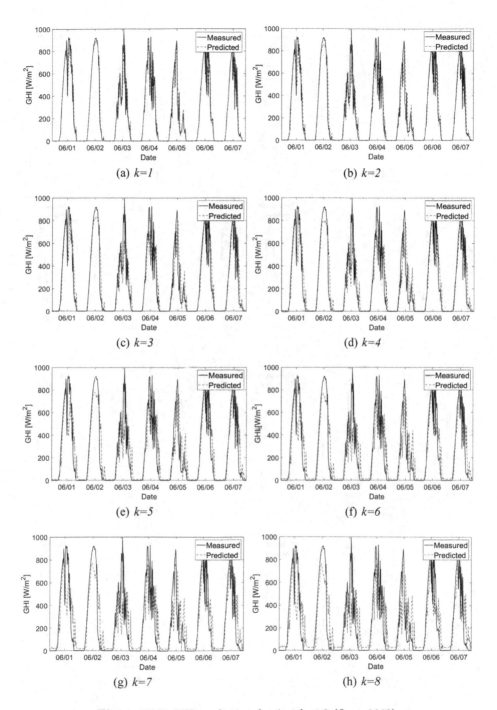

Fig. 4. NAR GHI prediction for $1 \leq k \leq 8$ (June 2013).

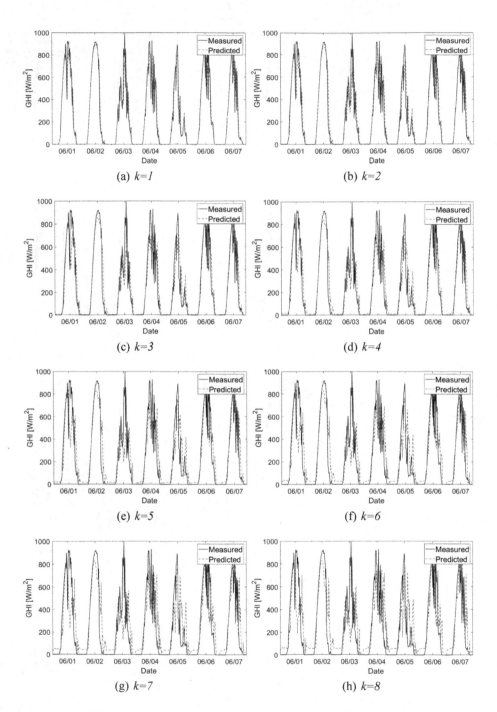

Fig. 5. NARMA GHI prediction for $1 \leq k \leq 8$ (June 2013).

the dataset described in Sect. 3. In this section, we present the obtained results and we also compare and discuss the two different architectures.

To evaluate the performance of our networks, we compare the results of our predictions with real measured values. To achieve this, we used a set of indicators introduced by Gueymard et al. [15] and briefly presented in the following. *Root Mean Square Difference (RMSD)* represents the standard deviation of differences between predicted and observed values. *Mean Absolute Difference (MAD)* represents a measure of statistical dispersion obtained by the average absolute difference of two independent values drawn from a probability distribution. *Mean Bias Difference (MBD)* measures the average squares of errors between predicted and measured values. *Coefficient of determination* (r^2) represents the proportion between the variance and the predicted variable. All these values are expressed in percentage. Finally, we also considered two other indicators to evaluate the overall network performance: *Willmott's Index of Agreement (WIA)* and *Legates's Coefficient of Efficiency (LCE)*. WIA represents the standardized measure of the degree of model prediction error [49]. LCE is the ratio between the mean square error and the variance in the observed data [24].

Figures 4 and 5 show the results of predictions given by proposed NAR and NARMA compared with real measured values sampled by weather station (dashed and continuous lines, respectively). These results include predictions with eight different time-steps, from $k = 1$ (i.e. next 15 min) to $k = 8$ (i.e next 120 min). Both cases refer to the first seven days of June 2013. Prediction trends of both architectures are very similar. Indeed, they follow with a good accuracy the real meteorological trends: i) clear sky, ii) cloudy and iii) rainy conditions, especially for $1 \leq k \leq 3$. Instead for $k > 3$, the prediction accuracy decreases. These aspects are better highlighted by Table 2 that reports the results of GHI predictions in terms of performance indicators considering the whole 2013, which is our validation-set for both architecture. These indexes highlight that the prediction performance worsens by increasing the predictive k-steps. Indeed, GHI predictions for high values of k has a higher error compared with real measurements. In both cases, the analysis of indexes highlights that the best GHI predictions are given with smaller time intervals. For example, *MAD* reveals that the forecast error grows as the prediction step k increases. Indeed, for $k = 1$, the error is about 12.96% and 12.81% for NAR and NARMA, respectively. Whilst for $k = 8$, the error exceeds the 55%. Also, *RMSD* has a similar trend. A good performance of r^2 is given when its values are closer to 1. In both cases, this happens for lower k values. For $k = 1$ and $k = 2$, r^2 is over 0.92 for both ANNs. For $k \geq 4$, it decreases down to about 0.70. This trend is also confirmed by both *LCE* and *WIA* that highlight a decreasing of the overall performance on high prediction steps. Under these circumstances, the performance indexes for $1 \leq k \leq 3$ are suitable to perform Photovoltaic energy estimations and simulation results will be discussed in the next Sect. 5. With this configuration, the maximum error rate for GHI prediction (expressed in *MAD*) is less than 25%.

To train and validate the proposed ANNs, we run our simulations in a server equipped with a CPU 2x Intel Xeon E5-2680 v3 2.50 GHz and 128 Gb of RAM. Table 3 reports the execution time for both ANNs considering the three main

Table 2. Performance indicators for GHI predictions.

Pred. steps	Time [min]	NAR neural network						NARMA neural network					
		MAD [%]	MDB [%]	r^2	RMSD [%]	LCE	WIA	MAD [%]	MDB [%]	r^2	RMSD [%]	LCE	WIA
$k=1$	15	12.94	0.16	0.95	35.31	0.89	0.99	12.80	0.36	0.95	35.03	0.90	0.99
$k=2$	30	19.47	0.81	0.92	46.80	0.84	0.98	19.15	1.06	0.92	46.07	0.84	0.98
$k=3$	45	24.87	1.80	0.89	54.41	0.80	0.97	24.67	2.23	0.89	53.65	0.80	0.97
$k=4$	60	30.16	3.06	0.86	61.05	0.76	0.96	30.23	4.09	0.86	60.24	0.76	0.96
$k=5$	75	35.67	4.77	0.83	67.29	0.71	0.95	36.35	6.86	0.83	66.82	0.71	0.95
$k=6$	105	41.78	7.23	0.79	73.93	0.66	0.94	43.30	10.46	0.79	74.16	0.65	0.94
$k=7$	115	48.90	10.65	0.75	80.94	0.60	0.92	50.61	14.57	0.74	81.88	0.60	0.92
$k=8$	120	56.90	15.23	0.70	88.51	0.54	0.90	58.18	19.01	0.69	89.89	0.53	0.90

Table 3. Computation time for both NAR and NARMA.

		NAR	NARMA
Execution time [hh:mm:ss]	ANN initialization before Pruning	00:01:13	00:02:24
	Pruning	01:04:12	01:47:58
	ANN initialization after Pruning	00:01:07	00:01:22
	Total	01:06:32	01:51:44
	Prediction step $k=1$	00:00:14	00:00:14
	$k=2$	00:00:13	00:00:14
	$k=3$	00:00:14	00:00:14
	$k=4$	00:00:16	00:00:18
	$k=5$	00:00:18	00:00:16
	$k=6$	00:00:19	00:00:19
	$k=7$	00:00:19	00:00:20
	$k=8$	00:00:20	00:00:21

phases: (i) *ANN initialization before Pruning*, (ii) *Pruning* and (iii) *ANN initialization after Pruning*.

ANN initialization before Pruning refers to the computational time needed to initialize ANNs with random values for the first training and validation. It includes all the steps needed before carrying out the network pruning. As shown in Table 3, NAR with 4 regressors needs about 1 min. Whilst, NARMA with 2 regressors needs about 2:30 min because its overall architecture is more complex with respect to NAR; hence, it needs more computational resources. This is clearly highlighted during the *Pruning* in Table 3, which refers to computational time to evaluate and eliminate unnecessary weights in order to optimize ANNs. This procedure takes around 1 h for NAR and about 1:48 h for NARMA. Thus, the optimization process is almost doubled for NARMA with respect to NAR. Finally, *ANN initialization after Pruning* is the time needed to train and validate the optimized ANNs. As highlighted in Table 3, it dropped to 1:22 min for NARMA with respect to the previous *ANN initialization before Pruning*. Whilst, it is almost constant for NAR.

Once both ANNs are pruned, the computation time to provide GHI forecasts varies between 14 and 21 s for $1 \leq k \leq 8$. This enables possible future applications where these ANNs are trained, validated and pruned on servers or cluster systems, since these phases need more computational resources. Then, the optimized ANNs can be deployed on embedded devices to provide GHI forecast. In a smart grid scenario, examples of application that can benefit from this forecast are: (i) energy dispatching and load balancing [47], (ii) battery management system [35], (iii) Demand/Response services [39] and (iv) vehicle-to-grid applications [36,51].

5   PV Energy Estimation

As already discussed in Sect. 4, the proposed ANNs forecast GHI in short-term time windows with a good accuracy. This allows estimating in advance energy produced by PV systems. To achieve this, we exploited the PV energy simulator (PVsim) presented in [6] that takes as input the GHI forecast resulting by both NAR and NARMA. The combination of both ANNs and PVsim unlocks development of novel services and control policies for a better management of future smart grids [39] that can also be tested and validated exploiting the methodology in [4].

PVsim is a GIS software infrastructure that simulates PV production in real-sky conditions. The inputs for these simulations are (i) a *Digital Surface Model* (DSM) and (ii) GHI trends. DSM is a digital elevation model that represents terrain elevation including all objects on it (i.e. buildings). It is used by PVsim to identify rooftops and to simulate the evolution of shadows in clear-sky conditions during the day. Then, this is combined with GHI trends to simulate solar incident radiation and, consequently, PV production in real-sky conditions with a time-resolution of 15 min. In a default configuration, PVsim retrieves real GHI trends from a weather station in our University Campus. To forecast PV energy production in short-term time intervals, we interpose our ANNs between weather station's data-source and PVsim. So that, both ANNs get the last real GHI measurements from the weather station and provide the resulting GHI forecast to PVsim.

As mentioned in Sect. 4, results of our ANNs for $1 \leq k \leq 3$ on GHI forecast are suitable to perform PV energy estimations. Hereafter, we present results obtained for these three time intervals, i.e. next 15, 30 and 45 min. To evaluate the error rate, we compared PVsim results of GHI forecast trends given by NAR and NARMA with those of real GHI trends retrieved by weather station. Figure 6 shows PVsim results for three significant days in June 2013 with different meteorological conditions: (i) sunny, (ii) cloudy and (iii) rainy. Blue continuous-line represents simulations given by real GHI trends, red dashed-line given by NAR GHI trends and green dashed-dotted-line given by NARMA GHI trends. As shown in Fig. 6, best performance is achieved when PVsim gets as input results of GHI trends from both ANNs with $k = 1$. This is also confirmed by performance indicators reported in Table 4 that considers the whole 2013.

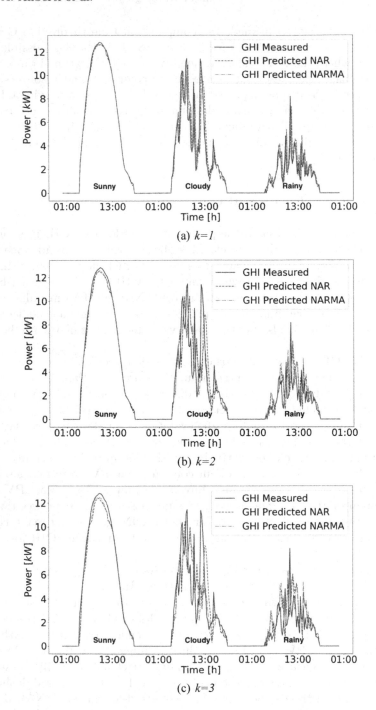

Fig. 6. Simulations of PV energy production given by real NAR and NARMA GHI trends for $1 \leq k \leq 3$ (June 2013). (Color figure online)

Indeed, the accuracy of PV energy estimations decreases by increasing the prediction step k. Regarding PVsim simulations preformed with NAR GHI trends, MAD increases from 10.31% to 19.22% for $k = 1$ and $k = 3$, respectively. Also $RMSD$ has a similar trend, increasing from 27.96% to 44.65%. MDB varies from -0.61 to -2.65. r^2 for $k = 1$ is equal to 0.97. Whilst, the error increases with an $r^2 = 0.92$ for $k = 3$. Finally, LCE varies from 0.92 to 0.84 and WIA decreases from 0.99 to 0.97. Similar trends are achieved by PVsim simulations preformed with NARMA GHI trends. MAD increases from 10.11% for $k = 1$ to 18.47% for $k = 3$. MDB is -0.17 for $k = 1$, -0.74 for $k = 2$ and -1.55 for $k = 3$. r^2 varies from 0.97 to 0.92. $RMSD$ rises from 27.86% to 43.97%. Finally, LCE varies from 0.91 to 0.85 and WIA decreases from 0.99 to 0.98.

Table 4. Performance indicator for PV simulation with NAR and NARMA.

Pred. steps	Time [min]	NAR neural network						NARMA neural network					
		MAD [%]	MDB [%]	r2	RMSD [%]	LCE	WIA	MAD [%]	MDB [%]	r2	RMSD [%]	LCE	WIA
$k = 1$	15	10.31	−0.61	0.97	27.96	0.92	0.99	10.11	−0.17	0.97	27.86	0.91	0.99
$k = 2$	30	15.45	−1.58	0.94	38.15	0.87	0.98	14.93	−0.74	0.94	37.66	0.88	0.98
$k = 3$	45	19.22	−2.65	0.92	44.65	0.84	0.97	18.47	−1.55	0.92	43.97	0.85	0.98

A comparison of these performance indicators highlights that NARMA GHI trends give slightly better PV energy estimations than NAR GHI trends. We can assert that both ANNs are able to simulate GHI trends in short-term periods with a good accuracy. This is also confirmed when we use ANNs' results to estimate PV energy production.

6   Conclusions

In this paper, we presented a methodology to implement two artificial neural networks for forecasting solar radiation in short-term time periods. In a smart grid scenario, this forecast is needed to estimate in advance the energy production of renewable energy sources enabling novel control strategies and services for grid management, such as Demand/Response policies [39].

The proposed ANNs implement two non-linear autoregressive neural networks, NAR and NARMA respectively, that exploit time-series data. We also analyzed their accuracy by comparing the obtained results with real values of solar radiation sampled by a real weather station. This analysis highlighted an overall good performance especially for a time horizon from future 15 to 120 min. We discussed strengths and weaknesses of both architectures, from both neural and computational viewpoints. Then, the results of these ANNs have been given as input to a Photovoltaic simulator (PVsim) [6] to estimate the energy production of Photovoltaic systems. The accuracy of these results is also acceptable especially for time horizon from future 15 to 45 min.

As future work, we will apply these ANNs together with PVsim to test services for smart grid management in a distributed test-bed environment, as depicted in [5].

Acknowledgements. Computational resources were provided by HPC@POLITO, a project of Academic Computing within the Department of Control and Computer Engineering at the Politecnico di Torino (http://www.hpc.polito.it).

References

1. Aghaei, J., Alizadeh, M.I.: Demand response in smart electricity grids equipped with renewable energy sources: a review. Renew. Sustain. Energy Rev. **18**, 64–72 (2013)
2. Aliberti, A., Bottaccioli, L., Cirrincione, G., Macii, E., Acquaviva, A., Patti, E.: Forecasting short-term solar radiation for photovoltaic energy predictions. In: Proceedings of the 7th International Conference on Smart Cities and Green ICT Systems - Volume 1: SMARTGREENS, pp. 44–53. INSTICC, SciTePress (2018). https://doi.org/10.5220/0006683600440053
3. Badescu, V.: Modeling Solar Radiation at the Earth's Surface. Springer, Heidelberg (2014)
4. Bottaccioli, L., Estebsari, A., Patti, E., Pons, E., Acquaviva, A.: A novel integrated real-time simulation platform for assessing photovoltaic penetration impacts in smart grids. Energy Procedia **111**, 780–789 (2017)
5. Bottaccioli, L., et al.: A flexible distributed infrastructure for real-time cosimulations in smart grids. IEEE Trans. Industr. Inf. **13**(6), 3265–3274 (2017)
6. Bottaccioli, L., Patti, E., Macii, E., Acquaviva, A.: GIS-based software infrastructure to model PV generation in fine-grained spatio-temporal domain. IEEE Syst. J. **12**(3), 2832–2841 (2017)
7. Box, G.E., Jenkins, G.M., Reinsel, G.C., Ljung, G.M.: Time Series Analysis: Forecasting and Control. Wiley, Hoboken (2015)
8. Brockwell, P.J., Davis, R.A.: Introduction to Time Series and Forecasting. Springer, Cham (2016). https://doi.org/10.1007/978-3-319-29854-2
9. Chandrashekar, G., Sahin, F.: A survey on feature selection methods. Comput. Electr. Eng. **40**(1), 16–28 (2014)
10. Cohn, D.A.: Neural network exploration using optimal experiment design. In: Advances in Neural Information Processing Systems, pp. 679–686 (1994)
11. Connor, J., Atlas, L.E., Martin, D.R.: Recurrent networks and NARMA modeling. In: Advances in Neural Information Processing Systems, pp. 301–308 (1992)
12. Demuth, H.B., Beale, M.H., De Jess, O., Hagan, M.T.: Neural Network Design. Martin Hagan (2014)
13. Dickinson, E.: Solar Energy Technology Handbook. CRC Press, Boca Raton (2018)
14. Expósito, A.G., Conejo, A.J., Canizares, C.: Electric Energy Systems: Analysis and Operation. CRC Press, Boca Raton (2016)
15. Gueymard, C.A.: A review of validation methodologies and statistical performance indicators for modeled solar radiation data: towards a better bankability of solar projects. Renew. Sustain. Energy Rev. **39**, 1024–1034 (2014)
16. Hamilton, J.D.: Time Series Analysis, vol. 2. Princeton University Press, Princeton (1994)

17. Han, S., Pool, J., Tran, J., Dally, W.: Learning both weights and connections for efficient neural network. In: Advances in Neural Information Processing Systems, pp. 1135–1143 (2015)
18. Hansen, L.K., Pedersen, M.W.: Controlled growth of cascade correlation nets. In: Marinaro, M., Morasso, P.G. (eds.) ICANN 1994, pp. 797–800. Springer, London (1994). https://doi.org/10.1007/978-1-4471-2097-1_189
19. Haykin, S., Network, N.: A comprehensive foundation. Neural Netw. **2**(2004), 41 (2004)
20. He, X., Asada, H.: A new method for identifying orders of input-output models for nonlinear dynamic systems. In: American Control Conference, pp. 2520–2523. IEEE (1993)
21. Hosenuzzaman, M., Rahim, N., Selvaraj, J., Hasanuzzaman, M., Malek, A., Nahar, A.: Global prospects, progress, policies, and environmental impact of solar photovoltaic power generation. Renew. Sustain. Energy Rev. **41**, 284–297 (2015)
22. Kaplanis, S., Kaplani, E.: Stochastic prediction of hourly global solar radiation profiles (2016)
23. Kubat, M.: Artificial neural networks. In: Kubat, M. (ed.) An Introduction to Machine Learning, pp. 91–111. Springer, Cham (2017). https://doi.org/10.1007/978-3-319-63913-0_5
24. Legates, D.R., McCabe, G.J.: A refined index of model performance: a rejoinder. Int. J. Climatol. **33**(4), 1053–1056 (2013)
25. Madanchi, A., Absalan, M., Lohmann, G., Anvari, M., Tabar, M.R.R.: Strong short-term non-linearity of solar irradiance fluctuations. Sol. Energy **144**, 1–9 (2017)
26. Makridakis, S., Wheelwright, S.C.: Adaptive filtering: an integrated autoregressive/moving average filter for time series forecasting. J. Oper. Res. Soc. **28**(2), 425–437 (1977)
27. Mandic, D.P., Chambers, J.A., et al.: Recurrent Neural Networks for Prediction: Learning Algorithms, Architectures and Stability. Wiley, Hoboken (2001)
28. Miller, G.F., Todd, P.M., Hegde, S.U.: Designing neural networks using genetic algorithms. In: ICGA, vol. 89, pp. 379–384 (1989)
29. Montgomery, D.C., Jennings, C.L., Kulahci, M.: Introduction to Time Series Analysis and Forecasting. Wiley, Hoboken (2015)
30. Nazaripouya, H., Wang, B., Wang, Y., Chu, P., Pota, H., Gadh, R.: Univariate time series prediction of solar power using a hybrid wavelet-ARMA-NARX prediction method. In: 2016 IEEE/PES Transmission and Distribution Conference and Exposition (T&D), pp. 1–5. IEEE (2016)
31. Norgaard, M., Ravn, O., Poulsen, N.K.L.: NNSYSID-toolbox for system identification with neural networks. Math. Comput. Model. Dyn. Syst. **8**(1), 1–20 (2002)
32. Norgaard, P.M., Ravn, O., Poulsen, N.K., Hansen, L.K.: Neural Networks for Modelling and Control of Dynamic Systems-A Practitioner's Handbook (2000)
33. Oancea, B., Ciucu, Ş.C.: Time series forecasting using neural networks. arXiv preprint arXiv:1401.1333 (2014)
34. Qazi, A., Fayaz, H., Wadi, A., Raj, R.G., Rahim, N., Khan, W.A.: The artificial neural network for solar radiation prediction and designing solar systems: a systematic literature review. J. Clean. Prod. **104**, 1–12 (2015)
35. Rahimi-Eichi, H., Ojha, U., Baronti, F., Chow, M.Y.: Battery management system: an overview of its application in the smart grid and electric vehicles. IEEE Ind. Electron. Mag. **7**(2), 4–16 (2013)
36. Rajakaruna, S., Shahnia, F., Ghosh, A.: Plug in Electric Vehicles in Smart Grids. Springer, Singapore (2016)

37. Rajamani, R.: Observers for lipschitz nonlinear systems. IEEE Trans. Autom. Control **43**(3), 397–401 (1998)
38. Refaeilzadeh, P., Tang, L., Liu, H.: Cross-validation. In: Liu, L., Özsu, M.T. (eds.) Encyclopedia of Database Systems, pp. 1–7. Springer, Boston (2016)
39. Siano, P.: Demand response and smart grids–a survey. Renew. Sustain. Energy Rev. **30**, 461–478 (2014)
40. Siegelmann, H.T., Horne, B.G., Giles, C.L.: Computational capabilities of recurrent NARX neural networks. IEEE Trans. Syst. Man Cybern. Part B (Cybern.) **27**(2), 208–215 (1997)
41. Srivastava, N., Hinton, G.E., Krizhevsky, A., Sutskever, I., Salakhutdinov, R.: Dropout: a simple way to prevent neural networks from overfitting. J. Mach. Learn. Res. **15**(1), 1929–1958 (2014)
42. Tealab, A., Hefny, H., Badr, A.: Forecasting of nonlinear time series using artificial neural network. Future Comput. Inf. J. **2**(1), 39–47 (2017)
43. Thimm, G., Fiesler, E.: Pruning of neural networks. Technical report, IDIAP (1997)
44. Vardakas, J.S., Zorba, N., Verikoukis, C.V.: A survey on demand response programs in smart grids: pricing methods and optimization algorithms. IEEE Commun. Surv. Tutor. **17**(1), 152–178 (2015)
45. Voyant, C., Darras, C., Muselli, M., Paoli, C., Nivet, M.L., Poggi, P.: Bayesian rules and stochastic models for high accuracy prediction of solar radiation. Appl. Energy **114**, 218–226 (2014)
46. Voyant, C., et al.: Machine learning methods for solar radiation forecasting: a review. Renew. Energy **105**, 569–582 (2017)
47. Weckx, S., Driesen, J.: Load balancing with EV chargers and PV inverters in unbalanced distribution grids. IEEE Trans. Sustain. Energy **6**(2), 635–643 (2015)
48. Weigend, A.S.: Time Series Prediction: Forecasting the Future and Understanding the Past. Routledge, Abingdon (2018)
49. Willmott, C.J., Robeson, S.M., Matsuura, K.: A refined index of model performance. Int. J. Climatol. **32**(13), 2088–2094 (2012)
50. Witten, I.H., Frank, E., Hall, M.A., Pal, C.J.: Data Mining: Practical Machine Learning Tools and Techniques. Morgan Kaufmann, Burlington (2016)
51. Xing, H., Fu, M., Lin, Z., Mou, Y.: Decentralized optimal scheduling for charging and discharging of plug-in electric vehicles in smart grids. IEEE Trans. Power Syst. **31**(5), 4118–4127 (2016)
52. Yadav, A.K., Chandel, S.: Solar radiation prediction using artificial neural network techniques: a review. Renew. Sustain. Energy Rev. **33**, 772–781 (2014)

Medical Freezers as Flexible Load
for Demand Response in a Business Park
Microgrid with Local Solar Power Generation

Rosa Morales González[1]([✉]), Madeleine Gibescu[3], Sjef Cobben[1], Martijn Bongaerts[2],
Marcel de Nes-Koedam[2], and Wouter Vermeiden[2]

[1] Eindhoven University of Technology, 5612AP Eindhoven, The Netherlands
{r.m.d.g.morales.gonzalez,j.f.g.cobben}@tue.nl
[2] Alliander NV, 6812AH Arnhem, The Netherlands
martijn.bongaerts@alliander.com, marcel.de.nes.koedam@qirion.nl,
wouter.vermeiden@exe.energy
[3] Copernicus Institute for Sustainable Development, Utrecht University,
3584CB Utrecht, the Netherlands
m.gibescu@uu.nl

Abstract. This work presents a day-ahead demand response (DR) scheduling framework that quantifies the flexibility in non-residential buildings by using thermodynamic modeling, and assesses the benefits of DR in terms of three separate optimization variants: net payment minimization, energy self-sufficiency, and peak power reduction. We test the framework in a case study of a medical research facility located in a business park with local solar power generation. The flexible loads are four groups of independently-controlled medical freezers. Our DR framework generates optimal freezer operation and solar power production/curtailment schedules that are compared against a business-as-usual scenario with no DR. We perform simulations for cases with and without end-of-horizon temperature constraints. Results show that the flexibility harnessed from the freezers' thermal mass for DR actions improves the price-responsiveness, energy independence, and peak power consumption of the system with respect to the business-as-usual scenario. Furthermore, adding end-of-horizon constraints ensures that the thermal buffer of the flexible load will be full for the next simulation time window.

Keywords: Demand response · Genetic algorithm · Smart grid ·
Local RES integration · Physical systems modeling

1 Introduction

Smart grids, evolved from traditional power systems, propose innovative energy and operational measures to cope with present-day industry challenges, such as meeting sustainability targets, decarbonizing the energy supply, and dealing with aging infrastructure [1]. One such measure is to increase distributed generation from renewable

This work was supported by Alliander N.V.

© Springer Nature Switzerland AG 2019
B. Donnellan et al. (Eds.): SMARTGREENS 2018/VEHITS 2018, CCIS 992, pp. 23–43, 2019.
https://doi.org/10.1007/978-3-030-26633-2_2

energy sources (DG-RES) like solar and wind. However, these resources cannot be ramped up or down to adapt to the load profile, as is the case with fossil fuels in traditional power plants, thus adversely impacting the flexibility—i.e. the ability to adapt to changes in consumption or generation patterns—of the power system value chain.

In order to solve this problem, smart grid technologies also propose different solutions to make up for the lost flexibility on the generation side by harnessing flexible resources from other parts of the power system value chain. For example, by enhancing monitoring and control functionalities, adding electrical and/or thermal storage, creating novel electricity market designs, and increasing demand-side flexibility through demand response (DR) programs [2,3]. In this paper, we focus on the latter, and define demand response as the set of "actions voluntarily taken by consumers [and/or prosumers] to change their energy usage—either in terms of quantity or timing—in response to an external control signal" [4], e.g., price or a direct command from the aggregator or system operator.

Thermostatically controlled loads such as water heaters [5], refrigerators [6], and heating, ventilation and air conditioning (HVAC) systems [7] have been widely used as sources of demand-side flexibility in DR programs. Many authors have focused on harnessing the flexibility of residential consumers with not quite satisfactory results due to the following drawbacks, which are discussed in more detail in [8–11]: that individual loads have to be aggregated in large numbers, yet consumer engagement, participation and retention are low; and setup investments are high, yet funding and operational resources are lacking and/or dependent on subsidies.

On the other hand, focusing on commercial and industrial (C&I) consumers for DR seems like an interesting prospect because of the following advantages [12,13]:

- These types of consumer sites have higher consumption footprints and higher peak demands than residential consumers [14]
- Resource aggregation is facilitated by the physical proximity of similar types of loads, since C&I consumers are usually located in business parks/industrial sites.

The history of demand-side management strategies may have started with targeting industrial consumers [15], but the *ad hoc* strategies proposed in works that feature industrial loads such as [16–18], have been unable to create the basis for a systematic, more widespread implementation of DR in this consumer sector due to two main problems: industrial consumers' energy needs vary greatly from one another, and applications for DR can be restricted in scope due to the industrial processes used as flexible loads [19,20].

In the realm of commercial consumers, extensive discussions on the flexibility potential of office buildings' passive thermal capacitance and HVAC controls have been taken place in the public scientific discourse [21–24]. The positive findings on applying DR to commercial buildings are especially relevant in the Netherlands, where the service industry is the second largest energy consumer behind heavy industry [25], and is the economic sector with the highest added value and employment numbers in the Dutch economy [26]. In particular, the health services sector has been consistently ranked in the top three sectors of the Dutch economy [27].

With the above in mind, in this work we propose a multiphysics DR framework to evaluate the flexibility potential of a medical freezing warehouse located in a business park microgrid with local solar photovoltaic (PV) generation. In our DR framework, freezer loads are shifted in time by automated actions scheduled on a day-ahead basis, controlling the medical freezers located at the consumer premises in four independent clusters, while treating the locally-available solar power generation as a curtailable resource.

We analyze the interactions between the thermal and electrical systems that make up our case study microgrid via an integrated, multiphysics simulation and optimization DR tool. Through this approach, we calculate the flexibility potential of the thermal mass of the freezer enclosure and contents in terms of energy shifted and/or saved. We also quantify the benefits in terms of energy self-sufficiency, price-responsiveness, and peak load reduction for the consumer, the local PV producer, and the operator of the business park microgrid. In order to test this framework, we designed two simulation experiments. In the first one, we make improvements to the practical implementation of our DR framework in MATLAB, with the hypothesis of improving computation times, by changing the way in which we optimize the design variables described in the problem formulation and comparing our results to those obtained in previous work [28]. The second simulation experiment was designed to add end-of-horizon temperature constraints to the original problem formulation. This was done in order to overcome a previous limitation of our model, in which the thermal inertia of the medical freezers was depleted at the end of the optimization horizon, requiring some recovery time during which DR could not be applied until the freezers could recharge their thermal buffers. The endpoint temperature constraints will limit the state of charge of the thermal buffer represented by the medical freezers.

The rest of the paper is organized as follows: Sect. 2 describes the methodology used; Sect. 3 describes the case study used for this work; Sect. 4 presents the results obtained from applying our DR framework to the case study; Sect. 5 discusses the results and the practical implications and limitations of our work; and, finally, Sect. 6 states the main conclusions of our work and gives a roadmap for future directions of the research.

2 Methodology

This section describes the mathematical models and algorithms that describe the optimization problems and physical systems that make up our DR framework.

2.1 Optimization Problem Formulation

Let the binary variable $\beta(i,t)$ signify the ON/OFF signal of the flexible thermostatic load of cluster i at time t. The net power imported from the grid of all I flexible loads, $P_{net}(t)$, after combining the predicted contribution of local DG-RES in the microgrid $P_{RES}(t)$ and the flexible load i at time t, $P(i,t)$, is expressed by (1):

$$P_{net}(t) = \sum_{i=1}^{I} \beta(i,t)P(i,t) - P_{RES}(t) \tag{1}$$

Our demand response optimization problem (2) will determine the flexible load operation $\beta(i,t)$ and PV production schedules $P_{RES}(t)$ over a given time horizon $t \in [t_o, t_f]$. The problem is constrained to:

- the safety temperature bounds $[T_{min}(i,t), T_{max}(i,t)]$ to which the flexible loads are subjected (2b);
- the physical constraints of local DG-RES production, $P_{RES}^{max}(t)$ (2c);
- the rated connection capacity, P_{max} (2d); and
- the state of charge of the thermal buffer by the end of the DR time window, $T_{ic}(i, t_f)$ (2e).

$$\min_{\beta, P_{RES}} \quad \Omega = \Phi \tag{2a}$$

$$\text{s.t.} \quad T_{min}(i,t) \leq T_{ic}(i,t) \leq T_{max}(i,t) \quad \forall i, t \tag{2b}$$

$$0 \leq P_{RES}(t) \leq P_{RES}^{max}(t) \quad \forall t \tag{2c}$$

$$|P_{net}| \leq P_{max} \tag{2d}$$

$$T_{ic}(i, t_f) = T_{min}(i, t_o) \forall i \tag{2e}$$

where Φ stands in for the three optimization variants that will be analyzed separately: minimizing energy exchanges with the regional grid Φ_e (3), peak power consumption Φ_p (4), and net energy payments Φ_c (8).

End-of-horizon temperature constraints (2e) are added to ensure that the thermal buffer will be replenished by the end of the optimization time window. This way, DR can be implemented again for the next time window without the need for recovery time, as was the case in [28].

The temperatures of the flexible thermostatic loads $T_{ic}(i,t)$ determine the overall available demand-side flexibility at any given time. T_{ic} and $P(i,t)$ are obtained from first-order dynamic models that will be discussed in Sect. 2.2.

$$\Phi = \Phi_e = \sum_{t=t_o}^{t_f} |E_{net}(t)| = \int_{t_f}^{t_o} |P_{net}(t)| dt \tag{3}$$

$$\Phi = \Phi_p = max(|P_{net}|) \tag{4}$$

For the net payment optimization problem, let $\lambda_{RES}(t)$ be the price the local consumer pays for buying locally-produced energy in the microgrid, $\lambda_{grid}(t)$ the price for buying electricity from the regional electricity supplier, and λ_{feedin} the tariff the local DG-RES producer gets for exporting energy to the regional distribution network (all in €/kWh). Let us assume that the DG-RES producer sells its electricity at a lower price than the consumer would pay for electricity from the regional electricity supplier, and that the feed-in tariff is considerably less than the monetary compensation it receives for selling electricity locally within the microgrid (5):

$$\lambda_{feedin} \ll \lambda_{RES}(t) < \lambda_{grid}(t) \quad \forall t \tag{5}$$

The consumer fees and revenue for the DG-RES producer are given in (6) and (7), respectively:

$$O_{cons} = \sum_{t=t_o}^{t_f} (\lambda_{RES}(t) E_{RES}(t) + \lambda_{grid}(t) E_{imports}(t)) \tag{6}$$

$$O_{prod} = \sum_{t=t_o}^{t_f} (\lambda_{RES}(t)E_{RES}(t) + \lambda_{feedin}(t)E_{exports}(t)) \qquad (7)$$

where $E_x(t) = \int_{t-1}^{t} P_x dt$, and x is a stand-in for subscripts *imports*, *exports*, and *RES*. $E_{imports}$ represents energy consumed from grid imports in the microgrid (i.e., when $E_{net} > 0$) at time t, and $E_{exports}$ signifies the locally produced energy from DG-RES fed back into the grid (i.e., when $E_{net} > 0$). Maximizing producer revenue and minimizing consumer fees, we have that the net payment is:

$$\Phi = \Phi_c = \sum_{t=1}^{T} (\lambda_{grid}(t)E_{imports}(t) - \lambda_{feedin}(t)E_{exports}(t)) \qquad (8)$$

2.2 Thermostatic Load Modeling

This section describes the thermostatic load modeling approach used to obtain the inputs for the optimization problem described in Sect. 2.1.

Thermostatic load behavior can be described by a first-order dynamic system, as detailed in works such as [29–31]. Said first-order system can also be represented schematically as a lumped parameter resistor/capacitor (RC) circuit model, as shown in Fig. 1, to understand how the thermal mass of buildings determine the available demand-side flexibility in terms of shifting power and duration. The main advantages of this modeling approach are:

- its capability of capturing first-order transients of the flexible loads with a reasonable degree of accuracy without the need for a heavily-detailed simulation;
- it can facilitate the real-time implementation of the optimization framework we use in our DR program, since the modeling effort and computation time are considerably less than those required to create and simulate a more sophisticated model.
- it integrates the thermal and electrical domains, for a multiphysics, multidisciplinary analysis of the energy usage of flexible thermostatic loads.

The system of equations describing the temperature evolution over time of the different components of the flexible thermostatic loads is given in (9):

$$(mc_p)_{ic}\frac{dT_{ic}(t)}{dt} = -\frac{T_{ic}(t) - T_{in}(t)}{R_{ic-in}} \qquad (9a)$$

$$(mc_p)_{in}\frac{dT_{in}(t)}{dt} = \frac{T_{ic}(t) - T_{in}(t)}{R_{ic-in}} - \frac{T_{in}(t) - T_{sup}}{R_{in-sup}} - \sum_{n=1}^{N}\frac{T_{in}(t) - T_{e,n}(t)}{R_{e,n,1} + R_{e,n,2}} \qquad (9b)$$

$$(mc_p)_{e,n}\frac{dT_{e,n}(t)}{dt} = \frac{T_{in}(t) - T_{e,n}(t)}{R_{e,n,1} + R_{e,n,2}} - \frac{T_{e,n}(t) - T_{amb}(t)}{R_{e,n,3} + R_{e,n,4}} \quad \forall n \in [1, N] \qquad (9c)$$

$$0 = \frac{T_{in}(t) - T_{sup}}{R_{conv}} + \beta(t)\dot{Q}_{sup}(t) \qquad (9d)$$

where $(mc_p)_x$ denotes heat capacity in J/K; $dT_x(t)/dt$, is the rate of change temperature with respect to time in K/s; and R_x signifies thermal resistance in K/W. The subscript x is a stand-in for the subscripts *ic*, *in*, *sup* and e, n, (see corresponding blocks

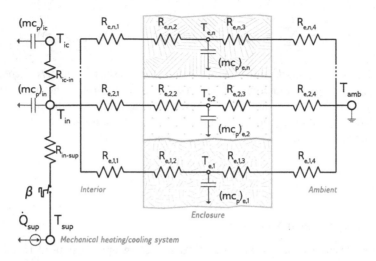

Fig. 1. Equivalent RC circuit of a flexible thermostatic load *(Adapted from* [28]*).*

in Fig. 1) which describe the flexible thermostatic load, indoor air, mechanical heating/cooling/refrigeration supply system, and n number of enclosure elements out of a total N (e.g., roof, walls, floor), respectively. $T_{amb}(t)$ is the temperature of the ambient or conditioned space in which the flexible thermostatic loads are kept as a function of time in degrees Kelvin, $\dot{Q}_{sup}(t)$ is the heat extracted or added by mechanical cooling/heating system in watts, and T_{sup} is the supply temperature of the mechanical heating/cooling/refrigeration system in K.

The coefficient of performance (COP) determines the proportionality between mechanical heat added/extracted to the system and electrical power consumption of the thermostatic load $\dot{W}_{el}(t)$ (10):

$$COP(t) = \dot{Q}_{sup}(t)/\dot{W}_{el}(t) \tag{10}$$

The assumption of a constant COP is reasonable when the conditioned space in which the flexible thermostatic loads are kept is maintained at a constant temperature to ensure an optimal operation. In that case, mechanical heat extracted is given by (11):

$$\dot{Q}_{sup}(t) = COP \times \dot{W}_{el}(t) \tag{11}$$

Assuming we can independently control the operation of the flexible loads in i groups, as discussed in the previous section, we can substitute Eq. (2d) with (12):

$$P_{net}(t) = \sum_{i=1}^{I} \beta(i,t)\dot{W}_{el}(i,t) - P_{RES}(t) \tag{12}$$

2.3   Model Interactions and Implementation of the DR Framework

Because we have both continuous and discrete decision variables and the constraints are nonlinear, finding the optimality conditions to solve our problem through traditional mathematical methods can be time-consuming and cumbersome [32]. We therefore need to employ iterative heuristic search techniques to solve our mixed-integer nonlinear optimization problem in order to keep the computation time within reason.

In previous work, $\beta(i,t)$ and $P_{RES}(t)$ were optimized simultaneously (see Fig. 2(a) [28]. In practice, the software implementation of the problem in MATLAB turned out to be quite costly in terms of the computation time and resources to find the optimality conditions for both sets of variables due to the limitations inherent to the software. Therefore, in this work, we propose to optimize $\beta(i,t)$ and $P_{RES}(t)$ separately (Fig. 2(b) in two sub-optimization routines, with the hypothesis that this will decrease the computation time and improve results. In principle, this decoupling might lead to suboptimal results. In order to mitigate this effect, however, we set $P_{RES}(t) = P_{RES}^{max}(t)$ in the thermostatic load sub-optimization routine to take full advantage of locally available DG-RES production, and then run the second sub-optimization routine to trigger DG-RES curtailment actions when necessary. The inputs and outputs of the proposed DR framework are shown in Fig. 3, which also shows the sequential optimization of the operation schedules of the thermostatic loads and DG-RES production.

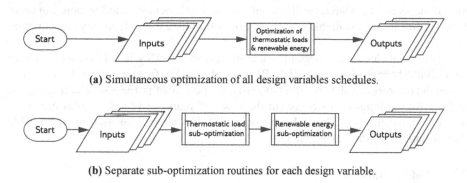

(a) Simultaneous optimization of all design variables schedules.

(b) Separate sub-optimization routines for each design variable.

Fig. 2. Demand response flowcharts.

As can be observed from the figure, our multiphysics DR framework consists of a cyclical interfacing of thermostatic load models with an optimization framework to: (1) calculate the available demand-side flexibility from the inherent thermal mass of the thermostatic loads; and (2) to devise optimal operation strategies for the flexible loads, such that the objectives of minimal net payment, maximal energy self-sufficiency or minimum peak load are achieved on a day-ahead basis. This means that the operation and PV production schedules are determined for the entire time horizon in advance of real-time, assuming perfect knowledge of wholesale and local day-ahead market prices, feed-in tariffs, as well as accurate forecasts of PV production.

3   Case Study

This section describes the case study and simulation experiments.

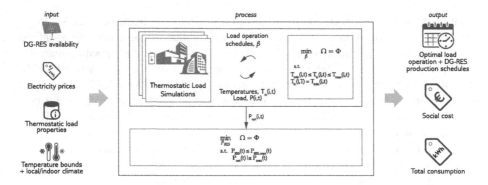

Fig. 3. Model interactions in the proposed DR framework *(Adapted from* [4]*).*

We test our proposed DR framework in a case study of a medical research facility in the Netherlands, which is located in a business park with a 250-kWp photovoltaic installation (1700 m^2 of crystalline PV panels with a 12% system efficiency). The administrators of the medical research facility would like to implement demand response in order better utilize locally-available PV generation and reduce their electricity consumption fees.

The annual electricity consumption at the research facility is 1.4 GWh/y, of which approximately 35% of the load (500 MWh/y) is due to 120 freezer units of 1.1 kW each. When the freezers are all ON simultaneously, the peak load is 132 kW. The freezers are utilized for the long-term storage (in the order of years) of blood samples preserved in a high-concentration glycerol solution at -80 °C, and will be used as our flexible thermostatic load for the case study.

3.1   Model Inputs

This section describes the inputs used for the MATLAB/Simulink thermostatic load models.

Best practices in cryogenic preservation of biomaterials require glycerolized blood samples to be stored continuously at -65 °C or colder. The samples can be subjected to temperature variations without detriment under the aforementioned conditions [33]. We set the flexibility temperature thresholds for the internal contents of the medical freezers to a conservative range: $T_{ic} \in [-80, -70]$°C. A tolerance of ± 0.3 °C is added to account for system delay.

The ultra-low-temperature freezers used in the medical research facility are kept at a constant ambient temperature of 25 °C. The COP at this temperature is 0.575, per manufacturer data. The physical properties of the enclosure materials and conditioned air inside the enclosure are listed in Table 1.

The amount of flexibility gained from the blood samples is given by:

$$Q_{flex} = (\rho V c_p)_{samples} \Delta T \tag{13}$$

where ρ and c_p are physical properties of the glycerolized blood samples, given in Table 1; $\Delta T = T_{max} - T_{min}$; and V is the total volume of the samples, which is 57.6 L

Table 1. Physical properties used to model the thermostatic loads.

Component	Density ρ [kg/m^3]	Specific heat capacity c_p [J/(kgK)]	Thermal conductivity k [W/(mK)]
Blood samples [33–35]	1063	1500	0.26
Air [36]	1	1000	0.02
Freezer enclosure [37,38]	186	650	0.01

when the freezer stores 1-ml samples and is at its full volumetric capacity. Substituting values in (13), we obtain that the total flexibility gained from the blood samples in the 120 freezers is $Q_{flex} = 30.61$ kWh per discharge cycle.

3.2 Assumptions

The assumptions made for the case study are enumerated below:

1. The heat transfer mechanisms considered for the thermostatic load modeling are conduction and convection. Radiation is deemed negligible due to the low emissivity values of the freezer enclosure materials and the high convective and conductive heat transfer rates from the air distribution system and evaporator coils in the freezers' interior.
2. Because the blood samples are kept in long-term storage, we assume that:
   (a) the internal contents of the freezer are already "at temperature"; i.e., the mechanical refrigeration system will only be used to maintain the product temperature; and
   (b) there is no in- or outflow of samples during the entirety of the DR time window.
3. Base electricity loads, loads triggered by human interaction (e.g. lighting), and heating/cooling loads required to balance ventilation and internal heat gains/losses within the medical research facility are neglected, since they are all considered inflexible loads.
4. Day-ahead electricity prices for the consumer and DG-RES producer (λ_{grid}, λ_{RES}), as well as the DG-RES feed-in tariffs (λ_{feedin}) are known.
5. PV generation can be forecasted with a reasonable degree of accuracy.

Expected day-ahead electricity prices[1] and PV generation values for typical irradiation days[2] used in the simulations are shown in Figs. 4 and 5.

3.3 Simulation Scenarios

We consider two simulation experiments for our DR program, in which we separately test three optimization variants:

- reduction of energy imports and exports from- and to the regional grid (3),

---

[1] Based on data from https://transparency.entsoe.eu/.

[2] Based on data from http://www.soda-pro.com/web-services#radiation.

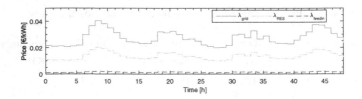

Fig. 4. Dynamic electricity prices for the end-users of the microgrid [28].

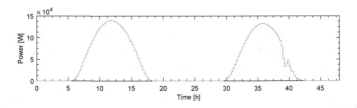

Fig. 5. PV production profiles for two consecutive average solar irradiation days in the Netherlands ($1700m^2$, system efficiency 12%) [28].

- net payment minimization (8), and
- peak load reduction (4).

In the first simulation experiment, we replicate the conditions of [28]: 48-h simulation window, 15-min resolution, no end-of-horizon temperature targets. Instead of optimizing our design variables $\beta(t)$ (772 elements) and $P_{RES}(t)$ (193 elements) simultaneously (966 design variables in total), we perform two separate sub-optimizations: one in which we solve for $\beta(t)$ with $P_{RES}(t) = P_{RES}^{max}(t)$, and a second one where we use the outputs of the first ($P_{opt}(t)$ in Fig. 3) to optimize $P_{RES}(t)$.

In the second simulation experiment, we apply end-of-horizon temperature constraints (2e) to see the effect of limiting the state of charge of the thermal buffer for all three optimization variants. We compare the results of these optimizations against a business-as-usual (BAU) scenario, where all freezers are operated as a single unit (worst-case scenario for peak load), and whose temperature controls consist of continuously-operating thermostats with a fixed setpoint and deadband based on the interior chamber temperature T_{in}. In this experiment, $\beta(t)$ has 388 elements and P_{RES} has 97 elements. In this scenario, we also optimize our design variables in separate sub-optimization routines as described in Sect. 2.3.

In both simulation exercises, we set P_{max} to the worst-case scenario for peak load, or 132 kW, in constraint (2d), and control our flexible load in four independent clusters of 30 freezers.

Simulations of our DR framework were carried out in MATLAB/Simulink using a double-processor Intel Xeon CPU with 28 cores and a clock speed of 2.6 GHz. The heuristic we chose for solving the optimization problem was the genetic algorithm (GA) as implemented by the MATLAB Optimization Toolbox, for its ability to deal with both continuous and discrete variables. We parallelized the search of feasibility conditions of the problem into 28 computational threads with the Parallel Computing Toolbox.

Because of the nature of the optimization problem and the iterative solution method we chose for it, it is not possible for us to obtain a global optimum. Instead, we found a number of local minima in successive simulation runs and selected the best ones to report in the next section.

4 Results

This section presents the simulation results for the two case studies detailed in Sect. 3.3.

4.1 Comparison Between Simultaneous and Separate Optimization of Design Variables

Figures 6, 7, 8 show the simulation results of the DR program when $\beta(t)$ and $P_{RES}(t)$ are optimized separately, for each of the optimization variants: energy, net payment and peak reduction, respectively. Each figure contains three subplots that are a function of time: (a) plots the temperature of the interior contents of each cluster of independently controllable freezers; (b) indicates how many groups of freezers are switched ON; and (c) graphs the electrical power consumption of the flexible load and the generation of the PV system, with positive values denoting consumption and negative values denoting generation.

In Fig. 6 we see that exchanges with the grid are kept as close to zero as possible during the day, when solar power generation is available (7:00–18:00 and 31:00–41:00 h),

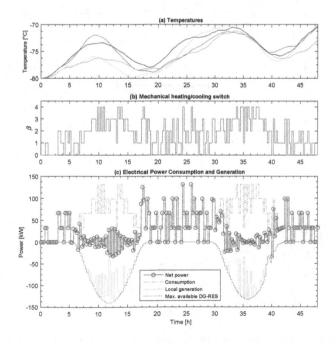

Fig. 6. Energy optimization with $\beta(t)$ and $P_{RES}(t)$ optimized separately.

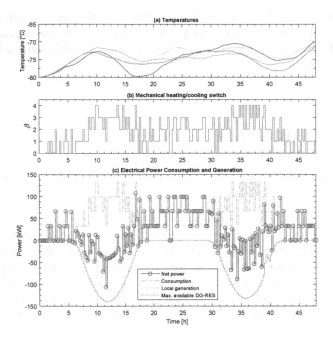

Fig. 7. Cost optimization with $\beta(t)$ and $P_{RES}(t)$ optimized separately.

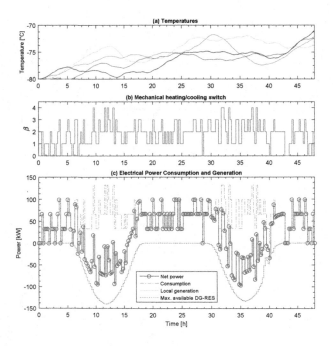

Fig. 8. Peak minimization with $\beta(t)$ and $P_{RES}(t)$ optimized separately.

and that, during the evening and early morning, the temperatures of the interior contents of the freezer are allowed to drift toward the upper bound by switching ON as few clusters of freezers as possible. In this scenario, we observe that PV generation is curtailed at several points during the day in order to keep the energy exchanges with the grid to a minimum, which comes at a detriment to the PV producer.

In Fig. 7 it is possible to observe that the flexible thermostatic loads are switched ON not only at the times where solar power is available, but also at the times when the electricity prices are low (approximately from 0:00–6:00, 15:00–19:00, 24:00–30:00 and 37:00–43:00 h). The general temperature trend during those hours is descending. In this scenario, PV production is fully utilized, thus maximizing the profit for the PV producer.

In Fig. 8, the peak power minimization objective is apparent: only three freezer clusters are ON simultaneously during the periods when there is no PV production. During daylight hours, all freezer clusters can be ON, since PV production offsets the load peak. In this scenario, PV production is also fully utilized.

Table 2 compares the results obtained by optimizing $\beta(t)$ and $P_{RES}(t)$ separately against those obtained by optimizing $\beta(t)$ and $P_{RES}(t)$ in a single genotype. The table shows the best and median values for the objective function evaluations, the computation times, and the PV utilization ratios from the successive simulation runs we performed for each scenario. From the figures and table, we can conclude that the results are comparable with one another, with the following notable improvements achieved by the sequential optimization of $\beta(t)$ and $P_{RES}(t)$:

- PV utilization rates increased.
- Better local minima were achieved in a slightly shorter amount of time.

The results confirm our hypothesis that optimizing our decision variables separately would decrease the computation time. We attribute this improvement to (1) a smaller search space due to the reduced number of variables, and (2) limiting the genotypes in the GA to either discrete or continuous elements instead of combining both types of variables in a single solution vector. The improved results obtained are attributable to an increased PV utilization rate, resulting from optimizing β assuming maximum PV production over the entire time horizon and then curtailing P_{RES} in the second suboptimization routine whenever necessary (see Fig. 2b).

4.2 Simulation Results Using Endpoint Constraints

This section presents and discussed the results obtained from the simulation experiments that included temperature end-of-horizon constraints (2e) in order to limit the state of charge of the freezers' thermal buffer, determined by Q_{flex} (13) and the heat loss rate through the the freezer enclosure elements (9c).

Table 3 shows the results for the three optimization variants with endpoint constraints, compared against the BAU scenario. In the table, the column entitled "Total exchange" is the sum of imports and exports from- and to the regional distribution grid. Figure 9 shows simulation results for the BAU scenario. This figure is analogous to Figs. 6, 7, 8, with the exception that subplot (a) shows the temperature evolution over time of the freezer contents (blue solid line) and indoor air temperatures

Table 2. Optimization results comparison.

Optimization variant	Objective function evaluation			Computation time [h:mm]		PV Utilization [%]	
	Best	Median	Unit	Best	Median	Best	Median
β and P_{RES} optimized simultaneously (from [28])							
Energy	1.52	1.77	MWh	1:22	1:34	77	64
Cost	36.92	42.69	€	1:21	1:46	88	87
Peak load	99	105.7	kW	1:11	1:20	53	49
β and P_{RES} optimized separately							
Energy	1.24	1.25	MWh	1:11	1:13	98	85
Cost	31.71	35.05	€	1:11	1:13	100	100
Peak load	99	103.0	kW	0:58	0:58	100	100

Table 3. Optimization results with endpoint constraints vs BAU scenario.

Optimization variant	Energy [kWh]			[€]	Reduction [%]			
	Consumption	Production	Total exchange	Net payment	Cost	Energy	Peak	PV utilization
BAU, no DR	1699.5	1006.7	1616.5	29.80	–	–	–	100
Energy	1489.1	666.42	840.5	22.45	25	48	5	66
Cost	1534.5	1006.7	1118.3	21.73	27	31	5	100
Peak load	1546.9	971.65	1154.01	22.76	24	29	29	97

(red solid line). Figures 10, 11, 12 graphically depict the simulation results for the energy, net payment and peak power minimization optimization variants for the endpoint constraints experiment.

In the BAU scenario, we can see that the uncontrolled infeed of power generated by the PV modules increases the peak from 132 kW (the peak output of the freezers) to 140 kW, because there is no consumption at the time when PV generation is highest (12:00 h). In the three optimization variants we can observe how the thermal buffer starts to deplete, but by around midday, the DR algorithm forces the freezers to start cooling again so that by the end of the horizon the temperature will be the same as the starting temperature −80 °C, and thus the thermal buffer will be full again. Because of the large time constant of the system and the relatively short simulation time horizon, we see that the temperatures never reach the upper bound of −70 °C. From this, we can conclude that adding endpoint constraints reduces the amount of flexibility available for DR actions, but eliminates the need for the system to recover (i.e., recharge its thermal buffers) after the DR time window has passed.

When comparing the results of this section to those obtained in Sect. 4.1, despite observing a difference in temperature evolutions brought about by the endpoint constraints (subplot a in Figs. 10, 11, 12), similar power consumption/generation trends can be observed for each optimization variant (subplot c in Figs. 10, 11, 12). In other words:

– The net energy exchanges with the electricity grid are reduced in the energy minimization scenario during times of solar energy production.

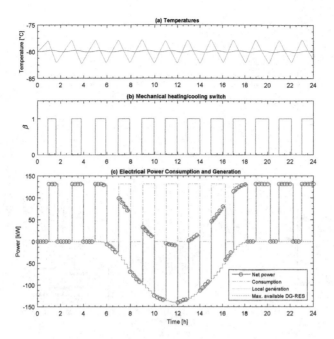

Fig. 9. BAU scenario 24-h.

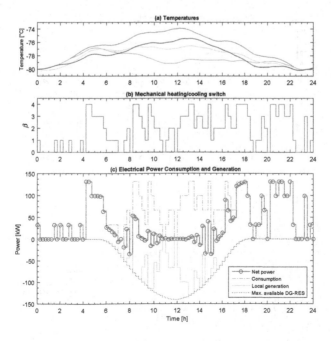

Fig. 10. Energy optimization with end-of-horizon temperature target.

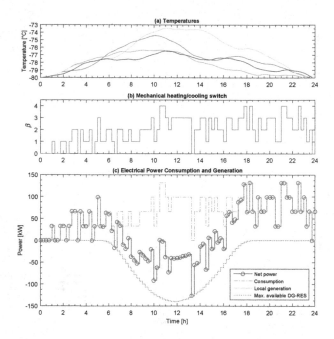

Fig. 11. Cost optimization with end-of-horizon temperature target.

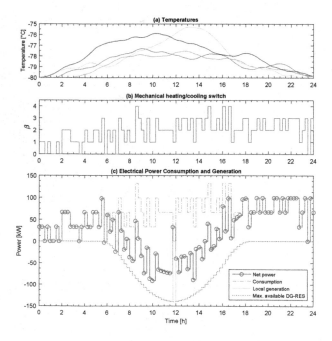

Fig. 12. Peak minimization with end-of-horizon temperature target.

- The periods of cheap electricity prices and solar energy production are taken advantage of in the net payment minimization scenario.
- The freezer clusters are operated three-at-a-time during periods of no solar power production, and are only allowed simultaneous operation during daylight hours.
- peak power is kept at less than or equal to the rated maximum power selected for these experiments in all three optimization variants.

The difference in electricity consumption between the results obtained when applying DR and the BAU scenario in Table 3 gives the total amount of flexibility gained from the freezers over the 24-h time horizon: 210 kWh for the energy minimization, 165 kWh for the net payment minimization, and 153 kWh for the peak load reduction objectives.

5 Discussion

This section further discusses the results obtained in the previous section and touches upon some limitations regarding the practical implementation of the proposed DR framework.

Results from the first simulation experiment confirm our initial hypothesis that optimizing the decision variables in separate, yet sequential optimization sub-problems would result in shorter computation times (22–30% less time) using the GA solver as implemented in MATLAB. We also achieved improvements in local minima and PV utilization rates by assuming maximum PV production for the thermostatic load scheduling sub-optimization routine and only curtailing DG-RES after obtaining an optimal load schedule. By reducing the number and type of variables for each sub-problem, the search spaces become smaller, and it takes a smaller number of generations to achieve the same or a better solution than solving the full optimization problem. However, it must be noted that separating the optimization problem into two (potentially suboptimal) subroutines is merely a compromise between achieving reasonable computation times and finding better local minima, given the chosen implementation in software of our DR framework. It would be worth investigating the effects of this using more powerful solvers.

The results from both Sects. 4.1 and 4.2 show the potential of implementing both price-responsive (net payment minimization) and direct control (peak load minimization) DR programs to harness flexibility from C&I customers' thermostatic loads. The employment of flexible loads brings about clear and attractive benefits in terms of reductions in the amount and overall electricity demand payments for consumers. Apart from the consumer benefits, the peak load reduction objective can also be beneficial for the network operator: the peak load reduction by 29% with respect to the BAU scenario with uncontrolled infeed of solar power could translate into deferrals in network reinforcement investments and/or lower connection fees.

Although the energy minimization case does not quite fall under the definition of DR programs, it still is an interesting variant to look at in terms of energy self-sufficiency for the consumer. However, the greater energy efficiency, while being in the interest of the microgrid as a whole, comes at a loss for the local PV producer due to occasional PV curtailment.

A possible expansion of our framework would be to combine all optimization variants into a single problem formulation by adding utilization constraints linked to the investment or operation expenses for the PV producer, and include peak capacity tariffs in the objective function.

Surmounting some of the assumptions made when computing the optimal schedules, especially with regards to dealing with errors in the PV forecasting data, will take additional effort before this DR framework can be rolled out into the field. In addition, although we have achieved shorter convergence times than in previous works, we need to take further steps to decrease the computation in order to move from the DR simulation environment into the the actual customer site. This issue can be resolved by using a more powerful commercial solver than those offered by the MATLAB Optimization Toolbox. Another possibility is to keep using MATLAB, but add a heuristic within the GA solver to filter out infeasible solutions based on heuristic calculations of the charging- and discharging rates of the system's thermal buffer, thus eliminating the need to perform the time-costly thermostatic load simulations in Simulink. A compromise between the quality of the solutions and the computational effort will be required when we scale up our DR framework to include more flexible sources in a business park.

6 Conclusions

This work presented a DR framework that schedules thermostatic loads and DG-RES production in advance of real-time (24–48 h) by using thermostatic load modeling techniques and a nonlinear optimization problem in order to quantify and deploy the demand-side flexibility in non-residential, C&I buildings. We assessed the benefits of DR in a series of case studies with and without end-of-horizon temperature constraints, where the flexible loads were 120 medical freezers containing blood samples, located in a research facility in a business park with local solar power generation.

Results show that the thermal buffer created by the thermal mass of the freezers' contents can be harnessed by automated DR actions to improve the price-responsiveness, energy independence and peak load of the system with respect to the business-as-usual scenario, by reducing load coincidence, improving consumer energy fees and equipment performance; and mitigating peak loads due to uncontrolled infeed of DG-RES that could allow the grid operator to defer investments in network reinforcements. Adding endpoint constraints reduces the amount of flexibility available for DR actions with respect to the scenario with no endpoint constraints, but eliminates the need for the system to recover (i.e., recharge its thermal buffers, represented by the medical freezers) immediately after the DR time window has passed.

Future work will extend the scope of our proposed DR framework to include the business park microgrid network constraints, and will add new flexibility sources in the business park, such as other building systems, thermal buffers (e.g. stratified hot water tanks), and/or electric vehicles.

Glossary

BAU Business-as-usual

C&I Commercial and industrial

COP Coefficient of performance

DG-RES Distributed generation from renewable energy sources

DR Demand response

GA Genetic algorithm

HVAC Heating, ventilation and air conditioning

PV Photovoltaic

RC Resistor/capacitor

References

1. Hewicker, C., Hogan, M., Mogren, A.: Power Perspectives 2030: on the road to a decarbonised power sector. Technical report, Roadmap 2050, Den Haag (2012)
2. Huber, M., Dimkova, D., Hamacher, T.: Integration of wind and solar power in Europe: assessment of flexibility requirements. Energy **69**, 236–246 (2014)
3. Alizadeh, M.I., Parsa Moghaddam, M., Amjady, N., Siano, P., Sheikh-El-Eslami, M.K.: Flexibility in future power systems with high renewable penetration: a review (2016)
4. Morales González, R., Shariat Torbaghan, S., Gibescu, M., Cobben, S.: Harnessing the flexibility of thermostatic loads in microgrids with solar power generation. Energies **9**, 547 (2016)
5. Gelažanskas, L., Gamage, K.A.A.: Distributed energy storage using residential hot water heaters. Energies **9**, 127 (2016)
6. Liu, W., Wu, Q., Wen, F., Ostergaard, J.: Day-ahead congestion management in distribution systems through household demand response and distribution congestion prices. Smart Grid, IEEE Trans. **5**, 2739–2747 (2014)
7. Yoon, J.H., Baldick, R., Novoselac, A.: Dynamic demand response controller based on real-time retail price for residential buildings. IEEE Trans. Smart Grid **5**, 121–129 (2014)
8. He, X., Keyaerts, N., Azevedo, I., Meeus, L., Hancher, L., Glachant, J.M.: How to engage consumers in demand response: a contract perspective. Util. Policy **27**, 108–122 (2013)
9. Klaassen, E., Frunt, J., Slootweg, J.: Method for evaluating smart grid concepts and pilots. In: IEEE Young Researcher Symposium 2014 (YRS 2014), Ghent, pp. 1–6. EESA (2014)
10. Dhulst, R., Labeeuw, W., Beusen, B., Claessens, S., Deconinck, G., Vanthournout, K.: Demand response flexibility and flexibility potential of residential smart appliances: experiences from large pilot test in Belgium. Appl. Energy **155**, 79–90 (2015)
11. Labeeuw, W., Stragier, J., Deconinck, G.: Potential of active demand reduction with residential wet appliances: a case study for Belgium. IEEE Trans. Smart Grid **6**, 315–323 (2015)

12. Ashok, S., Banerjee, R.: Load-management applications for the industrial sector. Appl. Energy **66**, 105–111 (2000)
13. Grünewald, P., Torriti, J.: Demand response from the non-domestic sector: early UK experiences and future opportunities. Energy Policy **61**, 423–429 (2013)
14. European Environment Agency: Final energy consumption by sector and fuel (2017)
15. Lampropoulos, I., Kling, W.L., Ribeiro, P.F., van den Berg, J.: History of demand side management and classification of demand response control schemes. IEEE Power Energy Soc. Gen. Meet. **2013**, 1–5 (2013)
16. Matthews, B., Craig, I.: Demand side management of a run-of-mine ore milling circuit. Control Eng. Pract. **21**, 759–768 (2013)
17. Mitra, S., Sun, L., Grossmann, I.E.: Optimal scheduling of industrial combined heat and power plants under time-sensitive electricity prices. Energy **54**, 194–211 (2013)
18. Finn, P., Fitzpatrick, C.: Demand side management of industrial electricity consumption: promoting the use of renewable energy through real-time pricing. Appl. Energy **113**, 11–21 (2014)
19. Samad, T., Kiliccote, S.: Smart grid technologies and applications for the industrial sector. Comput. Chem. Eng. **47**, 76–84 (2012)
20. Ton, D., Smith, M.: The U.S. department of energy's microgrid initiative. Electr. J. **25**, 84–94 (2012)
21. Zavala, V.M.: Real-time optimization strategies for building systems. Ind. Eng. Chem. Res. **52**, 3137–3150 (2013)
22. Ma, K., Hu, G., Spanos, C.J.: A cooperative demand response scheme using punishment mechanism and application to industrial refrigerated warehouses. IEEE Trans. Ind. Inform. **11**, 1520–1531 (2015)
23. Yin, R., et al.: Quantifying flexibility of commercial and residential loads for demand response using setpoint changes. Appl. Energy **177**, 149–164 (2016)
24. Hurtado, L.A., Mocanu, E., Nguyen, P.H., Gibescu, M., Kamphuis, I.G.: Enabling cooperative behavior for building demand response based on extended joint action learning. IEEE Trans. Ind. Inform **14**(1), 127–136 (2017)
25. Centraal Bureau voor de Statistiek: Energieverbruik; opbouw, bedrijfstak (2017)
26. Compendium voor de Leefomgeving: Bruto toegevoegde waarde en werkgelegenheid 1995–2016 (2017)
27. Centraal Bureau voor de Statistiek: Monitor topsectoren 2017 (2017)
28. Morales González, R., Gibescu, M., Cobben, J., Bongaerts, M., de Nes-Koedam, M., Vermeiden, W.: Demand response of medical freezers in a business park microgrid. In: SmartGreens 2015–7th International Conference Smart Cities Green ICT System, Funchal, SciTePress, pp. 1–10 (2018)
29. Kalsi, K., Chassin, F., Chassin, D.: Aggregated modeling of thermostatic loads in demand response: a systems and control perspective. In: 2011 50th IEEE Conference Decision Control European Control Conference (CDC-ECC), Orlando, pp. 15–20. IEEE (2011)
30. Hurtado, L., Mocanu, E., Nguyen, P., Kling, W.: Comfort-constrained demand flexibility management for building aggregations using a decentralized approach. In: 2015–4th International Conference Smart Cities Green ICT System SmartGreens, Lisbon, pp. 157–166 (2015)
31. Wilson, M.B., Luck, R., Mago, P.J.: A first-order study of reduced energy consumption via increased thermal capacitance with thermal storage management in a micro-building. Energies **8**, 12266–12282 (2015)
32. Sioshansi, R., Conejo, A.J.: Optimization in Engineering: Models and Algorithms. Springer, Cham (2017). https://doi.org/10.1007/978-3-319-56769-3
33. Eftekhar, J.G.: Some thermophysical properties of blood components and coolants for D5U. Technical report, University of Texas San Antonio, San Antonio (1989)

34. Wessling, F., Blackshear, P.: The thermal properties of human blood during the freezing process. Heat Transf. **95**, 246–249 (1973)
35. Zhang, A., Cheng, S., He, L., Luo, D., Gao, D.: Determination of thermal conductivity of cryoprotectant solutions and cell suspensions. Cell Preserv. Technol. **2**, 1–6 (2004)
36. Shpilrain, E.E.: AIR (PROPERTIES OF) (2011)
37. ASM Aerospace Specification Metals Inc.: (AISI Type 304 Stainless Steel)
38. MatWeb: Unifrax Excelfrax 200 VIP Vacuum Insulation Panel (2017)

A MPC Based Peak Shaving Application for a Household with Photovoltaic Battery System

Deepranjan Dongol$^{(\boxtimes)}$, Thomas Feldmann, Michael Schmidt,
and Elmar Bollin

Institute of Energy Systems Technology (INES), Offenburg University
of Applied Sciences, Am Güterbahnhof 1a, 77652 Offenburg, Germany
{deepranjan.dongol,thomas.feldmann,schmidt,
bollin}@hs-offenburg.de

Abstract. This paper presents the use of model predictive control (MPC) based approach for peak shaving application of a battery in a Photovoltaic (PV) battery system connected to a rural low voltage gird. The goals of the MPC are to shave the peaks in the PV feed-in and the grid power consumption and at the same time maximize the use of the battery. The benefit to the prosumer is from the maximum use of the self-produced electricity. The benefit to the grid is from the reduced peaks in the PV feed-in and the grid power consumption. This would allow an increase in the PV hosting and the load hosting capacity of the grid. The paper presents the mathematical formulation of the optimal control problem along with the cost benefit analysis. The MPC implementation scheme in the laboratory and experiment results have also been presented. The results show that the MPC is able to track the deviation in the weather forecast and operate the battery by solving the optimal control problem to handle this deviation.

Keywords: Model predictive control · Peak shaving · Battery storage

1 Introduction

A Photovoltaic (PV) system installed in a household allows the use of renewable energy at a local level. A distribution grid with a distributed number of such households can be considered to be an equivalent large PV plant with an aggregated load demand. Households with PV installations are typically under 10 kWp and comprise about 15% of the total installed PV power in Germany [1]. This poses a challenge to the distribution grid due to the mismatch in the power generation and the load demand. As distribution grids are resistive, the reverse power flows from the households to the grid leads to an increase in the voltage at the end of the distribution line. This situation can damage any installed electrical equipment in the grid such as the distribution transformer that have a specified nominal rating to deliver the power from the distribution grid to the households. According to the VDE-AR-N 4105 grid standard in Germany, for the defined nominal voltage of V_n, the permissible voltage rise at the coupling point of the end of the distribution line, V_{cp}, should follow the restriction

© Springer Nature Switzerland AG 2019
B. Donnellan et al. (Eds.): SMARTGREENS 2018/VEHITS 2018, CCIS 992, pp. 44–66, 2019.
https://doi.org/10.1007/978-3-030-26633-2_3

$V_{cp} \leq 1.03 \cdot V_n$ [2]. The regulation in Germany suggests the feed-in from the households with PV installations to be restricted to 70% of the installed peak PV power capacity [3]. In order to meet this feed-in limit, control strategies such as active power curtailment [4, 5] and reactive power control [6, 7] are available. However, this leads to a loss of useful energy. As such, a storage unit such as a battery is used to store the surplus PV energy and use it to meet the load demand.

Conventional operation of the PV battery, without the predictive control strategy, often leads to the battery being quickly charged and is unable to store any surplus PV energy during the peak power generation. As the battery technology is expensive, increasing the size of the battery is not a cost effective solution. Likewise, the battery is discharged as soon as there is a load demand and is unavailable to shave the peak load demand during the morning hours of the next day. The peak shaving strategy presented in [8] for a decentralized battery system in a residential network triggers the battery charging signal for each unit when the PV feed-in is higher than the threshold feed-in power defined. The threshold feed-in power limit is calculated from the sensitivity analysis of the voltage with respect to PV feed-in in the distribution grid. The authors in [9] have also presented the use of a battery to store PV energy when the PV feed-in limit is exceeded. The battery has been used as a buffer.

In this work, the challenge is to design a MPC for an individual household with a PV battery system connected to a rural distribution grid in a single electricity price scenario. The goals of the MPC are to shave the peaks in the PV energy and the peak load demand and maximize the use of the battery. The MPC would allow each individual household prosumer to conduct its own DSM autonomously and help postpone the need for varying the electricity price. This localized approach would be economically beneficial to the household by maximizing the use of self-produced electricity. At the same time, shaving peaks in the PV feed-in and the load demand would benefit the distribution grid by relieving it from the voltage stress.

This paper is also an extended version of our previous work presented in [10] and contains materials from our publication in [11].

1.1 Related Works

Several research works have been carried out to develop control strategies for a scheduled operation of the battery. The literature study was carried out to understand the existing research works on the predictive control strategies and cover the aspects of control approaches and the optimization problem formulations used by the researchers for this type of system.

In [12], the authors have presented a forecast based control strategy for the peak shaving application of battery in a PV battery system. In this approach, the battery SOC is provided as a set point for the charging or the discharging operation of the battery. The SOC set point is obtained by comparing the predicted PV power and the load demand with the available SOC in the battery over the defined time horizon and tuning it based on the current SOC of the battery. The battery is charged or discharged based on this battery SOC set point. A very similar forecast based control strategy has been used to dynamically set the PV feed-in limit using the battery [13]. In both [12, 13], the forecast based control strategies do not include an optimization problem but rather provide battery SOC set points to the local real time controller by using a decision based control (if then else) to operate the battery based on the forecast data.

The peak shaving strategy using the battery presented in [14] uses a model based predictive control approach. The economic operation of the battery is obtained by solving an optimization problem based on the varying price of electricity. The control strategy has two layers. The supervisory layer is the model based predictive control layer that provides the optimal values for the operation of the battery by solving the optimization problem at every 15 min time interval satisfying the operation constraints. The second layer is the decision based control layer (Fast Feedback Control Loop (FFCL) as mentioned by the authors) which handles any deviation between the measurement and the prediction during this interval in real time. The battery operation for peak shaving in [4] uses similar approach as in [14] , with an optimization layer and a decision based correction function defined in the real time controller which corrects the measurement-prediction deviation. In both [4] and [14] the battery is used as a buffer to store excess or to provide the lacking energy. In [14] the author has mentioned that using the battery as a buffer is a compromise with the optimal operation of the battery in order to deal with the model mismatch.

Researchers have used the principle of Model predictive Control (MPC) at the supervisory layer for the optimal operation of battery in renewable energy systems as in [15–18]. In these research works, the MPC has been used for the purpose of energy management strategy to offer an economic operation of the system components in a varying electricity price scenario. The economic operation of the system leads to a Linear Programming (LP) problem.The logical condition arising in the problem formulation such as the need to switch on-off of the system components or to avoid the concurrent charging and discharging of the storage unit, introduces binary variables that changes the LP problem to a Mixed Integer Linear programming (MILP) problem. Other objectives for the use of MILP based MPC problems might include a power commitment reference trajectory, such as in [19], for a PV power plant with battery storage where the battery operation is optimized to meet the required load demand. Some researchers have also used a quadratic degradation function of the storage components in the objective function for a hybrid storage system based micro grid with a battery and a hydrogen storage as in [20]. This degradation cost allows the optimization to decide on the optimal use of the hybrid storage components. This leads to a MPC based on a Mixed Integer Quadratic Programming (MIQP) problem. However, solving a MILP or a MIQP problems is not a big challenge as the constraints are linear which guarantees the convexity of the problem and can be efficiently solved using commercially available solvers such as IBM-CPLEX [21].

1.2 Comparison with Other Works

In this work, the MPC has been designed and implemented only as the supervisory layer. The correction function or the decision based control during the time interval, as implemented in [4, 14], has not used in the experiment as its application is trivial. In our work, the goal of the experiment is to capture the ability of the MPC as a supervisor layer to deal with the forecast uncertainties without compromising the optimal operation of the battery. The focus of this work is more towards the MPC problem formulation.

The MPC has been designed for a single electricity price scenario, with the feed-in tariff of 0.13 €/kWh and the grid electricity price of 0.31 €/kWh, in accordance with the regulation in Germany [12]. The cost of using the battery has been considered to be cheaper than using the grid electricity. The difference between the MPC designed in this work and other forecast based control strategies and the optimization problems for a grid connected PV battery system are as follows:

(i) The forecast based control strategies as mentioned in [12, 13] are focused on limiting the PV feed-in within the defined feed-in limit. In [12, 13] the SOC set point is tuned based on the PV and load demand forecast along with the measured and available storage capacity of the battery. If the measured SOC is less than the tuned SOC set point, the battery is charged as soon as there is surplus PV energy. When the SOC set point is exceeded, the battery operates in the peak shaving mode i.e. stores the PV energy only when the PV feed-in violates the feed-in limit. Similarly in [12, 13], the feed-in limit is tuned and the battery is charged accordingly. These strategies don't consider the peak shaving of the load demand. So during the evening period when there is a load demand, the battery is discharged to meet the load demand as in the conventional operation. This way, the battery is not available to shave the peaks in the load demand of the next morning. The MPC in our work considers both the peaks in the PV and the load demand and controls the charging and the discharging operation of the battery. The forecast based control strategies are suitable only for a large PV battery system where the surplus PV energy that violates the feed-in limit exceeds the energy demand. The stored surplus PV energy that exceeds the load demand is then later discharged to the grid. This type of case doesn't require an optimization problem formulation as the battery size is already big enough to store the surplus PV energy that can meet the entire load demand. Using an if-then-else conditions based on the forecast data is sufficient to operate the battery. The MPC designed in this work is more suitable for the cases where the energy demand during the off-sun time period is higher than the surplus PV energy stored in the battery. This requires controlling the battery power during the discharge to shave the peaks in the overall load demand in the prediction horizon. As the installation of the PV battery system is expensive, our MPC provides a peak shaving solution for a small scale PV battery system which is suitable for the households in the rural distribution grid.

(ii) The optimal control problem formulation in the research works mentioned in the literature study [14–18] is only suitable for a time varying electricity price scenario. The objective function is linear which is not suitable for a peak shaving application in a single electricity price scenario. This is because the optimization cannot differentiate between the peaks and non-peaks when the cost is the same. In our work, a quadratic objective function has been formulated in the optimal control problem which considers the difference between the predicted PV power and the load demand profile to ensure that the battery is fully utilized while prioritizing the peaks in the PV energy and the load demand. The optimal operation of the battery only influences the power profile of PV feed-in and the grid consumption and not the total energy exchanged. For our case, as the feed-in tariff is less than the grid electricity price, charging the battery from the grid and then discharging the battery to the grid is prohibited in the optimal control problem as it is not cost effective.

1.3 Power Flow Balance

A simplified schematic of a household with a grid-connected PV battery system is shown in Fig. 1. At any time interval i, $p_{vi} \geq 0$ is the AC output power of the installed PV system, $p_{L_i} \geq 0$ is the household load demand, $p_{bc_i} \geq 0$ is the battery charging power, $p_{bdc_i} \leq 0$ is the battery discharging power, $p_{gf_i} \geq 0$ is the power fed into the grid and $p_{gc_i} \leq 0$ is the grid power consumption. The sign convention of the respective variable is consistent throughout this paper. The power flow within the system satisfies the power-flow balance constraint which can be expressed as

$$p_{v_i} - p_{L_i} = p_{gf_i} + p_{bc_i} + p_{bdc_i} + p_{gc_i} \tag{1}$$

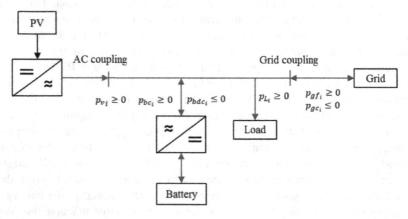

Fig. 1. A simplified schematic of the grid-connected PV battery system [10, 11].

1.4 Battery Storage Dynamics

A linear and discrete model is used to calculate the SOC of the battery. The battery model is obtained as

$$x_{i+1} = x_i + \eta_{ch} \cdot p_{bc_i} \cdot \Delta t + (1/\eta_{dch}) \cdot p_{bdc_i} \Delta t - L_{batt,loss} \cdot \Delta t \tag{2}$$

The total energy of the battery for a time interval $i+1$ is calculated as the sum of the energy available in the battery and the energy being stored or withdrawn during the battery operation at the time interval i Here, Δt is the duration of the time interval. The efficiency of the charging and discharging processes are defined by variables η_{ch} and η_{dch} respectively. For this problem, the constant values for both η_{ch} and η_{dch} have been considered. Otherwise, the model in Eq. 2 would become non-linear and stochastic if an interdependence of η_{ch} and η_{dch} with p_{bc_i} and p_{bdc_i} respectively are expressed. The problem would then become non-convex and very difficult to solve. The loss in the battery due to the self-consumption of the battery converter is represented by $L_{batt,loss}$. For the optimal control problem, if E_{batt} is the nominal capacity of the battery, the SOC of the battery is calculated as

$$SOC_{i+1} = (x_{i+1}/E_{batt}) \times 100 \tag{3}$$

In order to avoid the concurrent charging and discharging of the battery, a logical condition of $p_{bc_i} \cdot p_{bdc_i} = 0$ arises. It is represented as a linear inequality by using the binary variables as follows:

$$p_{bc_i} = \begin{cases} 0 \leq P_{bc_i} \leq P_{Max}, & \text{if } \delta_{bc} = 1 \\ 0, & \text{otherwise} \end{cases} \tag{4}$$

$$p_{bdc_i} = \begin{cases} -P_{Max} \leq p_{bdc_i} \leq 0, & \text{if } \delta_{bdc} = 1 \\ 0, & \text{otherwise} \end{cases} \tag{5}$$

For the optimal control problem, Eqs. 4 and 5 can be reformulated as

$$0 \leq p_{bc_i} \leq P_{Max} \cdot \delta_{bc_i} \tag{6}$$

$$-P_{Max} \cdot \delta_{bdc_i} \leq p_{bdc_i} \leq 0 \tag{7}$$

Here, P_{Max} is the maximum rated capacity of the battery converter. Equations 4 and 5 suggest that the charging or discharging of the battery only occur when the binary variable δ_{bc} or δ_{bdc} is equal to 1 respectively. The concurrent charging and discharging of the battery is avoided by defining a binary inequality constraint as

$$\delta_{bc_i} + \delta_{bdc_i} \leq 1 \tag{8}$$

The maximum storage capacity of the battery is restricted by its rated capacity. Likewise, the allowable discharge of the battery is restricted by the Depth of Discharge (DOD) provided by the battery manufacturer. This operational constraint on the battery SOC can be expressed as

$$X_{Min} \leq x_{i+1} \leq X_{Max} \tag{9}$$

$$X_{Min} = (1 - DOD) \cdot X_{Max} \tag{10}$$

Here, $X_{Max} = E_{batt}$ is the rated capacity of the battery.

1.5 Interaction with the Grid

As in the case of the battery, binary variables are introduced to avoid the concurrent feed-in to the grid and the grid power consumption to reformulate the logic constraint of $p_{gf_i} \cdot p_{gc_i} = 0$ as

$$P_{gf_i} = \begin{cases} 0 \le P_{gf_i} \le P_{v_i}, & \text{if } \delta_{gf} = 1 \\ 0, & \text{otherwise} \end{cases} \qquad (11)$$

$$P_{gc_i} = \begin{cases} -P_{g_{Max}} \le P_{gc_i} \le 0, & \text{if } \delta_{gc} = 1 \\ 0, & \text{otherwise} \end{cases} \qquad (12)$$

$$\delta_{gf_i} + \delta_{gc_i} \le 1 \qquad (13)$$

For the optimal control problem, Eqs. 11 and 12 can be expressed as

$$0 \le P_{gf_i} \le P_{v_i} \cdot \delta_{gf_i} \qquad (14)$$

$$-P_{g_{Max}} \cdot \delta_{gc_i} \le P_{gc_i} \le 0 \qquad (15)$$

In Eq. 14, the maximum grid feed-in is restricted by the PV power p_{v_i}. However, a very high positive scalar value, much greater than the installed peak PV capacity, could also be used instead of p_{v_i} as this restriction is just to bring the binary variable δ_{gf_i} into action. In Eq. 15, $P_{g_{Max}}$ is defined by the maximum possible grid power consumption for the system which is set to a very high positive scalar value that is even higher than the maximum peak load demand. This is in order to ensure that the grid consumption is always available when required. This doesn't affect the optimal solution due to the power-flow balance constraint in Eq. 1. The concurrent grid feed-in and grid consumption is avoided using Eq. 13. Furthermore, the power flow between the battery and the grid and vice versa has been disallowed as the optimal control problem is designed for the maximum usage of the self-produced electricity using the battery. This leads to the logical conditions $p_{bc_i} \cdot p_{gc_i} = 0$ and $p_{bdc_i} \cdot p_{gf_i} = 0$, which are then expressed as

$$\delta_{gf_i} + \delta_{bdc_i} \le 1 \qquad (16)$$

$$\delta_{gc_i} + \delta_{bc_i} \le 1 \qquad (17)$$

1.6   PV Power Prediction

A physical model was used to predict PV power along with the procedure as described in [22]. The sun's position is calculated from the site-specific information in terms of the latitude and the longitude, the time zone and the calendar day. From these data, the solar azimuth, the elevation angle of the sun and the extraterrestrial irradiation are calculated. The global solar irradiation obtained from the weather data is then separated into diffused and direct insolation. From the position of the sun, the direct and the diffused global solar irradiance on the horizontal plain and the orientation and the tilt of the PV modules, irradiation, G_h, is calculated on the inclined surface of the PV panel. After having obtained this irradiation, the photovoltaic DC output is calculated as

$$P_{v_{dc}} = P_{v,\text{STC}} \cdot \left(G_h/G_{h,\text{STC}}\right) \cdot \left[1 - \lambda \cdot (T_c - 25)\right] \tag{18}$$

$P_{v_{dc}}$ is PV power, $P_{v,\text{STC}}$ is PV power under Standard Test Conditions (STC), $G_{h,\text{STC}}$ is irradiance under STC, λ is the temperature coefficient at the maximum power point, and T_c is the cell temperature. The calculation for cell temperatures is obtained from as

$$T_c = K_{Gt} \cdot G_h + T_{amb} \tag{19}$$

A correction factor of $K_{\text{GT}} = 0.037 \,°\text{C}/\text{m}^2 \cdot \text{W}$ was introduced to the cell temperature by assuming a linear relation between the cell temperature T_c and the solar irradiance G_h on the PV panels, where T_{amb} is the ambient temperature. According to [23], K_{GT} is calculated using the Nominal Operating Cell Temperature (NOCT) information as $K_{\text{GT}} = (\text{NOCT} - 20\,°\text{C})/0.8\,\text{kW} \cdot \text{m}^2$. NOCT is defined as the cell temperature at an ambient temperature of 20 °C, solar irradiance at $0.8\,\text{kW} \cdot \text{m}^2$ and a wind speed of $1\,\text{m} \cdot \text{s}^{-1}$. In this work, each Bosch Solar Module c-Si M 60 EU 30117 in the installed array has a NOCT value of 49.6 °C.

The efficiency of the PV inverter for the conversion of DC to AC power, which follows the European standard, is obtained as

$$\eta_{\text{W}_r} = 0.833 + 0.684 \cdot (P_{v_{dc}}/P_{\text{N}}) - 1.29 \cdot (P_{v_{dc}}/P_{\text{N}})^2 + 0.662 \cdot (P_{v_{dc}}/P_{\text{N}})^3 \tag{20}$$

$P_{v_{dc}}$ is the DC input power to the inverter from PV, and P_{N} is the nominal rating of the inverter. The AC output of PV power is calculated as

1.7 Load Demand

For this work, no load prediction model has been used as there was no real case available. The load demand is taken from the database for the experiment.

2 Model Predictive Control

A MPC requires that an optimal control problem is solved repeatedly based on the measurement update of the system variables at each time step. For the MPC design, the PV prediction model from Sect. 3.4 is used to predict the PV power. The weather data are available from the weather service provider. The load demand is obtained from the database and has been considered to be perfect. An optimal control problem has been formulated which is solved for the prediction horizon from i to $i + N - 1$, where N is the total number of time steps.

The optimal operation of the battery depends on the solution of the optimal control problem formulation. The objective function needs to be solved within the defined set of system constraints. For this system, as the power flow balance has to be maintained as per Eq. 1, the entire performance of the system is based on the optimal operation of the battery. A detailed mathematical formulation of the optimal control problem has been presented. The economic benefit of the optimal control problem has also been evaluated.

2.1   Optimal Control Problem

The PV power output is obtained as $\underline{P_v} = \begin{bmatrix} p_{v_i} \ldots p_{v_{i+N-1}} \end{bmatrix}^T$ in a $N \times 1$ vector over the prediction horizon. Similarly, the load demand over the prediction horizon is obtained in a $N \times 1$ vector as $\underline{P_L} = \begin{bmatrix} p_{L_i} \ldots p_{L_{i+N-1}} \end{bmatrix}^T$. The difference between the predicted PV power and the predicted load demand over the prediction horizon for each time interval is obtained in a new $N \times 1$ vector as $\underline{P_{in}} = \underline{P_v} - \underline{P_L} = \begin{bmatrix} p_{in_i} \ldots p_{in_{i+N-1}} \end{bmatrix}^T$. The vector $\underline{P_{in}}$ provides the reference for the battery operation over the prediction horizon. For a prediction horizon of 24 h, the number of time steps N with a time interval of 10 min is obtained as $N = (24 \times 60)/10 = 144$. The time interval of 10 min was chosen as a standard for the supervisory layer in this work. The objective of the optimal control problem formulation is to find the optimal values for p_{bc_i} and p_{bdc_i} so as to reduce the peaks in $\underline{P_{in}}$. As the problem has a reference and a target variable along with the binary constraints, the optimal control problem has been formulated as a MIQP problem as

$$J = \min_u \sum_i^{i+N-1} \frac{1}{2} u_i^T R u_i \tag{22}$$

Subject to: Eqs. 1–3, Eqs. 6–9 and Eqs. 13–17

$$\text{Where, } u_i = \begin{bmatrix} p_{in_i} - p_{bc_i} \\ p_{in_i} - p_{bdc_i} \\ p_{gc_i} \end{bmatrix} \text{ and } R = \begin{bmatrix} 100 & 0 & 0 \\ 0 & 100 & 0 \\ 0 & 0 & 2000 \end{bmatrix} \tag{23}$$

The objective function in Eq. 22 can be represented in an equivalent form as

$$J = \min \sum_{i=1}^{i+N-1} \underbrace{R_{11} \cdot (p_{in_i} - p_{bc_i})^2}_{J_1} + \underbrace{R_{22} \cdot (p_{in_i} - P_{bdc_i})^2}_{J_2} + \underbrace{R_{33} \cdot p_{gc_i}^2}_{J_3} \tag{24}$$

When the objective function J is minimized, the quadratic penalty on $p_{gc_i}^2$ ensures that the grid power consumption is very low with reduced peaks. The penalties on the squared differences in expression J_1 and J_2 ensure that the battery power flow reaches as close as possible to the reference $\underline{P_{in}}$, thereby prioritizing the peaks.

For the situations $p_{in_i} > 0$, minimization of J results in $p_{bc_i} \rightarrow p_{in_i}$ as $p_{bc_i} \geq 0$. In this case, as $p_{bdc_i} \leq 0$, minimization of J results in the minimization of the variable p_{bdc_i}. But due to the constraint defined in Eq. 8, $p_{bdc_i} = 0$. Similarly, for the situations $p_{in_i} < 0$, minimizing J results in $p_{bdc_i} \rightarrow p_{in_i}$ and $p_{bc_i} = 0$. For the situation, when $p_{in_i} = 0$, there is no battery power flow i.e. $p_{bc_i} = p_{bdc_i} = 0$, due to the constraints defined in Eqs. 16 and 17. Due to the power flow balance constraint in Eq. 1, the value of p_{gf_i} is obtained automatically from the optimal solution.

The objective function defined in Eq. 22 is quadratic. The convexity of a quadratic function with linear constraints is trivial and can be verified by finding the Hessian of the function which should be positive semi-definite [24]. From Eq. 23 as $R > 0$, the Hessian matrix is positive semi-definite. Therefore the optimal control problem is convex and has a global minimum.

2.1.1 Economic Benefit Assessment

As the objective function J in Eq. 24 is not dictated by price, its solution has been compared with the solution of the optimization problem for an economic operation of the system. The idea is to compare the economic benefits and the resulting grid power profile in a single grid electricity price scenario. The objective function for the price based optimization problem was formulated using [15] as the reference and is expressed as

$$Cost = min \sum\nolimits_{i=1}^{i+N-1} -C_{bdc} \cdot p_{bdc_i} - C_{gf} \cdot p_{gf_i} - C_{gc} \cdot p_{gc_i} \qquad (25)$$

Subject to: Eqs. 1–3, Eqs. 6–9 and Eqs. 13–15

Here, $C_{gf} = 0.13$ €/kWh and $C_{gc} = 0.31$ €/kWh are the feed-in tariff and the grid electricity price respectively. $C_{bdc} = 0.02$ €/kWh is the wearing cost of the battery used in this paper and has been considered only for the discharging process. The expressions $-C_{bdc} \cdot p_{bdc_i}$ and $-C_{gc} \cdot p_{gc_i}$ have a negative sign respectively in the objective function as $p_{bdc_i} \leq 0$ and $p_{gc_i} \leq 0$. But the expression $-C_{gf} \cdot p_{gf_i}$ has a negative sign as $p_{gf_i} \geq 0$, and minimizing it would maximize the cost benefits from the feed-in tariff. The battery charging p_{bc_i} is provided by the solver from the power flow balance constraint in Eq. 1.

The constraint in Eq. 14 changes to $0 \leq p_{gf_i} \leq P_{vMax} \cdot \delta_{gf_i}$. Here P_{vMax} is the PV feed-in limit usually defined by the regulation or the grid operator. This is because, as feed-in to the grid earns cost benefit from the feed-in tariff, not providing this limit would lead to peaks in the PV feed-in to the grid. For this problem, an arbitrary $P_{vMax} = 3.5$ kW has been considered. The constraints in Eqs. 16 and 17 have not been used here. The optimal solution decides if the interaction between the battery and the grid brings any cost benefits for a single electricity price scenario.

The optimization problems were solved using PV and load demand data for a week using the system specification of Table 1. The solutions of the two different optimization problems - peak shaving (our optimal control problem) and for an economic operation of the system (as defined in Eq. 25), were evaluated with respect to the increase in the nominal battery size as shown in Fig. 2a. The value of the objective function *Cost* in Eq. 25 gradually decreases with an increase in the battery size which is an indicator of the reduction in the operational cost. It saturates at the battery size of 15 kWh. This is because any surplus PV energy beyond that is required to meet the load demand will not be stored in the battery as the battery feeding energy to the grid would not be cost beneficial due to the loss of energy during the battery operation. Therefore, there is no battery feed-in to the grid. On the other hand, the value of the objective function J in Eq. 24 decreases with an increase in the battery size even for the battery size greater than 15 kWh. This is because the objective function J maximizes the use of the battery and stores as much of surplus PV energy as possible. The objective function J is formulated in the way that it always decreases with the increase in the use of the battery.

Since the work is based on a single electricity price scenario, the economic benefit analysis can be carried out in terms of the energy exchanged for both the optimization problems cases. This can be explained in terms of the Self-Consumption and the Self-Sufficiency which according to [4] is defined as

$$Self-Consumption = \frac{E_{DU} + E_{BC}}{E_{PV}} \tag{26}$$

$$Self-Sufficiency = \frac{E_{DU} + E_{BD}}{E_L} \tag{27}$$

Where, E_{DU} is the PV energy directly used, E_{BC} is the energy stored in the battery during charging, E_{PV} is the overall PV energy, E_{BD} is the energy used from the battery during discharging and E_L is the total energy demand.

The Self-Consumption and the Self-Sufficiency of the system obtained from both the optimization cases are shown in Fig. 2b. For the price based optimization, the Self-Consumption increases with the increase in the battery size and saturates at the battery size of 15 kWh, which is also where the operational cost benefit of the system saturates. This again indicates that any surplus PV energy beyond that is required to meet the load demand will not be stored in the battery. In contrast, the Self-Consumption of the system obtained from the solutions of the peak shaving optimization is the same as that for the price based optimization until the battery size of 15 kWh and tends to increase even when the battery size is increased beyond 15 kWh. This is again because the objective function J maximizes the use of the battery and stores as much of surplus PV energy. The surplus PV energy stored exceeding the load demand could have been used to earn the feed-in tariff benefits. However, it is understood that the battery size beyond 15 kWh for this system would not be economically beneficial either. The Self-Sufficiency calculated from the solutions of both the optimization problems is the same. Therefore, our optimal control problem ensures the same operational cost benefits as the price based optimization problem if the battery size has been chosen to bring the economic benefits. This comparative evaluation also justifies the use of constraints defined in Eqs. 16 and 17 for our optimal control problem.

2.1.2   Reduction in the Peaks of the Grid Power Flow

The grid power flow profiles obtained from solving the optimization problems using the same data and the system as in Sect. 3.1. As the energy exchanged with the grid is the same for both the optimization problems, the optimal control problem used in our work only influences the grid power profile by shaving the peaks as shown in Fig. 3. The PV feed-in has been restricted to 3.2 kw even though the feed-in limit was set to 3.5 kW. Likewise, the grid power consumption has been restricted to 0.43 kw.

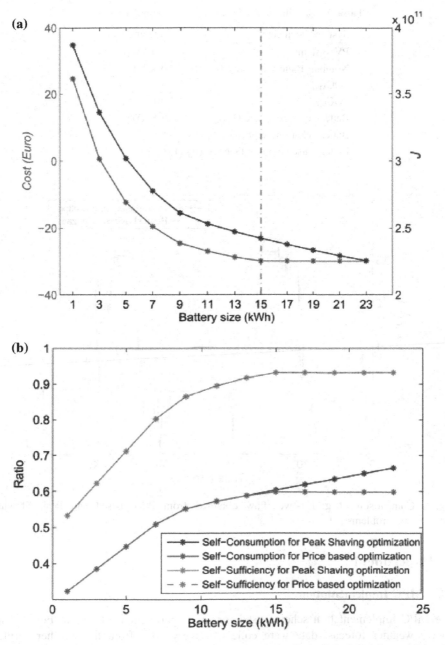

Fig. 2. a (Above). Cost benefit using the price based optimization and the behaviour of J for the peak shaving optimization with the increase in the nominal battery capacity. b (Below). Self-Sufficiency and Self-Consumption for the price based optimization and the peak shaving optimization with the increase in the nominal battery capacity [11].

Table 1. Specification of parameters for simulation [11].

System parameters	Specification
PV system	6.5 kWp
Nominal Battery capacity (E_{batt})	3 kWh
SOC_{Max}	80%
SOC_{Min}	20%
Battery converter size (P_{Max})	1.8 kWp
Battery charging efficiency (η_{ch})	85%
Battery discharging efficiency (η_{dch})	95%

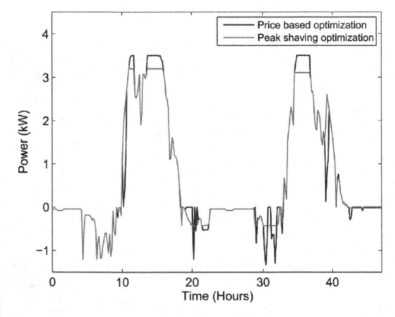

Fig. 3. Comparison of grid power flow obtained from Price based and Peak Shaving optimization problems [11].

3 Experiment

3.1 MPC Implementation

The MPC implementation scheme used for the experiment is shown in Fig. 4. The hourly weather forecast data were collected every 24 h from the weather service provider. The weather forecast data were used to predict the PV power using the prediction model described in Sect. 3.4. The predicted hourly PV power profile was then interpolated using Piecewise Cubic Hermite Data Interpolation (PCHIP) for every 10 min which is also the time resolution of the MPC.

A generic household load profile was used which was collected from the database with the peak load demand of 1.03 kWp. The Load demand was available for each time

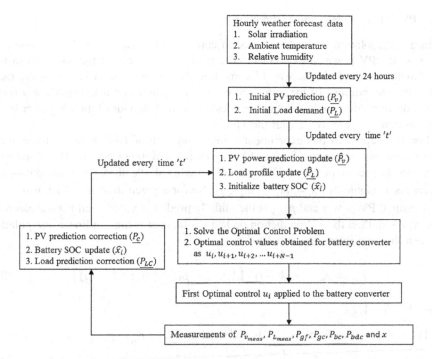

Fig. 4. MPC implementation in the experiment [10, 11].

step and was considered to be perfect. The load demand is virtual as there was no real load available due to the limitations in the laboratory infrastructure. The optimal discharging of the battery was fed to the internal micro-grid. The reduction in the load demand and the expected grid power consumption were calculated from the power-flow balance in Eq. 1.

At the time interval i when the experiment was run, the predicted PV data, $\underline{P_v}$ along with the day's load profile, $\underline{P_L}$, and the initialized battery SOC, $\hat{x}_i$ from the measurement, were provided to the optimal control problem. The optimal solution results in a sequence of optimal control values: $u_i, u_{i+1}, u_{i+2}, \ldots u_{i+N-1}$ for each time step. Only the first solution u_i for the first control interval i was applied to the battery converter. At the end of each control time interval, the measured PV power was used to correct the PV prediction, obtained as $\underline{P_c}$, which then updated the predicted PV power profile as $\widehat{P_v}$. The load profile was automatically updated from the database as $\widehat{P_L}$. The measured battery SOC was again used to update and initialize before another optimal control problem was solved. The prediction horizon is updated every 24 h that also slides at the end of each control interval as the optimal control problem is solved. This process was repeated online.

3.2 PV Power Prediction Correction

A linear interpolation method was used to correct and update the PV prediction data based on the PV power measurement. The prediction correction method used in this experiment is a very simple way of correcting the predicted data based on the measurement. The purpose of the introduction of our method is not to introduce a novel prediction correction method but rather to estimate the behavior of the PV power based on measurements and use it with the MPC.

For the purpose of this experiment a time resolution of 10 min, as for the optimal control problem, was used for the PV power prediction-correction. This correction procedure is shown in Fig. 5. The initially predicted PV data from the day-ahead forecast is available as $\underline{P_v} = \begin{bmatrix} p_{v_i} & \cdots & p_{v_{i+N-1}} \end{bmatrix}$. So for a given time interval i, if $p_{v_{meas_i}}$ is the measured PV power and $p_{v_{i+6}}$ is the initially predicted value at an hour-ahead time interval $i + 6$, then the PV prediction update is obtained using the linear interpolation between the time intervals i and $i + 6$ as

$$\widehat{p}_{v_k} = p_{v_{meas_i}} + (k - i) \cdot \left(\left(p_{v_{i+6}} - p_{v_{meas_i}} \right) / ((i+6) - i) \right) \tag{28}$$

where $k \in [i+1, i+5]$.

The updated data from Eq. 28 is collected as $\underline{P_c} - \begin{bmatrix} \widehat{p}_{v_{i+1}} & \widehat{p}_{v_{i+2}} & \cdots \widehat{p}_{v_{i+5}} \end{bmatrix}$. The PV data is then updated as $\widehat{\underline{p}}_v = \begin{bmatrix} p_{v_i} & \widehat{p}_{v_{i+1}} & \widehat{p}_{v_{i+2}} & \cdots & \widehat{p}_{v_{i+5}} & p_{v_{i+6}} & \cdots & p_{v_{i+N-1}} \end{bmatrix}$ between the time interval i and $i + 6$.

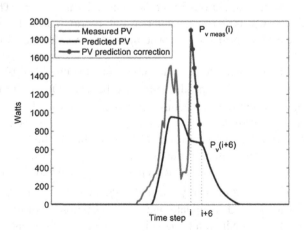

Fig. 5. PV prediction-correction method by using linear interpolation.

3.3   Experiment Setup

The schematic of the MPC implemented in the laboratory system is shown in Fig. 6. The experiment setup consisted of an installed 2.1 kWp PV system. The PV installation was AC-coupled with the experimental micro-grid by a 2.2 kWp PV inverter. A 1.8 kWp battery converter connected the battery to this micro-grid. A deep-discharge 3 kWh lithium-ion battery was used for the experiment. The battery capacity was used from 15% to 100% of its rated capacity as suggested by the battery manufacturer. As mentioned before, the load demand is virtual and has only been shown for the sake of representation. It should be noted that the $p_{v_{meas_i}}$, p_{gf_i}, p_{bc_i}, p_{bdc_i} and x_i were measured directly from the real system. Since p_{L_i} is virtual, p_{gc_i} was obtained from the calculation. The system parameters used for the experiment are shown in Table 2.

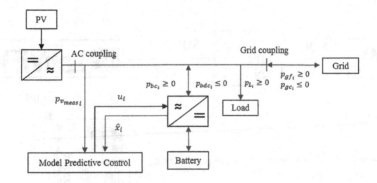

Fig. 6. Schematic of the experiment setup using the proposed MPC strategy.

Table 2. System specification in the experiment setup [10, 11].

System parameters	Specification
Installed PV	2.1 kWp
Installed PV inverter	2.2 kWp
Nominal battery capacity (E_{batt})	3 kWh
SOC_{Max}	100%
SOC_{Min}	15%
Battery converter size (P_{Max})	1.8 kWp
Battery charging efficiency (η_{ch})	85%
Battery discharging efficiency (η_{dch})	95%

For this experiment, the schematic of the communication between the hardware and the software interface is shown in Fig. 7. This approach was chosen because the MATLAB 2014a version does not support the OPC UA protocol [25]. All the relevant measurements and the required weather forecast and the load data are stored in the MS-SQL (Microsoft – Structured Query Language) server database. These data are then fetched into the MATLAB using the SQL commands. The optimal control problem was formulated in MATLAB and solved using the IBM- CPLEX solver. The optimal value of the battery power flow is then written from the MATLAB into the MS-SQL server database using the SQL commands. The PLC reads this optimal value and sets it into the battery converter via CAN bus. LABVIEW was used as an interface between the MS-SQL server database and the CX2040 Beckhoff Programmable Logic Controller (PLC) by using the OPC UA communication protocol to visualize the process. Otherwise, the PLC could also directly read and write from and to the MS-SQL server database. All the measurements are written to the MS-SQL server database by the PLC.

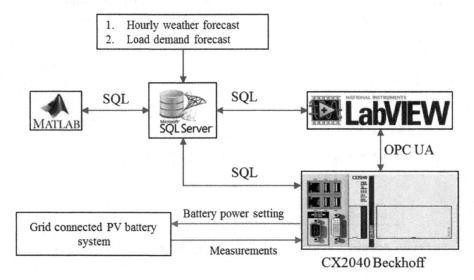

Fig. 7. Schematic of the communication used in experiment [10, 11].

3.4   Experiment Results

The experiment was conducted for a consecutive two cloudy days. These cloudy days were chosen based on the weather forecast data in order to verify the effectiveness of the MPC to deal with the forecast uncertainty. All the experiment results have been presented with a time resolution of 10 min.

The predicted PV power using the weather forecast data before the start of the experiment and the measured PV power after the end of the experiment are shown in Fig. 8. The resulting power flow in the system obtained from applying the MPC in the experiment is shown in Fig. 9. The loss in the battery due to the self-consumption of the power electronics in the converter was measured to be approximately about 10 W. This has been reflected in the battery power flow between 0 and 7 h and likewise between 25 and 31 h during the measurement.

The plot of the surplus power represented by the variable P_{in} in the optimal control problem and the battery power flow obtained from the experiment is shown in the Fig. 10. The results show that the random peaks in the PV power due to the clouds

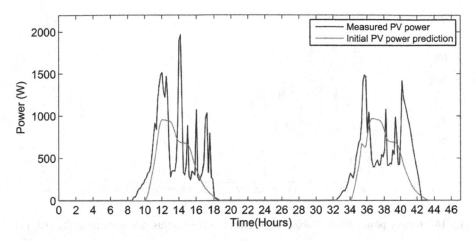

Fig. 8. Predicted and measured PV power output from the two consecutive experiments days [10, 11].

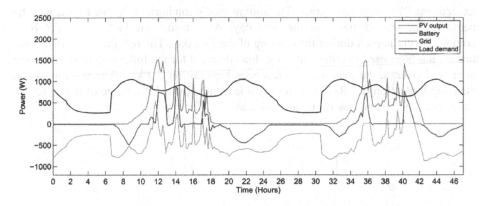

Fig. 9. Power flow results from the experiment [10, 11].

have been detected. The MPC was able to control the charging of the battery when the peaks in PV power occurred. As the MPC was used only for the supervisory purpose, it was not able to handle the deviations in the PV power that occurred during the 10 min control time interval. Due to this, between hour 11 and 13, the battery charging power was at times more than the surplus PV power. This situation has also occurred between the hour 17 and 18 as well as between hour 34 and 36. So during these time slots, the grid power has been consumed from the internal micro-grid to charge the battery. Also the PV power at hour 16, 38 and 39 was not able to be charged to the battery as the deviation occurred during the control time interval. If the system were run rule based, the battery would have been able to store all the surplus PV energy. The error in this experiment is due to the time resolution of the MPC. For this experiment, the Root Mean Square Error (RMSE) between the surplus PV power available and the battery charging power using the MPC was calculated to be 82.28 W.

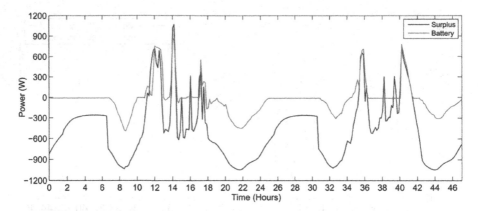

Fig. 10. Battery power flow obtained with respect to the surplus power variable $\underline{P_{in}}$ [10, 11].

The optimal discharge of the battery has reduced the peaks in the load demand. The battery is seen to have been discharged also during the day time when the load demand exceeds the PV power production. The sliding prediction horizon is able to consider the peaks in the load demand for the next day. As a result, the battery has not been completely discharged during the evening of the first day. The remaining energy in the battery has been used to reduce the peak load demand for the following morning of the next day. Overall, the load demand has been kept within 0.9 kW. The resulting Load Demand Reduction (LDR) obtained only due to the optimal discharge of the battery is shown in Fig. 11 and has been calculated as

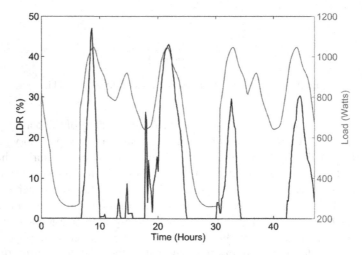

Fig. 11. Load Demand reduction (LDR) using battery [10, 11].

$$\text{LDR}(\%) = (p_{bdc_i}/p_{L_i}) \times 100 \tag{29}$$

The battery SOC profile obtained in this experiment is shown in Fig. 12 with respect to the battery power flow. As a linear model of the battery was used in the MPC to estimate the battery SOC, there is a mismatch of this model with the measurement of the SOC from the Battery Management System (BMS). For instance, there was a much more increase in the battery SOC between 17 and 18 h during the battery charging as compared to during the hour 40. However, the battery SOC follows the battery operation. The continuous update of the SOC in the MPC has restricted the battery operation within its defined SOC boundary condition. The operation of the battery is well within the defined constraints in the MPC. It should be noted that despite the linear power-flow model of the battery is effective for the MPC application, the battery safety still needs to be ensured by a local BMS which also provides the measurement of the battery SOC.

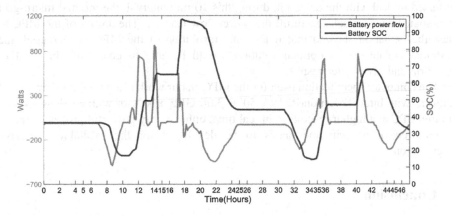

Fig. 12. Experimental results for the battery SOC profile.

4 Results and Discussion

The economic benefit analysis showed that our optimal control problem brings the same operational cost benefits as by the optimization for an economic operation of the system. The nominal battery capacity should be chosen so as to bring the economic benefits. Based on this economic benefit analysis the following criteria have been proposed for the selection the battery storage capacity for a single electricity price scenario:

1. The nominal battery capacity should be sufficient to store the peak PV energy to keep the PV feed-in within the permissible limit. This condition serves as the lower boundary condition. As the optimal control problem has been designed to shave the peaks, with this requirement fulfilled, the PV feed-in and hence the voltage at the coupling point is restricted within the permissible limits.

2. The initial investment in the battery should bring operational cost benefit to the user. For a single electricity price scenario, the nominal battery capacity should not exceed the energy demand. This provides us with the upper boundary condition.

If the battery storage capacity is chosen within these two boundary conditions, then for a given PV battery system design, the optimal control problem will always bring maximum operational cost benefit to the user.

The MPC design was implemented in the laboratory and the experiment result was able to capture the ability of the MPC to deal with the weather forecast deviation. The MPC was implemented online which repeatedly updated and solved the optimal control problem at each time step. The measurement updates of the PV power and the battery SOC allowed the MPC to track the deviation of the PV power from its predicted value and operate the battery accordingly within its defined constraints. In this experiment, as the MPC was used only as a supervisory layer, the optimal solution applied to the battery converter was constant for 10 min before another optimal control problem was solved and the optimal solution was applied. As no other local controller was used to deal with the deviation during this 10 min interval, the internal micro-grid participated automatically to fulfill the power flow balance. The ability of the MPC to track the deviation showed that if the time resolution of the MPC is increased, the continual update of the optimal solution should be able to deal with the weather deviation and give better results.

The computer specification used for the MPC in our work is a 64 bit Windows 2010 platform with Intel(R) Xenon(R) W3350 @ 3.06 GHz processor with 8 GB RAM. To run the MPC at a higher resolution in real time, either a very powerful processor might be required or a technique needs to be developed for the available processor specifications.

5 Conclusion

The MPC has been designed to maximize the use of the battery by prioritizing the peaks in the PV energy and the load demand for a single electricity price scenario. This has been achieved by the quadratic formulation of the objective function in the optimal control problem. If the forecast based control strategy were to be used for a small scale PV battery system, as in our experiment, the stored PV energy in the battery would be completely discharged during the evening of the first day. But with our MPC, the optimal discharge of the battery has allowed to shave the overall peak load demand for the evening as well the following morning.

This MPC is only suitable for a single electricity price scenario where the cost of battery degradation is less than the grid electricity price. As such maximizing the use of the battery is cost effective rather than using the grid electricity. Therefore, our MPC is not dictated by the electricity price but rather by the predicted PV power and the load-demand profile.

Also in this work, a simple PV prediction correction method based on measurement was used in the MPC to estimate the behavior of the PV power output over a short horizon of one hour. Similarly, a load prediction model needs to be included in the

MPC so that the load forecast uncertainty can be dealt as well. The PV and load prediction models are independent of the optimal control problem formulation. Therefore, depending upon the site specific weather and load forecast data, such prediction models can be easily integrated within the MPC design.

References

1. Harry, W., Schneider, K.: Recent facts about photovoltaics in Germany. Report from Fraunhofer Institute for Solar Energy Systems (2013)
2. Stetz, T., Marten, F., Braun, M.: Improved low voltage grid-integration of photovoltaic systems in Germany. IEEE Trans. Sustain. Energy 4(2), 534–542 (2013)
3. Spring, A., Witzmann, R.: CIRED Workshop - Rome, 11–12 June 2014 Paper 0079 Grid Voltage Influences of Reactive Power Flows of Photovoltaic Inverters with a Power Factor Specification of One Cired Workshop - Rome, 11–12 June 2014 Paper 0079, no. June, pp. 11–12 (2014)
4. Weniger, J., Bergner, J., Quaschning, V.: Integration of PV power and load forecasts into the operation of residential PV battery systems. In: 4th Solar Integration Workshop, pp. 383–390 (2014)
5. Castillo-Cagigal, M., et al.: PV self-consumption optimization with storage and active DSM for the residential sector. Sol. Energy 85(9), 2338–2348 (2011)
6. Weckx, S., Gonzalez, C., Driesen, J.: Combined central and local active and reactive power control of PV inverters. IEEE Trans. Sustain. Energy 5(3), 776–784 (2014)
7. Turitsyn, K., Sulc, P., Chertkov, M.: Local control of reactive power by distributed photovoltaic generators, pp. 79–84
8. Marra, F., Yang, G., Træholt, C., Østergaard, J., Larsen, E.: A decentralized storage strategy for residential feeders with photovoltaics. IEEE Trans. Smart Grid 5(2), 974–981 (2014)
9. Von Appen, J., Stetz, T., Braun, M., Schmiegel, A.: Local voltage control strategies for PV storage systems in distribution grids. IEEE Trans. Smart Grid 5(2), 1002–1009 (2014)
10. Dongol, D., Feldmann, T., Bollin, E.: A model predictive control based peak shaving application for a grid connected household with photovoltaic and battery storage. In: Smartgreens, pp. 54–63 (2018)
11. Dongol, D., Feldmann, T., Schmidt, M., Bollin, E.: Sustainable energy, grids and networks a model predictive control based peak shaving application of battery for a household with photovoltaic system in a rural distribution grid. Sustain. Energy Grids Netw. 16, 1–13 (2018)
12. Braam, F., Hollinger, R., Engesser, M.L., Müller, S., Kohrs, R., Wittwer, C.: Peak shaving with photovoltaic-battery systems, pp. 1–5 (2014)
13. Zeh, A., Witzmann, R.: Operational strategies for battery storage systems in low - mounted solar power systems. In: IRES, pp. 1–11 (2013)
14. Manjunatha, A.P., Korba, P., Stauch, V.: Integration of large battery storage system into distribution grid with renewable generation
15. Wu, Z., Tazvinga, H., Xia, X.: Demand side management of photovoltaic-battery hybrid system. Appl. Energy 148, 294–304 (2015)
16. Zhang, Y., Liu, B., Zhang, T., Guo, B.: An intelligent control strategy of battery energy storage system for microgrid energy management under forecast uncertainties. Int. J. Electrochem. Sci. 9(8), 4190–4204 (2014)
17. Parisio, A., Rikos, E., Tzamalis, G., Glielmo, L.: Use of model predictive control for experimental microgrid optimization. Appl. Energy 115, 37–46 (2014)

18. Zhang, Y., Zhang, T., Wang, R., Liu, Y., Guo, B.: Optimal operation of a smart residential microgrid based on model predictive control by considering uncertainties and storage impacts. Sol. Energy **122**, 1052–1065 (2015)
19. Perez, E., Beltran, H., Aparicio, N., Rodriguez, P.: Predictive power control for PV plants with energy storage. IEEE Trans. Sustain. Energy **4**(2), 482–490 (2013)
20. Garcia-torres, F., Bordons, C.: Optimal economical schedule of hydrogen-based microgrids with hybrid storage using model predictive control. IEEE Trans. Ind. Electron. **62**(8), 5195–5207 (2015)
21. IBM Corp. and IBM, V12. 1: User's Manual for CPLEX, Int. Bus. Mach. Corp., vol. 12, no. 1, p. 481 (2009)
22. Schmelas, M., Feldmann, T., da Costa Fernandes, J., Bollin, E.: Photovoltaics energy prediction under complex conditions for a predictive energy management system. J. Sol. Energy Eng. **137**(3), 31015 (2015)
23. Luque, A., Hegedus, S.: Handbook of Photovoltaic Science
24. Goldfarb, D., Idnani, A.: A numerically stable dual method for solving strictly convex quadratic programs. Math. Program. **27**(1), 1–33 (1983)
25. Schleipen, M.: OPC UA supporting the automated engineering of production monitoring and control systems. In: IEEE International Conference of Emerging Technologies and Factory Automation, ETFA, pp. 640–647 (2008)

cloud.iO: A Decentralised IoT Architecture to Control Electrical Appliances in Households

Pierre Roduit[1]([✉]), Dominique Gabioud[1], Gillian Basso[1,2], Gilbert Maitre[1], and Pierre Ferrez[1]

[1] HES-SO Valais-Wallis, Sierre, Switzerland
pierre.roduit@hevs.ch
[2] École Polytechnique Fédérale de Lausanne, Lausanne, Switzerland

Abstract. Demand Response (DR) systems exist since decades in most industrialised countries. It started with phone calls to big industrial plants to reduce their consumption in time of need. Gradually, other solutions were installed by distributors to control the electricity consumption in their grid. Two well-known systems are the two-tariff system and ripple control. The second was installed to shave the consumption peak, sending telegrams on the distribution grid to cut some high consumption loads, such as heating appliances, water boilers, or white appliances. This solution is mainly open loop as the same command is sent to multiple households at the same time and only the global utility load curve is monitored. This blind switching of mass of appliances at the same time has also side effects, such as synchronising the restart of most appliances when the controlling relays are simultaneously released, provoking a rebound effect in the form of a power surge that can exceed the shaved peak.

The last decades saw the advent of Internet of Things (IoT) as well as the deployment of a more sustainable energy generation (photovoltaic, wind energy, etc.). The second makes the generation more decentralised, less predictable, and less controllable, increasing the need for more flexibility to balance it. On the other hand, the development of IoT technologies provides means to acquire more data and have a more precise control on the appliances, and all that with reduced costs.

This paper presents how the flexibility of space and domestic hot water heating in existing residential buildings can be controlled for grid services. It focuses on the Internet of Things (IoT) framework including both hardware and software to connect existing buildings to a central Virtual Power Plant (VPP) intelligence. It also presents field experiments that were performed during the European FP7 SEMIAH project.

Keywords: Demand Side Management (DSM) ·
Demand Response (DR) · Internet of Things (IoT) · Smart grid ·
Cloud computing · cloud.iO · Time series consumption

© Springer Nature Switzerland AG 2019
B. Donnellan et al. (Eds.): SMARTGREENS 2018/VEHITS 2018, CCIS 992, pp. 67–89, 2019.
https://doi.org/10.1007/978-3-030-26633-2_4

1 Introduction

Clean energy is becoming one of the most important challenges of today's world – as witnessed by the ratification of the Paris Agreement within the United Nations Framework Convention on Climate Change [19]. To address this challenge, an intermittent and non-dispatchable renewable generation (photovoltaic, wind energy, etc.) has grown dramatically in Europe and elsewhere over the last few decades. The geographical distribution of new renewables as well as their hard to predict intermittent behaviours pose a double challenge to electrical grid operators:

- keeping a global balance between production and generation,
- avoiding congestion at the local grid level.

Two categories of solutions can be distinguished: energy storage or management of flexible consuming processes. The latter solution is a priori interesting, as it requires only a control infrastructure and no new power infrastructure.

Demand Response (DR) "is the intentional modification of normal consumption patterns by end-use customer.... It is designed to lower electricity use at times of high wholesale market prices or when system reliability is threatened" [2]. Space heating and Domestic Hot Water (DHW) heating are appropriate processes for DR in households, as they both involve non-negligible energy amounts and as consumption shifting has minimal impact on the comfort of inhabitants [17].

Section 2 presents the context of the European FP7 SEMIAH project during which the proposed solution was developed, deployed and tested. Section 3 presents the most related works. The underlying ICT architecture is presented in Sect. 4. Finally, Sect. 5 describes the pilot of the project and its impacts on the electrical grid.

This article is an extended version of a SmartGreens 2018 conference article [10].

2 Context

The European FP7 SEMIAH project (2014–2017) pursued "a major technological, scientific, and commercial breakthrough by developing a novel and open ICT infrastructure for the implementation of automated Demand Response (DR) in households so as to enable shifting the energy consumption of major loads to off-peak consumption periods or to periods with high generation from Renewable Energy Sources (RES)". The developed DR framework had to cope with existing appliances and electrical installations in households, which were not designed for DR. It aimed also at using the domestic internet connection for communication. The project aimed to provide real-time DR with a response time in the range of seconds.

The SEMIAH project addressed the full chain required for the deployment of DR services in households as illustrated in Fig. 1:

1. a Virtual Power Plant (VPP) providing an aggregated view of the controlled households for grids and markets,
2. a Household Manager component turning an individual building into a dispatchable unit by processing monitoring signals and generating command signals,
3. the Household Infrastructure, made up of a set of connected sensors and actuators installed on the heating and electrical infrastructure of the building.

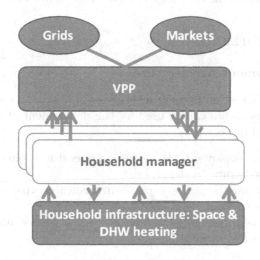

Fig. 1. SEMIAH architecture for DR in households (from [10]).

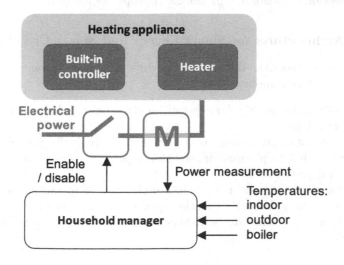

Fig. 2. Control loop for DR service (from [10]).

The VPP component used in the SEMIAH project was IWES.vpp developed by Fraunhofer IWES. The Household Manager was an ad-hoc component also developed by Fraunhofer IWES. The control loop performed by the Household Manager is illustrated in Fig. 2. Since heating appliances have their own built-in controllers, the role of Household Managers is limited to enable or disable power supply (either using a power relay or by a signal to a controller). Input measurement parameters for Household Managers were the amount of electrical power consumed by the heating appliance and three temperatures (inside, outside, and boiler).

This article focuses on the distributed part of the ICT architecture, ranging from existing appliances in buildings to Household Managers.

3   Related Works

3.1   DR Deployment Architectures

A survey of DR schemes and programs is given in [25].

Three main approaches can be used for the deployment of a closed-loop DR service as described in Sect. 2:

- The DR service is deployed by the metering operator as part of the Advanced Metering Infrastructure (AMI) [1,18].
- The DR service makes use of a platform dedicated to Demand Response. OpenADR [8] is an example of such a platform.
- The DR service is implemented as a service over a generic multi-service Internet of Things (IoT) platform.

As the DR service in SEMIAH was implemented on an IoT platform, the rest of the section presents IoT platforms appropriate for DR.

3.2   IoT Architectures for Smart Energy and Smart City Services

From an ICT perspective, the DR service has similar requirements as smart energy and smart city applications:

- Applications make use of a large set of highly distributed and heterogeneous sensors/actuators.
- As collected data may belong to several owners (typically inhabitants), the underlying technical platform must enforce privacy rules according to data owners requirements.
- The elaboration of actuator set points makes use of instantaneous and historical sensor data, forecasts (weather, prices...), and user preferences.
- Applications run in real-time, with time constraints in the order of magnitude of seconds.

IoT platforms offer services for integration of distributed "things" and programming interfaces for domain specific applications [23]. Several platforms provide in addition big data and analytics tools with straightforward access to IoT data [22]. Hence, it is no surprising that many smart energy/city services rely on IoT platforms completed with a cloud based infrastructure for central services [14,20,24]. The components of IoT/cloud ecosystems along with the main standards for interoperability are described in [9] and [11]. The exponential growth of IoT has triggered the development of IoT/cloud platforms released either under commercial or open source licenses (surveys in [11,12,26]).

From an architectural point of view, platforms can be classified into two categories, depending on the capabilities of the distributed gateways acting as a hub for local sensors and actuators:

- IoT platforms with smart gateways: The gateways distributed in households implement logic for local control, sensor signal processing and/or process supervision. This concept known as "edge computing" [21] can address concerns such as latency, nodes' limited capabilities, bandwidth, safety, and privacy. A typical open source member of this category is the he modular platform Eclipse Kapua [5]. Its companion framework Eclipse Kura provides services for the implementation of logic in distributed nodes [15].
- IoT platforms with bridge gateways: The gateways act only as a bridge between local sensors and actuators on ones side, and the cloud on the other side. Locally implemented logic is limited to put local processes in a safe state when the link with cloud hosted central services is lost. FIWARE [6] is an open-source platform belonging to this category. It promotes "open sustainable ecosystem around public, royalty-free, and implementation-driven software platform standards that will ease the development of new Smart Applications in multiple sectors". FIWARE includes tools for big data and analytics.

Household Manager components can be either hosted in distributed gateways (smart gateway model) or centrally in the cloud (bridge gateway model).

4   Distributed ICT Architecture

4.1   Overview

The control strategy requires the deployment of the following sensors (generating monitoring signals) and actuators (consuming command signals) in participating buildings:

- temperature sensors for space (living room, outdoor) and for hot water (boiler),
- sub-meters to measure the power consumption of heating appliances,
- a meter to measure the household total consumption, and
- power relays to enable/disable power supply to heating appliances (electric heaters and heat pumps).

These devices, together with an internet connected gateway, form a wireless Home Area Network (HAN). Wireless networking is required to limit installation costs in existing buildings [13]. The Process Image is an image, mirrored in a central data store, of the current status of monitoring and command signals. Four applications interact with the Process Image, as illustrated in Fig. 3:

- Household Managers (considered as a single Application),
- a supervision system, independent of the DR intelligence, detecting faulty conditions and generating alarms accordingly,
- a provisioning system supporting the deployment of the DR service in new participating buildings, and
- a web-based interface for consumers.

4.2 The Home Area Network

The HAN is based on ZigBee, with the gateway acting as coordinator and the sensors/actuators as devices. ZigBee devices are compliant with the Home Automation or the Smart Energy profiles defined by the ZigBee Alliance.

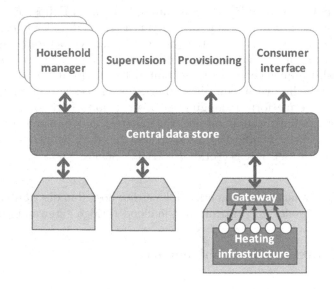

Fig. 3. Distributed part of the SEMIAH ICT architecture (from [10]).

4.3 The cloud.iO IoT Framework

Despite the availability of (too) many IoT/cloud platforms, an in-house developed framework named cloud.iO [3] was selected for the SEMIAH project. cloud.iO can be seen as a collection of field-proven open source components widely used for internet services, completed by a limited set of uncoupled cloud.iO specific modules with limited complexity. Despite its simplicity, cloud.iO implements all core features of an IoT platform: object model to abstract sensor values and monitor set points, APIs for smart applications, searchable database storing the object models of connected gateways, information security, access control (read/write access rights at the level of individual data points can be assigned to each smart application), access to past values of data points (historical database). Big data and analytics tools are not integrated in the platform. As its modules can be clustered, the platform features a high level of scalability and availability.

Vision and Architecture. The cloud.iO IoT framework aims to simplify the development of embedded and distributed "Things" (called endpoints in cloud.iO) and of cloud-hosted applications interacting with them.

The heart of cloud.iO is the Process Image, which contains an up-to-date centralised mirror of the status of distributed Endpoints. An Endpoint updates the Process Image when the value of a monitoring signal has changed. Applications can subscribe to monitoring signal updates and are notified on new values. Applications can modify set points of command signals in endpoints (see Fig. 4). cloud.iO provides dedicated APIs for the development of applications and endpoints. The Process Image contains two databases:

- the Process Database, with the current status of the endpoints (connection state, list of signals with their current values), is a searchable database containing the full information models of all endpoints.
- the History Database, storing time series for monitoring and command signals.

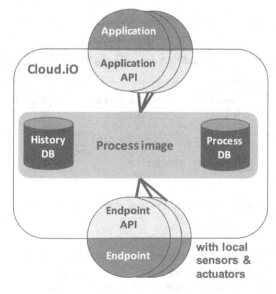

Fig. 4. cloud.iO architecture (from [10]).

cloud.iO Class Model and Endpoint Data Model. The cloud.iO class model is derived from the IEC 61850 class model [16]. IEC 61850 is the ICT standard for power utility automation. The cloud.iO class model features a tree-shaped structure and is composed of Endpoints, Nodes, Objects, and Attributes classes. A cloud.iO Endpoint is evidently the equivalent of an Endpoint instance. The cloud.iO class model features a tree-shaped structure and is composed of Endpoints, Nodes, and Objects. An Endpoint object represents a distributed gateway. It is composed of a set of Nodes, themselves composed of Objects. Attributes, in Objects, are the leaves of the tree. Attributes can be classified in read Attributes (monitoring signals and status parameters) and write Attributes (command signals and configuration parameters). AttributeItems objects store the value of an Attribute at a given point in time. The definition of Objects, Nodes, and Attributes instances is not constrained by cloud.iO. The resulting class model is presented in Fig. 5.

The instances of Nodes, Objects and Attributes in an Endpoint form its information model. cloud.iO allows the use of either a free information model, without a predefined structure, or of a constrained information model (i.e. an information model compliant with some schema). Schemas are defined by interfaces (similar to Logical Nodes in IEC 61850) and classes (similar Common Data Class in IEC 61850).

An Attribute is identified by its full label, which is made up by the concatenation of Endpoint, Object, and Attribute labels according to the following pattern (assuming no recursion in Objects):

<Endpoint−UUID>/<nodeLabel>/<objectLabel1>/<attributeLabel>

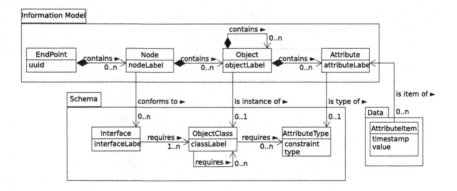

Fig. 5. The cloud.iO class model (from [10]).

Messaging System. Applications, endpoints, and databases inside the Process Image are clients of a messaging system. Messages are composed of a routing topic and of a message content. Once a client has subscribed to a topic, it receives all messages featuring that topic. Table 1 presents the message routing concept used in cloud.iO.

Table 1. Message routing for an EndPoint (from [10]).

Messaging client	Subscribes to topics:	Generates message with topic
EndPoints	/@ set/<Endpoint-UUID>/*	/@ update/<read_attr_full label>
Applications	/@ update/<read_attr_full label>	/@ set/<write_attr_full label>
Database	/*	-

Hence, an application is notified of any change on its subscribed read Attributes and it can at any time update write Attributes in endpoints. Of course, applications may only read or write Attributes if corresponding access rights have been granted. It is foreseen that applications access databases through the messaging service, but this function is not yet implemented in cloud.iO. Message contents are JSON encoded, with a cloud.iO specific schema. They notably contains a value (different types, arrays supported) and a timestamp.

Security and Privacy. Endpoints connect to the message broker using SSL/TLS with X.509 certificate based client and server authentication. The canonical name in endpoint certificates must be the Endpoint UUID. SSL/TLS provides state-of-the-art confidentiality, authentication, and access control. cloud.iO allows managing access rights to Attributes: an Endpoint belongs to a User (either a person or an organisation). Users may grant read/write access permissions on individual Attributes of their endpoints to applications. Hence cloud.iO is capable to implement any privacy requirements. For example, it would be possible to grant access to Attributes to an application only with the explicit authorisation of a User. This pattern is well-known in the smart phone world, where Users must grant applications the right to access peripheral devices.

Implementation. cloud.iO design philosophy is to take advantage of the power and reliability of open source components, with minimal specific code development. The central component is the message broker RabbitMQ. It connects Endpoints, Applications and Databases using the MQTTS and AMQPS protocols. The databases can be deployed using any database management system. In the reference implantation of cloud.iO, InfluxDB and MongoDB are used for respectively the history database and the real-time database. If performance is required, all components of the reference implementation can be deployed as clusters.

4.4   The cloud.iO Framework Applied for SEMIAH

Gateways in participating households play the role of cloud.iO Endpoints. The SEMIAH names for participating buildings are used to construct Endpoint

UUIDs. Nodes, Objects, and Attributes labels provide a logical view of a building: a Node label indicates the process ("boiler"), an Object label refers to a command or monitoring signal ("temperature") and an Attribute label identifies a parameter of the signal, typically its "value". The mapping between the ZigBee and endpoint data models is made in a configuration file elaborated during the provisioning operation. Hence, the Household Managers dispose of a logical model for a building, which is independent of ZigBee.

5 System Deployment

In the framework of the European FP7 SEMIAH project, a pilot with 200 households was in operation between October 2016 and May 2017. The deployment was performed under the responsibility of local Distribution System Operators (DSOs). One hundred households were located in Norway in the Adger region (DSO: Adger Eneri Net) and another hundred in Switzerland, canton of Valais (DSO: SEIC Teledis and EnAlpin). Most of the participating households were single-family houses. To interface the households, hardware from the Danish company Develco Products [4] was used. This hardware is presented in Fig. 6. It encompasses:

(a) A Squid gateway, based on the ARM9-454 MHz CPU, with 256 MB of RAM. It was connected to the household internet connection modem through a RJ45 cable in Switzerland, and through GSM in Norway. It also acts as a 2.4 Ghz ZigBee hub for the Home Area Network (HAN) that was deployed.
(b) A smartplug, allowing to measure the consumption and to cut electrical power to connected loads up to a limit of 10A.
(c) A one phase relay, allowing to measure the consumption and to switch off connected loads up to a limit of 16A. It was used either as a unit in a group of three relays acting together as a three-phase relay (cutting power supply to boilers in Switzerland), or as a simple command relay to act on heat pump controllers. This relay was DIN mounted in electrical cabinets.
(d) A boiler temperature sensor, specially developed for this application, which was built on a DS18b20 1-Wire temperature probe. The probe was in contact with water tanks, in order to measure the water temperature. This sensor was used to ensure the comfort of the household inhabitants.
(e) A pulse meter, used in conjonction with electronic meters from the DSOs. It counts the pulses emitted by the meters every time energy consumed exceeds a given amount (most of the time, 10 Wh per pulse). It thus allows to acquire the global load curve of households.
(f) A power meter (prosumer meter), used to acquire the consumption of heat pumps. As it is not appropriate to cut the power to a heat pump, with the risk of interrupting abruptly one of its cycles, commands were sent directly to the heat pump controller. However, it was necessary to measure the consumed power, and three-phase power meters were therefore used. This device was also DIN mounted in electrical cabinets.

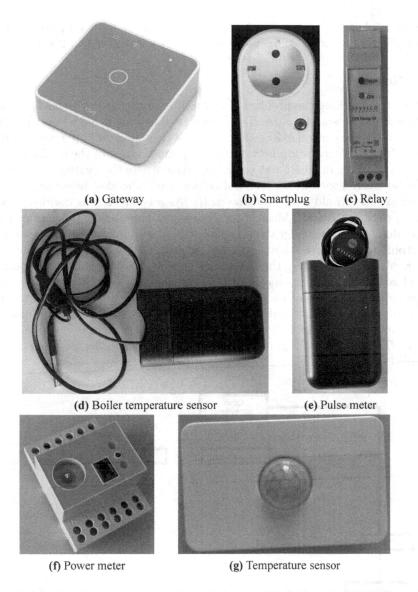

(a) Gateway   (b) Smartplug   (c) Relay

(d) Boiler temperature sensor   (e) Pulse meter

(f) Power meter   (g) Temperature sensor

Fig. 6. Develco hardware used to interface the households during the SEMIAH project.

(g) A temperature sensor, used to acquire the temperature of the main room of the household. It encompasses a passive infrared sensor that was not used. The temperature sensor was used to ensure the comfort of the household inhabitants.

The gateway was communicating with all other devices through ZigBee. The location of the devices were defined by electrical distribution in the household and the appliances location. Both temperature sensors were supplied with batteries, whereas all other components were directly connected to 230 V.

5.1   Norway

In Norway, attacking the problem of controlling domestic hot water or building heating systems caused trouble. Direct electrical heating is quite common. However, as no ripple control exists, electrical supply is structured per room and not with a dedicated separation between heating and the rest of the appliances (e.g. lighting). As a result, there was no central place where the heating consumption could be easily controlled. Electrical cables are embedded into the walls and accessing them would have been too costly. As a result, it was decided to focus only on electrical boilers. Most of the Norwegian households are equipped with a one phase electrical boiler that is connected to a standard electrical socket. A smartplug was thus used to measure the consumption and cut the supply to the boiler. Moreover, as using the household inhabitants' internet connection was considered as too cumbersome, a GPRS USB dongle was used with the gateway to provide an easier way to install the hardware. To finalise the installation, two additional sensors were deployed: a boiler temperature sensor to insure the inhabitant's comfort, as well as a pulse meter to measure the global consumption of the households. Figure 7 describes the way the different elements were installed.

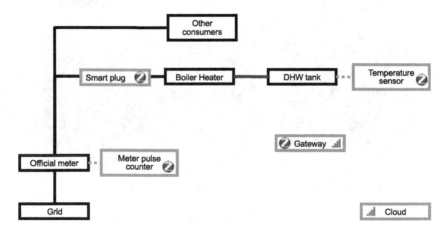

Fig. 7. Schematic of the installations in Norway with electrical boiler.

5.2   Switzerland

For decades, a DR system called Ripple Control (RC, shown in Fig. 8) has been in operation in Swiss residential buildings as a tool for peak shaving on the distribution grid. Every house is equipped with a RC receiver, which is configured with a multicast address. A RC manager generates telegrams (broadcasted

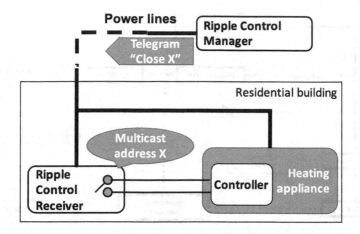

Fig. 8. Principle of Ripple Control (RC) (from [10]).

using Power Line Communication) containing orders to switch on or off relays configured with a certain multicast address. RC implements a "blind" open loop control strategy. The SEMIAH Household Manager drives the control input on heating appliances, hence replacing the RC receiver. The SEMIAH control differs from RC control in two ways: the SEMIAH control is unicast (each appliance can be controlled individually) and is closed loop (temperature and electrical measurements are input parameters for the Household Manager). Finally, since the heating appliances have their own controllers, the SEMIAH Household Managers cannot force them on, but can only turn them off, through a cut of the power supply or through the interface of heat-pump controllers that is used by RC. As RC is mandatory in Switzerland, for domestic hot water and building heating, as well as for washing machines and tumble dryers, the electrical supply distribution in households is made completely differently than in Norway. There is a clear separation between the supply distribution to theses appliances and to the rest of the appliances. This separation is made generally in the electrical cabinet where the fuses are located. As a result, smart relays could be used in those cabinets to act on the heating appliances.

Two major types of installations were done in Switzerland. The first was to control only electrical boilers. Unlike in Norway, most electrical boilers in Switzerland have three phases and are not connected to a standard socket. As a result, it was not possible to use smart plugs. The simplest way the measure the consumption and cut the supply to the boilers was thus to use three one-phase relays that replace the existing RC relays located in the fuse cabinet. Figure 9 shows the installation schematic for this type of installation. Three one-phase relays are used to replace the existing RC relay dedicated to the boiler. A boiler temperature sensor was added to insure the inhabitant confort, as well as a pulse counter to measure the global consumption of the household. All these elements were communicating through ZigBee with the gateway that was connected to

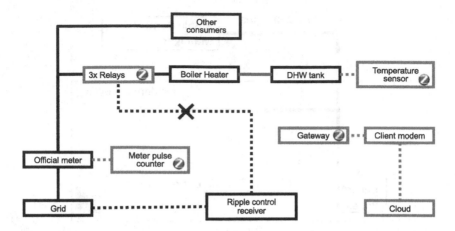

Fig. 9. Schematic of the installations in Switzerland with an electrical boiler.

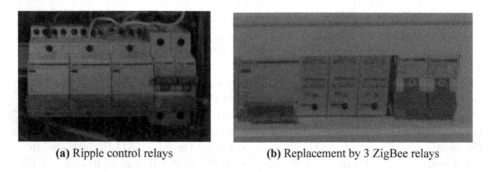

(a) Ripple control relays   (b) Replacement by 3 ZigBee relays

Fig. 10. Electrical cabinet before and after the installation. On the left, three ripple control relays can be observed. They are used for the boiler, the direct electrical heating, and the washing machine. On the right, the existing three phase relay for the boiler was replaced by three one-phase relays that allows to cut power supply and measure the consumption.

the inhabitant internet connection (router) with a RJ45 cable. Figure 10 shows how the relays were installed in the electrical cabinet.

The second type of installation was done to control heat-pumps. Figure 11 shows the schematic of the installation. It differs from the boiler installations in a few ways. First, as it is not advised to cut directly the supply to a heat pump, a relay was used to replace the existing RC relay that was connected to the heat-pump controller. Second, a power meter was used to measure the consumption of the heat-pump. Third, a ambiant temperature sensor was installed in the main room of the household to insure the inhabitant confort. This was required as heat-pump are generally used for both heating the building and providing domestic hot water. All these element were communicating in the same way as with the previous type of installation.

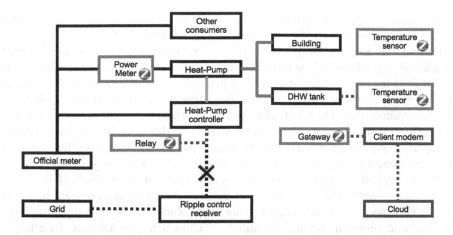

Fig. 11. Schematic of the installations in Switzerland with a heat pump.

Fig. 12. Real installation. The prosumer meter (top center) has been installed and wired in the existing electrical cabinet. A pulse meter can also be observed mounted on the official meter on the right.

Figure 12 shows an example of how the hardware was deployed in a specific household with an heat-pump. The wiring work can be observed with a power meter installed in the electrical cabinet. Even if this picture shows that the solution had to be installed by a professional, there was always sufficient space in the electric cabinets to fit the SEMIAH hardware.

5.3   System Deployment Costs

In Norway, as no electrician was needed for the installation (no wiring work as only smart-plugs were used), it was decided to send the components directly to the clients and let them handle the installation. This proved to be problematic as most of the clients had difficulties to install the hardware themselves, leading to a lot of intervention by the support team to make it work.

During the Swiss pilot deployment, two technicians went to the different households to perform the installation. The first one was an electrician, working for the DSO in charge of the area, who did the electrical wiring work. The second one was an IT specialist who installed the gateway and checked the ZigBee and internet connectivity. The whole cloud.iO infrastructure was deployed and tested before the installation, to reduce the duration of the installation. Installations were performed in about 1 h. With training and more experience, installations could be done by only one technician who would do the wiring and the IT checks. Taking into account travel costs (~1 h), hardware costs (~300 CHF), and labour costs (~200 CHF), the total cost per installation could go down to about 500 CHF. However, in the scope of this pilot phase, development, debugging, updates, and problem solving amounted to a much bigger amount. In a larger scale deployment, the relative importance of these costs would proportionally decrease.

5.4   Installation Weaknesses and Drawbacks

Several problems occurred during the pilot phase of the SEMIAH project but most of them were quickly detected and resolved soon after. However, one of the most important remaining problem was range issues of the ZigBee communication. Swiss buildings are especially strongly built with thick walls that were damping too much the communication signal. Being often close to the limit had two main effects. It first increased the communication losses and thus induced many interruptions of data collection. Moreover, lost packets lead to repeated communication at increased transmission power, taking an heavy toll on consumption and thus on battery life expectancy that dropped sometime to just a few months. This problem could not be easily solved by increasing the meshing with smart plugs, as sometime signal damping was already too consequent through a single wall.

The installation of an innovative technology in households did also sometimes show unpredictable behaviours of the household inhabitants. For example, some participants were turning off their gateway during part of the day. Some placebo effects were also observed, with pilot participants complaining about a lower than usual room or hot water temperature, when no control was yet performed on their heating appliances.

6   Tests

6.1   Purpose and Execution

To make a verification of the good behaviour of the cloud.iO infrastructure, as well as a first evaluation of the flexibility of the households that were controlled, manuel cuts through cloud.iO were performed. They aimed at validating multiple objectives:

- verify the effective real relation between the cloud.iO abstraction and the installed hardware (actuators are really operated),
- evaluate the reactivity of the system (delay),
- evaluate the impact of power cuts of various durations on both temperatures and load curves.

The first two points were easily verified, with simple cut performed in real household through the cloud.iO infrastructure. Commands were sent and relays were acting according to those commands. It was also verified that the reactivity of the system was good enough, with a latency of about 1 second between the sending of the command and the mechanical reaction of the relays.

6.2 Heating Cuts

The third point was evaluated only using the Swiss infrastructure with both types of households: those equipped with boilers and those with heat-pumps. A series of heating cuts were conducted during one week, with enough time between two consecutive cuts to ensure that previous cuts had no effect on the current one. The power cuts were performed during week 8 in 2017 (February 20th to 24th), a quite cold period. Five heating power cuts of 1 h were performed between February 20th and 21st, four heating power cuts of 2 h were performed between February 21st and 22nd and 2 heating power cuts of 4 h were performed between February 23th and 24th.

Two different but complementary results based on these power cuts are presented in this paper. The first one analyses the influence on power and temperature curves of a 4-h cut in one household. The second one analyses the decrease of the consumed energy and the impact on the electrical grid when simultaneously performing cuts in several households.

Figures 13 and 14 respectively present the consumption and the temperatures measured for one household. Two observations can be made based on these figures: it is clear that, during the cuts, the amount of energy consumption is drastically reduced. Moreover, a 4-h cut in winter does not significantly influence the temperature inside the household. We can observe that the indoor temperature (blue curve in Fig. 14) slightly increase during the first cut. This is due to the large increase of the outdoor temperature (green curve in Fig. 14).

Figures 15 and 16 respectively present the aggregated consumption and temperature of 5 households during two synchronised cuts of 4 h. Three observations can be made based on these Figures:

- A diminution of the consumption can be observed during the first cut. Indeed, the mean power during a 4-h time window before the cut is 7776 W with a deviation of 2675 W. During the cut, the mean power is 3064 W with a deviation of 1522 kW. This means an average reduction of power consumption of about 900 W per household during the cuts.

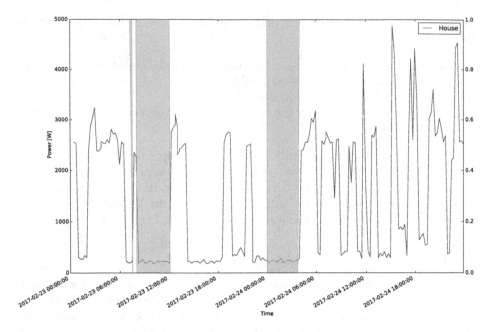

Fig. 13. Consumption of one household during 48 h, with two 4-h cuts (in red). A really short cut (test) before the first 4-h cut can also be observed (from [10]). (Color figure online)

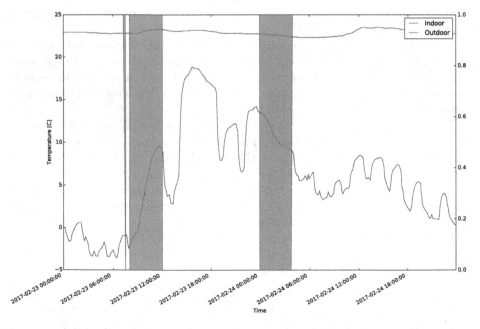

Fig. 14. Temperature of household during 48 h, with two 4-h cuts (in red) (from [10]). (Color figure online)

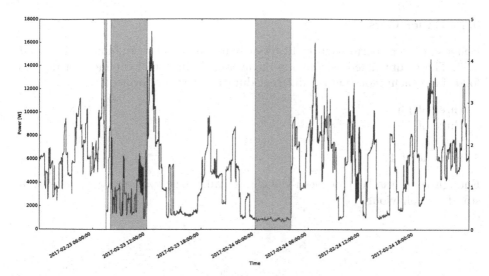

Fig. 15. Sum of consumption of 5 households during 48 h, with two 4-h cuts (in red). (Color figure online)

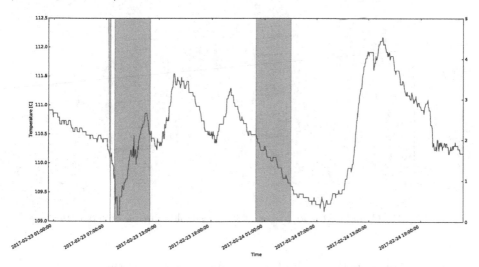

Fig. 16. Sum of temperature of 5 households during 48 h, with two 4-h cuts (in red). (Color figure online)

- A "rebound effect" appears just after both cuts. The fact that all the heating systems start simultaneously explains the consumption peak.
- A delay between the start of heating system and the increase of the temperature inside households can be observed. This is especially visible after the second cut, a delay of 4 h occurs before the temperature begins to increase.

6.3 Boiler Cuts

Boiler cuts were performed on 12 Swiss households between January 23th and 27th. These cuts aimed at verifying the average influence of cutting boilers. The following synchronous cuts of different duration were performed:

- three of 1 h,
- three of 2 h,
- two of 3 h,
- and one of 4 h.

Enough time was kept between the cuts to allow the systems to go back to a standard behaviour.

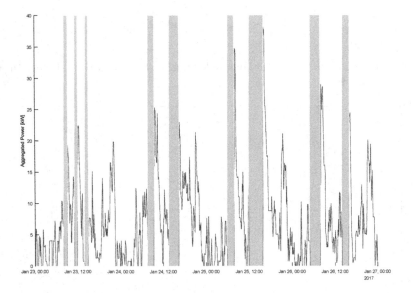

Fig. 17. Cumulated load curves of 12 households during boilers cuts.

Figure 17 presents the result of theses cuts in the form of the cumulated load power of the 12 boilers involved. As only the power of the boilers were measured, a cumulated power of 0 W can be observed during the cuts. The cumulated power outside of the cuts was 4.58 kW, leading to an average cut of about 380 W per household. After the 4 h cut, a big "rebound effect" can be observed with a peak cumulated power of 30 kW, more than 6 times the average power outside of the cuts.

The maximum water temperature drop in the boilers tank was about 0.6 °C per hour, whereas the average temperature drop was of about 0.2 °C per hour. For short cuts of a few hours, these decreases of temperature can be considered as negligible.

7   Conclusion

This article presents how the cloud.iO IoT infrastructure was developed to offer a virtualisation in the cloud of sensors and actuators installed in households. This infrastructure was used with heating appliances (boilers and heat-pumps) to evaluate the feasibility of using such a solution to perform demand side management. The infrastructure was deployed in 100 households in Norway and 100 households in Switzerland. The installation costs show that such a solution could be deployed at a larger scale. Field experience showed however the difficulty of working with ZigBee devices, as it was sometime difficult to achieve a correct meshing of the network. It was especially the case in Switzerland where household are often built with heavy walls, sometime in concrete, and where the heating appliances are often installed underground in dedicated technical rooms.

The article presents also the influence of cutting the appliances on the load curves of the households. It shows that a good flexibility is available without impacting the comfort of the inhabitants.

After this trial phase and based on the communication problems arising from the high radio frequency used by ZigBee devices (2.4 GHz), creating difficulties to go through concrete walls, a new communication technology (Z-Wave) working at a lower frequency (800–900 MHz) was selected to be used in the trial phase of a new project, GOFLEX [7], where the cloud.iO infrastructure will be deployed on more than 200 households in Switzerland.

Acknowledgment. This research was supported by the European FP7 research grant 619560 (SEMIAH project, Scalable Energy Management Infrastructure for Aggregation of Households).

References

1. Advanced metering infrastructure, netl modern grid strategy, powering our 21st-century economy. Technical report, National Energy Technology Laboratory for the U.S. Department of Energy, Office of Electricity Delivery and Energy Reliability (2008)
2. Demand response - empowering the european consumer. Setis Magazine - Smart Grid, pp. 21–22, March 2014. https://setis.ec.europa.eu/setis-reports/setis-magazine/smart-grids/demand-response-empowering-european-consumer
3. cloud.iO (2018). http://cloudio.hevs.ch/
4. DEVELCO products (2018). https://www.develcoproducts.com/
5. Eclipse Kapua (2018). https://www.eclipse.org/kapua/
6. FIWARE (2018). https://www.fiware.org/
7. Goflex project (2018). https://goflex-community.eu/
8. OpenADR (2018). http://www.openadr.org/
9. Al-Fuqaha, A., Guizani, M., Mohammadi, M., Aledhari, M., Ayyash, M.: Internet of things: a survey on enabling technologies, protocols, and applications. IEEE Commun. Surv. Tutor. **17**(4), 2347–2376 (2015). https://doi.org/10.1109/COMST.2015.2444095

10. Basso, G., Gabioud, D., Roduit, P.: IoT architecture for decentralised heating control in households. In: Proceedings of the 7th International Conference on Smart Cities and Green ICT Systems - Volume 1: SMARTGREENS, pp. 70–77. INSTICC, SciTePress (2018). https://doi.org/10.5220/0006692400700077
11. Botta, A., de Donato, W., Persico, V., Pescapé, A.: Integration of cloud computing and internet of things: a survey. Future Gener. Comput. Syst. **56**, 684–700 (2016). https://doi.org/10.1016/j.future.2015.09.021, http://www.sciencedirect.com/science/article/pii/S0167739X15003015
12. Derhamy, H., Eliasson, J., Delsing, J., Priller, P.: A survey of commercial frameworks for the internet of things. In: 2015 IEEE 20th Conference on Emerging Technologies Factory Automation (ETFA), pp. 1–8, September 2015. https://doi.org/10.1109/ETFA.2015.7301661
13. Gill, K., Yang, S.H., Yao, F., Lu, X.: A zigbee-based home automation system. IEEE Trans. Consum. Electron. **55**(2), 422–430 (2009). https://doi.org/10.1109/TCE.2009.5174403
14. Jin, J., Gubbi, J., Marusic, S., Palaniswami, M.: An information framework for creating a smart city through internet of things. IEEE Int. Things J. **1**(2), 112–121 (2014). https://doi.org/10.1109/JIOT.2013.2296516
15. Lee, Y.H., Nair, S.: A smart gateway framework for IoT services. In: 2016 IEEE International Conference on Internet of Things (iThings) and IEEE Green Computing and Communications (GreenCom) and IEEE Cyber, Physical and Social Computing (CPSCom) and IEEE Smart Data (SmartData), pp. 107–114, December 2016. https://doi.org/10.1109/iThings-GreenCom-CPSCom-SmartData.2016.44
16. Mackiewicz, R.: Overview of IEC 61850 and benefits. In: Power Systems Conference and Exposition, 2006, PSCE 2006, 2006 IEEE PES, pp. 623–630. IEEE (2006)
17. Maître, G., Basso, G., Steiner, C., Gabioud, D., Roduit, P.: Distributed grid storage by ordinary house heating variations: a swiss case study. In: 2015 Euromicro Conference on Digital System Design (DSD), pp. 241–249. IEEE (2015)
18. Mohassel, R.R., Fung, A., Mohammadi, F., Raahemifar, K.: A survey on advanced metering infrastructure. Int. J. Electr. Power Energy Syst. **63**, 473–484 (2014). https://doi.org/10.1016/j.ijepes.2014.06.025, http://www.sciencedirect.com/science/article/pii/S0142061514003743
19. Rogelj, D., et al.: Paris agreement climate proposals need a boost to keep warming well below 2 c. Nature **534**(7609), 631–639 (2016)
20. Santos, P.M., et al.: Portolivinglab: an IoT-based sensing platform for smart cities. IEEE Int. Things J. **5**(2), 523–532 (2018). https://doi.org/10.1109/JIOT.2018.2791522
21. Shi, W., Dustdar, S.: The promise of edge computing. Computer **49**(5), 78–81 (2016). https://doi.org/10.1109/MC.2016.145
22. Strohbach, M., Ziekow, H., Gazis, V., Akiva, N.: Towards a big data analytics framework for IoT and smart city applications. In: Xhafa, F., Barolli, L., Barolli, A., Papajorgji, P. (eds.) Modeling and Processing for Next-Generation Big-Data Technologies. MOST, vol. 4, pp. 257–282. Springer, Cham (2015). https://doi.org/10.1007/978-3-319-09177-8_11
23. Suciu, G., Vulpe, A., Halunga, S., Fratu, O., Todoran, G., Suciu, V.: Smart cities built on resilient cloud computing and secure internet of things. In: 2013 19th International Conference on Control Systems and Computer Science, pp. 513–518, May 2013. https://doi.org/10.1109/CSCS.2013.58
24. Theodoridis, E., Mylonas, G., Chatzigiannakis, I.: Developing an iot smart city framework. IISA **2013**, 1–6 (2013). https://doi.org/10.1109/IISA.2013.6623710

25. Vardakas, J.S., Zorba, N., Verikoukis, C.V.: A survey on demand response programs in smart grids: pricing methods and optimization algorithms. IEEE Commun. Surv. Tutor. **17**(1), 152–178 (2015). https://doi.org/10.1109/COMST.2014.2341586
26. Zdravković, M., et al.: Survey of Internet-of-Things platforms. In: 6th International Conference on Information Society and Techology, ICIST 2016, vol. 1, pp. 216–220. Kopaonik, Serbia, February 2016. https://hal.archives-ouvertes.fr/hal-01298141. ISBN: 978-86-85525-18-6

A SaaS Implementation of a New Generic Crypto-Classifier Service for Secure Energy Efficiency in Smart Cities

Oana Stan[1]([✉]), Mohamed-Haykel Zayani[2], Renaud Sirdey[1,2],
Amira Ben Hamida[2], Mallek Mziou-Sallami[2], and Alessandro Ferreira Leite[2]

[1] CEA, LIST, Point Courrier 172, 91191 Gif-sur-Yvette Cedex, France
{oana.stan,renaud.sirdey}@cea.fr
[2] IRT SystemX, Palaiseau, France
{mohamed-haykel.zayani,renaud.sirdey,amira.benhamida,
mallek.mziou-sallami,alessandro.ferreiraleite}@irt-systemx.fr

Abstract. More and more, accessing data remotely in a secure manner appears like the backbone for providing new advanced and customized functionalities. The proliferation of social media and domotics urges a new kind of ubiquity where different kinds of features are deployed everywhere atop of the everyday life small devices and even embedded in our surroundings. While we measure the opportunities offered by such advancements in improving people lifestyles and obtaining immediate and useful services, it is necessary to consider the real impact on our privacy. Recently, a newly adopted European standard, the General Data Protection Regulation aims at codifying the rules of personal data use. We strongly believe in the necessity for a Smart City of adopting such privacy regulation while benefiting at the same time from new services, in a generic and easy way.

In that sense, we build an approach that is at the frontier of the cryptoscience domain for a better privacy and the Micro Service-Oriented Architectures for an increased use by tiers. Indeed, our service is accessible in a Software-as-a-Service (SaaS) manner and uses encryption to ensure data privacy. The particularity of our system lies in the fact that the server performs a classification algorithm without any information about the sensitive data and without the capability to decrypt it. The underlying cryptographic technology used is homomorphic encryption, allowing to perform calculations directly on encrypted data. Our service is generic by design and could be applied over several metrics.

We adopt an energy efficiency use case and propose a service for buildings energy diagnosis and classification towards renovations and/or reductions of the electric consumption. We showcase our prototype of crypto-classification service by involving different actors of a Smart City community. Finally, we assess our proposal thanks to a set of real data collected from an Irish residential district. Our SaaS crypto-classifier achieves acceptable performances in terms of security, execution times and memory requirements.

© Springer Nature Switzerland AG 2019
B. Donnellan et al. (Eds.): SMARTGREENS 2018/VEHITS 2018, CCIS 992, pp. 90–115, 2019.
https://doi.org/10.1007/978-3-030-26633-2_5

Keywords: Smart city · Secure classification · Data privacy ·
Homomorphic encryption

1 Introduction

One of the key concepts of the smart city relies in the intensive usage of ICT (Information and Communication Technologies) not only for the deployment and interconnection of all the complex subsystems but also for increasing the "smartness" through new services and functionalities. However, the smart information technologies rise multiple privacy issues related to the data they manipulate from its collection (via smart devices) to its transmission and remote analysis.

Other fundamental piece in building a smart city, on which we particularly concentrate in this paper, is the energy infrastructure and the smart grids. In some countries and regions, privacy concerns are the main barriers for the large scale adoption of smart grid infrastructures and of the associated services one could benefit from (e.g., in Netherlands, the senate has refused in 2009 to make compulsory the installation of E-meters for consumers because of data protection issues).

These problems of privacy and more generally data protection and computer security are making the object of various reports and recommendation documents. For example, [1] is advanced by the NIST (National Institute of Standards and Technology) in the USA as well as [2] by the Canadian authorities. In France, the CNIL (Commission Nationale de l'Informatique et des Libertés) has published in November 2012 a compliancy kit for the communication meters [3], conceived as a guide of best practices for the innovation process in the electrical industry by integrating data protection directly in the definition of new services, i.e. the "privacy by design". More recently, the General Data Protection Regulation (GDPR) [4] has been voted by the EU Member states and has the objective to provide a common data privacy framework across Europe such that data privacy of the EU citizens is respected.

It is in this context, of a real concern of citizens about their energy data privacy and the need of innovative services, making use of modern cryptographic primitives such as homomorphic cryptosystems, that our work arose.

We assist lately to the emergence of more and more smart devices (smart meters, sensors, actuators, etc.) for which the energy domain is a particularly suitable application field. In order to achieve their functionality, these smart devices require the collection and the treatment of different sort of personal data, such as, for example, a customer's energy consumption. Indeed, the smart meters interacting with electrical appliances and measuring the end user power consumption are further communicating the information to the smart grids providers for optimization and monitoring.

Or, despite their advantages, the smart metering systems and in general the monitoring of smart devices and the services for the energy domain cause serious security and privacy concerns.

A reporting too fine-grained on a user consumption can reveal behavioral patterns and thus may infringe on his/her privacy. For example, the daily measurements can reveal whether a house is inhabited or not or when the inhabitants are away. In the same manner, the 15-min or even the hourly reports can reveal a person timetable and habits making him/her vulnerable (see Fig. 1). These sensitive private information could be accessible if stored outside a person house and not protected (e.g. the server of a grid operator or the cloud) and could be further exploited for various criminal actions.

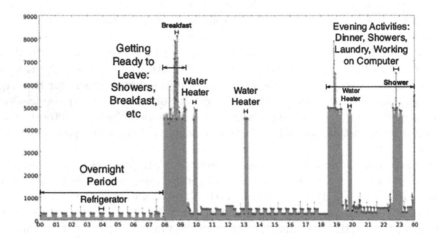

Fig. 1. Inferring user activity from a daily consumption data [5].

Finally, a longer-term insight in someone energy consumption allows data mining and profiling which can be further seen as a form of intrusion (e.g. targeted advertising on domestic appliances). Here are some possible scenarios of security attacks, as suggested in [6]:

- Compromise of the smart meters in order to manipulate power usage and energy costs;
- Attacks of the power system (e.g. overload of a nuclear plant) by simulating a large scale consumption;
- Control and management of electrical devices by attackers via smart meters;
- Inferring private activities and habits of a victim by hacking the power company database.

The aim of this work is thus to propose a new privacy preserving classification service architecture, using homomorphic cryptography, in which the privacy of the energy data is assured by design. The design of this web service remains generic and could be further applied to other private data.

The system prototype proposed here is a service for a smart district made of residential buildings, performing classification and labeling remotely, without having access to sensitive data such as energy consumption or households characteristics (surface, number of inhabitants, etc.). Since one of the main issues with homomorphic cryptosystems are their costs in terms of applicability and performances, we are focusing here more on the required effort needed to implement a privacy preserving service based on this kind of technology. As such, we analyse the requirements in terms of protocol as well as the performances when using an additive homomorphic cryptosystem [7], more easy to use but allowing only additions on encrypted data, and also a leveled homomorphic scheme (e.g. [8]). The latter is more recent and more complex but allows to execute, beside additions on the encrypted domain, a predefined number of consecutive multiplications. Let us also insist on the fact that, in this paper, we focus only on the privacy-preserving of the second step of a classification process, i.e. the operational phase of predicting the label for a given secured-through-encryption data, based on an already acquired model. We are not interested in the first step of the classification system, in which we suppose that the model has been learned using clear datasets.

To summarize, the main contributions in this paper are: (a) the proposal of a new and generic type of services for the smart city which are secured-by-design; (b) a Gaussian classifier for predicting the class of encrypted data (here, readings of smart meters); (c) the use of two appropriate homomorphic encryption schemes to protect energy data and, finally, (d) a description of a working demonstrator and a detailed analysis of its performances.

This work is organized as follows. In Sect. 2, we present some prior work related to the data privacy in the smart energy field with a focus on the privacy preserving data mining approaches as well as the applications of homomorphic encryption as a security solution for the energy domain. Section 3 describes the overall architecture of the classifier and its the generic SaaS implementation as well as the underlying mechanisms for performing the required operations using homomorphic properties. The prototype, the dataset description and an evaluation of the associated performance results are given in Sect. 5. Lastly, the final section gives some insight about future works and perspectives.

2   Related Work

2.1   Existing Works on Energy Consumption Analysis

The notion of energy classification is intrinsically related to the one of energy rating, i.e. designing of a method to assess energy usage quality. Such an example of an energy rating system for residential profiles is the Home Energy Rating System (HERS) of the Energy Star program. It measures the relative energy efficiency of a house based on its thermal envelope, glazing strategies, HVAC (Heating, Ventilation and Air-Conditioning) systems etc. Beside its standard assumptions (standard occupant behavior, typical weather and so on), another drawback of this kind of approaches is its need of a detailed knowledge of the behavior of the domestic appliances of a household.

Many other approaches (e.g. [9,10]) deal with the so called Non-Intrusive Load Monitoring (NILM). By analyzing the measurements of the electricity readings at a high frequency, they have as purpose to determine the contribution of the individual appliances to the overall energy consumption. Their aim is thus substantially different from the one of the work presented here and, moreover, we do not require such a fine granularity of data sampling.

A large body of related literature is dedicated to the identification of patterns in the electricity consumption data either to predict future energy usage or to recognize different consumption behavior or routines [11–13]. This kind of approaches analyzes the energy consumption recorded at larger intervals than the NILM systems (intervals of the order of minutes or hours) but they do not correlate this data with other characteristics of the household (e.g. surface).

Other unsupervised learning methods study the problem of determining clusters of consumers with similar energy usage. For example, [14] uses several clustering techniques in order to analyze the energy load patterns of around 400 non-residential consumers in Italy and group them with the aim to find the inefficient billing, by correlating these data with the current tariff for each consumer. In [15], a k-means clustering algorithm is used to determine groups of residences having similar hourly electricity usage within each season for a dataset formed by 103 homes in Austin. Another category of such approaches use Self-Organizing Maps (SOMs), based on neural networks allowing to automatically extract clusters from potentially unstructured data (e.g. [16,17]). More notably, [18] used annual energy meter readings and corresponding dwelling attributes to group consumers and provide recommendations.

Finally, from the supervised learning studies, one can cite as examples [19] and [20]. First of them shows, using a linear regression model, that certain household attributes such as the number of beds are highly correlated with the electricity consumption. The last work combines four classifiers: KNN, LDA, Mahalanobis and SVM taking into input electricity consumption residential data and providing as output the estimated values of properties such as the floor area or the number of persons living in them. As such, its purpose, of automatic discovering the households characteristics, is different from ours, which is to find the class of a house in function of its energy consumption and other known properties, all by keeping this private data nondisclosed. However, the approach from [20] shows that the metric we used here, taking into account the house surface and the number of occupants is a relevant one.

2.2 Data Mining Over Encrypted Data

According to the mechanisms they rely on, we can distinguish between three main categories of privacy preserving data mining approaches:

- Data perturbation methods (e.g. [21,22])
  Before outsourcing the data and sending it to an external service which will perform the data mining, the data is perturbed by adding random noise such that the final distribution seems different from the one of the actual data.

Due to the addition of noise, data mining results may be significantly less accurate. Additionally, the data perturbation techniques do not offer strong cryptographic security properties such as the semantic security [23].

– Data distribution or partitioning methods (e.g. [24,25])
  The main disadvantage of this type of methods is that they rely on heavy cryptographic mechanisms with high computational and communication overheads.

– Other cryptography-based techniques.
  In this category, we include the studies which are also using homomorphic encryption schemes beside other cryptographic techniques (e.g. [26–29]). Since there are only a few existing studies and this is the particular setting we are interested in, we will insist on this family of studies and provide more details for describing the classification algorithms belonging to this class.

The purpose of a privacy-preserving classification is to keep secret to one or several of the involved parties the feature vector and/or the learned model. Most of existing studies are dedicated to preserving privacy during the training phase in which a model is learned (using or not homomorphic encryption machinery, e.g. [27,28]) and only a few address the prediction step. Since, as stated previously, our approach addresses data privacy in the operational step of the classification process, we will describe further on the existing studies using homomorphic encryption during the labeling process.

The authors in [27] propose a machine learning confidential protocol based on homomorphic encryption in which both the training and the classification occur on encrypted data. A Linear Means classifier and a Fisher's Linear Discriminant Classifier using a gradient descent based approximation are designed and implemented based on an extended version of the encryption scheme from [30]. For both classifiers, the experimental results on a standard Wisconsin Breast Cancer dataset [31] show a slow down of 6–7 orders of magnitude when performing on encrypted data instead on plaintexts. For example, the classification of a test vector using a Linear Means Classifier with 100 training vectors and 30 attributes takes roughly 6 s while the classification of test vectors with 10 features takes 20 s using the division free Fischer's Classifier.

In [26], only the privacy for the classification process is addressed, by ignoring how the model has been build (either directly from plaintext data or from protected data). As such, they are first conceiving a library with three building blocks which is further used as support for implementing classifiers such as hyperplane decision based, Naive Bayesian, decision trees and AdaBoost. The building blocks are protocols between two parties for which the inputs and outputs are in clear or encrypted using additive homomorphic schemes and which performs three types of operations: comparison of two inputs, *argmax* over encrypted data and computation of dot products of two vectors. The performances vary in function of the complexity of the classifier and the number of classes of the model, with ~320 ms for a linear classifier, more than 1600 ms for a Naive Bayes Classifier on 5 classes and 9 features and more than 4000 ms for a decision tree with 6 nodes and a depth of 4. We remark however an important overhead due to the communication times (more than 70% of the total execution).

Here, we present a Gaussian classifier with the prediction performed on encrypted data, tailored to be applied for the protection of smart energy data readings.

2.3   Applications of Homomorphic Encryption for the Smart City

In this section, we describe some of the existing homomorphic-based approaches treating the privacy of data collected at the smart meter level (i.e. energy consumption readings) in smart grids. Most of the existing studies concentrate on data aggregation as the main application of homomorphic cryptography for smart grids (e.g. [6, 32–34]).

In [32], the usage of homomorphic cryptography in a smart grid environment is assessed via two possible application scenarios: direct aggregation and spatial/temporal aggregation. In the first one, based on the Paillier cryptosystem [7], the usage data from each smart meter is encrypted with the public key of the power company and then sent to the entity performing the aggregation. The overall encrypted consumption is then sent to the power company which decrypts it with its secret key. In the second case, the usage data consists of the identifier of the smart meter and the time interval in which the data was recorded. The experimental results based on a Java Smart Grid Simulator showed that the overall process (encryption, decryption and aggregation) for the first case is 10 times longer and 8 times more energy consuming than a non-homomorphic encryption scheme. However, due to the recent and continuous advances in the practical implementation of homomorphic-based algorithms, it is expected that the performances obtained back in 2012 can be highly improved in the coming years, if not already now.

The effects of using homomorphic encryption for aggregating data on the performance of the Smart Grid network are also analyzed in [35]. The network composing the smart grid is modeled as a hierarchical network tree in which there is one gateway as sink node and several smart meters as leafs. Each smart meter sends its encrypted consumption data to its parent in the tree and these nodes perform either End-To-End (ETE) homomorphic aggregation or Hop-By-Hop (HBH) operations. The experimental results, based on a Java simulation of a secure aggregation using Paillier cryptosystem, showed that even if HBH has a computational overhead at intermediate nodes (as expected), the overall latency and the size of the fixed data crossing the network is comparable with that of the ETE homomorphic encryption.

In [34], a smart metering architecture is proposed, it can be deployed in a cloud environment, when the database of energy reports of customers is being outsourced. The energy consumptions are encrypted with the additive homomorphic scheme from [36] and, for protecting against malleability attacks, a homomorphic Message Authentication Code (MAC) [37] is also used. The smart metering architecture consists of a key authority, an Energy Management System (EMS), a set of customers and a set of services (offered by the grid provider

- GP, the energy provider - EP). Several protocols are defined: the GP installs a meter, a customer establishes/cancels a contract with the EP, a smart meter reports its reading to the EMS and the EMS is SQL-queried for aggregated consumptions. For a 16-bit encrypted consumptions, querying the sum of 30 million records (with a MySql 5.1 server) lasts up to 10 s (same as querying plaintext data). To this time, one has to add the querying time for the sum of the 30 million MAC tags which takes 12 s. The storage requirements increase linearly with the number of stored consumptions (e.g. for 100 million records and their MAC tags, 1.8 GB of storage against 200 MB for plaintext consumptions).

Finally, other approaches, such as [38], suggest a new design of smart grid architectures, following the slogan "power to the meter", in which the security is assured by a trusted computing element (e.g. a smart card), included in the smart meter. Under this assumption of existence of a such trusted card, [38] provides several basic protocols of communication with the smart meters, including a non-leakage additively homomorphic-based protocol for aggregation.

3 Service Architecture

In this section, we present different architectural global views for employing the classification private service, as well as, at the end, a way of going generic and exposing the classifier for further usages. The difference between the architectures presented below lies in the manner the service is exploited by the actors in a smart city. In the scenario of a residential district, between the main users of such privacy-preserving classification energy service, one can enumerate:

- Owners of residential buildings, providers of energy data and other household characteristics (surface, number of inhabitants, revenues, etc.)
- A district management entity. One of his main concerns is how to ensure the district energy cost effectiveness based on district energy data. Estimating the energy efficiency of the district buildings is an interesting way towards the identification of greedy consumers. It is also a valuable feedback for future strategic decisions. However, for different reasons (legal or ethics, lack of resources or experience in data mining, focus on his core business) he does not perform the classification service by his own.
- A qualified remote third-party. This service provider designates a major actor of the use case and is able to process data, perform energy classification and assign ratings or labels. It can be perceived as an energy stakeholder having a valuable experience with classification or an energy consulting service supported by an energy provider/governmental programs [39]. Typically, these services are built over conceived metrics and defined ratings [40]. They are extracted from users' feedback, investigations, surveys and simulations about residential electricity consumption and householders information. Thereby, sharing such data with the energy rating service is obviously necessary. Nevertheless, if sharing plain data threatens the privacy of inhabitants, this would compromise the rating process. The use of the homomorphic cryptography, in this situation, is a credible solution to overcome this constraint.

Attributing labels or ratings to the buildings, the same way it is done for some home appliances, could be helpful in providing synthetic indications about the energy efficiency throughout the district. Many architectures can be proposed in this sense but we will describe here two kinds of architectures. On the one hand, a three-tier architecture that involves the energy rating service, the district buildings and a district management entity. The latter role can be assumed by a district manager, (an) energy program administrator(s) or state/local authorities. According to the entity right access to district energy data, two subtypes of this architecture variant can be defined. On the other hand, if the process only concerns buildings and the energy rating service, a two-tier architecture fulfills the use case requirements.

We address the following questions: Concretely, how do a district management entity or district buildings communicate with the energy rating service? What are the requirements that allow the energy rating service to process data and guarantee the exclusive access to the plain results to the district manager?

3.1 First Variant of the Three-Tier Architecture

As shown in Fig. 2, this architecture supposes that the district management entity collects the data and leads the encrypted data exchange with the energy rating service. This requires that the district management entity securely collects the energy data throughout the district (for example using standard cryptography techniques such as symmetric encryption). Then, when the district management entity needs to rate the energy efficiency of residential buildings, he launches the encryption of the data with her homomorphic public key. The encrypted data is sent to the third-party service to be processed and to determine encrypted ratings expressing the energy efficiency. In order to assign a rating to

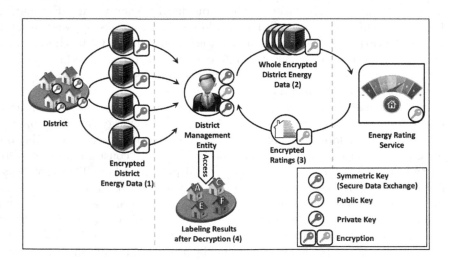

Fig. 2. First variant of the three-tier architecture [41].

residential building in a secure way, an encrypted distance is computed between its energy efficiency metric and the one of each reference rating. The reference metrics are also encrypted with the public key of the district management entity. The sharing of the homomorphic public key can be realized by sending it from the district manager to the third-party service or by the recourse to a public key infrastructure (PKI).

Finally, after the secure rating process, the district management entity collects the encrypted classification results. Her private key ensures that he has the exclusive right to decrypt the outputs of the energy rating service and obtain the energy efficiency for all the district he administrates.

3.2 Second Variant of the Three-Tier Architecture

Fig. 3 depicts a second variant of the three-tier architecture. In this case, the district buildings send the encrypted data to the energy rating service to perform the secure classification. As for the district management entity, he collects the encrypted ratings. The three tiers share the same public key, meanwhile, the district management entity possesses the private key which enable her to decrypt the service output in order to access the labeling results. Here, the architecture offers a credible solution when it is preferred that the district management entity has no visibility on plain data.

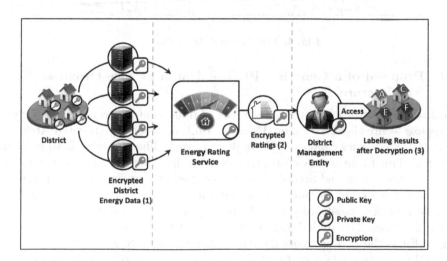

Fig. 3. Second variant of the three-tier architecture [41].

3.3 Two-Tier Architecture

When the process does not involve a district management entity, we head for a two-tier architecture as depicted in Fig. 4. The public key is shared between the district and energy rating service sides. A private key is possessed by each one of the buildings in the district. In this case, a householder who wants to obtain an energy efficiency evaluation launches the sending of his own encrypted data. Then, the energy rating service processes this data and returns the encrypted rating to the householder. Finally, he decrypts the service answer with his private key to access his evaluation. In this case, we assume either the existence of a PKI or that each district building has previously sent the public key to the energy rating service.

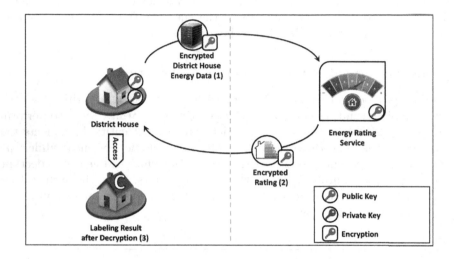

Fig. 4. Two-tier architecture [41].

3.4 Proposal of a Generic API Based on a Service-Oriented Architecture

We also aimed at developing a generic API (Application Programming Interface) to realize secure classification on data. It is built on a Service-Oriented Architecture and offers a user interface through Swagger[1]. The objective is to securely affect a class to an observation. This can be done for various use cases that handle private data and according to determined class references (see Fig. 6).

The service relies on three major components: the encryption, the distance computation for classification and the decryption of the distance results to find the right class. The underlying secure classification process is represented in Fig. 5. First, the API encrypts the data using the already generated public key. Typically, x represents a vector with n features and stands for an observation to classify. Then, encrypted distances with class references (formatted as the observations) are computed. Thereafter, these distances are decrypted by the private key and the class of the observation is determined. In the following, more details about how classification is driven by the homomorphic encryption are given in Sect. 4. The proposal of the system prototype we propose for energy efficiency classification is addressed in Sect. 5.

---

[1] https://swagger.io/.

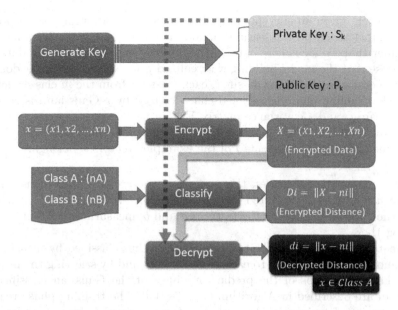

Fig. 5. Secure classification process.

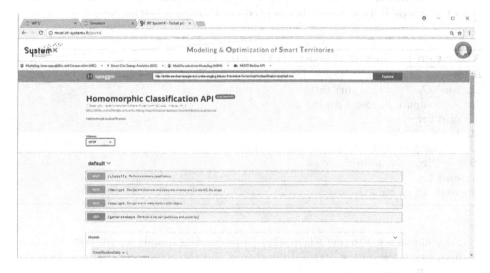

Fig. 6. Homomorphic classification API.

4   Private Classification Algorithm

4.1   General Description

For showing the feasibility of our approach, we have chosen a basic Gaussian classifier which was adapted in order to execute the prediction step on encrypted data. As such, given an encrypted attribute vector x, the purpose is to predict its class label based on the learning model acquired during the training step. Remember that we focus here only on the labeling step using private data and we suppose that the model building was realized previously in the clear domain.

In the case of a Gaussian Classifier, each class C_j from the m classes defined during the training phase is assumed characterized by a Gaussian distribution with a mean μ_j and a covariance matrix Σ_j.

The mean of a class C_j is the vector $\mu_j \in \mathbb{R}^n$: $\mu_j^\mathsf{T} = [\mu_{j_0}, \mu_{j_1}, \ldots, \mu_{j_n}]$ with μ_{j_i} the mean for the components i of the examples vectors x belonging to class C_j (i.e. $\mu_{j_i} = \frac{\sum_i^n x(i)}{n}$).

For vectors with n features, the covariance matrix of a class C_j is a semi-positive $n \times n$ matrix computed as: $\Sigma_j = \{c(a,b)\}$ with $a, b \in \{1, \ldots, n\}$ and $c(a,b)$ the covariance between the features a and b, measuring their tendency to vary together.

A feature vector x from the training set T is thus classified by measuring a Mahalanobis distance from x to each of the classes and by selecting the minimal norm. The main steps of the prediction phase of the Gaussian classification algorithm are described in Algorithm 1, Steps 4–6. The training phase realized on T_0, the set of training vectors x_0, has been realized before, resulting in a model with m classes. After computing the mean and the covariance of each class C_j (Steps 1–3), a class label is predicted for each testing vector $x \in T$.

Algorithm 1. Gaussian classifier - prediction step.

Require: $T_0 = \{x_0 \in \mathbb{R}^n\}$; $T = \{x \in \mathbb{R}^n\}$; m classes C_j
1: **for** $\forall C_j, j \in \{1, \ldots, m\}$ **do**
2:     compute μ_j and Σ_j using x_0
3: **end for**
4: **for** $x \in T$ **do**
5:     compute $d_M(x, C_j), \forall j \in \{1, \ldots, m\}$
6:     $C(x) \leftarrow argmin(d_M(x, C_j))$
7: **end for**
Ensure: $C(x), \forall x \in T$

As you can see, the prediction algorithm consists mainly on the computation of distances between the attribute vector x and the classes. Let us now explain how this distance can be evaluated on homomorphic encrypted data.

4.2   Homomorphic Distance Evaluation

Given a vector x and a class C_j, the Mahanalobis distance from x to class C_j is defined as:

$$d_M^2(x, C_j) = (x - \mu_j)^\mathsf{T} \Sigma_j^{-1} (x - \mu_j).$$

Note that in the particular case where the features are uncorrelated or of a unidimensional feature vector the Mahalanobis distance is equivalent to the

Euclidean distance. In contrast to Euclidean distance, this metric allows to also take into account the correlation existing between different features and it can provide curved as well as linear decision boundaries.

For simplification reasons, let us note Σ_j^{-1} as S, μ_j simply as μ and $r = d_M^2(x, C_j)$. Thus, the distance metric becomes:

$$r = (x - \mu)^\mathsf{T} S(x - \mu) = x^\mathsf{T} S x - 2\mu^\mathsf{T} S x + \mu^\mathsf{T} S \mu.$$

Let suppose that we want to protect x and that μ and S were previously computed on plaintexts. Thus, the computation of the distance has to be realized using the encrypted form of x leading to an encrypted r. The last term is only using plaintext data so it is easy to calculate it and to add it to the other terms using the properties of the underlying homomorphic scheme. Also, since μ^T is a vector with the same dimension as x, the term $\mu^\mathsf{T} S x$ is linear (the scalar tensor between a plaintext vector and an encrypted one) and can be computed with an additive homomorphic scheme. The first term $\alpha = x^\mathsf{T} S x$ is a little bit more complicated. If $\sum_{j=1}^n s_{ij} x_j = y$ then:

$$\alpha = \sum_{i=1}^n x_i y_i = \sum_{i=1}^n \sum_{j=1}^n s_{ij} x_i x_j = \sum_{i=1}^n \sum_{j=1}^n s_{ij} z_{ij} \tag{1}$$

with $z_{ij} = x_i x_j$. So, if we have at our disposal the n ciphertexts x_i and the $n(n-1)/2$ ciphertexts z_{ij}, we can use an additive homomorphic cryptosystem.

If we want to avoid the transfer of the quadratic terms from the client to the server, we can also make appeal to a homomorphic cryptosystem with a multiplicative depth of at least 1. An example is the encryption scheme from [42], extension of Paillier cryptosystem, allowing to perform one multiplication over encrypted data. One can also use the so-called leveled homomorphic cryptosystems, such as the Ring-LWE-based (e.g. [8]), more complex but with more computing capabilities and quantum-safe.

Let us remember that the multiplicative depth, notion defining the number of consecutive multiplications one can execute on encrypted data, is a important characteristic of these leveled homomorphic schemes, related to the maximum allowable level of noise for a given set of parameters (the multiplication operation inducing a much bigger noise than the addition).

In the following, for simplicity sake, we explain the case of a classical architecture, in which the client has some private data, a single attribute vector, and makes appeal to a classification service in order to obtain a label for this data only. Of course, the protocols described below still can be applied if, instead of a single instance, we have to label k such instances, as is the case with the district manager in the scenarios described in Sect. 3.

4.3 Prediction Step on Homomorphic Encrypted Data

Additive Homomorphic Encrypted Data. Let us suppose that the system relies on an additive homomorphic cryptosystem and analyze more in details the overall protocol required by the classification service.

The client having the sensitive data to be protected in the form of an attribute vector x of size n, has to encrypt, using his public key, for each vector each component x_i as well as the products $x_i x_k$, with $i, k \in \{1 \ldots n\}$ and $i \le k$. He send these encrypted data to the service provider which has the model build on clear data, i.e. for the Gaussian classifier, the m classes mean μ_j and the inverse of the covariance matrix Σ_j for $j \in \{1, \ldots, m\}$. When receiving an encrypted vector to be labeled, the server computes the distances as described in the previous section and sends these encrypted m ciphertexts to the client. The client decrypts the distances using his secret key, then performs the sorting and selects the minimal distance, corresponding to the classes his data belongs. Moreover, the access to all clear distances can give the client an idea not only of the class he belongs to now but also how far is it from the other classes and, in some way, the needed effort in order to target a better label. The main drawback is the communication overhead induced by sending the quadratic terms from the client to the server.

Leveled Homomorphic Encrypted Data. If the underlying homomorphic scheme allows to realize at least one multiplication on the ciphertext, there are some slight modifications in the protocol for the labeling step. This time, the client having the attribute vector x of size n will encrypt only the components $\{x_i\}$ and send them to the service provider. As such, the quantity of upload information is in this case linear in the number of attributes. The server computes the m encrypted distances as previously, with the mention that now it is able to compute alone the first term α since one multiplication is allowed. The remaining of the protocol is similar to the previous one, on the client side.

Moreover, this protocol can be improved due to the batching technique [43], allowing to pack and encode data for processing it in parallel in a SIMD (Single Instruction Multiple Data) fashion without any extra cost. As such, all the m distances can be embedded in slots and encrypted with a single ciphertext, computed in parallel by the service provider, and send in a single shot to the client (and thus reducing the download communication cost).

Threat Model. For both protocols, one could argue that the client could infer the properties model of the server from the information he has access to, through repeated requests and statistical inference. We focus in this paper more on protecting the client data from a honest-but-curious or not secured enough service provider and one could easily imagine protection mechanisms also for the server side (e.g. no more than a given number of requests). Note also that the security model we present here is not designed to assure the model nondisclosure in the case of collusion between several clients. As for the underlying homomorphic cryptosystems, they assure semantic security [23].

Let us now give some details about the homomorphic schemes we used for testing the feasibility of our approach, with the remark that the general principles remain the same if other additive or leveled homomorphic schemes are deployed.

4.4   Homomorphic Cryptosystems

Paillier Additive Encryption Scheme. As described previously, it appears that an additively homomorphic system is enough in order to execute the classification algorithm. We have chosen Paillier cryptosystem [7] a well-known and popular additively homomorphic cryptosystem. Let us recall here some of its main characteristics allowing the distance computation in the encrypted domain.

Let p and q denote two large primes and $n = pq$. Then, the cleartext domain of the Paillier system is $\mathbb{Z}_n$ and the ciphertext domain is $\mathbb{Z}_{n^2}$. Additionally, let $\lambda = \mathrm{lcm}(p-1, q-1)$ and $g < n^2$ be randomly chosen such that

$$\gcd(L(g^\lambda \mod n^2), n) = 1,$$

with $L(u) = \frac{u-1}{n}$. The public (encryption) key is provided by n and g whereas the private (decryption) key in given by p and q or, equivalently, λ. Then, encryption is done by computing

$$c = \mathrm{enc}(m) = g^m r^n \mod n^2, \tag{2}$$

where $m < n$ is the message and r is uniformly chosen in $\mathbb{Z}_n$. Letting $D = L(g^\lambda \mod n^2)$ and D^{-1} its multiplicative inverse in $\mathbb{Z}_n$, decryption is then performed by evaluating

$$m = \mathrm{dec}(c) = L(c^\lambda \mod n^2) \times D^{-1} \mod n.$$

More importantly for the present purpose, this cryptosystem has the following homomorphic properties:

1. $\mathrm{dec}(\mathrm{enc}(m_1)\mathrm{enc}(m_2)) \mod n^2 = m_1 + m_2 \mod n$ (addition of two encrypted messages).
2. $\mathrm{dec}(\mathrm{enc}(m)g^k) \mod n^2 = m + k \mod n$, for all $k \in \mathbb{Z}_n$ (addition of an encrypted message to a clear integer).
3. $\mathrm{dec}(\mathrm{enc}(m)^k) \mod n^2 = km \mod n$, for all $k \in \mathbb{Z}_n$ (multiplication of an encrypted message by a clear integer).

BGV Encryption Scheme. This leveled homomorphic encryption scheme, based on the Ring-Learning with Errors problem, uses a series of different integer modulus for ciphertexts evaluation, allowing the modulus switching between these modulus in order to reduce the noise. Let $\mathbb{A} = \mathbb{Z}[x]/\Phi_m(x)$ be the ring of integers modulo the m-th cyclotomic polynomial. The ciphertext space is composed of vectors over the polynomial ring $\mathbb{A}_q = \mathbb{A}/q$ where q is an odd modulus evolving during homomorphic evaluation. The cleartext domain is the ring of polynomials $\mathbb{A}_t$, with the native plaintext being $t = 2$ but larger modulus allowing to execute operations on integers modulo t are also possible.

In its batching version, the plaintext space ring $\mathbb{A}_t$ is factored into sub-rings (through CRT-factorization of $\Phi_m(x)$ modulo t) such that the operations of addition and multiplication can be applied on each sub-ring independently. As such, it is possible to pack several several messages into the slots of a single ciphertext and execute the homomorphic operations in parallel on all messages at once.

Let us enumerate some of the important homomorphic operations supported by this cryptosystem:

1. $Keygen(1^\lambda)$ with λ security parameter (generation of the secret key sk, the public key pk and of an additional set of evaluation keys evk for key-switching in homomorphic operations).
2. $enc_{pk}(m)$ (encryption of the plaintext message $m \in \mathbb{A}_t$ using pk).
3. $dec_{sk}(ct)$ (decryption of the ciphertext ct using sk).
4. $dec_{sk}(Add(ct_1 ct_2)) = dec_{sk}(ct_1) + dec_{sk}(ct_2)$ (addition of two encrypted messages).
5. $dec_{sk}(Mult(ct_1, ct_2, evk)) = dec_{sk}(ct_1) * dec_{sk}(ct_2)$ (multiplication of two encrypted messages using if needed key-switching for reducing the noise).

More details are to be found in the original paper [8].

5   System Prototype

5.1   Load Profiles Dataset and Energy Efficiency Rating

In order to reproduce the scenario of the residential district, we have used the CER Smart Metering Project dataset[2]. It represents a comprehensive data source as it encompasses several residential load profiles (4225 load profiles in total) with related environmental information.

The electricity consumption measurements, expressed in kW, were gathered every 30 min during one and a half year. (from July 14th, 2009 to December 31st, 2010). Therefore, the daily load profiles have 48 measures. On top of proposing electricity consumption information, the dataset provides specific indications about the householders owners. Indeed, they accepted to volunteer for a survey about the electricity consumption feedback behavior and answered various questions in that sense. Especially, residential profiles are enlivened with various details about residential buildings (type, construction year, surface, number of occupants, home appliances, etc.) which are useful to express the energy efficiency. Subsequently, we chose 40 residential load profiles among the available ones to create our district. The selected profiles have to fulfill the following conditions:

- No missing data between January 1st, 2010 and December 31st, 2010.
- Householders of the retained load profiles must have completed the information about the surface of the residential building and the number of occupants.
- Electric heating systems are installed in these buildings.

These conditions are defined so to enable us to express the energy efficiency of a residential building.

---

[2] www.ucd.ie/issda/data/commissionforenergyregulationcer/.

Regarding the ratings, we proposed to create clusters from the metrics for each load profile, each cluster defined by a label (ranged from 'A', heavy consumers, to 'F', light consumers) and an average metric (expressed in kWh/(year.m^2.occupant)). For this purpose, we simply applied a k-means [44] and we set the number of cluster at 6. This choice proposed the maximum number of rating levels where no cluster has a size of one. Table 1 summarizes the clustering results and indicates the references that are used by the energy rating service we proposed for the demonstrator. To determine the category of a residential building, a distance is computed between its metric and the ones of each cluster using homomorphic encryption.

Table 1. Labeling references.

Label/Cluster	Average metric	Cluster size
A	7.967	6
B	14.794	10
C	22.272	6
D	30.472	11
E	45.464	5
F	66.096	2

5.2   Performances Results

All the experiments were realized using a standard workstation, with a processor Intel Core I7 at 2.6 GHz, with 16 GB of RAM memory and Ubuntu 16.04 as operating system (on 64 bits). The performance tests use a home made C++ implementation of Paillier additive cryptosystem (based on GMP library) as well as HElib [45], the open-source library from IBM, implementing the BGV cryptosystem. For the version based on Paillier, the code has parallelized sections for the encryption part and the distance evaluation (using pragma omp instructions). For the HElib-based tests, we implemented two basic solutions both using batching but one of them being more optimized.

As described in the previous section, the metric we used is the annual energy consumption per square meter per inhabitant. Therefore, the attribute vectors are mono-dimensional and the Gaussian classifier uses a simple Euclidean distance in order to label them.

Results for Paillier-Based Prototype. Our experiments showed that, as expected, the size of the upload data increases with the number of instances we want to label and, also, with the number of attributes for each instance and their quadratic products. The download data is proportional with the number of households' instances to classify, the dimension of the attribute vector for each household (one dimension for our demonstrator) and the number of classes the model presents.

Table 2 shows the size, in bytes, of one ciphertext for different security levels (i.e. the modulus size) as well as the latency in seconds for uploading the encrypted data (column "UP") and downloading the 6 distances (column "DW") for all of the 40 instances, when considering a network with a throughput of 10 Mbps.

We have also been interested in measuring the processing times of the encryption, distance computation and decryption steps according to the size of the key. For this evaluation we defined a scenario by a couple of parameters: the key size and the step to execute. We considered 2 key sizes for this purpose, by analyzing the execution times when using 1024- and 2048-bit keys for the encryption of the 40 residential profiles, the computation of the distances for these instances with regards to the 6 classes and the decryption of the results for all the households. We collected valuable information after executing each scenario 40 times. Table 3 summarizes these execution times for each step and each key size. As expected, the larger the key size, the longer the execution times are, for each of the steps. This is particularly remarkable for the distance computation step, taking the most important part of the overall computation. Besides its dependency on the key size, the labeling is also proportional with the number of instances to classify (here 40), their dimension (here 1) and the number of the reference classes (here 6). The execution times for the encryption depend on the number of instances to classify and their dimension while the decryption processing times depend on the dimension and the number of references.

Table 2. Data communication for different key sizes [41].

Bits	Size/ciphertext (bytes)	Latency (sec)	
		UP	DW
1024	617	0.03	0.12
2048	1233	0.08	0.23

Table 3. Execution times (sec) of labeling steps for different keys [41].

Bits	Step	Avg.	Min.	Max.
1024	Encryption	0.76	0.42	2.25
	Labeling	3.97	3.23	5.73
	Decryption	0.49	0.34	1.91
2048	Encryption	3.96	3.19	5.45
	Labeling	19.84	17.97	22.85
	Decryption	2.69	2.47	4.34

Results for HElib-Based Prototype. For the first solution based on HElib tests (named "SOL 1") and for a given attribute vector x with n elements, each of the attributes x_i, with $i \in \{1, \ldots, n\}$ is embedded in a different plaintext slot in the form of an integer modulo p^r where p is an arbitrary prime (which does not divide m) and r a small positive integer. This allows to encrypt all the attributes of x in the same ciphertext. The references, i.e. the means of the classes, are represented as m vectors of dimension n. As such, for one instance to label, we obtain m ciphertexts corresponding to the encrypted distances to each class. When such a ciphertext is decrypted, the sum on the slots for the obtained plaintext gives the clear distance to the associated class (modulo p^r). The details of solution "SOL 1" are shown in Fig. 7.

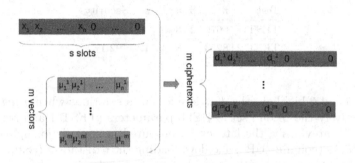

Fig. 7. First packing solution (SOL1) using Helib library.

In the second solution, named "SOL 2" and shown in Fig. 8, we take advantage of the free plaintexts slots (usually the number of slots is much larger than the number of attributes) and, for a single instance x of dimension n to label with regards to m classes, we replicate it m times and embedded into the slots

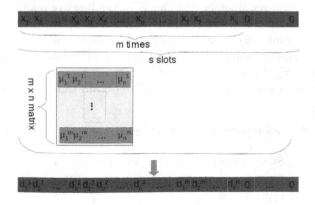

Fig. 8. Second packing solution (SOL2) using Helib library.

of a plaintext, by padding with 0 the remaining space. In this configuration, the means are expressed as a single array of dimension $m \times n$ and we can compute all the distances in the same time using a single ciphertext. Once received and decrypted, one can obtain the clear distances by making the sum on sub-sets of successive slots. The necessary condition for this approach is that the number of slots has to be higher or equal to $m \times n$.

Table 4 shows two configuration of parameters for HElib testing we chosen in order to have s, the right number of slots, (sufficient but not too large) and a security level of at least 80.

Table 4. Parameters for HElib tests [41].

Test	m	p	r	L	s	Security
TEST 1	6679	2	8	3	42	180.46
TEST 2	8253	2	8	4	12	92.17

Tables 5 and 6 highlight the data size for both solutions when using the first and respectively the second set of HElib parameters (TEST 1 and respectively TEST 2). As previously, the latency is computed in seconds for uploading the encrypted data (column "UP") and downloading the 6 distances (column "DW") for all of the 40 instances, when considering a network with a throughput of 10 Mbps. This time, the size of a ciphertext is much larger than the one for a Paillier encrypted data (several thousands of kbytes versus thousands of bytes), due to the complexity of BGV cryptosystem. We also note that the second solution allows to decrease the download latency. In fact, instead of sending m ciphertexts, only one is sent back to the client for decryption.

Tables 7 and 8 summarize the execution times obtained for the first and respectively second solution, when using the above configurations of parameters, for labeling the 40 households relying on 6 references. We consider that the context reading (the parameters and the keys reading) is realized once for all the 40 instances and, as the results indicate, depends on the set of initial HElib parameters. The results of execution times of the second optimized solution (SOL 2) are of better quality than for the first solution for the labeling and decrypting step, which looks right since we are executing the homomorphic evaluation and the decryption on a single ciphertext. Also, we obtain that for the second set of

Table 5. Data communication for different key sizes (TEST 1) [41].

SOL	Size/ciphertext (kbytes)	Latency (sec)	
		UP	DW
(1)	290.98	9.31	55.87
(2)	290.98	9.31	23.14

Table 6. Data communication for different key sizes (TEST 2) [41].

SOL	Size/ciphertext (kbytes)	Latency (sec)	
		UP	DW
(1)	204.61	6.54	98.30
(2)	204.61	6.54	16.38

Table 7. Execution times (sec) of labeling steps for different key sizes (TEST 1) [41].

SOL	Step	Avg.	Min.	Max.	Context reading
(1)	Enc.	0.67	0.60	0.79	7
	Label	9.56	9.02	10.51	
	Dec.	27.49	25.64	31.44	
(2)	Enc.	0.71	0.64	0.91	7.15
	Label	1.65	1.48	2.10	
	Dec.	4.36	4.05	5.02	

Table 8. Execution times (sec) of labeling steps for different key sizes (TEST 2) [41].

SOL	Step	Avg.	Min.	Max.	Context reading
(1)	Enc.	0.83	0.80	0.98	4.06
	Label	14.57	13.55	15.32	
	Dec.	9.80	9.25	10.55	
(2)	Enc.	0.90	0.81	1.31	4.31
	Label	2.45	2.31	3.27	
	Dec.	1.58	1.38	2.57	

parameters (TEST 2), aiming a smaller security level, the processing times are smaller that the ones for the first set (TEST 1) which seems quite normal.

Finally, when comparing the second optimized solution with Paillier-based prototype on 2048 modulus, we remark that in general the execution times for encryption and labeling steps are faster but the decryption takes longer.

Of course, these are just some preliminary tests using HElib and a more thoughtful analysis of the parameters setting is necessary. Moreover, we can imagine several solutions for improving the performances. One of the problems we have in the current form is that most of the time passes in the context reading. Also, for now, the 40 instances are executed sequential and in the future this treatment could be also parallelized.

We would like to remark however that, overall, it is difficult to compare the Paillier-based prototype with the one using Helib library (BGV cryptosystem) since they have different security parameters. Indeed, their security relies on distinct hard problems (Decisional Composite Residuosity Problem vs. Learning with Errors Problem).

6   Conclusion and Perspectives

This paper presents a generic SaaS architecture for private data classification to be deployed in a Smart City. It also describes the associated demonstrator of a practical implementation of a secure energy data classifier. The system was tested with a homomorphically additive cryptosystem and a leveled homomorphic scheme and achieves performances acceptable in a real-world setting. The results obtained attested the effectiveness of our proposal and the ability of our solutions to perform processes on data while guaranteeing privacy.

We think that the advances described in this work can be exploited for other types of data and applications, especially thanks to the generic API (for example, a healthcare dedicated solution able to detect a disease using the encrypted checkups).

This is just a first proposal of a secure rating energy service using homomorphic encryption and thus many improvements can be imagined.

First at all, we plan to implement and test the classification algorithm using other homomorphic cryptosystems (e.g., more recent, third generation homomorphic schemes such as [46]). At the same time, we will focus on the scalability of such an application and the subsequent impacts on processing performance.

Secondly, one could imagine a more complex classification algorithm, less naive than the Gaussian one along with a more thorough evaluation process of the accuracy of the proposed service. Moreover, due to the web API exposing only main and generic methods for encryption, decryption and classification, the new classification algorithm could be easily deployed, without major changes, on the backend of existing architectures.

Last but not least, one has to think of the way the labeling obtained by this outsourced service could be usefully exploited by other tools, such as optimization scenarios, in order to endow the Program Administrator with a cost efficient overall solution and to provide a complete optimization tool for the Smart City.

References

1. NIST: Guidelines for smar grid cyber security. Technical report (2010)
2. Cavoukian, A., Polonetsky, J., Wolf, C.: Smartprivacy for the smart grid: embedding privacy into the design of electricity conservation. Identity Inf. Soc. **3**, 275–294 (2010)
3. CNIL: Pack de conformite sur les compteurs communicants. Technical report (2012)
4. EU: General data protection regulation (GDPR) (2016). http://www.europarl. europa.eu/oeil/popups/ficheprocedure.do?lang=en&reference=2012/0011 %28COD%29
5. Molina-Markham, A., Shenoy, P., Fu, K., Cecchet, E., Irwin, D.: Private memoirs of a smart meter. In: Proceedings of the 2nd ACM Workshop on Embedded Sensing Systems for Energy Efficiency in Building, BuildSys 10, pp. 61–66. ACM (2010)
6. Li, F., Luo, B., Liu, P.: Secure information aggregation for smart grids using homomorphic encryption. In: 2010 First IEEE International Conference on Smart Grid Communications (SmartGridComm), pp. 327–332 (2010)

7. Paillier, P.: Public-key cryptosystems based on composite degree residuosity classes. In: Stern, J. (ed.) EUROCRYPT 1999. LNCS, vol. 1592, pp. 223–238. Springer, Heidelberg (1999). https://doi.org/10.1007/3-540-48910-X_16

8. Brakerski, Z., Gentry, C., Vaikuntanathan, V.: Fully homomorphic encryption without bootstrapping. Cryptology ePrint Archive, Report 2011/277 (2011). http://eprint.iacr.org/

9. Kim, H., Marwah, M., Arlitt, M., Lyon, G., Han, J.: Unsupervised disaggregation of low frequency power measurements. In: In Proceedings of SIAM Interational Conference on Data Mining, pp. 747–758 (2010)

10. Zeifman, M., Akers, C., Roth, K.: Nonintrusive monitoring of miscellaneous and electronic loads. In: 2015 IEEE International Conference on Consumer Electronics (ICCE), pp. 305–308 (2015)

11. De Silva, D., Yu, X., Alahakoon, D., Holmes, G.: A data mining framework for electricity consumption analysis from meter data. IEEE Trans. Ind. Inform. **7**, 399–407 (2011)

12. Verdu, S.V., Garcia, M., Senabre, C., Marin, A.G., Franco, F.J.G.: Classification, filtering, and identification of electrical customer load patterns through the use of self-organizing maps. IEEE Trans. Power Syst. **1**(4), 1672–1682 (2006)

13. Birt, B.J., Newsham, G.R., Beausoleil-Morrison, I., Armstrong, M.M., Saldanha, N., Rowlands, I.H.: Disaggregating categories of electrical energy end-use from whole-house hourly data. Energy Build. **50**, 93–102 (2012)

14. Chicco, G., Napoli, R., Postolache, P., Scutariu, M., Toader, C.: Customer characterization options for improving the tariff offer. IEEE Trans. Power Syst. **18**, 381–387 (2003)

15. Rhodes, J., Cole, W.J., Upshaw, C.R., Edgar, T.F., Webber, M.E.: Clustering analysis of residential electricity demand profiles. Appl. Energy **135**, 461–471 (2014)

16. Figueiredo, V., Rodrigues, F., Vale, Z., Gouveia, J.B.: An electric energy consumer characterization framework based on data mining techniques. IEEE Trans. Power Syst. **20**, 596–602 (2005)

17. McLoughlin, F., Duffy, A., Conlon, M.: Analysing domestic electricity smart metering data using self organising maps. In: IET Conference Proceedings, (1), pp. 319–319 (2012)

18. Räsänen, T., Ruuskanen, J., Kolehmainen, M.: Reducing energy consumption by using self-organizing maps to create more personalized electricity use information. Appl. Energy **85**, 830–840 (2008)

19. McLoughlin, F., Duffy, A., Conlon, M.: Characterising domestic electricity consumption patterns by dwelling and occupant socio-economic variables: an irish case study. Energy Build. **48**, 240–248 (2012)

20. Beckel, C., Sadamori, L., Santini, S.: Automatic socio-economic classification of households using electricity consumption data. In: Proceedings of the Fourth International Conference on Future Energy Systems, e-Energy 2013, pp. 75–86 (2013)

21. Agrawal, R., Srikant, R.: Privacy-preserving data mining. SIGMOD Rec. **29**, 439–450 (2000)

22. Bayardo, R., Agrawal, R.: Data privacy through optimal k-anonymization. In: Proceedings 21st International Conference on Data Engineering, 2005, ICDE 2005, pp. 217–228 (2005)

23. Goldwasser, S., Micali, S.: Probabilistic encryption and how to play mental poker keeping secret all partial information. In: Proceedings of the Fourteenth Annual ACM Symposium on Theory of Computing, STOC 1982, New York, NY, USA, pp. 365–377. ACM (1982)

24. Lindell, Y., Pinkas, B.: Privacy preserving data mining. In: Journal of Cryptology, pp. 36–54. Springer-Verlag (2000)
25. Kantarcıoğlu, M., Clifton, C.: Privately computing a distributed k-nn classifier. In: Boulicaut, J.-F., Esposito, F., Giannotti, F., Pedreschi, D. (eds.) PKDD 2004. LNCS (LNAI), vol. 3202, pp. 279–290. Springer, Heidelberg (2004). https://doi.org/10.1007/978-3-540-30116-5_27
26. Bost, R., Popa, R., Tu, S., Goldwasser, S.: Machine learning classification over encrypted data. Cryptology ePrint Archive, Report 2014/331 (2014). http://eprint.iacr.org/
27. Graepel, T., Lauter, K., Naehrig, M.: Ml confidential: machine learning on encrypted data. IACR Cryptol. ePrint Arch. **2012**, 323 (2012)
28. Samanthula, B., Elmehdwi, Y., Jiang, W.: k-nearest neighbor classification over semantically secure encrypted relational data. CoRR (2014)
29. Zhan, J., Chang, L., Matwin, S.: Privacy preserving k-nearest neighbor classification. Int. J. Netw. Secur. **1**, 46–51 (2005)
30. Lyubashevsky, V., Peikert, C., Regev, O.: On ideal lattices and learning with errors over rings. In: Gilbert, H. (ed.) EUROCRYPT 2010. LNCS, vol. 6110, pp. 1–23. Springer, Heidelberg (2010). https://doi.org/10.1007/978-3-642-13190-5_1
31. UCI: Machine learning repository (2016)
32. Zirm, M., Niedermeier, M.: The future of homomorphic cryptography in smart grid applications. In: Procedeedings of the 3rd IEEE Germany Student Conference Passau 2012 (2012)
33. Saputro, N., Akkaya, K.: Performance evaluation of smart grid data aggregation via homomorphic encryption. In: Wireless Communications and Networking Conference (WCNC), 2012 IEEE, pp. 2945–2950 (2012)
34. Vetter, B., Ugus, O., Westhoff, D., Sorge, C.: Homomorphic primitives for a privacy - friendly smart metering architecture. In: SECRYPT, pp. 102–112 (2012)
35. Thoma, C., Cui, T., Franchetti, F.: Secure multiparty computation based privacy preserving smart metering system. North Am. Power Symp. (NAPS) **2012**, 1–6 (2012)
36. Castelluccia, C., Mykletun, E., Tsudik, G.: Efficient aggregation of encrypted data in wireless sensor networks. In: The Second Annual International Conference on Mobile and Ubiquitous Systems: Networking and Services, 2005, MobiQuitous 2005, pp. 109–117 (2005)
37. Agrawal, S., Boneh, D.: Homomorphic MACs: MAC-based integrity for network coding. In: Abdalla, M., Pointcheval, D., Fouque, P.-A., Vergnaud, D. (eds.) ACNS 2009. LNCS, vol. 5536, pp. 292–305. Springer, Heidelberg (2009). https://doi.org/10.1007/978-3-642-01957-9_18
38. Garcia, F.D., Jacobs, B.: Privacy-friendly energy-metering via homomorphic encryption. In: Cuellar, J., Lopez, J., Barthe, G., Pretschner, A. (eds.) STM 2010. LNCS, vol. 6710, pp. 226–238. Springer, Heidelberg (2011). https://doi.org/10.1007/978-3-642-22444-7_15
39. Energy rating (2016). http://www.energyrating.gov.au/
40. Nikolaou, T., Kolokotsa, D., Stavrakakis, G., Apostolou, A., Munteanu, C.: Review and state of the art on methodologies of buildings' energy-efficiency classification. In: Nikolaou, T., Kolokotsa, D., Stavrakakis, G., Apostolou, A., Munteanu, C. (eds.) Managing Indoor Environments and Energy in Buildings with Integrated Intelligent Systems. GET, pp. 13–31. Springer, Cham (2015). https://doi.org/10.1007/978-3-319-21798-7_2

41. Stan, O., Zayani, M., H., Sirdey, R., Ben Hamida, A., Ferreira Leite, A., Mziou-Sellami, M.: A new crypto-classifier service for energy efficiency in smart cities. In: Proceedings of the 7th International Conference on Smart Cities and Green ICT Systems (2018)
42. Catalano, D., Fiore, D.: Boosting linearly-homomorphic encryption to evaluate degree-2 functions on encrypted data. Cryptology ePrint Archive, Report 2014/813 (2014). http://eprint.iacr.org/2014/813
43. Smart, N.P., Vercauteren, F.: Fully homomorphic simd operations. Des. Codes Crypt. **71**, 57–81 (2014)
44. MacQueen, J.B.: Some methods for classification and analysis of multivariate observations. In: Cam, L.M.L., Neyman, J. (eds.) Proceedings of the Fifth Berkeley Symposium on Mathematical Statistics and Probability, vol. 1, pp. 281–297. University of California Press (1967)
45. Halevi, S.: Helib - an implementation of homomorphic encryption (2013). https://github.com/shaih/HElib
46. Gentry, C., Sahai, A., Waters, B.: Homomorphic encryption from learning with errors: conceptually-simpler, asymptotically-faster, attribute-based. In: Canetti, R., Garay, J.A. (eds.) CRYPTO 2013. LNCS, vol. 8042, pp. 75–92. Springer, Heidelberg (2013). https://doi.org/10.1007/978-3-642-40041-4_5

Identification of Environment- and Context-Specific Key Factors Influencing the User's Thermal Comfort

Antonios Karatzoglou[1,2]([⊠]), Yannick Meny[1], and Michael Beigl[1]

[1] Karlsruhe Institute of Technology, Karlsruhe, Germany
yannick.meny@student.kit.edu,
{antonios.karatzoglou,michael.beigl}@kit.edu
[2] Robert Bosch, Corporate Sector Research and Advance Engineering,
Stuttgart, Germany
antonios.karatzoglou@de.bosch.com

Abstract. The indoor climate conditions in a working environment are extremely important, since these affect the employees' mental state and may lead to a higher or lower productivity. For this reason, the focus in the last years rests on developing sophisticated and adaptable HVAC control systems. The respective systems attempt usually to regulate the users' thermal comfort while keeping the energy consumption low. Recently launched products in this field deliver promising but still perfectible results with space for improvement. This could be attributed to the degree of awareness of current control approaches and the fact that they take only a limited number of environmental (e.g., temperature, humidity) and no context-specific factors (e.g., human activity and emotional state) into account. In this work, we explore whether and to what extend a number of environment- and context-specific factors influence the users' sense of well-being. For this purpose, we deployed a server-based survey framework and conducted a 8-week long field study in an office environment. After performing a number of descriptive and inferential statistical analysis methods on the resulting data, it can be shown that there exist several factors, apart from temperature and humidity, that are capable of affecting significantly the users' thermal comfort. The results presented in this paper could support the development of an improved, context- and emotion-aware generation of HVAC control systems.

Keywords: Smart buildings · HVAC systems · Thermal comfort · Model Predictive Control (MPC) · Context awareness · Light intensity and temperature color · Noise level · Human activity · Emotional state

1 Introduction

Office workers spend 90% of their time indoors [1]. The office environment is a significant factor for a healthy and satisfactory working atmosphere. There exists a strong connection between the performance of office workers and the environment in which they find themselves. A good working atmosphere can lead to an

© Springer Nature Switzerland AG 2019
B. Donnellan et al. (Eds.): SMARTGREENS 2018/VEHITS 2018, CCIS 992, pp. 116–138, 2019.
https://doi.org/10.1007/978-3-030-26633-2_6

up to 10% high performance boost [2]. At the same time, suboptimal conditions often produced negative emotions. Clements-Croome et al. showed that employees, who are dissatisfied with their environment, are most likely also dissatisfied with their occupation [3], a fact that further highlights the importance of work environment conditions.

Previous studies and temperature control systems refer primarily to the impact of individual environmental factors such as temperature [4] or noise. However, there is a lack of research that keep the big picture in mind, that is the entirety of all potential factors and their complex interaction affecting the overall working conditions.

In the presented work, we lay our focus on a set of diverse context and environmental factors (e.g., light temperature color, human activity, mental state, among others) and their impact on the user's thermal comfort. The outcome of our study could help develop smarter temperature controllers that control beside temperature and humidity other insofar unconsidered thermal comfort affecting parameters as well. In particular, we will attempt to provide evidence for the following formulated hypotheses.

Hypothesis I: Noise has no significant influence on thermal comfort.

Hypothesis II: Illumination influences the thermal comfort.

Hypothesis III: Light color temperature influences the thermal comfort.

Hypothesis IV: The type of activity influences the perception of thermal comfort.

Hypothese V: The emotional state has an influence on thermal comfort.

Our work is structured as follows. First, Sect. 2 goes briefly through some of the most related works. Then, in Sect. 3 we provide insight into the basic terms, concepts and scales found in our work. Section 4 describes in detail the design of our experiment, while the respective results are discussed in Sects. 5, 6 and 7. Finally, we conclude our outcomes in Sect. 8 and point at potential future work.

2   Related Work

A certain degree of dissatisfaction with the environmental conditions in their workplace is a typical issue among employees. A questionnaire of Huizenga et al. with 34169 participants revealed that there were more dissatisfied than satisfied employees. Furthermore, only in 11% of 215 buildings were 80% of the workers or more satisfied [5]. A further survey evaluation including 7500 participants in 80 office buildings showed similar results. Depending on the building 15–55% of the employees were dissatisfied. However, even the buildings with the highest rates of satisfaction were assessed as a dissatisfying working environment by up to 20% of employees [6].

The thermal comfort depends on multiple factors, with the room temperature being the most significant one. Seppänen et al. reviewed 24 case studies investigating the influence of room temperature on productivity. They specifically chose studies that relied their evaluation on objective criteria considered to be of relevance to office tasks. The weighting of these studies depended on the number of participants as well as on their relevance to real-world conditions. Their review showed that performance increases up to a room temperature of 21–22 °C and decreases beyond 23–24 °C [7]. Further studies, as the one of Kamarulzaman et al. confirm Seppänen et al.'s result. Their analysis confirms a strong correlation between decreasing performance and higher room temperatures. According to their work, productivity decreases by 2% per degree Celsius above 25 °C [8]. In general, thermal comfort can be associated with certain fixed temperature intervals. In a study of Fang et al., thermal comfort was assessed as neutral at 23 °C, as slightly cold at 20 °C and as slightly warm at 26 °C [9]. The works of Jaakkola et al. [10], Tanabe et al. [11], Lan et al. [12] and Vimalanathan et al. [13] show similar findings. Lan et al. in [14] investigate how high or low temperatures affect human performance in an office environment. They came to the conclusion that deviations from the thermal comfort optimum produce a clear negative impact on the overall performance. Furthermore, they establish a relation between energy saving system designs and a reduced performance of office workers. Amasuomo et al. in [15] tested the stress behavior of students in lecture rooms. Their results indicate that discomfort leads to less concentration, more tiredness and irritation. A similar project was conducted by Steinmetz et al. [16], where he showed that the response behavior differs in cold and warm environments.

Beside room temperature, thermal comfort depends on the perception of air quality, which in turn depends on the room humidity. Air with low humidity is perceived as fresher [9] and less odor-intensive [17].

Noise is also a considerable factor that is able to influence the overall comfort feeling and which has already been investigated thoroughly in previous works. Based to Fischer, employees in open-plan offices assess noise as the main reason for discomfort and low productivity [18]. However, this observation is not applicable to office environments with few employees, since the higher the number of workers in an open-plan office the higher the noise levels. Silent environments show on the other hand a low susceptibility to errors and a high productivity [8]. However, this condition cannot be obtained in practice.

Banbury et al. and Smith report a light deterioration of concentration due to noise as well [19,20]. In addition, Smith found that individuals working with earplugs or hearing protection show a 12% higher productivity. However, other studies suggest that there exist only few certain tasks where noise has some influence when performing them. According to Witterseh et al., noise resulted in a 3% decrease of the performance, but had no significant impact on the satisfaction with regard to the spatial environmental conditions [21]. Jahncke et al. found a significant effect of noise on remembering words, whereas other cognitive tasks seemed not to be negatively influenced by it [22]. Veith [23] and Sundstrom et al. [24] obtained similar results. In his literature review Roelofsen found no significant association between certain noise levels and performance [25].

Another important influencing factor is the lighting of the working space. Juslen analyzed five field studies in which illumination at work was increased and found an increase in productivity by 3–7% [26,27]. All five studies were carried out in an industrial working environment. According to Aries, regular office tasks require an illumination of 500 lux, but levels of 800 lux and more were preferred more by office workers [28]. Analog outcomes have been also confirmed by other works too. For instance an illumination of 1000 lux yields higher performance levels compared to the one 500 or 750 lux [13]. Begemann et al. observed that the preferred illumination level of artificial light in office buildings depends on daylight illumination levels. On cloudy days study participants preferred approximately 1000 lux additional illumination, while on clear weather the preferred illumination level decreased from 1200 to 500 lux with increasing daylight illumination levels [29].

Beside illumination levels it is feasible that the light temperature affects the performance of office workers as well. Study participants of Mills et al. were asked to provide feedback about their well-being feeling and their performance capacity under high light temperature conditions of 14.000 °K [30]. They evaluated high light temperatures as performance- and efficiency-enhancing.

Apart from the aforementioned external environmental factors, it is quite conceivable that other context information such as the physical and mental activity of the occupants as well as their the emotional and mental state (e.g., stressed, angry, etc.) play also a major role when it comes to thermal comfort. In the book [31], the authors discuss that stress adversely affects the skill of processing information in complex tasks and causes negative emotions, which subsequently has again an impact on their comfort. Thus, it seems possible that employees working under stress have different requirements regarding their physical environment and their thermal comfort. Furthermore, comfort is highly relative and depends strongly on the current situation. In [32] for instance, Ahmadpour confirms a high correlation between humans' concerns, like control, privacy, accessibility, style, etc., the situation in which they find themselves, and their general comfort experience. Auliciems [33] did a study to get the correlation between the mental state and different atmospheric parameters like warmth, humidity, cloudiness, intensity of sunlight and windiness. They found that increased outdoor temperature and windiness lead to aggression. But increased humidity and cloudiness increased liking of school.

There exists a great variety of temperature and HVAC[1] control approaches. They all have two major goals in common, namely to raise the participants' thermal and not only comfort levels while keeping the energy consumption low. State of the art works rely on various sensor-gained data, such as the indoor and outdoor temperature, the humidity and the air pressure and its quality to name a few. At the same time, an increasing number of research use additional context information in order to enhance their functionality. Karatzoglou et al. presented in [34] a climate control approach based on both a Support Vector Regression (SVR)-driven occupancy prediction model and a respective rule base that takes

---

[1] Heating, Ventilation, and Air Conditioning.

certain activities of users into account, on top of a PID controller. Their approach was able to enhance the thermal comfort, while keeping the energy consumption low at the same time. In their recent work, Karatzoglou et al. extend their previous work by introducing an adaptable PMV- and Model-based Predictive Control (MPC) based framework [35]. They show that the adaptive behaviour of their approach can lead to a more personalized and therefore improved user experience. Shi et al. in [36] use an occupancy prediction model as well to improve their MPC controller achieving a similar high comfort and energy efficiency. Vesely et al. [37] propose an extension of HVAC systems in order to be able to control microclimates and promote that way both personalized air conditioning and energy performance.

However, prediction is not restricted in occupancy when it comes to temperature control. Ellis et al. in [38] use temperature sensors, gas meter sensors, outdoor temperature sensors and boiler time in order to predict the indoor temperature itself. By predicting the temperature they are able to provide a more accurate control. In [39], the authors make use of the weather forecast as an additional factor for a more efficient temperature control. Finally, Feldmaier et al. swear by a great number of fixed and portable sensors in [40]. At the same time, they collect the users' feedback about their thermal comfort by letting them push one of three buttons (hot, cold and neutral). A control module collects all information and decides whether to open or close the window or change the temperature.

3   Basic Definitions

3.1   Thermal Comfort

In general, *comfort* describes a satisfying and enjoyable human experience. *Thermal Comfort* is more specific and according to the ANSI/ASHRAE Standard 55-2010 it is defined as follows [41]:

> *A condition of mind that expresses satisfaction with the thermal environment and is assessed by subjective evaluation.*

In addition, ASHRAE defines a 7-value comfort index scale displayed in Table 1. Reaching and keeping the optimal thermal comfort reflects the major objective of HVAC systems. There are many factors that have an effect on thermal comfort, like air temperature, clothe insulation and air velocity to name a few.

Table 1. ASHRAE comfort index.

Cold	Cool	Slightly cool	Neutral	Slightly warm	Warm	Hot
−3	−2	−1	0	1	2	3

3.2   Environmental Noise

In this work, environmental noise refers to any intended or unintended sound of which the pressure level can be measured and specified via the decibel unit (dB). The acoustic pressure level is a logarithmic value. Humans perceive a +10 dB raise as twice so loud. The noise level in a quite office ranges from 20–30 dB. The voice of a speaking person reaches 40–60 dB.

3.3   Color Temperature

The color temperature reflects the color impression of a light source. It is expressed in ° Kelvin (K). Figure 1 illustrates the color temperature distribution.

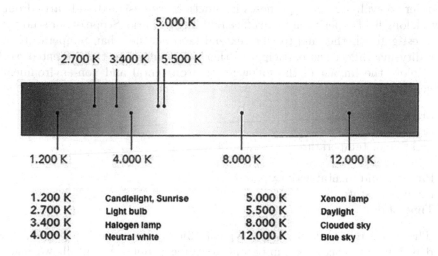

1.200 K	Candlelight, Sunrise	5.000 K	Xenon lamp
2.700 K	Light bulb	5.500 K	Daylight
3.400 K	Halogen lamp	8.000 K	Clouded sky
4.000 K	Neutral white	12.000 K	Blue sky

Fig. 1. The range of color temperature [42].

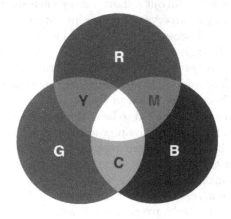

Fig. 2. RGB: Additive color model [43]. (Color figure online)

The average color temperature of daylight depends on the weather conditions and ranges between 5300K and 6000K [29].

3.4 RGB Color Model

The RGB model represents an additive color space, whereby R, G and B refers to the basic colours Red, Green and Blue (see Fig. 2). Usually, RGB values are expressed by 24 Bits, 8 Bits for each prime color. Thus, each basic color part can take 256 numerical values.

4 Experiment - User Study

In order to evaluate our hypotheses in practice, we designed and carried out a 8-week long field experiment in an office building scenario. Scope of our study was to investigate whether and to what extend factors other than temperature and humidity may affect the participants' thermal comfort. In the presented work, we explore the impact of the following environmental and non-environmental influencing factors:

- Light intensity
- Light color
- Light color temperature
- Noise level
- Physical and mental activity
- Emotional state
- Time of day

The user study took place in a typical office environment. In particular we used 6 different offices containing one to three people. All in all, we had 11 persons participating in our study. During the study, the participants were asked on a regular basis (hourly) to fill out a short survey via a smartphone application. The questions asked in the surveys aimed mainly at getting feedback from the users about their thermal sense of well being. These were used to derive the corresponding thermal comfort index (see Sect. 3). An extra group of questions focusing on gaining a comprehensive view of the state of the user, such as her current activity and level of workload experienced at that time, complemented the questionnaires. This can be shown in Fig. 3.

During our experiment, we strived to keep the temperature and humidity levels at a constant level by applying the predictive control mechanism introduced in [35]. In addition, the windows were kept closed and the window blinds at a constant level in order to maintain the same conditions. Besides, the participants were asked not to change their daily clothing level (e.g. taking off their jacket, etc.) in order to prevent related false study results. The radiators in the office environment used for our study are connected with exposed (outside the walls) heating pipes to each other. So, when a person turns on one of the radiators, the heating pipe in all previous rooms are getting hot too, which in turn has an

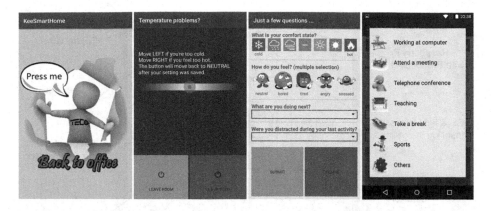

Fig. 3. Login screen, default UI screen, survey screen (displayed hourly), and activity survey screen (displayed hourly) (from the left to the right) [35].

effect on their temperature. To avoid such uncontrolled influences of following radiators we used an 22 mm polyethylene pipe insulation with a thickness of 9 mm to cover all exposed pipes within the test rooms. After that, heating tests showed no demonstrable influence of the water flow initiated by other radiators in the heating system.

4.1 Experimental Setup - Deployment

In this section, we discuss the deployed hardware infrastructure of our experiment. Figure 4 gives an overview of a typical sensor and HW installation in one of the office rooms. The rest of the rooms are of similar size and architecture.

Each room was equipped with sensors to measure the prevailing environmental conditions. An HDC1080 temperature and humidity sensor was mounted indoors in every room, near to the participants and close to their working desk. We installed the same sensor outside the building on the same floor in an appropriate weather resistant shell to get the outdoor temperature and humidity values. Apart from that, we used it also in the corridor to infer eventual temperature gaps between the offices and the corridor. On the other hand, a DS1820 temperature sensor was fixed with insulation tape in the middle of the radiator front to measure directly its temperature. In order to control the hot water flow in each of the rooms, we mounted a wireless FHT8V valve operating mechanism on the radiators. The door state was monitored by a magnet switch and one to two motion detectors, depending on the size of the room, were mounted on the ceiling above the users. In addition, we used RGB-sensors to keep watch over the light conditions.

In order to collect the thermal comfort votes of the users, we deployed a smartphone with an app running on it, which was designed in [35] (see Sect. 4.2), at every workspace serving as a user interface. At the same time, we used the smartphones' sensors to measure the brightness and the ambient sound level near the user. We used clams to fix permanently the smartphones at the monitors in

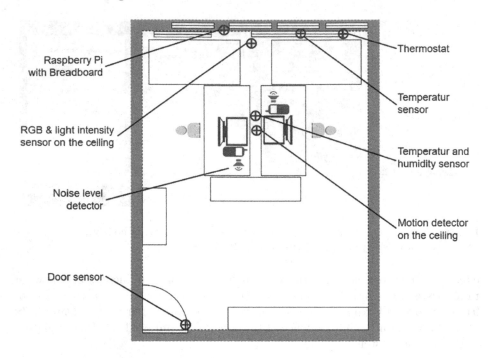

Fig. 4. Sensor and HW deployment [35].

sight of the users as shown on the right of Fig. 5, so that they could send their comfort feedback in the most comfortable way. Moreover, with the smartphone at sight we were able to remind our participants to fill-out the survey by blinking smoothly the screen instead of annoying them with ringtones or other alerting functions. Figure 5 shows a sample of pictures of the deployed sensors and the UI.

Fig. 5. Sensors and UI. Outdoor temperature, motion detection, door, RGB, radiator temperature sensor, Raspberry Pi, and UI (from the left to the right) [35].

All sensor data were collected locally by a Raspberry Pi[2] board that served as a measurement server and forwarded the data to the central server for further processing. For this purpose, each sensor had to be connected through an appropriately designed prior circuit to the boards.

---

[2] https://www.raspberrypi.org/.

In order to keep the temperature stable and regulated, a Raspberry Pi equipped with a 868 MHz dongle was setup outside the test rooms and acted as a central valve control server for the overall temperature controlling approach controlling the mounted valve operating mechanisms mentioned above. The respective data transmission was realized with the help of the FHEM[3] framework and protocol which allows to register and control the FHT8Vs.

4.2 SW Infrastructure and User Interface

For our study, we made use of the server based architecture presented in [35]. It consists of three major components: a valve control server, a central data server and a sensor layout deployed in every room. In this section, we explain in detail our SW architecture. Figure 6 gives an overview of the deployment and illustrates the participating components and their connections.

The valve setting functionality is encapsulated by a HTTP valve control server with an appropriately defined interface to allow the server to control the valves of every test room over the local network as described in [35]. The interface was written in Python and we used the Tornado Web Server[4] for providing the HTTP commands to set and get the valve state.

The central server system processes can be divided into three categories: data storage, system monitoring and controlling. Each service on the server communicates over the local network via the HTTP-protocol. The data storage component consists of two databases. On the one hand, a special time series database (TSDB) is used to store the sensor values and the controller loggings. We have

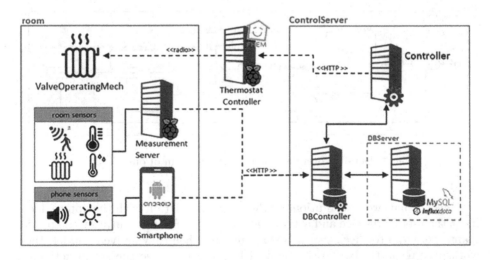

Fig. 6. Deployment diagram of the used framework [35].

---

[3] https://fhem.de/.

[4] http://www.tornadoweb.org/.

chosen the open solution *influxdata*[5] for this purpose. All comfort feedbacks made by the users during the study are also logged in the time series database. On the other hand, a *MySQL*[6] Database was used to store the complete surveys of the users. Like in the valve control server, all database transactions were handled by a HTTP server to encapsulate the database access. The same interface can be used to link other database systems as well. To identify sensor and HW malfunctions and check if everything works fine, the system was continuously monitored with the help of *Kapacitor*, a component of influxdata. Kapacitor allows sending automatic messages if predefined conditions do not match for a specific period. Additionally, we used influxdata's visualization tool *Chronograph* to check the measured data.

An Android application was written to allow users to inform the central control server about their current comfort state and interact with our controller (*virtual thermostat*). The android application has two different default views: the survey and the default UI view. The survey view shows a set of questions and is used to perform the interviewing of the users. It is called regularly every hour. The default UI view enables the users to give feedback about their current thermal comfort on a scale from very hot over neutral to very cold visualized as a gradient line from red to blue. The swipe button's position is mapped to a corresponding ASHRAE comfort index value and is in turn sent to the central server. After sending the comfort feedback, the swipe button switches back to neutral and is ready for the next feedback. The application's workflow is described in Fig. 7, where both the default UI view, as well as the Survey functionality can be seen.

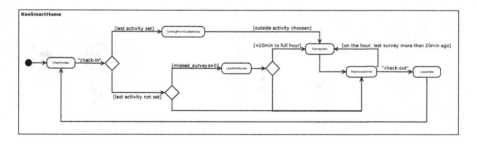

Fig. 7. Detailed overview of the Flow diagram of our UI [35].

Beyond that, we use additionally the users' interaction with the app to document the users' presence and activity ground truth. For this purpose, the participants were told to check themselves in and out when they arrived and left their workspace respectively. On the right of Fig. 3, we can see the set of activities, that users could choose of.

---

[5] https://www.influxdata.com/.
[6] https://www.mysql.com/.

5   Evaluation I: Descriptive Statistical Analysis

The following sections outline our evaluation results. Since the correlation between temperature and humidity has already been thoroughly studied, in our work we focus rather on following potential influencing factors: light intensity, color and color temperature, noise level, time of day, human activity and mental state. Thus, this work explores whether and to what extend the aforementioned factors may affect the thermal comfort. We strived to keep both the temperature and the humidity levels at a constant level throughout the whole study. We use both descriptive and inference statistics to evaluate our data and test our hypotheses formulated in the introductory section. The user study was conducted in the spring. During the user study, the outdoor temperature ranged between $-2°$ (at night) and $+21\,°C$ (at daytime) with a stable daytime average of approximately $14\,°C$.

Figure 8 shows on the left the average thermal comfort vote distribution among the study participants. On the right, we can see the overall thermal comfort vote distribution. All in all, the average comfort votes are close to the neutral comfort 0. A slight tendency towards positive values can be recognized,

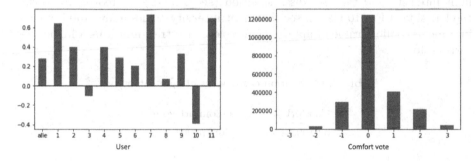

Fig. 8. Average user thermal comfort votes (left) and overall thermal comfort distribution (right).

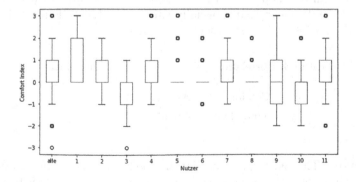

Fig. 9. Box plot of average user comfort votes.

with an overall average comfort vote of +0.279. This could reflect the fact that humans are more sensitive against heat than against coldness.

The respective interquartile ranges can be found in the box plot in Fig. 9. It shows that the interquartile range of most users covers two values of the ASHRAE scale. The neutral and a slightly unsatisfied value (−1 or +1).

5.1   Correlation Coefficient Analysis

In order to make qualitative assessments about the satisfaction of the office workers, the absolute value of comfort indexes has to be used. By definition only a neutral vote implies that the user is satisfied. A deviation shows a dissatisfaction regardless of the value. As a consequence, correlation coefficients were based on the absolute value of comfort indexes. Positive correlations imply that with increasing value of the respective variable discomfort of users increases as well. In the following, "absolute comfort index" describes the absolute value of comfort indexes. If no other value is stated, all of the following correlation coefficients are statistically significant ($p < 0.001$).

Light Intensity. There seems to be a slight negative correlation between the light intensity and the user dissatisfaction (see Table 2). Moreover, by looking the left side of Fig. 10 we can see that light intensity values above 150 lux result in a mean comfort value of approximately zero (neutral) and thus a higher user satisfaction.

Table 2. Correlation coefficients of light intensity.

Comfort vote	Abs. comfort vote
0,016931663	−0,066790968

Light Color Temperature. The slight positive correlations in Table 3 suggest that the environment is perceived as warmer and generally not satisfying. The right part of Fig. 10 shows that especially values over 12000 °K result in a higher dissatisfaction. These values represent bluish light.

Table 3. Correlation coefficients of color temperature.

Comfort vote	Abs. comfort vote
0,061443361	0,076574087

Light Color. The light color correlation coefficients are generally very low. Solely the white color shows some significant correlation value. This fact together with white being one of the brightest colours supports the outcome in Sect. 3.3 where high light intensities improve the users' satisfaction (Table 4).

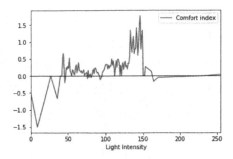 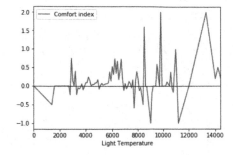

Fig. 10. Average comfort index with respect to light intensity (lux) (left) and color temperature (K) (right).

Table 4. Correlation coefficients and mean values of statistically significant colours.

Color	Color name	C. mean value	Corr. c. index	Corr. abs.
	Black	-0,390374332	-0,061201723	-0,022178096
	Navy	0,682593857	0,032623417	0,012380342
	Purple	-0,042502952	-0,063366712	-0,086063532
	Gray	0,206272159	-0,07087336	-0,023201669
	Fuchsia	-0,32	-0,014113506	-0,007725475
	White	0,038510101	-0,065773897	-0,100928869

Noise. There is a slight positive correlation with the comfort index (Table 5). Thus, higher noise levels are associated with a environment perceived as slightly too warm. The slight negative correlation with the absolute comfort index shows that users are more satisfied when their environment features some kind of sound. However, the dissatisfaction increases rapidly if noise values exceed 80 dB (see Fig. 11).

Time of Day. The correlation coefficients imply that later in the day the thermal comfort is rated as colder. It is also noticeable that the satisfaction decreases after 8.00 pm (Fig. 11). If one assumes that office workers working at these times generally have longer working hours, this effect may be attributed to the long work and the related exhaustion. Haynes also concluded that the longer employees stay in their office the physical environment grows more important [44] (Table 6).

Emotional State. The "stressed" state stands clearly out from the rest. Being stressed results in the perception of a too warm and more dissatisfying envi-

Table 5. Correlation coefficients of noise (dB).

Comfort vote	Abs. comfort vote
0,05895337	−0,111926239

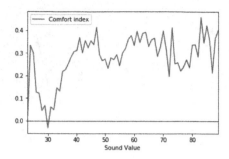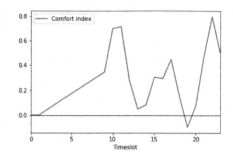

Fig. 11. Average comfort vote with respect to noise (left) and time of day (right).

Table 6. Correlation coefficients of time of day (represented by hourly time slots).

Comfort vote	Abs. comfort vote
−0,115492451	−0,148407276

ronment. Being "angry", at first sight surprisingly, shows the least influence. However, this could be explained by the fact that users tended to annotate their state as "stressed" in both cases. This led to an overall low number of stated angry states. The emotional states "neutral", "tired" and "bored" yield similar effects regarding their correlation coefficients and the corresponding mean values. They all seem to have a minimal affection the thermal effect (Table 7).

Table 7. Correlation coefficients and mean value of the moods.

Emotional state	C. mean value	Corr. c. index	Corr. abs. c. index
neutral	0,230694119	−0,075278429	0,051755537
müde	0,183150183	−0,068425682	−0,043157023
gelangweilt	0,226020893	−0,011708214	−0,066482122
wütend	0,095447871	−0,022721167	−0,021829285
gestresst	0,538833333	0,100605178	0,178662233

Activities. The correlation coefficients of the activities are also low. It can be observed that a meeting or a taking a break increases dissatisfaction of the users. This may be due to metabolic processes. For instance, users move more during a break compared to working at their desk. Levine et al. found that even low-intensity activities such as walking result in a increased rate of caloric expenditure [45]. This effect and the adaptation of the human body may lead to a increased dissatisfaction regarding the thermal comfort (Table 8).

Ablenkungen. We let the participants to distinguish between distractions due to business affairs and other reasons (e.g., friend passes by, small talk with the

Table 8. Correlation coefficients and mean values of activities.

Activity	C. mean value	Corr. c. index	Corr. abs. c. index
Calling	0	−0,019089409	−0,048968955
Break	0,074390244	−0,039666042	0,051528453
Meeting	0,049019608	−0,039966151	0,038769464
Teaching	0,279726729	−0,014357674	−0,03683091
Working on PC	0,250066527	−0,031182718	−0,094145261

colleague, etc.) We found out that if users were distracted by business affairs, they generally perceived their environment as too cold. The particular dissatisfaction was higher in the business-related case compared to the other type of distractions. A possible explanation could be the fact that in the first case, participants are forced to lay their focus on a completely other task and refocus on their previous one, while the distraction in the second case does not require their full attention and thus it is easier for them to refocus (Table 9).

Table 9. Correlation coefficients and mean values of distractions.

Distraction	C. mean value	Corr. c. index	Corr. abs. c. index
Business	−0,018275967	−0,153983409	0,031410005
Other	0,356650246	0,030291192	−0,041516978

5.2 Multiple Linear Regression Analysis

Performing a multi-linear regression analysis on our data confirmed the outcome of the above correlation coefficient analysis. As we can see in Table 10, the greatest influence on the dependent variable of the thermal comfort is humidity. It is followed by the time of the day and the temperature, with time of the day being higher. The influence factors with the lowest, but in no way insignificant, impact are noise, light intensity and color temperature.

From the rest of the factors considered in our study, the multi-regression analysis showed that the emotional state "stressed", as well as the activities "calling" and "taking a break" have also a significant impact on the thermal comfort.

5.3 Cluster Analysis

Finally, we performed a cluster analysis, which resulted in 21 clusters. Thereof, five groups are outliers and represent only one single data set. It has to be taken in account that the ASHRAE standard defines unsatisfying comfort votes as greater or lower than zero. Therefore, only cluster midpoints whose values are

Table 10. Coefficients of environmental variables in the linear regression.

Influence factor	Coefficient	p-value
Noise	0,209	0,000
Color temperature	−0,309	0,000
Light intensity	−0,21	0,005
Temperature	−0,458	0,000
Humidity	−0,95	0,000
Time of day	−0,634	0,000
Outdoor temperature	0,325	0,000

greater than one or lower than minus are applicable for the evaluation. For this reason, only ten cluster remain for further analysis. In this section, we describe the two clusters that contain the highest dissatisfaction rates, that is, with the most extreme positive and negative average thermal comfort vote midpoints. For each cluster we list the five top influence factors, that showed the highest relative change in comparison with the mean values at a neutral thermal comfort .

Cluster 1. Comfort mean value: 2
This cluster groups data sets where office workers were distracted by a non business-related issue and that were generally in a stressed emotional state. This resulted in a high comfort index value, although the light intensity was at the maximum value, which as we saw before usually led to a high satisfaction. The values were generally recorded later in the day, a fact that could be the explanation for the overall increased dissatisfaction of the users (Table 11).

Table 11. Midpoint deviations of cluster 1.

Influence factor	Value	Reference value	Rel. change
Emotional state: stressed	1	0,038	25,223
Distraction: others	1	0,0801	11,481
Light intensity	255	115,069	1,216
Time of day	22	15,574	0,412
Outdoor temperature	10	13,288	−0,247

Cluster 2. Comfort mean value: −1, 4
Cluster 2 groups thermal comfort votes that were gathered in an environment with low light intensity. In addition, the users were distracted by business-related matters. This combination shows a high dissatisfaction despite the fact that the noise level is very low (Table 12).

Table 12. Midpoint deviations of cluster 2.

Influence factor	Value	Reference value	Rel. change
Distraction: business	0,6	0,188	2,196
Light intensity	18,411	155,069	−0,84
Emotional state: neutral	1	0,657	0,522
Noise	32,58	49,59	−0,343
Activity: PC	0,4	0,538	−0,257

6 Evaluation II: Inferential Statistical Analysis

This chapter includes significance tests of our data sample.

6.1 t-Test

The t-test allows examining statistically significant differences in the comfort votes of the users. The null hypothesis in this case is that there is no difference comparing different samples. Comparing all users pairwise shows that the null hypothesis is rejected in every case ($p < 0.95$). Only the votes of user two and four were equal: $t = 0.012$, $p = 0.984$. Therefore, the findings suggest that there are individual differences in the perception of thermal comfort. Furthermore, no equal comfort index values were observed in different rooms.

The t-test also allows to compare the results of other studies with the comfort values of the underlying study in this work. Huizenga et al. reviewed 34,000 survey results in 215 buildings [5]. The average thermal comfort value was −0.1. Comparing our study values with Huizenga et al.'s mean value the null hypothesis was rejected by the t-test. There are several possible explanations for this result. For instance, 90% of the office buildings that were included in Huizenga et al.'s study were in North America. Furthermore, most of the surveys have been conducted in the summer. The negative mean value could be due to air conditioning which could be set as too cold because of high outdoor temperatures. In addition, it is possible that certain cultural differences in the perception of the thermal environment exist resulting in different comfort values.

6.2 Chi-Squared Test

Beside the average value, Huizenga et al.'s work also describes the overall deviation and distribution of the annotated comfort votes. In order to compare the comfort vote distribution of our user study with their outcomes, we used the Chi-squared test technique. Like in the case of the t-test, this test rejected the null hypothesis as well. This can be again attributed to the same reasons as in the t-test case.

The comparison with the deviation of the data set of our work (see Fig. 12) shows that the number of dissatisfied votes in the external study is higher. Furthermore, extreme dissatisfied values, e.g., comfort index >=2 or comfort index

<=2, were committed more often. In addition, there was a tendency to values representing a cold thermal comfort whereas in our work a tendency to a warm thermal comfort was found. The distribution difference may be due to the fact that Huizenga et al. took 215 office buildings into account, of which only 11% were occupied by at least 80% satisfied office workers. Therefore, the high number of votes representing dissatisfaction were committed in buildings, which generally had dissatisfying working conditions.

7 Hypothesis Testing

In this section, we evaluate the hypotheses that were formulated in the introductory section.

Hypothesis I: Noise has no significant influence on thermal comfort.

The data analysis showed a slight negative correlation of noise with the absolute comfort index value. This implies that increasing the noise level up to a certain degree, in contrast to completely silent work places, raises the satisfaction with the working environment. Looking at out noise level mean values, it is apparent that a low noise level of 30 dB is optimal. However, a noisy environment with levels of 80 dB or more lead to a rapid decrease of the thermal comfort. It seems that noise between these two values has no influence on the thermal comfort. Hence, there is a statistically significant effect of noise. However, this influence can only rarely be observed because there is no effect under normal noise levels. Studies of Kamarulzaman et al. [8] and Smith [20] have shown that silent environments support a higher employee productivity, while Roelofsen found no effect of noise that does not lead to hearing damage [2].

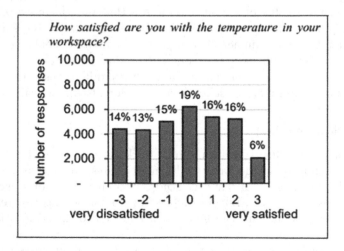

Fig. 12. Distribution of survey results with respect to the satisfaction with the thermal environment [5].

Their results confirms the outcome of our work, where relative silence acts positively and loud noise negatively, while mid-level noise in-between shows no effect.

Hypothesis II: Illumination influences the thermal comfort.

Higher illumination levels correlate slightly negatively with the absolute value of the comfort index votes. Increasing light intensity leads to an increased satisfaction with the thermal environment as well. "White" is the color with the highest light intensity. The fact that higher light intensities are associated with higher satisfaction levels implies the fact that the color "white" features a high correlation with the environmental satisfaction as well. These results confirms the previously proposed hypothesis. In addition, the cluster analysis showed that low light intensities combined with other factors resulted in a high dissatisfaction. Related works also showed an increase of productivity linked to bright environments [13, 26, 28], which in turn can be attributed to a higher satisfaction with the working environment.

Hypothesis III: Light color temperature influences the thermal comfort.

The work of Mills et al. shows a higher satisfaction of individuals at the very high color temperature of 14,000 °K [30]. In contrast, the outcome of our study suggests that color temperature levels above 12,000 °K increase dissatisfaction levels. In general, color temperature seems to slightly correlate with the participants' dissatisfaction. Therefore, the may be a relation between the color temperature and the thermal comfort.

Hypothesis IV: The type of activity influences the perception of thermal comfort.

If we compare the correlation coefficients of the different activities regarding thermal comfort we come up with a negative influence of "breaks" and "meetings" on the users' thermal satisfaction. This could be attributed to the fact that the change of the environment or stopping doing routine tasks may lead to a more intense awareness of the working environment and consequently to being more sensitive in identifying dissatisfying environmental variables. In addition, activities associated with tasks that may increase the users' stress levels may in turn increase dissatisfaction with respect to thermal comfort (see next hypothesis). The cluster analysis confirms this assumption as well.

Hypothesis V: The emotional state has an influence on thermal comfort.

The correlation analysis already showed that a stressed emotional state correlates with a higher thermal dissatisfaction. It is noteworthy that this effect is greater than of any environmental influence factor. While the emotional states "tired", "bored" and "angry" showed light but no significant differences in the regression analysis compared to the reference value of a "neutral" mood, "stress" had a noticeable influence. Moreover, several in the cluster analysis identified groups that showed a higher dissatisfaction included "stress" as a significant feature. Many of the times, "stress" was accompanied by some distraction. So it is possible that in these cases the distraction caused the stress.

8 Conclusion

In the present work, we explore the impact of a number of environment- and context specific factors on the users' thermal comfort. In particular, we go beyond the usual suspects, such as temperature and humidity, and investigate whether and to what extend light conditions (intensity and color temperature), environmental noise, human activity and mental state, as well as time of day affect their sense of well-being. In order to evaluate our preliminary hypotheses, we designed and conducted a 8-week long field study in an office environment. For this purpose we deployed a server-based survey framework. After preprocessing the resulting data, we performed a number of descriptive (e.g., correlation analysis, multi-linear regression, cluster analysis) and inferential statistical analysis (t-test, chi-square-test). Our outcomes show that several factors, like the light intensity and color temperature as well as the emotional state, have a significant impact on the users' thermal comfort. This fact could contribute to developing a new generation of smart indoor temperature controllers that control beside temperature and humidity other insofar unconsidered thermal comfort affecting parameters as well. In the future work, we plan to gradually integrate the presented results into a predictive indoor climate control system and evaluate their practical feasibility.

References

1. Klepeis, N.E., et al.: The national human activity pattern survey. A resource for assessing exposure to environmental pollutants. J. Expo. Sci. Environ. Epidemiol. **3**, 231–252 (2001)
2. Roelofsen, P.: The impact of office environments on employee performance: the design of the workplace as a strategy for productivity enhancement. Health Facil. Manag. **1**, 247–264 (2002)
3. Clements-Croome, D., Baizhan, L.: Productivity and indoor environment. Proc. Healthy Build. **1**, 630–633 (2000)
4. Lan, L., Lian, Z., Pan, L., Ye, Q.: Neurobehavioral approach for evaluation of office workers' productivity: the effects of room temperature. Build. Environ. **44**, 1578–1588 (2009)
5. Huizenga, C., Abbaszadeh, S., Zagreus, L., Arens, E.: Air quality and thermal comfort in office buildings: results of a large indoor environmental quality survey. Proc. Healthy Build. **3**, 393–397 (2006)
6. Leaman, A.: Dissatisfaction and office productivity. Facilities **13**, 13–19 (1995)
7. Seppänen, O., Fisk, W.J., Lei, Q.: Effect of temperature on task performance in office environment. Technical report, Helsinki University of Technology (2006)
8. Kamarulzaman, N., Saleh, A.A., Hashim, S.Z., Hashim, H., Abdul-Ghani, A.A.: An overview of the influence of physical office environments towards employees. Procedia Eng. **20**, 262–268 (2011)
9. Fang, L., Wyon, D.P., Clausen, G., Fanger, P.O.: Impact of indoor air temperature and humidity in an office on perceived air quality, SBS symptoms and performance. Indoor Air **14**, 78–81 (2004)

10. Jaakkola, J., Heinonen, O., Seppänen, O.: Sick building syndrome, sensation of dryness and thermal comfort in relation to room temperature in an office building: need for individual control of temperature. Environ. Int. **15**, 163–168 (1989)
11. ichi Tanabe, S., Nishihara, N., Haneda, M.: Indoor temperature, productivity, and fatigue in office tasks. HVAC&R Res. **13**, 623–633 (2007)
12. Lan, L., Lian, Z., Pan, L.: The effects of air temperature on office workers' well-being, workload and productivity-evaluated with subjective ratings. Appl. Ergon. **42**, 29–36 (2010)
13. Vimalanathan, K., Babu, T.R.: The effect of indoor office environment on the work performance, health and well-being of office workers. J. Environ. Health Sci. Eng. **12**, 113 (2014)
14. Lan, L., Wargocki, P., Lian, Z.: Optimal thermal environment improves performance of office work. REHVA Eur. HVAC J. **2**, 12–17 (2012)
15. Amasuomo, T.T., Amasuomo, J.O.: Perceived thermal discomfort and stress behaviours affecting students' learning in lecture theatres in the humid tropics. Buildings **6**, 18 (2016)
16. Steinmetz, J., Posten, A.C.: Physical temperature affects response behavior. J. Exp. Soc. Psychol. **70**, 294–300 (2017)
17. Reinikainen, L.M., Aunela-Tapola, L., Jaakkola, J.J.K.: Humidification and perceived indoor air quality in the office environment. Occup. Environ. Med. **54**, 322–327 (1997)
18. Vischer, J.C.: The effects of the physical environment on job performance: towards a theoretical model of workspace stress. Stress Health **23**, 175–184 (2007)
19. Banbury, S., Berry, D.: Office noise and employee concentration: Identifying causes of disruption and potential improvements. Ergonomics **48**, 25–37 (2005)
20. Smith, A.: Noise, performance efficiency and safety. Int. Arch. Occup. Environ. Health **62**, 1–5 (1990)
21. Witterseh, T., Wyon, D.P., Clausen, G.: The effects of moderate heat stress and open-plan office noise distraction on SBS symptoms and on the performance of office work. Indoor Air **14**, 30–40 (2004)
22. Jahncke, H., Hygge, S., Halin, N., Green, A.M., Dimberg, K.: Open-plan office noise: cognitive performance and restoration. J. Environ. Psychol. **31**, 373–382 (2011)
23. Veitch, J.A.: Office noise and illumination effects on reading comprehension. J. Environ. Psychol. **10**, 209–217 (1990)
24. Sundstrom, E., Town, J.P., Rice, R.W., Osborn, D.P., Brill, M.: Office noise, satisfaction, and performance. Environ. Behav. **26**, 195–222 (1994)
25. Roelofsen, P.: The impact of office environments on employee performance: the design of the workplace as a strategy for productivity enhancement. J. Facil. Manag. **1**, 247–264 (2002)
26. Juslén, H.: Lighting and productivity in the industrial working place. Light. Eng. **14**, 53–62 (2006)
27. Jusléna, H., Wouters, M., Tenner, A.: The influence of controllable task-lighting on productivity: a field study in a factory. Appl. Ergon. **38**, 39–44 (2007)
28. Aries, M.B.C.: Human lighting demands: healthy lighting in an office environment. Technische Universiteit Eindhoven (2005)
29. Begemann, S., van den Beld, G., Tenner, A.: Daylight, artificial light and people in an office environment, overview of visual and biological responses. Int. J. Ind. Ergon. **20**, 231–239 (1997)

30. Mills, P.R., Tomkins, S.C., Schlangen, L.J.: The effect of high correlated colour temperature office lighting on employee wellbeing and work performance. J. Circadian Rhythm. **5**, 2 (2007)

31. Hancock, P.A., Szalma, J.L.: Performance Under Stress. Ashgate Publishsing, Burlington (2008)

32. Ahmadpour, N.: Comfort experience in everyday life events. In: Chung, W., Shin, C. (eds.) Advances in Affective and Pleasurable Design, vol. 483, pp. 625–632. Springer, Cham (2017). https://doi.org/10.1007/978-3-319-41661-8_61

33. Auliciems, A.: Mood dependency on low intensity atmospheric variability. Int. J. Biometeorol. **22**, 20–32 (1978)

34. Karatzoglou, A., Janssen, J., Srikanthan, V., Ding, Y., Beigl, M.: Comfort-efficiency-equilibrium: a proactive, at room level individualized climate control system for smart buildings (2017)

35. Karatzoglou, A., Jann, J., Srikanthan, V., Urbaczek, C., Beigl, M.: A predictive comfort- and energy-aware MPC-driven approach based on a dynamic PMV subjectification towards personalization in an indoor climate control scenario. In: Proceedings of the 7th International Conference on Smart Cities and Green ICT Systems - Volume 1: SMARTGREENS, INSTICC, pp. 89–100. SciTePress (2018)

36. Shi, J., Yu, N., Yao, W.: Energy efficient building hvac control algorithm with real-time occupancy prediction. Energy Procedia **111**, 267–276 (2017)

37. Veselỳ, M., Zeiler, W.: Personalized conditioning and its impact on thermal comfort and energy performance-a review. Renew. Sustain. Energy Rev. **34**, 401–408 (2014)

38. Ellis, C., Hazas, M., Scott, J.: Matchstick: a room-to-room thermal model for predicting indoor temperature from wireless sensor data. In: Proceedings of the 12th International Conference on Information Processing in Sensor Networks, pp. 31–42. ACM (2013)

39. Oldewurtel, F., et al.: Use of model predictive control and weather forecasts for energy efficient building climate control. Energy Build. **45**, 15–27 (2012)

40. Feldmeier, M., Paradiso, J.A.: Personalized HVAC control system. In: Internet of Things (IOT), 2010, pp. 1–8. IEEE (2010)

41. American Society of Heating, Refrigerating and Air-Conditioning Engineering: ANSI ASHRAE standard 55-2010. Standard 55-2010 (2010)

42. Energie Burgenland AG: Energieeffiziente beleuchtung (2017)

43. Kunkel, V.: RGB-farbmodell (2017)

44. Haynes, B.P.: An evaluation of the impact of the office environment on productivity. Facilities **26**, 178–195 (2008)

45. Levine, J.A., Schleusner, S.J., Jensen, M.D.: Energy expenditure of nonexercise activity. Am. J. Clin. Nutr. **72**, 1451–1454 (2000)

Vehicle Technology and Intelligent Transport Systems

Information System Development for Seamless Mobility

Markus C. Beutel[1,3]([✉]), Sevket Gökay[1,3], Eva-Maria Jakobs[2],
Matthias Jarke[1,3], Kai Kasugai[4], Karl-Heinz Krempels[1,3], Fabian Ohler[1,3],
Christian Samsel[1,3], Felix Schwinger[3], Christoph Terwelp[1,3], David Thulke[1],
Sara Vogelsang[2], and Martina Ziefle[4]

[1] Information Systems, RWTH Aachen University, Aachen, Germany
{jarke,samsel,thulke}@dbis.rwth-aachen.de
[2] Textlinguistics and Technical Communication, RWTH Aachen University,
Aachen, Germany
{e.m.jakobs,s.vogelsang}@tk.rwth-aachen.de
[3] Fraunhofer Institute of Applied Information Technology, Sankt Augustin, Germany
{beutel,goekay,krempels,ohler,schwinger,terwelp}@fit.fraunhofer.de
[4] Communication Science, RWTH Aachen University, Aachen, Germany
{kasugai,ziefle}@comm.rwth-aachen.de

Abstract. Today, combining diverse mobility services during a single itinerary across different regions is still bristled with obstacles. Although developments concerning Mobility as a Service (MaaS) concepts, Advanced Travel Information Systems (ATIS) or Mobility Service Platforms (MSP) fostered integration, there are still various limitations. Manifold reasons, ranging from technical problems like heterogeneous system landscapes up to strategic business considerations, cause barriers on different levels. Within this work, we present a high level methodology to develop an integrated travel information system to overcome some of these barriers. We describe the practical applications as well as the method evolution in two German research projects. One project developed an IT platform to realize the interoperability of mobility services, whereas the second project focuses on the generalization of the approach by defining a reference framework. In addition, we discuss the lessons learned from half a decade of mobility and information systems research to suggest implications for future research.

Keywords: Advanced travel information systems · Digitization · Intermodal mobility · Transportation service interoperability · Software engineering · Mobility platforms

1 Introduction

Nowadays, various heterogeneous modes of transportation lead to a diversified mobility behavior and often to *intermodal* traveling, which is defined as the switching between various heterogeneous modes of transportation during one

© Springer Nature Switzerland AG 2019
B. Donnellan et al. (Eds.): SMARTGREENS 2018/VEHITS 2018, CCIS 992, pp. 141–158, 2019.
https://doi.org/10.1007/978-3-030-26633-2_7

single trip [1]. Intermodal transportation enables travelers to travel flexibly and individually, but is at the same time highly complex. This results in a wide range of user requirements towards (travel) information systems [2,3]. According to [4], Advanced Travel Information Systems (ATIS) use information and communication technology to provide travel information to a wide range of users, who use various different modes of transportation with a diversity of characteristics. The assistance through advanced travel information systems goes beyond the provision of information and enables to manage the complexity of planning, booking and utilization of intermodal travel chains [5]. Thus, the characteristics of travel information systems move from former standalone solutions to comprehensive systems especially incorporating the service distribution.

Beyond usability and ecological benefits, service integration offers economical potentials as well. From the transportation providers perspective, it offers potentials to increase the provider's market share through adding complementary services and synergistic effects.

In [6], we described the method of project *Mobility Broker* with the aim to combine, integrate and digitize heterogeneous mobility services into one mobility service platform. Hereby, we continue this work by presenting lessons learned from Mobility Broker and introduce the refined method of the follow-up project *Open Mobility Platform (OMP)*.

In Sect. 2, selected related projects are presented to identify method-critical core activities. Afterwards, Sect. 3 introduces the step-by-step integration method. Section 4 demonstrates the integration of mobility services in research project Mobility Broker whereas Sect. 5 generalizes the concept in project OMP. Finally, Sect. 6 reflects, discusses, and concludes the work.

2   Related Projects

As a starting point, we base our work on the activities of the software engineering process by [7]. It consists of *requirements engineering, application analysis, application outline, implementation, test* and *maintenance*. To specify the method even further, we initially investigate related development projects to identify essential core activities.

2.1   econnect Germany

The aim of the project "econnect Germany" (2012–2014) was to develop electric mobility in Germany. Multiple work packages in the areas of smart traffic, smart grid, smart home, tourism, and intermodal travel information helped advancing the introduction of electric vehicles in Germany. Involved in the project were multiple universities and research institutes, (heavy-)industry and IT companies and municipal utilities. A work package focused on intermodal personal mobility was guided by an outline aiming to offer attractive and environmentally friendly mobility. To offer such a service, a mobile application called "CityNavigator" was developed and tested [8], which integrated (electric) shared vehicles into public transport travel information. The communication interface between the travel information system and the vehicle sharing backend has been standardized as IXSI [9,10].

The identified core activities in this project were the specification of *use cases*, *processes* and *data models* for the service integration.

2.2 SUPERHUB

"SUPERHUB" (SUstainable and PERsuasive Human Users moBility in future cities) is a European research project, aiming to develop a system that supports "[...] an integrated and eco-efficient use of multi-modal mobility systems in an urban setting." In more detail, the system "[...] provides a user-centric, integrated approach to multi-modal smart urban mobility systems, through an open platform able to consider in real time various mobility offers and provide a set of mobility services able to address user needs [...]" [11]. It combines heterogeneous mobility services with the help of intermodal routing [12]. The offerings are additionally provided via a mobile application. The system uses a flexible best price solution. Moreover, sustainable mobility behavior should be encouraged by a behavior management component [13].

Above the fundamental steps of the software engineering process, the investigation of the SUPERHUB project showed indeed valuable additional process parts. As part of a basic analysis, we identified especially *business model analysis* as a core activity to ensure economical reliability. Moreover, the chronology of developing described system components seems reasonable and expedient.

3   Integration Method

The mobility service integration process method we propose, provides a structured solution to compose existing and integrate new mobility services with diverging characteristics on the basis of an (travel) information system. The structure is based on the fundamental work by [14]: A method fragment is closely interwoven with the concept of method components and is characterized by exactly one draft result of a method. The separation into method fragments reduces the inherent complexity of the described method through dividing the overall project into comprehensible parts with defined milestones. On the one hand this eases the description, on the other hand it facilitates the applicability of the method [15].

A special focus is on the software development methodology. One characteristic of current software systems is their connectedness with other software systems. The Internet became the de facto platform for integration, and more and more software systems are built as *distributed systems*. This is partly due to the growing complexity of developing software, since the current generation of software aims to be more powerful and capable than previous generations. One side effect is division of labor: Software components are built by specialized developers or teams, who mainly concentrate on their subset of tasks (component level). At the same time, it is also necessary to monitor/manage the efforts for their convergence towards the bigger picture (top level). In the fundamental software development process by [7], *analysis* plays an important role. The concept states *requirements engineering* and *application analysis* as two analytical starting points. Our work relies on this basis, but complements it with the step of *mobility service analysis*.

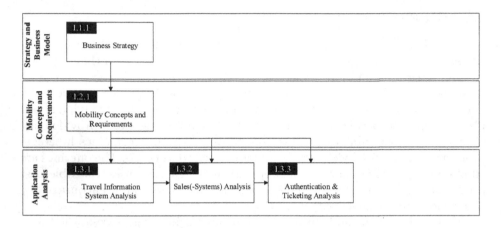

Fig. 1. Method part I: Concepts and requirements.

As a starting point (cf. Fig. 1), a *business strategy* (I.1.1) has to be defined. It is crucial to define these collaboration strategies because this configuration affects related *business models* significantly. After defining the overall business strategy of each party, the *requirements* towards the intended information system have to be evaluated. Especially in the mobility sector, which we are focusing on, *mobility concepts* (I.2.1) play an important role. Suitable concepts that fit the requirements have to be reviewed and analyzed. This step helps to improve the knowledge of specific mode characteristics and integration solutions. Afterwards, an *analysis* of related information systems (I.3.1–I.3.3) to provide the services takes place.

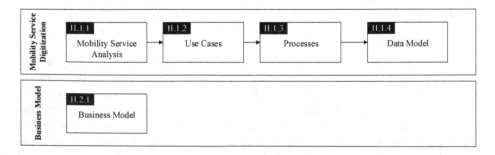

Fig. 2. Method part II: mobility service digitization.

This knowledge base is necessary for the *mobility service digitization* phase (cf. Fig. 2). Herewith, specific mobility service characteristics and processes have to be identified and represented in a suitable data model (II.1.1–II.1.4). Derived of the business strategy, an actual business model has to be specified (II.2.1).

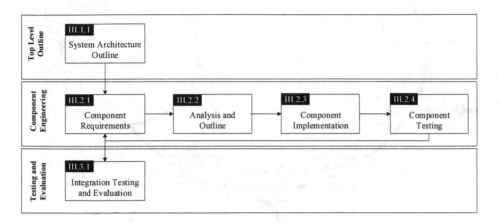

Fig. 3. Method part III: system implementation and evaluation.

This leads to a *top level outline* (III.1.1) of the system architecture (cf. Fig. 3). The top level phases determine fundamental requirements and guidelines for the system. But for each system component, e.g., the user-interface, backend and data-interfaces, *specific engineering processes* occur (III.2.1–III.2.2). After implementing the system components (III.2.3), *integration testing* and *evaluation* (III.3.1) of the solution takes place. In case of adding a *new service* (or improvements of the system), the loop starts from the beginning.

Combining these steps and adding a loop-characteristic for incremental improvement, which has proven its worth in various software engineering techniques, results in the development cycle depicted in Fig. 4. Here, one can notice two cycles, top and component level, influenced by iterative and incremental development. It can also be seen that the stages planning, requirements, analysis, evaluation and testing occur at both levels. While top level focuses on the abstract conceptualization (incl. business and use cases), the actual realization is delegated to partners. For research projects, usually at most one top level iteration can be conducted. On the component level, partners receive input (concept and goals) from top level and at this point it is their responsibility to perform a more technical examination, e.g., analysis and requirements engineering specific to their domain and tasks.

The described method was only specified partly before the start of project Mobility Broker. Hence, these explanations are descriptive and were streamlined after the project.

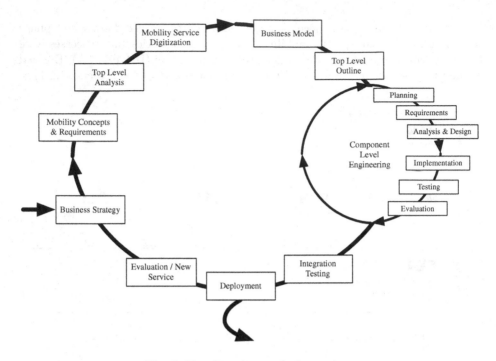

Fig. 4. Development method overview.

4   Overall Integration of Mobility Services with Respect to Seamless Mobility – The Project Mobility Broker

Goal of the project Mobility Broker is the unification of heterogeneous mobility services by distinct providers based on an ATIS to enable and support flexible intermodal travel behavior. Such a service includes seamless travel information, booking, ticketing and accounting for multiple mobility services. The following section summarizes the course of action in the project.

4.1   Concept and Requirements

There are different exemplary strategies for the integration scenario. An organization (e.g. an IT company) provides the system infrastructure for integration, whereas the mobility services are supplied by third parties. A different approach would be an established mobility service provider offering a platform to provide several different in-house services. In addition, it can integrate services from third party providers as well.

In Mobility Broker, the second approach, i.e. a major public transportation provider integrating sharing services from other providers, was carried out.

For the requirement analysis (method part I, cf. Fig. 1), we conducted – among many – the following two studies. Firstly, we carried out a literature based investigation considering different types of requirements from a user's perspective that deal with traveling using the transportation modes public transportation, (e-)carsharing and (e-)bikesharing in [2]. Our review showed that there was a lack of knowledge on intermodal trips and related travel information applications. Our results revealed, that the heterogeneous transportation modes lead to a high amount of user requirements. To reduce the complexity and provide a clear representation of the investigated demands, we categorized the identified requirements. Several different types of user requirements could be differentiated: travel-related (e.g., time-related demands) and app-related requirements (e.g., information quality, usability). The category of travel-related requirements consists of two subcategories:

- travel task-related requirements: planning a trip, renting and sharing a vehicle, reacting to unpredictable barriers, etc.
- transport-related requirements: public transport (passenger volume, real time information), carsharing (availability of cars and parking lots), bikesharing (weather conditions, bicycle infrastructure), electric vehicles (technology-related information), etc.

Secondly, we investigated intermodal travel chains to examine traveler's needs for phase- and activity-related assistance in [16]. For that, we combined two methods: literature-based modeling and scenario-based modeling. The results of both were compared and used for a systematic modeling of uni- and intermodal travel chains. The literature-based modeling of travel chains indicated that there is a lack of knowledge about intermodal travel chains; regarding unimodal travel chains, they have hardly been systematically investigated and the described chains were inconsistent. Our modeled travel chains were, e.g., more comprehensive and consistent than the ones described in the literature. The modeled travel chains include phase-/step-related activities and related information needs. Not only the planning of the trip was taken into account, but the whole trip including the first and last mile.

Afterwards, we analyzed several mobility concepts for intermodal traveling (I.2.1). A mobility concept defines essential parameters of people's (urban) mobility, e.g., mode characteristics, infrastructure, economic considerations, mobility behavior. Based on this information, we formed a fundamental guideline for system design, which was to maximize user's flexibility in switching heterogeneous modes of transportation in urban environments. To achieve this, the information system should allow to query, reserve, book and utilize different modes of transportation. Beyond that, an integrated ticketing, accounting and pricing should be established. Moreover, we decided to establish sharing provision especially to the first and last mile of intermodal travel chains. To realize such a comprehensive system corresponding to the fundamental guideline, a detailed application analysis took place. In principle, the analysis was conducted in four workshops with members of all project partner institutions. Each workshop followed a structure, such that at first relevant state-of-the-art information related to the specific topic were given and then selected problems were solved and tasks were done in an interactive idea generation part. Initially, known mobility concepts were analyzed with a special focus on identifying gaps (I.2.1). Followed by a more technical analysis of existing travel information applications (I.3.1). The next workshop analyzed transportation service sales systems and marketing (I.3.2). Finally, the analysis part was completed by a workshop concerning authentication and ticketing solutions (I.3.3).

4.2   Mobility Digitization

Based on detailed service analysis (II.1.1, cf. Fig. 2) and a fundamental guideline, we created use cases (II.1.2) for further development steps in [17]. Subsequently, mobility specific mobility service processes were described, compared and consolidated (II.1.3) to specify the underlying data model of the system (II.1.4). From the analysis of user interactions with mobility services we deduced the following interaction phases: *information/planning* (before trip), *reservation* (before trip), *booking* (before trip), *travel assistance and navigation* (on trip), *payment* (before trip or after trip), *customer service* (specific during all the other phases), and the optional interaction phases: *cancellation* (before trip or on trip) and *replanning* (before trip or on trip). With these knowledge foundations, project partners formed their specific business models (II.2.1). Therefore, several products for specific customer segments were considered. Recent developments of information systems for Mobility as a Service systems, mobility service integration patterns, cooperation scenarios among participating actors, and suitable business models for mobility platforms are discussed in [18] and [19].

4.3   System Implementation and Evaluation

To develop a working system architecture to support intermodal traveling, we initially reviewed and designed various draft possibilities for different purposes and conditions in [20]. Based on these initial results, the architecture depicted in Fig. 5 was developed and implemented for Mobility Broker (III.1.1, cf. Fig. 3). The traveler interacts with the system using a *mobile application* or a *web portal* which communicates with the backend using standardized communication interfaces. All requests from mobile applications and the web frontend are served by the *dispatcher* component, acting as a single endpoint. Door to door routing queries are processed by the *intermodal router*. This component serves as a merger of the different routing techniques. The *individual transport router* serves pedestrian and (private) bicycle routing queries. Routing information supplied by the *intermodal router* is augmented by the *pricing module* with pricing information. The *accounting/billing module* collects all billing information from service providers to allow a real time cost check as well a monthly billing. The *user management* component is responsible for creating and modifying user accounts and user authorization. Second party sharing mobility services are integrated with the help of the *communication adapter*. During the design of the IXSI interface [9,10] all the identified interaction phases from Sect. 4.2 were considered to support the integration of one sharing mobility service provider based on one

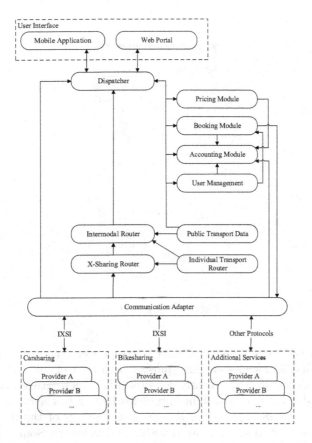

Fig. 5. Mobility Broker system architecture and information flows [17].

contract and one system link. The *X-Sharing router* component supplements the *intermodal router* with routing specific to *sharing mobility services*, it employs real time vehicle availability data to calculate route segments. The architecture is described in more detail in [21].

To develop the mobile application, respectively the user interface, human-centered software development methods were employed. Based on the gained insight about current mobile travel information applications (I.1.1, cf. Sect. 4.1) and the planned features (III.2.1) for the project, paper prototypes were created. Using the paper prototypes and features descriptions in textual form (III.2.2), the software developers created a functional Android prototype (III.2.3). Crucial for the success of travel information applications is their usability [22]. Therefore, we iteratively conducted usability evaluations (III.3.1) of the developed mobile application with qualitative methods, e.g., from the perspective of communicative usability in [23–25]. Three usability experts conducted the assigned tasks from the perspective of three personas. The used methodological design was a combination of the exploratory walkthrough ($n = 3$) and the user-centered method user test ($n = 10$). The user tests were conducted in a lab setting ($n = 4$)

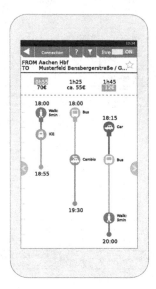

Fig. 6. GUI prototype.

and in a field test $(n = 6)$; the examined groups were students, staff members of the university, and senior citizens (mostly with respect due to the designated group of customers). In total, nearly 300 usability issues with varying degrees of severity were detected. The usability problems belong to the categories *naming, formulation, structure, and visual design*. The findings of the iterative testing have been presented to and discussed with the developers. Some problems were easy and cost-effective to improve but some were more complex and could not be solved during the project. Figure 6 shows an initial design mockup, the implemented version is shown in Fig. 7.

Fig. 7. User interfaces of the Mobility Broker mobile application showing route planning, route results, map view and booking history.

5 Conceptual Generalization: Development of a Reference Model in the Project OMP

While we developed a functional system for project Mobility Broker, which was successfully put in productive operation in multiple regions, feasibility still needs to be investigated for different business models. Regarding business strategy and business model aspects, there were various limitations during the project. An explicit, structured and definite specification of business aspects were missing, which made it impossible to communicate them in a transparent way to all project partners and involved mobility service providers. As a result, the willingness to participate varied among mobility services providers, because they weighted potentials and risks of our solution differently.

Furthermore, technical scalability and interoperability of the resulting system architecture were not the main focus. Thus, the system is not enabled to integrate a structural distinct mobility service, e.g., ridesharing integration is not possible in the current implementation.

Consequently, we are currently working on a generalization of the platform – the development of a reference model for intermodal mobility service platforms with a special focus on the specification of business model aspects.

This model is developed in a more structured and formal process covering a wider range of aspects and requirements. The business model analysis, the requirements engineering and the software engineering process were adapted from the initial process (given in Sect. 3) with respect to the universal character of a reference model and its applicability for different deployment scenarios. The overall developed methodology is based on TROPOS [26,27], following the phases: early and late requirements engineering, architecture design, and design refinement. Considering the different aspects from Multiagent Systems Iterative View Engineering [28] and the requirements and software engineering tasks from Multiagent System Engineering [29], we developed the system development methodology given in Fig. 8.

Starting with the analysis of *actor scenarios* (interactions among actors), *interaction scenarios* (interactions between actors and the system), and *system scenarios* (system internal interactions), we identified and specified suitable user and system *tasks*. Furthermore, we extended the presented aspects of human-centered development in terms of personas and use cases in [30]. *Roles* were defined and specified as representatives for groups of tasks. The *role relationship model* was deduced from the analysis and iterative simulation of the overall system function. The analysis of cooperation scenarios was done using a morphological box describing all the user interaction phases of a mobility service, the underlying business model for the mobility platform, and the customer relationship. We deduced four archetypes for mobility platform *cooperation scenarios*: information portal, market place, broker, and reseller/provider. The archetypes were used to define the system limits of the mobility platform system architecture. With the help of the identified roles and the role relationship diagram as well as a platform typology, we analyzed *cooperation scenarios* among the participants of the mobility platform context. On the one hand, this serves as

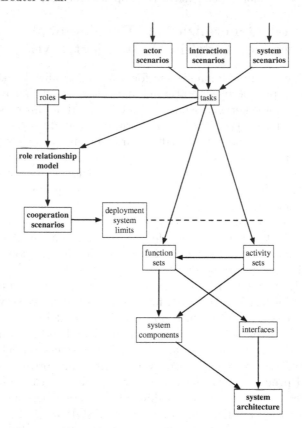

Fig. 8. Adapted requirements engineering process for the development of the reference model for the system architecture for open mobility platforms.

a knowledge base for conceptualization and development phases, on the other hand this helps to determine the specific extent of the system. The initial analysis and formalization of business models, roles, and relationships is presented in [19].

All specified tasks were mapped to technical *function and activity flows* describing task solutions. Activities were assigned to *functional system components*. All function flows between two functional system components define the corresponding *interface*.

Based on these formal specifications, a *reference model* for technical architectures for mobility platforms is currently being developed. The reference model describes the required functional components, the corresponding interfaces, and underlying conceptual models for the development of a system architecture for mobility platforms. This will enable a wide variety of organizations, e.g., mobility service providers, vehicle manufacturers, IT companies, and municipalities to create a heterogeneous, but still interoperable, region-specific mobility service platform. An early version of the reference model for the development of system architectures for open mobility platforms is given in Fig. 9.

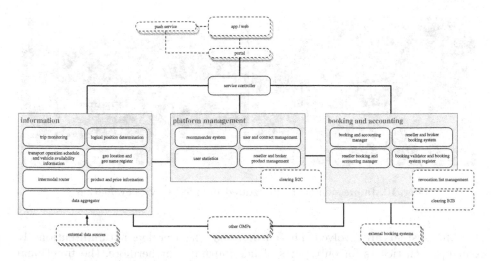

Fig. 9. Reference model for open mobility platform system architectures.

We identified three main functional groups: *information, platform management,* and *booking and accounting.* The interworking among all functional components of the main functional groups is provided by the *service controller* component. This component serves as the interface for functional user requests provided by a *mobile application* or *web interface* to the mobility platform.

The first functional group *information* consists of the functional components: *intermodal router, product and price information,* and the underlying *data aggregator.* Furthermore, it contains the additional supportive functional components: *transport operation schedule and vehicle availability information, geolocation and location name register, trip monitoring,* and *logical position determination.* The functional group *information* collects all the required information via the *data aggregator* component from *external data sources* including public transport schedules, public transport real time information, shared vehicles information and availability, traffic flow information, car park information, toll information, and ride sharing information. Furthermore, the functional group information is interconnected with data aggregator components of other mobility platforms (for other geographical regions).

The second functional group *platform management* comprises functional components central to the management of users, customer contracts and platform products. This also includes authentication and authorization of users. Furthermore, it contains supportive functional components integrating user statistics and a recommender system.

The third functional group *booking and accounting* provides all services in the context of booking, ticketing, usage data transmission, and accounting. It is connected to the *external booking systems* of all mobility service providers integrated in the mobility service platform. The manager components inside this group provide transactional behavior in situations where multiple external

Fig. 10. Impression of the integrated mobility service evaluation.

booking systems are involved. This ensures that the user does not unintentionally end up with tickets for only parts of her journey. Furthermore, the functional group *booking and accounting* handles the decomposition of product bundles presented to the end user.

The development of detailed specifications of the mentioned reference model with functional components and interfaces is the objective of the R&D project "Digitalisierte Mobilität – die offene Mobilitätsplattform (DiMo OMP)". All the results will be forwarded to the Association of German Transport Companies (Verband Deutscher Verkehrsunternehmen) as proposals for normative models for system architectures for open mobility platforms.

6 Lessons Learned and Conclusion

In this work, we presented the methodology and results of the development of an integrated intermodal travel information system, combining many mobility services of the region Aachen, Germany as well as the first steps of a generalization of such an approach.

Combining heterogeneous transportation services via travel information systems can enable and support flexible intermodal mobility behavior. Various evaluations of integrated solutions underline beneficial synergies in different areas [31–33]. As a result of individual characteristics, heterogeneous modes are suitable for specific use cases and therefore can complement each other instead of substituting them. This offers potentials for mobility providers to increase utilization by offering a more exhaustive and high quality service to customers. Nevertheless, developing a suitable solution is challenging for mobility providers. This work suggests a guideline method to develop travel information systems which enable seamless intermodal traveling. Carefully selected use cases have influenced the method design as well as the application in the presented research projects. Our method complements the fundamental software engineering process with additional steps in order to refine and specify it according to the domain. Thus, we identified mobility service analysis as a key step for a suitable development, because mode characteristics significantly determine information system design.

In particular, the project Mobility Broker focused on an extensive analysis phase at the beginning of the project to derive fundamental requirements. For testing and evaluating travel information systems as realistically and comprehensively as possible, a well-developed mobility infrastructure is recommendable. During the project, the infrastructure was built and new mobility services, e.g., ebike sharing, were established (cf. Fig. 10). This allowed a holistic evaluation of the IT systems and the mobility service [34], gaining additional insight compared to assessing the travel information system individually. Still, some aspects, e.g., changing between different modal types in an intermodal journey, could only be tested to a limited extend, because of organizational constraints.

Project OMP, with its focus on a structured methodology, showed that there is a need for support in collaborative design to create a specification for a complex infrastructure like an intermodal mobility service platform [35]. Moreover, a reference architecture offers beneficial potentials, e.g., less implementation efforts/ modularity of components because of uniform terminologies, functional descriptions of system components as well as (standardized) interface specifications.

Crucial for the success of such projects is the cooperation of the interdisciplinary team, which comprises experts from academia and industry. During the whole life cycle of the projects, regular meetings between the teams of developers and researchers were held. Thereby, the experts kept each other informed about their current status, interim results, and discussed them in the interdisciplinary team as well as agreed on further actions. Experience shows that the meetings are effective and necessary for the project process. At the same time, the differing perspectives of the industry and science emerge. Scientists primarily develop recommendations for actions and designs based on their findings; developers act in an economical manner (e.g., lay a focus on the requirements of mobility services providers instead of user requirements such as help features) and expect concrete proposals (e.g., paper prototypes). Thus, it is important to get to know the various points of view and working methods to coordinate, e.g., distributed work accordingly, and achieve a successful interdisciplinary cooperation.

Acknowledgments. This work was funded by the German Federal Ministry of Economic Affairs Energy for the project Mobility Broker (01ME12136) and by the German Federal Ministry of Transport and Digital Infrastructure for the project Digitalisierte Mobilität - die offene Mobilitätsplattform (DiMo OMP) (19E16007A).

We would like to thank to all the industrial and academic partners from the research projects Mobility Broker and DiMo OMP for their cooperation, support, problem related discussions, and finally their great hospitality for project meetings and visionary discussions.

References

1. Nobis, C.: Quantitative Analyse multimodalen Verkehrshandelns [Quantitative Analysis of Multimodal Travel Behavior]. Ph.D. thesis, Humboldt-Universität zu Berlin (2013)

2. Vogelsang, S., Digmayer, C., Jakobs, E.M.: User requirements on intermodal traveler information systems. In: 2015 IEEE International Professional Communication Conference, IPCC 2015, Limerick, Ireland, 12–15 July 2015, pp. 1–9. IEEE (2015)

3. Stopka, U., Pessier, R., Fischer, K.: User requirements for intermodal mobility applications and acceptance of operating concepts. In: Kurosu, M. (ed.) HCI 2015, Part I. LNCS, vol. 9169, pp. 415–425. Springer, Cham (2015). https://doi.org/10.1007/978-3-319-20901-2_39

4. McQueen, B., Schuhman, R., Chen, K.: Advanced Traveler Information Systems. Artech House Inc., Norwood (2002)

5. Beul-Leusmann, S., Jakobs, E., Ziefle, M.: User-centered design of passenger information systems. In: IEEE International Professional Communication 2013 Conference, Vancouver, BC, Canada, 15–17 July 2013, pp. 1–8. IEEE (2013)

6. Beutel, M.C., et al.: Integrated provision of heterogeneous mobility services. In: Helfert, M., Gusikhin, O. (eds.) Proceedings of the 4th International Conference on Vehicle Technology and Intelligent Transport Systems, VEHITS 2018, Funchal, Madeira, Portugal, 16–18 March 2018, pp. 204–213, SciTePress (2018)

7. Sommerville, I.: Software Engineering, 8th edn. Pearson Education Limited, Essex (2007)

8. Beul-Leusmann, S., Habermann, A.L., Ziefle, M., Jakobs, E.: Unterwegs im ÖV. Mobile Fahrgastinformationssysteme in der Usability Evaluation [Traveling using Public Transport. Usability Evaluation of Mobile Travel Information Systems]. In: Prinz, W., Borchers, J.O., Jarke, M. (eds.) Mensch und Computer 2016, Tagungsband, Aachen, Germany, 4–7 September 2016. Gesellschaft für Informatik e.V. (2016)

9. Kluth, W., Beutel, M.C., Gökay, S., Krempels, K.H., Samsel, C., Terwelp, C.: IXSI - interface for X-sharing information. In: Monfort, V., Krempels, K.H., Majchrzak, T.A., Turk, Z. (eds.) WEBIST 2015 - Proceedings of the 11th International Conference on Web Information Systems and Technologies, Lisbon, Portugal, 20–22 May 2015, pp. 293–298. SciTePress (2015)

10. Beutel, M.C., Gökay, S., et al.: MobilityBroker Schnittstelle mit Smartcar Erweiterung basierend auf IXSI - Interface for X-Sharing Information Version 4 (2016). https://github.com/RWTH-i5-IDSG/ixsi. Commit: 3643589babb7b437338ac7fd6f0db2b24d3bbb31

11. SUPERHUB-Consortium: Seventh Framework Programme: SUPERHUB - SUstainable and PERsuasive Human Users moBility in future cities. Technical report (2011)

12. Hrncír, J., Jakob, M.: Generalised time-dependent graphs for fully multimodal journey planning. In: 16th International IEEE Conference on Intelligent Transportation Systems, ITSC 2013, The Hague, The Netherlands, 6–9 October 2013, pp. 2138–2145. IEEE (2013)

13. Wells, S., Forbes, P., Masthoff, J., Gabrielli, S., Jylhä, A.: SUPERHUB: integrating digital behaviour management into a novel sustainable urban mobility system. In: Love, S., Hone, K.S., McEwan, T. (eds.) BCS-HCI 2013 Proceedings of the 27th International BCS Human Computer Interaction Conference, Brunel University, London, UK, 9–13 September 2013, p. 62. British Computer Society (2013)

14. Gutzwiller, T.: Das CC RIM-Referenzmodell für den Entwurf von betrieblichen, transaktionsorientierten Informationssystemen. Physica, Heidelberg (1994)

15. Bucher, T.: Ausrichtung der Informationslogistik auf operative Prozesse - Entwicklung und Evaluation einer situativen Methode. Ph.D. thesis, Universität St. Gallen (2009)

16. Digmayer, C., Vogelsang, S., Jakobs, E.M.: Designing mobility apps to support intermodal travel chains. In: Proceedings of the 33rd Annual International Conference on the Design of Communication, SIGDOC 2015, Limerick, Ireland, 16–17 July 2015, pp. 44:1–44:11 (2015)
17. Beutel, M.C., et al.: Heterogeneous travel information exchange. In: Internet of Things. IoT Infrastructures - Second International Summit, IoT 360 2015, Rome, Italy, 27–29 October 2015, Revised Selected Papers, Part II, pp. 181–187 (2015)
18. Aapaoja, A., Eckhardt, J., Nykänen, L.: Business models for MaaS. In: Proceedings of the 1st International Conference on Mobility as a Service, ICoMaaS 2017, Tampere, Finland, 28–29 November 2017 (2017)
19. Beutel, M.C., et al.: Mobility service platforms - cross-company cooperation for transportation service interoperability. In: Hammoudi, S., Smialek, M., Camp, O., Filipe, J. (eds.) Proceedings of the 20th International Conference on Enterprise Information Systems, ICEIS 2018, Funchal, Madeira, Portugal, 21–24 March 2018, vol. 1, pp. 151–161. SciTePress (2018)
20. Beutel, M.C., Gökay, S., Kluth, W., Krempels, K.H., Samsel, C., Terwelp, C.: Product oriented integration of heterogeneous mobility services. In: 17th International IEEE Conference on Intelligent Transportation Systems, ITSC 2014, Qingdao, China, 8–11 October 2014, pp. 1529–1534. IEEE (2014)
21. Beutel, M.C., et al.: Information integration for advanced travel information systems. J. Traffic Transp. Eng. **4**, 177–185 (2016)
22. Beul-Leusmann, S., Samsel, C., Wiederhold, M., Krempels, K.-H., Jakobs, E.-M., Ziefle, M.: Usability evaluation of mobile passenger information systems. In: Marcus, A. (ed.) DUXU 2014, Part I. LNCS, vol. 8517, pp. 217–228. Springer, Cham (2014). https://doi.org/10.1007/978-3-319-07668-3_22
23. Wirtz, S., Jakobs, E.: Improving user experience for passenger information systems. Prototypes and reference objects. IEEE Trans. Prof. Commun. **56**, 120–137 (2013)
24. Jakobs, E.M.: Des Nutzers Lust und Frust. Kommunikative Usability hypermedialer Systeme. Int. J. Lang. Data Process. **1**, 7–19 (2010)
25. Jakobs, E.M.: Kommunikative Usability, 1st edn. Marx, Konstanze and Schwarz-Friesel, Monika (2012)
26. Giorgini, P., Kolp, M., Mylopoulos, J., Pistore, M.: The tropos methodology: an overview. In: Bergenti, F., Gleizes, M.P., Zambonelli, F. (eds.) Methodologies and Software Engineering For Agent Systems, pp. 1–20. Kluwer Academic Publishing, New York (2003)
27. Bresciani, P., Perini, A., Giorgini, P., Giunchiglia, F., Mylopoulos, J.: A knowledge level software engineering methodology for agent oriented programming. In: Proceedings of the Fifth International Conference on Autonomous Agents, AGENTS 2001, pp. 648–655. ACM Press, New York (2001)
28. Lind, J.: The conceptual framework of MASSIVE. In: Lind, J. (ed.) Iterative Software Engineering for Multiagent Systems. LNCS (LNAI), vol. 1994, pp. 97–120. Springer, Heidelberg (2001). https://doi.org/10.1007/3-540-45162-5_4
29. DeLoach, S.A., Wood, M.F., Sparkman, C.H.: Multiagent systems engineering (2001)
30. Steinert, T., et al.: Definition und Dokumentation der Nutzeranforderungen an eine offene Mobilitätsplattform [Definition and Documentation of User Requirements for an Open Mobility Service Platform]. Technical report (2018)
31. Huwer, U.: Public transport and car-sharing - benefits and effects of combined services. Transp. Policy J. World Conf. Transp. Res. Soc. **11**, 77–87 (2004)

32. Hoffmann, C., et al.: Bewertung integrierter Mobilitätsdienste mit Elektrofahrzeu-genaus Nutzerperspektive [Assessment of integrated mobility services using electric vehicles from a user perspective]. InnoZ-Baustein 11 (2012)
33. Beutel, M.C., Zaunbrecher, B.S., Himmel, S., Krempels, K.H., Ziefle, M.: Evaluation of an integrated intermodal travel service. In: Klein, C., Donnellan, B., Helfert, M. (eds.) SMARTGREENS 2016 - Proceedings of the 5th International Conference on Smart Cities and Green ICT Systems, Rome, Italy, 23–25 April 2016, pp. 363–371. SciTePress (2016)
34. Himmel, S., Zaunbrecher, B.S., Ziefle, M., Beutel, M.C.: Chances for urban electromobility. In: Marcus, A. (ed.) DUXU 2016, Part II. LNCS, vol. 9747, pp. 472–484. Springer, Cham (2016). https://doi.org/10.1007/978-3-319-40355-7_45
35. Ohler, F., Beutel, M.C., Gökay, S., Samsel, C., Krempels, K.: A structured approach to support collaborative design, specification and documentation of communication protocols. In: Proceedings of the 13th International Conference on Evaluation of Novel Approaches to Software Engineering, ENASE 2018, Funchal, Madeira, Portugal, 23–24 March 2018, pp. 367–375 (2018)

Car Accident Detection and Reconstruction Through Sound Analysis with Crashzam

Matteo Sammarco[1(✉)] and Marcin Detyniecki[1,2,3]

[1] AXA Data Innovation Lab, 48 rue Carnot, 92150 Suresnes, France
matteo.sammarco@axa-groupsolutions.com, marcin.detyniecki@axa.com
[2] Sorbonne Universités, UPMC Univ Paris 06, CNRS, LIP6 UMR 7606,
4 place Jussieu, 75005 Paris, France
[3] Polish Academy of Sciences, IBS PAN Newelska, 6, Warsaw 01-447, Poland

Abstract. A car accident is a dangerous and extremely stressful moment involving many actors: one or more drivers, passengers, rescues, police force, as long as repairmen and insurance companies. In such circumstances, smart connected vehicles have the opportunity to provide really helpful services like an automatic crash detector for quick first aid alerting, first notification of loss, proactive claim management, settlement estimation, and damage assessment. While until now crash detection and reconstruction is completely based on accelerometer sensor time series analysis, this paper presents an innovative way to detect any type car accidents, called Crashzam, which relies on another source of information: the sound produced by a car impact that reverberates inside the car cabin. In the manuscript we introduce an original dataset we have beforehand built composed by in vitro and in vivo crash sounds, the overall system design, model and classification built upon features extracted from the time and frequency domain of the audio signal and from its spectrogram image, and a possible approach for crash reconstruction. Results show that the proposed model is able to easily identify crash sounds from other sounds reproduced in-car cabins, even in presence of noise.

Keywords: Real-time incident detection · Road safety · Connected vehicle · Audio signal processing.

1 Introduction

Although car manufacturers make evaluate passive and active security of their vehicles by car crash test programs like the European New Car Assessment Programme (Euro NCAP) [1] or the National Highway Traffic Safety Administration (NHTSA) [2], and the effort in launching road safety programs in many countries, road traffic death figures remain stable worldwide at nearly 1.2 million since 2004 [3]. Causes of such a plague are diverse: speed, drink-driving,

© Springer Nature Switzerland AG 2019
B. Donnellan et al. (Eds.): SMARTGREENS 2018/VEHITS 2018, CCIS 992, pp. 159–180, 2019.
https://doi.org/10.1007/978-3-030-26633-2_8

drug-driving, unused safety belt, bad weather and road conditions, and bad car break and wheel conditions. It results essential to promptly notify a crash for first aid, if possible through an Automatic Crash Notification (ACN) system, as a correlation between delaying emergency medical care and mortality rate has been proved [4,5].

Some car manufacturers offer for their high-end products an automatic collision notification which mainly monitors the airbag deployment to detect a severe collision and calling assistance with the embedded cellular radios. The BMW's Automatic Crash Notification System and the GM's OnStar are just two examples. These products remain mostly restricted as option to luxury market sectors and a large part of the circulating vehicles do not embed an OEM automatic accident detection and notification system.

Relatively cheaper third party solutions foreseen the installation of boxes under the hood, wind-screen boxes or OBDII dongles which embed an acceleration sensor, a third party sim card as along as a proprietary algorithm to detect bumps.

Smartphones embed, among other sensors, a three axes accelerometer. Nevertheless, smartphone data is hard to analyze due to calibration, noise and rotation issues. In addition, it is not clear the optimal frequency for acceleration samples and the time window width to record. Also, in many situations, relying only on acceleration data may lead to false predictions: street bumps, holes and bad street conditions trigger false positives, whereas collisions coming from the back while standing still may be classified as normal accelerations. Also as regards the a posteriori crash reconstruction, acceleration data is not suitable to reconstruct side impacts.

As electric lamps were not invented by improving candles, the goal of this work is not to improve accelerometer-based car crashing detection algorithms, but to detect crashes by sound. Crashzam is an innovative way to detect car crashes based on sound recognition techniques [6]. It does not suffer from neither calibration and sensor configuration problems nor frequency parametrization. The unique assumption is that a crash produces a sound. It can take advantage of the presence of microphones inside car cabins: hands free car kits, Bluetooth kits, car audio systems with voice command, wind-screen SOS boxes, dash cameras and smartphones are some hardware equipments embedding microphones, which are usually present in a vehicle. It does not matter where and with which angle respect to the horizon these devices are placed in the car cabin, since the received sound will not be affected by calibration or device rotation.

Nevertheless, in order to perform, Crashzam must take into account the presence of environmental noise and any other overlapping sound usually reproduced in a car cabin (engine rotation, car horn, radio music, road side noise, etc.).

The main contribution of this paper is the design of a ACN system through a crash sound detection model. It can detect crash sounds and distinguish other sounds generated inside the car cabin. To this aim, we collect a novel dataset of crash sounds recorded from inside the car cabin. Then, we create and select a set of features computed from the time and frequency sound signal domain and from the sound spectrogram image. Finally we propose a combination of machine learning models for the automatic classification of sounds reproduced inside vehicles. In addition, we propose a method for crash reconstruction, still uniquely based on sound analysis.

This manuscript is structured as follows: in Sect. 2 we provide a summary of works related to crash and sound detection already present in the literature, while in Sect. 3 we describe our solution Crashzam in a top-down approach. In Sects. 4 and 5 we explore in detail the model to detect crashes from audio clips. Section 6 contains the description of the dataset that we have built and used to train and test our model. In Sects. 7 we evaluate the model in different conditions and we discuss about performances in according to the model parameters. In Sect. 8, instead, we propose a method to reconstruct a crash relying uniquely on the sound information. Finally, we give our conclusions and perspectives in Sect. 9.

2 Related Work

State of the art solutions for car crash detection employ accelerometer data to detect more or less severe impacts triggered by the sudden variation of acceleration on one or more axes [7–13]. Although the use of accelerometer sensors leads to a precise impact identification and severity, dedicated hardware must be professionally installed and calibrated to achieve the maximum accuracy.

The most cost effective and practical solution, instead, relies on acceleration time series recorded on drivers' smartphones. On these bases, some mobile applications like Zendrive, SOSmartapp and TrueMotion are already available on the market [14–16]. This solution reduces costs but calibration and rotation issues.

As a trendy solution, social networks and microblogs provide a global source where to share what we experience and see around us. Car accidents usually attract people curiosity, who might post tweets and photos of the event [17]. Although this provides a zero-cost solution, many disadvantages affect it: especially in rural areas accidents could not be immediately advertised, people might provide confused or misleading information, necessary third party people identification comes with privacy issues. Not least important, the use of smartphones during driving is a source of accident itself.

Recently, sound analysis is acquiring more and more attention, especially regarding speech-to-text, music generation, scene classification and speaker identification. Saggese et al. propose two levels of feature extractions and a combination of K-means clustering with bag of words to classify environmental urban sounds [18,19]. Their dataset includes a small amount of crashes too, but being road surveillance the main aim of their work and not drivers' safety, such sounds are recorded from the road side and not from inside the car cabin.

Rabaoui et al. use a set of dedicated time and wavelet-based audio features to classify 9 sound classes (human screams, gunshots, glass breaks, explosions, door slams, dog barks, phone rings, children voices, and machines) [20]. They prefer to use a SVM classifier to a Hidden Markov Model (HMM) or a Gaussian

Mixture Model (GMM) which are instead adopted by other authors in specific fields (e.g., medical telesurvey) [21–24].

Latest works employ Deep Neural Networks (DNNs) for sound classification, in particular authors in [25] use a Recurrent Neural Network (RNN) with bidirectional long short-term memory (BLSTM) cells, while Salamon and Bello use Convolutional Neural Networks (CNN) considering the spectrogram image as input [26].

3   System Design

Crashzam hardware requirements include a microphone, network access, accelerometer sensor and a limited computational capability. Smartphones completely satisfy such requirements, beyond providing a low cost and widely deployable solution. In case of Crashzam running on a smartphone, it acquires an additional twofold advantage: cost is extremely low as no extra hardware is needed, and protection is not coupled to a specific vehicle. Crashzam mobile application owners are protected all along their journeys, including multimodal transports.

Considering Crashzam running as a smartphone application, we show in Fig. 1 the high level system design. Android and iOS operating systems provide an activity recognition mechanism which starts at time t_0 the recording of a PCM samples buffer simultaneously to the detection of driving activity. The sliding buffer has a duration of T_b seconds. In our proof of concept we set $T_b = 5\,s$, with PCM sampled at 16kHz and quantized at 16 bits at least. At t_0, also the location service (GPS) and the accelerometer sensor are activated.

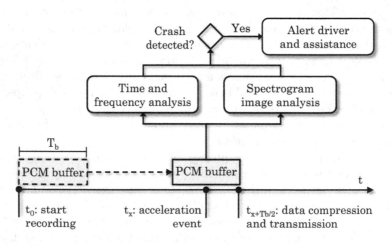

Fig. 1. Crashzam high level system design: while driving, the microphone records a sliding buffer of PCM samples which are analyzed if an acceleration event occurs (e.g., acceleration norm is over a certain threshold). Accelerometer is used as a mere trigger. If Crashzam detects a crash, the driver is solicited and assistance is alerted in case of no answer from the driver [6].

We use the accelerometer as a mere trigger: if at time t_x the norm of the three acceleration axes exceeds $2.5g$, then we continue recording for $T_b/2$ s before analyzing data. In this way we use half of the buffer to record what happened before a probable impact event and the other half to record what happened after it. In fact, a typical crash event includes tire skidding or horn sounds before the crash and human screams before or after it. Thus, in the following we train our models to distinguish between car impact sounds which are high energy, percussive sounds and other sounds which are likely to be produced during a crash but not necessarily like car horn or harsh deceleration sounds. It is worth to note that Crashzam can also work in combination with a traditional accelerometer-based car crash detection.

At time $t_x + T_b/2$, the array of PCM is compressed and transmitted to the server as along as the last GPS position, as a JSON object to a server dedicated to analyze the recorded sound. Data is independently analyzed by two models detailed in Sects. 4 and 5. Finally, both results are combined by a weighted voting classifier. The first model focuses on time and frequency aspects of the sound. It mainly detects high energy, abrupt changing hollow sounds. But since car horn or engine starting are such kind of sound too, we include a second model based on spectrogram image analysis calibrated on the detection of percussive sounds, which correspond to crashes.

A side effect feature of having two independent models, is that the system is modular and the first model can be reused in other application fields (e.g., glass breaking detection).

The result of the classification $\widehat{y}$ is based on a linear combination of the probabilities p_{ij}, outputs from the two models $j \in 1, 2$ in according to the relation:

$$\widehat{y} = \arg\max_i \sum_{j=1}^{2} w_j p_{ij},$$ (1)

where $i \in 0, 1$ represents the sound class ("Other" or "Crash" sound).

At the end of the classification pipeline, if a crash is detected, the driver is solicited for an interaction (e.g., pushing a safe button or answering to a call), otherwise assistance is alerted.

As a mobile application, Crashzam must monitor drivers and passengers' safety all along their journeys, all day long. A smartphone microphone drains about 80 mAh, thus not impacting the overall battery daily duration.

4   Model 1: Time and Frequency Analysis

A large set of metrics and features can be extracted from audio signals [27]. For the first model, we have selected some time and frequency-based features largely adopted in the literature for tasks of audio event detection or sound classification. In particular, Eq. (2)–(13) are extracted from Sammarco et al. [6].

4.1   Time Domain Features

Let us consider $x(t)$ a discrete audio signal of $\mathcal{N}$ samples. We extract the following time domain features from $x(t)$:

- **Zero-Crossing Rate** (ZCR). The rate a discrete signal $x(t)$ changes sign during its duration N is a key feature to recognize percussive sounds [28,29].

$$ZCR_x = \frac{1}{2N} \sum_{t=0}^{N-2} |sgn(x(t+1)) - sgn(x(t))|, \qquad (2)$$

where $sgn(x(t)) = \begin{cases} 1, \text{if } x(t) \geq 0, \\ -1, \text{if } x(t) < 0. \end{cases}$

- **Signal Power.** It is the sum of squares of the signal values normalized by the signal length.

$$P_x = \frac{1}{N} \sum_{t=0}^{N-1} |x(t)|^2 \qquad (3)$$

We expect crash sounds to show high power.

- **Entropy.** Entropy of a discrete random variable X with possible values $x_1, ..., x_n$ and probability function $P(X)$ is usually defined as:

$$H(x) = - \sum_{i=1}^{n} P(x_i) \log_b P(x_i). \qquad (4)$$

We consider $P(x_i) = e_j = \frac{E_{frame_j}}{E_x}$, where $E_x = \sum_{t=0}^{N-1} |x(t)|^2$ is the signal energy and E_{frame_j} is the energy of the jth of K fix-sized sub-frames the signal is split into. Thus, our entropy becomes:

$$H(x) = - \sum_{j=1}^{K} e_j \log_2(e_j). \qquad (5)$$

Entropy is usually interpreted as a measure of abrupt changes in energy [30,31]. We expect crash sounds having high entropy.

4.2   Frequency Domain Features

It is often useful to analyze discrete signals in the frequency domain through a Discrete Fourier Transform (DFT). The original signal is split in fixed-size smaller frames, and the DFT is applied on each frame returning an array of coefficients having the same length of the number of samples in the frame. Let us consider $X_i(k), k = 1, \ldots, M$, the magnitude of DFT coefficients of the ith frame.

We compute average and standard deviation over all frames for the following metrics:

- **Spectral Centroid** (SC). For the ith frame, SC is the average of frequencies present in the signal, weighted by their amplitudes:

$$SC_i = \frac{\sum_{k=1}^{M} kX_i(k)}{\sum_{k=1}^{M} X_i(k)}, \tag{6}$$

The SC represents the barycenter of the spectrum and higher values correspond to brighter sounds [32]. Crash sounds typically have a low SC.

- **Spectral Spread** (SS). It represents the deviation from the SC:

$$SS_i = \sqrt{\frac{\sum_{k=1}^{M}(k - SC_i)^2 X_i(k)}{\sum_{k=1}^{M} X_i(k)}} \tag{7}$$

Low values of SS correspond to signals whose spectrum is concentrated around the spectral centroid. Usually crash sounds present a high SS value.

- **Spectral Flux** (SF). SF represents the spectral change by comparing the power spectrum of two consecutive frames:

$$SF_{i,i-1} = \sum_{k=2}^{M} \left(\frac{X_i(k)}{\sum_{l=1}^{M} X_i(l)} - \frac{X_{i-1}(k)}{\sum_{l=1}^{M} X_{i-1}(l)}\right)^2 \tag{8}$$

SF is mainly used for onset detection, thus applicable to crash detection too [33].

- **Spectral Rolloff** (SR). The SR is the frequency below which 90% of the magnitude distribution of the spectrum is concentrated. SR is the frequency which satisfies the following relation:

$$\sum_{k=1}^{SR} X_i(k) = 0.9 \sum_{k=1}^{M} X_i(k). \tag{9}$$

It is useful to discriminate sounds like human voice signals whose energy is concentrated under 4 kHz and music.

- **Spectral Entropy** (SE). Similarly to the entropy in the time domain, let us consider the spectrum divided in k fixed-size frequency sub-bands, SE is:

$$SE = -\sum_{i=1}^{k} P_i \log_2(P_i), \tag{10}$$

where $P_i = \frac{E_i}{\sum_{i=1}^{k} E_i}$ and E_i is the energy in the $i^{t}h$ sub-band. In crash sounds, SE should have low values as the energy is spread on all the sub-bands.

- **Chroma Vector** (CV). With the Chroma Vector we group all the DFT coefficients into 12 bins corresponding to the 12 pitches of an equal tempered scale. Each element of the vector is the mean of DFT coefficients:

$$v_k = \sum_{f \in F_k} \frac{X_i(f)}{|F_k|}, \quad k \in [1 - 12], \tag{11}$$

where F_k is the set of frequencies included in the same bin. CV is widely used for audio matching [34, 35].
- **Mel-Frequency Cepstral Coefficients** (MFCCs). MFCCs are 13 coefficients forming a cepstral representation where the frequencies are distributed according to the mel scale. The mapping between the mel and frequency scale using k triangular overlapping windows is the following:

$$Mel(f) = 2595 \log_{10}(1 + \frac{f}{100}). \tag{12}$$

Then, MFCCs are computed as the discrete cosine transform (DCT) of cepstrum powers at each mel frequency:

$$c(k) = DCF \log |DFTm(n)|. \tag{13}$$

MFCC are useful to analyze abrupt changes in the spectrum and widely employed in human speech domain where they are particularly effective [36–39].

5   Model 2: Spectrogram Image Analysis

The second model is based on spectrogram image features and it is specifically designed to discern between percussive and sustained sounds. The former have high amplitude values distributed on all the frequencies at a certain time, while the latter present high values of amplitude at certain frequencies for relatively long time. The intuition behind this model is that a crash is a percussive sound, while many other sounds reproduced in car like car horn, harsh acceleration or tire skidding are sustained sounds.

5.1   Specific Spectrogram Image Features

A spectrogram is essentially a matrix of amplitudes of a particular frequency (row) at a certain time (column). Starting from a spectrogram images like the ones in Fig. 2, we extract the amplitude matrix and we select a constellation of peaks, which are points, located in time and frequency, exceeding a certain amplitude threshold A_{th}. Such peaks are local maxima, meaning that in a region with size D, they show the maximum value. If more points in a region are candidate to be a peak (i.e., they have the same amplitude), all of them are selected. Thus, we convert the amplitude matrix to a matrix P which localizes a

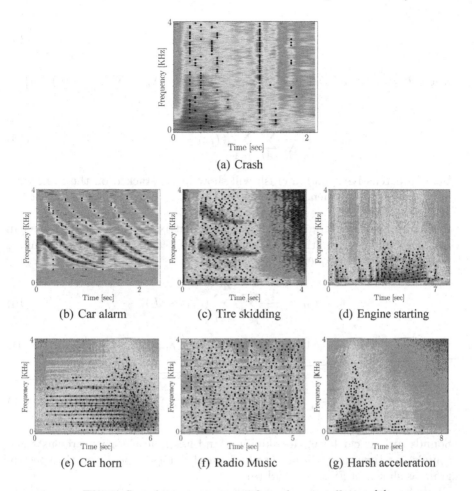

(a) Crash

(b) Car alarm   (c) Tire skidding   (d) Engine starting

(e) Car horn   (f) Radio Music   (g) Harsh acceleration

Fig. 2. Sound spectrograms with peaks constellation [6].

constellation of peaks p_{ft} and we analyze the patterns created by such peaks. P is a $F \times T$ binary, sparse matrix, where $f \in F$ denotes a frequency in the range $[0, \frac{sampling\ rate}{2}]$ and $t \in T$ denotes a small time bin the original signal is split into to compute the DFT.

A considerable advantage considering peaks extracted from the spectrogram is that we filter out noise and background sounds. From the constellation, we extract the following metrics through Eqs. (14)–(18) selected from Sammarco et al. [6]:

– **Peaks Vertical Alignment.** Given the matrix of peaks, we get the mean μ_V and standard deviation σ_V from the distribution of frequency gaps among peaks in the same time bin.

$$\mu_V = \frac{1}{N_v} \sum_{t \in T} \sum_{j=1}^{|I|-1} (I_{j+1} - I_j), \tag{14}$$

where $I = \{i \in F | p_{it} \neq 0 \ and \ \sum_i p_{it} > 1\} \forall t$, and $N_v = \sum_{t \in T} [(\sum_{f \in F} p_{ft}) - 1]$.

$$\sigma_V = \sqrt{\frac{1}{N_v} \sum_{t \in T} \sum_{j=1}^{|I|-1} [(I_{j+1} - I_j) - \mu_V]^2}. \tag{15}$$

Being a percussive sound, a crash will show peaks stacked on the same time bin along all the frequency range as shown in Fig. 2(a). Thus, we expect low average and standard deviation values.

- **Peaks Horizontal Alignment.** Given the matrix of peaks, we get the mean μ_H and standard deviation σ_H from the distribution of time delays among peaks at the same frequency.

$$\mu_H = \frac{1}{N_h} \sum_{f \in F} \sum_{i=1}^{|J|-1} (J_{i+1} - J_i), \tag{16}$$

where $J = \{j \in T | p_{fj} \neq 0 \ and \ \sum_j p_{fj} > 1\} \forall f$, and $N_h = \sum_{f \in F} [(\sum_{t \in T} p_{ft}) - 1]$.

$$\sigma_H = \sqrt{\frac{1}{N_h} \sum_{f \in F} \sum_{i=1}^{|J|-1} [(J_{i+1} - J_i) - \mu_H]^2}. \tag{17}$$

Sounds such as car horn, tire skidding, and harsh acceleration are sustained sounds and thus they will present horizontal stripes of peaks on the spectrogram as shown in Figs. 2(c) and (e).

- **Peak Entropy.** Entropy of the peak constellation is computed similarly to the entropy in the time and the frequency domain. We split the spectrogram in k time bins and for the ith bin, we compute the ratio between peaks included in that bin and all the peaks in the constellation: $e_p = \frac{\sum peaks_i}{\sum peaks}$.

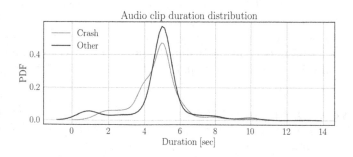

Fig. 3. PDF for samples duration in the dataset.

$$PE = -\sum_{i=1}^{k} e_p \log_2(e_p). \tag{18}$$

6 Dataset

In Spring 2016, AXA Winterthur has set the annual crash test campaign in Switzerland. During this occasion, the AXA Data Innovation Lab collected about 6.2 GB of data, including audio files recording crashes from inside the car cabins. This original dataset is composed by 46 signals of crash and, to the best of our knowledge, it is the only dataset collecting crash sounds from inside the car cabin[1]. Moreover, each test was controlled in impact speed and angle, thus such dataset has been essential to study crash dynamics.

In order to extend the set of positive samples, we extracted sounds recorded by dash cameras published on the "Car Crash Time" Youtube channel which provides several hours of crash recordings [41]. With respect to the controlled dataset, such sounds are very realistic and genuine, including background noises like rain, hail or screams before the impacts. Overall, we collected 500 crash sounds recorded inside the cabin. Most of them (92%) come from "Car Crash Time" and the rest from the AXA Winterthur crash test campaign. We kept 150 samples per class aside as test set.

As negative samples, we choose to include in the dataset any sound which might be generated or listened to inside a car cabin like radio music, people talking, engine starting, car door opening or closing. We also include sounds that are often linked to car bumps like car horn, harsh decelerations, and tire skidding to control the false positive rate. Such sounds have been mostly imported from FreeSound [42] and Urban Sound Dataset [43]. Although gathering negative sounds is a simpler task compared to the positive samples, we collected an equal number of samples in order to have a balanced dataset. Table 1 summarize the dataset distribution into categories "Crash" and "Other" and sub-categories.

All audio clips are sampled at 16 KHz, quantized at 16 bits and all amplitudes are normalized. They represent a mix of collision types: vehicle to barrier, vehicle to vehicle, frontal impact, side impact, and at different speeds.

A crash can occur between two or more cars, thus it can last more or less time. Figure 3 shows the distribution of sample durations. The vast majority of crashes involve only two cars and last five seconds, while the longest crash can last also the double. We selected negative samples in order to follow the same distribution as crash sounds.

---

[1] There exist a dataset of sounds provided by the MIVIA Computer Science department of Università di Salerno (Italy) for research purposes which includes crash sounds recorded only from outside the car cabin [40]. Thus, such sounds were not eligible to include in our dataset. Nevertheless it also contains tire skidding and scream sounds.

Table 1. Dataset classes and sub-classes repartition.

Class	Sound type	%
Crash	AXA Winterthur crash campaign	8
	Car Crash Time	92
Other	Harsh acceleration or deceleration	10
	Car horn	10
	Car door opening and closing	6
	Radio music	15
	People talking	16
	Tire skidding	10
	Car alarm	7
	Rain, hail, strong wind	10
	Engine during driving	16

7   Model Evaluation

Both time-frequency domain and spectrogram image classifiers are random forest classifiers trained with cross validation using the Python scikit-learn library. Number of trees are 200 and 100 respectively while all the other default parameters are left unchanged.

Figures 4 shows ROC and precision-recall curves for classification done by the two models independently and by combining their result probabilities together. The time and frequency based classifier (Model 1) performs in line with other models presented in the literature on sound detection like gun shots or human screams for surveillance purposes [44]. Its accuracy, computed as the ratio $\frac{\sum(True\ Positive)+\sum(True\ Negative)}{\sum Samples}$, is equal to 0.84. Nevertheless, it is wrong for some specific sub-types of sounds with abrupt changes and high energy like car horn or tire skidding.

As the spectrogram based classifier (Model 2) is specifically designed to discern between sustained and percussive sounds, it is able to help the first models in such ambiguous situations. Although in absolute terms Model 2 performs worse than Model 1, the combination of the two (Model 3) in according to Eq. 1 brings the overall accuracy to 0.86. Models weights in Eq. 1 are set to $w_1 = 0.6$ and $w_2 = 0.4$ respectively. They come from an exhaustive research to obtain the best results on the training set.

Most of the final misclassifications correspond to slammed door sounds.

7.1   Classification Accuracy with Environmental Noise

A car cabin is an endogenous and exogenous noisy environment. Therefore, in this Section we want to appreciate the model sensibility to additive noise, namely road side noise and white Gaussian noise. The former simulates a urban scenario

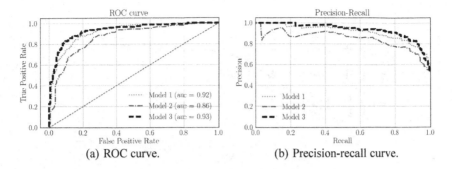

(a) ROC curve. (b) Precision-recall curve.

Fig. 4. Comparison of accuracy, precision and recall among singular models (Model 1 and 2) and the combination of such models in according to Eq. 1 (Model 3).

where the noise of people and other vehicles passing by as long as street works enter in the car cabin, while the latter emulates a generic disturbance, interference or microphone defect.

To this aim, we reclassify all the sounds $s(t)$ in the test set, adding an attenuated noise $n(t)$ in order to obtain a given SNR. We indicate with P_s the original sound signal power and with $P_{n\_rescaled} = \frac{1}{N}\sum_{i=0}^{N-1}(kn(i))^2 = \frac{k^2}{N}\sum_{i=0}^{N-1}(n(i))^2 = k^2 P_n$ the power of the noise signal rescaled by k. Setting a SNR_{target}, we find the rescaling coefficient k:

$$SNR_{target} = 10\log_{10}\frac{P_s}{P_{N\_rescaled}} \Rightarrow 10^{\frac{SNR_{target}}{10}} = \frac{P_s}{k^2 P_n} \Rightarrow k = \sqrt{\frac{P_s}{10^{\frac{SNR_{target}}{10}}P_n}}. \quad (19)$$

$P_n = 1$ for a white Gaussian noise of average 0 and variance 1.

Figure 5(a) shows the classification average and standard deviation accuracy for Model 1, 2 and their combination Model 3, adding 10 different road side noises to original sounds. The target SNR is in the range $[0 - 33]dB$, that is P_s is from 1 to 15 times greater than P_n. Both Model 1 and 2 barely achieve 60% accuracy when the target SNR is less than 10 dB. Model 1 is uncertain though, showing a positively skewed distribution of classification probability (Fig. 5(b)). For a SNR from 10 dB up, both models improve their classification achieving a steady state at 20 dB SNR. Also the probability distribution becomes initially uniform, then more and more negatively skewed. Even if in such conditions Model 2 in performs worse with respect to Model 1, Model 3 takes advantage of it, slightly improving the overall classification.

The presence of a white Gaussian noise produces the same negative effect as a road side noise for a SNR below 10 dB as shown in Fig. 6(a). Nevertheless, this time both models reveal a classification probability distribution centered close to 1 (Fig. 6(b)). It means that the presence of a white noise with high power heavily confuses both models. With higher SNR ratios, Model 1 starts to better classify sounds, while Model 2 gives a valid contribution only starting at 30 dB SNR.

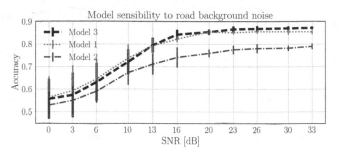

(a) Classification accuracy for Model 1, 2 and 3.

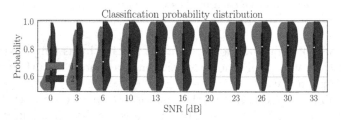

(b) Classification result probability distributions for Model 1 and 2.

Fig. 5. Classification results in presence of multiple road side noises with different SNR.

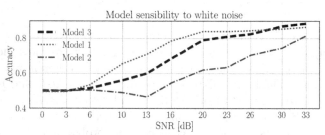

(a) Classification accuracy for Model 1, 2 and 3.

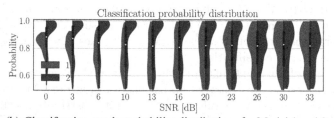

(b) Classification result probability distributions for Model 1 and 2.

Fig. 6. Classification results in presence of white Guassian noise with different SNR.

7.2   Classification Accuracy Tuning Spectrogram Parameters

Creating the constellation of peaks is highly dependent from the spectrogram image in background. Spectrogram is created spitting the time series of PCM in small windows having a certain overlap and computing the Fourier transform in each window. Being samples also quantized at 16 bits, the constellation of peaks will be depended by the number of samples per window (NFFT) and by the overlap between consecutive windows. A short window will tend to produce many peaks at the same frequency since the same sound amplitude will be replicated for many windows. Having a large overlap will have the same impact. On the other hand, a large window will increment horizontal peak gaps, but will tend to reduce vertical frequency gaps among peaks. Figure 7 shows how the accuracy on the training dataset changes, varying both NFFT and the overlap, where the overlap is at most equal to NFFT. The impact of such parameters is quite important since the accuracy scale is in the range [0.65–0.82]. Intermediate values for NFFT, 256 or 512, introduce the least offset and they are more independent to the overlap, thus we choose $NFFT = 512$ and $overlap = 354$. Once the NFFT and overlap set, the accuracy varies a little changing the threshold and the distance to find the local peaks. We have set a threshold $A_{th} = 50 \quad dB$ and a minimum distance $D = 3$.

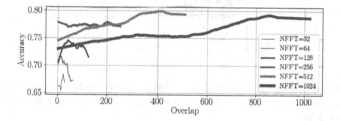

Fig. 7. Effects on classification tuning the number of data points used in each block for the Fast Fourier Transform (NFFT) to create the spectrogram and the number of overlapped points [6].

8   Crash Reconstruction

Subsequently a car impact and a prompt rescue alerting, a series of actions are taken in order to discriminate the guilty driver who could incur in a damage reimbursement, a higher insurance premium, and even in a legal process.

Crash reconstruction is the process which aims to recreate the dynamic of the accident, possibly estimating the point of impact, as long as the angle and the severity. The knowledge of the point of impact is necessary and sufficient for a fast damage assessment, the identification of the closest garage having new spare parts and for fraud detection.

Acceleration data has the advantage to allow an easy crash reconstruction, at least for recognizing head-on and back collisions. On the other hand, side impacts are much more ambiguous as a bottom/top right/left side impact could provoke the same rotation to the vehicle.

Sound analysis comes in help also regarding the discovery of the point of impact. It is a sound source localization problem, well known in literature as many animal species auditory system, as long as humans themselves are able to localize the provenance of a sound [45–54].

The problem of detecting the point of impact needs more than one microphone though. Some smartphones are equipped with a double microphone, but the installation of a microphone array board like the ReSpeaker or the XMOS xCORE in the center of the car cabin roof, as shown in Fig. 8, is better suited. For sake of simplicity, we decide to deploy the microphones at the vertex of a square having the barycenter coincident with the barycenter of the car cabin and having a size $d \ll l$, where l is the car cabin width. Other deployment shapes are possible, e.g., microphones at the vertex of an heptagon or octagon.

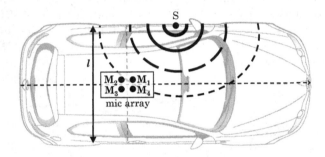

Fig. 8. A car equipped with a microphone array board placed at the cabin roof barycenter receiving a bump at point S. Sound waves will eventually reach microphones M_i at different time delay.

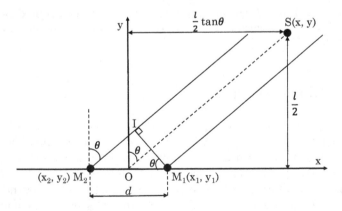

Fig. 9. Finding the point of impact considering the middle point of microphones as origin of axes.

Nevertheless, more microphones means more computational complexity for the next signal analysis.

We foresee two steps to figure out the point of impact:

1. Identification of the impact side with respect to the forward direction of the vehicle. In Fig. 6, the impact is at the left side of the vehicle.
2. Discovering the point of impact S laying on the side identified before.

Since bumps do not occur on the top or the bottom of the vehicle, we assume that the sound propagates on a two dimensional plane, coplanar to the transversal section of the vehicle.

Let us consider $m_i(t)$ with $i \in [1 - M]$ the signal recorded by the ith microphone and M the cardinality of microphones in the array. When an accident happens, a new sound $s(t)$ is produced. Thus, microphones will record the signal

$$m_i(t) = s(t + \tau_i) + n(t), \quad \forall 1 \leq i \leq M, \tag{20}$$

where $s(t + \tau_i)$ is the bump sound delayed by a time τ_i called Time Difference of Arrivals (TDOA) and $n(t)$ is the noise already present in the car cabin. The Interaural Time Difference (ITD) τ_{ij} is the arrival time difference of the same signal at two microphones i and j. A method to compute the ITD is detecting the maximum peak from the cross-correlation of the two signals:

$$\tau_{ij} = \arg\max_{\tau} (\sum_{t=-\infty}^{\infty} m_i(t)m_j(t + \tau)). \tag{21}$$

τ_{ij} is positive if $m_j(t)$ is delayed with respect to $m_i(t)$ and negative otherwise. Once all the $\frac{1}{2}\frac{M!}{(M-2)!}$ interaural time differences among microphones are computed, it is straightforward to identify microphones closer to the sound origin. In ascending order, the first two microphones in the array are the ones closest to the vehicle side where the bump happened.

Let us assume without loss of generality that S is the impact point and M_1 and M_2 are the closest microphones as shown in Fig. 6. In this case, the impact comes from the left side of the vehicle. Let us now consider the middle point between M_1 and M_2 as the origin of axes of a Cartesian plane with positive x in the forward direction of the vehicle and positive y through the left vehicle side as shown in Fig. 9. We want to find out the coordinate of the impact point $S = (x, y)$. Since $d \ll l$, sound waves are parallel and incident on the $y = 0$ plane. M_1 if first reached, then M_2 after a delay

$$\tau_{12} = \frac{\overline{IM_2}}{c} = \frac{d \sin \theta}{c}, \tag{22}$$

being $c = 345\frac{m}{sec}$ the sound travel speed in air at 20 degrees Celsius and $\theta = $ arcsin $\frac{c\tau_{12}}{d}$ the angle between the incident sound to the microphone array baseline and the perpendicular to the baseline itself.

Since the microphones are aligned at the center of the vehicle, we already know that $S_y = \frac{l}{2}$ and we can conclude that the point of impact on the left side is at

$$S = (\frac{l}{2}\tan\theta, \frac{l}{2}). \tag{23}$$

9 Summary and Outlook

This manuscript introduces Crashzam, an innovative way to detect car accidents with sound recorded by smartphones or any other suitable microphone-equipped device installed in cars. The goal is to enhance drivers and passengers' safety with a low cost solution, capable to propose domain specific services like medical assistance alerting or First Notification Of Loss (FNOL).

Sounds are analyzed by two models based on time, frequency and spectrogram features and the final detection result reflects a combination of both of them.

In order to evaluate our model, we set up an original dataset of crash sounds beforehand, since no dataset of crash sounds recorded inside the car cabin exist.

Detection results show an accurate classification between crash sounds and other sounds likely to be reproduced in car. Also, combining models analyzing specific aspects of sound signals (time series, frequency, spectrogram) helps the system to be more accurate and reliable when the environment is noisy. In fact, models are evaluated adding environmental and white Gaussian noises.

Finally we propose an approach to reconstruct the impact relying always on sound analysis and on a microphone array board installed inside the car cabin.

A wide range of perspectives are possible. We propose Crashzam in the context of driving safety and connected car, but the same concept could be applied to other domains such as the connected home and the connected health. For instance, Minut, a Scandinavian startup, is specialized on sound-based home surveillance [55]. Their devices are able to detect alarm or glass breaking. Remaining in a the telematics context, the detection of repetitive car horn, accelerations and tire skidding sounds gives an insight on the drivers' driving style.

As regards the system design, the current tendency is to embed models into devices, e.g., shrinking TensorFlow models inside mobile devices. In the safe driving context, having an autonomous system that gets rid of server requests would mean a full time detection availability. Also, the use of V2X communication with adequate protocols is suitable to quicker disseminate alerts to closer drivers [56].

Although microphone array boards are not expensive, crash reconstruction could be totally smartphone based if such devices have a double microphone and are placed in a fixed known position.

References

1. Euro NCAP, European New Car Assessment Programme (2018). https://www.euroncap.com/en. Accessed 03 May 2018

2. NHTSA, National Highway Traffic Safety Administration (2018). https://www. nhtsa.gov. Accessed 03 May 2018
3. World Health Organization: Global status report on road safety (2015). http:// www.who.int/violence_injury_prevention/road_safety_status/2015/en/. Accessed 03 May 2018
4. Plevin, R.E., Kaufman, R., Fraade-Blanar, L., Bulger, E.M.: Evaluating the potential benefits of advanced automatic crash notification. Prehospital Disaster Med. **32**, 156–164 (2017)
5. Evanco, W.M.: The impact of rapid incident detection on freeway accident fatalities (1996)
6. Sammarco, M., Detyniecki, M.: Crashzam: sound-based car crash detection. In: Proceedings of the 4th International Conference on Vehicle Technology and Intelligent Transport Systems, VEHITS 2018, Funchal, Madeira, Portugal, March 16–18, 2018, pp. 27–35 (2018)
7. Snyder, J.S., Ferguson, D., Irey, G.: Automatic crash detection. U.S. Patent 9 767 625 B1, 13 April 2015
8. White, J., Thompson, C., Turner, H., Dougherty, B., Schmidt, D.C.: Wreckwatch: automatic traffic accident detection and notification with smartphones. Mob. Networks Appl. **16**, 285–303 (2011)
9. Thompson, C., White, J., Dougherty, B., Albright, A., Schmidt, D.C.: Using smartphones to detect car accidents and provide situational awareness to emergency responders. In: Cai, Y., Magedanz, T., Li, M., Xia, J., Giannelli, C. (eds.) Mobile Wireless Middleware, Operating Systems, and Applications, pp. 29–42. Springer, Heidelberg (2010)
10. Zaldivar, J., Calafate, C.T., Cano, J.C., Manzoni, P.: Providing accident detection in vehicular networks through obd-ii devices and android-based smartphones. In: 2011 IEEE 36th Conference on Local Computer Networks (LCN), pp. 813–819. IEEE (2011)
11. Punetha, D., Kumar, D., Mehta, V.: Article: design and realization of the accelerometer based transportation system (ATS). Int. J. Comput. Appl. **49**, 17–20 (2012). Full text available
12. Lahn, J., Peter, H., Braun, P.: Car crash detection on smartphones. In: Proceedings of the 2nd International Workshop on Sensor-Based Activity Recognition and Interaction. WOAR 2015, pp. 12:1–12:4. ACM, New York (2015)
13. Aloul, F.A., Zualkernan, I.A., Abu-Salma, R., Al-Ali, H., Al-Merri, M.: ibump: smartphone application to detect car accidents. Comput. Electr. Eng. **43**, 66–75 (2015)
14. Zendrive: Safer Drivers, Safer Roads (2017). http://www.zendrive.com/. Accessed 03 May 2017
15. Sosmartapp: Automatic car crash detection app (2017). http://www.sosmartapp. com. Accessed 03 May 2017
16. TrueMotion: Driving Intelligence (2017). https://gotruemotion.com/. Accessed 03 May 2017
17. Schulz, A., Ristoski, P., Paulheim, H.: I see a car crash: real-time detection of small scale incidents in microblogs. In: Cimiano, P., Fernández, M., Lopez, V., Schlobach, S., Völker, J. (eds.) ESWC 2013. LNCS, vol. 7955, pp. 22–33. Springer, Heidelberg (2013). https://doi.org/10.1007/978-3-642-41242-4_3
18. Carletti, V., Foggia, P., Percannella, G., Saggese, A., Strisciuglio, N., Vento, M.: Audio surveillance using a bag of aural words classifier. In: 2013 10th IEEE International Conference on Advanced Video and Signal Based Surveillance, AVSS 2013 (2013)

19. Foggia, P., Petkov, N., Saggese, A., Strisciuglio, N., Vento, M.: Audio surveillance of roads: a system for detecting anomaloussounds. IEEE Trans. Intell. Transp. Syst. **17**(1), 279–288 (2016)
20. Rabaoui, A., Davy, M., Rossignol, S., Ellouze, N.: Using one-class SVMs and wavelets for audio surveillance. IEEE Trans. Inf. Forensics Secur. **3**, 763–775 (2008)
21. Vacher, M., Istrate, D., Besacier, L., Serignat, J.F., Castelli, E.: Sound detection and classification for medical telesurvey. In: ACTA Press, C. (ed.) 2nd Conference on Biomedical Engineering, pp. 395–398. Innsbrück, Austria (2004)
22. Clavel, C., Ehrette, T.: Fear-type emotion recognition and abnormal events detection for an audio-based surveillance system. WIT Trans. Inform. Commun. Technol. **39**, 471–479 (2008)
23. Valenzise, G., Gerosa, L., Tagliasacchi, M., Antonacci, F., Sarti, A.: Scream and gunshot detection and localization for audio-surveillance systems. In: 2007 IEEE Conference on Advanced Video and Signal Based Surveillance, AVSS 2007 Proceedings, pp. 21–26 (2007)
24. Ntalampiras, S., Potamitis, I., Fakotakis, N.: Exploiting temporal feature integration for generalized sound recognition. EURASIP J. Adv. Signal Process. **2009**, 807162 (2009)
25. Parascandolo, G., Huttunen, H., Virtanen, T.: Recurrent neural networks for polyphonic sound event detection in real life recordings. In: 2016 IEEE International Conference on Acoustics, Speech and Signal Processing (ICASSP), pp. 6440–6444 (2016)
26. Salamon, J., Bello, J.P.: Deep convolutional neural networks and data augmentation for environmental sound classification. IEEE Signal Process. Lett. **24**, 279–283 (2017)
27. Peeters, G., Rodet, X.: A large set of audio feature for sound description (similarity and classification) in the cuidado project. Technical report, Ircam, Analysis/Synthesis Team, 1 pl. Igor Stravinsky, 75004 Paris, France (2004)
28. Gouyon, F., Pachet, F., Delerue, O.: On the use of zero-crossing rate for an application of classification of percussive sounds. In: Proceedings of the COST G-6 Conference on Digital Audio Effects (DAFX 2000) (2000)
29. Gouyon, F., Delerue, O., Pachet, F.: Classifying percussive sounds: a matter of zero-crossing rate ? In: Proceedings of DAFX 2000, Verona (It) (2000)
30. Pikrakis, A., Giannakopoulos, T., Theodoridis, S.: Gunshot detection in audio streams from movies by means of dynamic programming and bayesian networks. In: Proceedings of the IEEE International Conference on Acoustics, Speech, and Signal Processing, ICASSP 2008, March 30 - April 4, 2008, Caesars Palace, Las Vegas, Nevada, USA, pp. 21–24 (2008)
31. Giannakopoulos, T., Pikrakis, A., Theodoridis, S.: A multi-class audio classification method with respect to violent content in movies using Bayesian networks. In: IEEE 9th Workshop on Multimedia Signal Processing, MMSP 2007, Chania, Crete, Greece, October 1–3, 2007, pp. 90–93 (2007)
32. Grey, J.M., Gordon, J.W.: Perceptual effects of spectral modifications on musical timbres. J. Acoust. Soc. Am. **63**, 1493–1500 (1978)
33. Dixon, S.: Onset detection revisited. In: Proceedings of the International Conference on Digital Audio Effects (DAFx 2006), Montreal, Quebec, Canada, pp. 133–137 (2006)
34. Kurth, F., Müller, M.: Efficient index-based audio matching. IEEE Trans. Audio Speech Lang. Process. **16**, 382–395 (2008)

35. Muller, M., Kurth, F., Clausen, M.: Chroma-based statistical audio features for audio matching. In: IEEE Workshop on Applications of Signal Processing to Audio and Acoustics 2005, pp. 275–278 (2005)
36. Gonzalez, R.: Better than MFCC audio classification features. In: Gonzalez, R. (ed.) The Era of Interactive Media, pp. 291–301. Springer, New York (2013). https://doi.org/10.1007/978-1-4614-3501-3_24
37. Sengupta, N., Sahidullah, M., Saha, G.: Lung sound classification using cepstral-based statisticalfeatures. Comput. Biol. Med. **75**, 118–129 (2016)
38. Ganchev, T., Fakotakis, N., Kokkinakis, G.: Comparative evaluation of various MFCC implementations on the speaker verification task. In: Proceedings of the SPECOM 2005, pp. 191–194 (2005)
39. Müller, M.: Information Retrieval for Music and Motion. Springer, Secaucus (2007). https://doi.org/10.1007/978-3-540-74048-3
40. Foggia, P., Petkov, N., Saggese, A., Strisciuglio, N., Vento, M.: Audio surveillance of roads: a system for detecting anomalous sounds. IEEE Trans. Intell. Transp. Syst. **17**, 279–288 (2016)
41. Car Crash Time: Youtube channel (2017). https://www.youtube.com/channel/UCwuZi_C_yFtHsfCicthqygw. Accessed 03 May 2017
42. FreeSound: On-line free sound samples (2017). www.freesound.org. Accessed 03 May 2017
43. Urban Sound Dataset (2017). https://serv.cusp.nyu.edu/projects/urbansounddataset/urbansound8k.html. Accessed 03 Sept 2017
44. Crocco, M., Cristani, M., Trucco, A., Murino, V.: Audio surveillance: a systematic review. ACM Comput. Surv. **48**, 1–44 (2016)
45. Alameda-Pineda, X., Horaud, R.: A geometric approach to sound source localization from time-delay estimates. IEEE/ACM Trans. Audio Speech Lang. Process. **22**, 1082–1095 (2014)
46. Karbasi, A., Sugiyama, A.: A new doa estimation method using a circular microphone array. In: 2007 15th European Signal Processing Conference, pp. 778–782 (2007)
47. Chen, L., Liu, Y., Kong, F., He, N.: Acoustic source localization based on generalized cross-correlation time-delay estimation. Procedia Eng. **15**, 4912–4919 (2011)
48. Fernández, C., María, S., Ortega, D.B.: Direction of arrival estimation - a two microphones approach. Ph.D. thesis, Blekinge Institute of Technology School of Engineering Department of Signal Processing (2010)
49. Qinqin, Z., Linghua, Z.: Study of delay estimation in acoustic source localization based onmicrophone array. In: 2015 IEEE Advanced Information Technology, Electronic and Automation Control Conference (IAEAC), pp. 664–667 (2015)
50. Kumar Dhull, S.: Review on acoustic source localization techniques. Eur. J. Adv. Eng. Technol. **2**, 72–77 (2015)
51. Lopez-Poveda, E.A.: Development of fundamental aspects of human auditory perception. In: Development of Auditory and Vestibular Systems, pp. 287–314. Elsevier (2014)
52. Cobos, M., Antonacci, F., Alexandridis, A., Mouchtaris, A., Lee, B.: A survey of sound source localization methods in wireless acousticsensor networks. In: Wireless Communications and Mobile Computing 2017 (2017)
53. Khaddour, H.: A comparison of algorithms of sound source localization based on time delay estimation. Elektrorevue **2**, 31–37 (2011)
54. Argentieri, S., Danès, P., Souères, P.: A survey on sound source localization in robotics: from binaural to array processing methods. Comput. Speech Lang. **34**, 87–112 (2015)

55. Minut: Home surveillance (2017). https://minut.com/. Accessed 03 May 2017
56. Belblidia, N., Sammarco, M., Costa, L.H.M.K., de Amorim, M.D.: Epics: fair opportunistic multi-content dissemination. IEEE Trans. Mob. Comput. **14**, 1847–1860 (2015)

A Multi-domain Co-simulation Ecosystem for Fully Virtual Rapid ADAS Prototyping

Róbert Lajos Bücs[✉], Pramod Lakshman, Jan Henrik Weinstock,
Florian Walbroel, Rainer Leupers, and Gerd Ascheid

Institute for Communication Technologies and Embedded Systems,
RWTH Aachen University, Aachen, Germany
{buecs,lakshman,weinstock,walbroel,leupers,ascheid}@ice.rwth-aachen.de

Abstract. In the last decades, vehicular control applications evolved to comprehensive Advanced Driver Assistance Systems (ADAS) with exploding complexity. Several simulation-driven approaches can ease their development, e.g., model-based design and driving simulators, which are often limited to functional traits. To bridge this gap, virtual platforms can be used for accurately simulating the entire hardware/software layer, while validating beyond-functional properties (e.g., task execution times). Moreover, multi-domain co-simulation standards enable combining such distinct ecosystems beyond tool and model boundaries. Based on these concepts, this work presents a joint set of frameworks for virtualizing the ADAS prototyping flow via whole-system simulation. The focus of the work lies in the design of an automotive-flavor virtual platform, ensuring accurate and fast hardware/software simulation. To highlight the advantages of the framework system, two ADAS applications were prototyped in various configurations. Lastly, algorithmic and system-level analyses are presented, alongside simulation performance evaluation.

Keywords: ADAS prototyping · Driving simulators ·
Virtual platforms · Multi-domain co-simulation ·
Near real-time execution

1 Introduction

Vehicles have evolved from mainly mechanical to complex hardware/software (HW/SW) driven systems in the last decades. Vehicular SW covers vast areas, ranging from infotainment, over safety-critical control tasks, heading all together

This work was supported by the German Federal Ministry of Education and Research (BMBF) via the PARIS project (**PAR**allele **I**mplementierungs-**S**trategien für das Hochautomatisierte Fahren - funding code 16ES0602) aiming at the development of efficient hardware architectures for highly automated and autonomous driving.

© Springer Nature Switzerland AG 2019
B. Donnellan et al. (Eds.): SMARTGREENS 2018/VEHITS 2018, CCIS 992, pp. 181–201, 2019.
https://doi.org/10.1007/978-3-030-26633-2_9

towards highly automated driving. Furthermore, recent HW trends reflect strong integration, i.e., fewer Electronic Control Units (ECUs) with multi and many-core CPUs. The resulting architecture of Advanced Driver Assistance Systems (ADAS) consist of up to 100 networked ECUs with 250 embedded and graphic processors [19], executing an estimated 100 million lines of code [11].

Moreover, frequent factory recalls were observed in the past years with various manufacturers, most of which were caused by failures in the electronic system [38]. This called attention to secure HW/SW design, test and validation for which the automotive industry agreed on functional safety standards, e.g., the ISO 26262 [25]. Such standards define strict rules to ensure functional safety by design for the HW/SW layer and recommend full-system simulation to provide early guarantees. However, with the sheer complexity of the electronic and electrical system and the demanding requirements posed by functional safety standards, ADAS development and validation has become immensely difficult.

Model-Based Design: Such tools can tackle the aforementioned challenges by offering early algorithmic prototyping, in-tool testing and often ISO-certified code generation. Model-based design tools accelerate the *design-validation-refinement cycle* of ADAS via a simulation-driven approach. Moreover, such frameworks further refine validation steps via *x-in-the-loop* methods; particularly, Model-, Software- and Hardware-In-the-Loop (MIL, SIL, HIL) techniques assist to reduce late nonconformities. Yet, model-based design frameworks are limited to *(i)* rigid artificial inputs/outputs (I/O) and *(ii)* model only algorithmic aspects of ADAS. Although road tests can be conducted to overcome these shortcomings, non-reproducible driving scenarios and the possibility of property and personal damage shift the applicability of test drives to later design stages.

Driving Simulators: Such frameworks address the aforementioned limitations by providing realistic I/O via their virtual driving environment. This enables ADAS evaluation/refinement using virtual test drives, while having the freedom to experiment with various traffic and environmental conditions, as well as vehicle types (e.g., cars, trucks). Furthermore, driving simulators ensure deterministic test repeatability, which is essential if spurious errors occur. Moreover, they can also include a driver in the ADAS evaluation, thus capturing real human reactions. However, driving simulators are limited to model only functional aspects of ADAS. In addition, they are restricted to their confined simulation environment, making a joint usage with further tools challenging.

Virtual Platforms (VPs): This technology addresses the second limitation of model-based design tools by extending the simulation to the ADAS HW/SW system. VPs consist of simulation models of hardware blocks and their interconnection, created by using *electronic system-level* specifications, e.g., SystemC/TLM-2.0 [1]. Such standards enable modeling and simulation of full systems including, e.g., CPUs, buses, memories and various peripheral devices. Further, VPs enable HW/SW co-design by simulating the complete ADAS SW layer as executed by the platform. In contrast to model-based design tools, VPs enable exploring system properties beyond functional boundaries, e.g., HW/SW partitioning, task mapping, schedulability and dynamic worst-case execution time analysis. VPs also assist and accelerate system prototyping by maintaining full HW/SW visibility, debuggability and non-intrusive monitoring, while ensuring execution determinism. However, such frameworks are generally limited by either their simulation speed or modeling accuracy. In addition, similarly to driving simulators, VPs are limited beyond their simulation environment.

Multi-domain Co-simulation: This technique extends the boundaries of application-specific simulation tools/models by providing means for cross-domain interconnection and joint control. The multi-domain approach may be used to fulfill the ISO 26262 requirement of full-system validation by co-simulating various vehicular subsystems. Conceptually, this would allow to connect, e.g., a virtual platform with the environment of a driving simulator, among others. Tool-agnostic standards are defined for such purposes, overcoming the inflexibility of point-to-point coupling solutions. Yet, target tools/models need to be made compliant to multi-domain co-simulation standards for joint usage.

Contributions: This chapter is based on the work presented in [7], and its contributions are as follows. To reap their mutual benefits, we propose joining the preceding tools and techniques to facilitate and accelerate ADAS prototyping via full virtualization and whole-system simulation. Putting this in practice, a joint set of frameworks is presented, composed of carefully chosen tools and standards, that mutually resolve their aforementioned limitations as follows:

#1. To overcome the artificial I/O limitation of model-based design tools, the realistic virtual environment of driving simulators shall be utilized.
#2. To extend the functional simulation capability of model-based design tools and driving simulators, virtual platforms shall be used to ensure beyond-functional modeling and exploration.
#3. The chosen frameworks shall be interconnected by providing compliance for all target tools to a selected multi-domain co-simulation standard.
#4. To aim at the speed/accuracy trade-off of VPs, an automotive-flavor platform shall be created, simultaneously offering detailed and fast simulation.
#5. Pursuing near real-time whole-system co-simulation execution, to be able to involve the developer in the virtual ADAS test driving process.

The envisioned simulation system allows ADAS testing in a closed-loop manner, i.e., *(i)* capturing the environment of a driving simulator via virtual sensors *(ii)* inputting the gathered data and executing the target ADAS on a VP and *(iii)* applying regulatory feedback on the virtual vehicle within the driving simulator. Lastly, to highlight its advantages, ADAS applications shall be prototyped using the proposed full-system simulator.

2 Selection of Tools and Standards

The previously presented ideas pose strict requirements on simulation ecosystems, such as high flexibility and accuracy, while achieving near real-time execution speed. Thus, various tools and standards were carefully compared to select the most suitable combination fulfilling the prerequisites.

In this work, Simulink [26] was chosen as model-based design tool in the ADAS design automation flow, as it provides advanced modeling semantics, a vast block set and in-tool simulation features. Moreover, its certified code generator ensures safe and continuous ADAS integration onto target HW devices.

The requirements for a driving simulator in the proposed approach are availability, adaptability and a realistic virtual environment. Several open-source (e.g., TORCS [41], Rigs Of Rods [31]) as well as commercial frameworks (e.g., CIVITEC Pro-SiVIC [13], carSIM [27]) were carefully examined. From all tools, an open-source racing game, Speed Dreams 2 [34], was selected as it supports various environmental conditions (e.g., precipitation), different car types and configurable vehicle dynamics. Moreover, the chosen game is an extension of TORCS, a simulator frequently used in research for, e.g., ADAS development and even automated driving [10, 22]. In this work, Speed Dreams 2 was adapted for urban traffic simulation and ADAS virtual test driving in such environments. Lastly, compliance to a selected multi-domain co-simulation standard was added, ensuring connectivity beyond its simulation environment.

The virtual platform technology is concerned with the strictest requirements in the proposed methodology and was the main focus of this work. The envisioned framework needs to accurately model and simulate the complete ADAS HW/SW stack. On the HW side, this requires assembling a scalable distributed system, consisting of a configurable number of modular subsystems connected over a communication bus. Further, the envisioned platform needs to execute the complete ADAS SW stack, including the target algorithms, and ideally a full-fledged automotive Operating System (OS). Due to its magnitude and complexity, the VP is expected to be the performance bottleneck of the whole framework system. Thus, to avoid slowing down the full-system simulation, the platform needs to achieve execution speeds close to real-time. Considering these serious requirements, numerous SystemC-based simulation technologies were carefully examined, as this is the de facto *electronic system-level* design standard. Herein several open-source (e.g., OVPsim [24], SoCLib [36]) and commercial frameworks (e.g., Synopsys Virtualizer [35]) were examined. Among them, a technology named GreenSoCs [21] emerged as the best choice. At its heart, GreenSoCs uses the QEMU [5] fast system emulator to overcome the strongest performance bottleneck of a VP, the CPU model. In this regard, QEMU can be also configured to contain multiple instances of the CPU module in a single package, still maintaining high execution efficiency. Its performance lies in the *just-in-time compilation* engine, translating and caching target CPU instructions to code blocks of the simulation host at run-time. Yet, due to the nature of system emulation, QEMU lacks timing annotation, which degrades the overall simulation accuracy. To address this issue, the GreenSoCs technology provides a dedicated SystemC wrapper around QEMU, thus integrating the CPU models into the timed SystemC environment. Herewith, GreenSoCs-based platforms can leverage both, fast simulation and temporal accuracy at CPU instruction level. The necessary timing management is achieved by synchronizing the global simulation time whenever QEMU is ahead of the current SystemC time by more than an

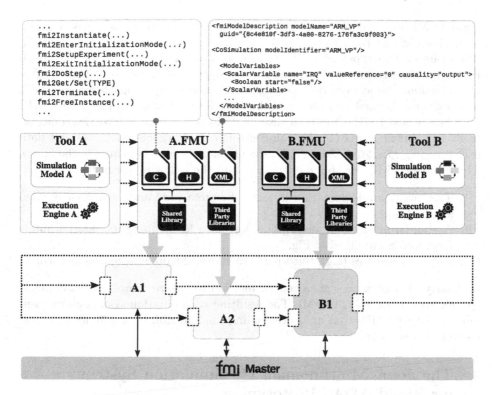

Fig. 1. Example on FMU generation, model taxonomy and FMI-based co-simulation.

amount called *quantum*. Based on GreenSoCs, this work presents an advanced automotive-flavor VP that supports distributed multi-core setups while maintaining high execution efficiency. Lastly, to ensure connectivity beyond its environment, the VP has been made compliant to a multi-domain co-simulation standard.

In this regard, various standards were compared to join the previously presented distinct simulation ecosystems beyond tool and domain boundaries via a dedicated co-simulation. Herein a centralized orchestration was envisioned for joint co-simulation control. State-of-the-art standards were carefully analyzed, such as CosiMate [12], the High Level Architecture [14] and the Functional Mock-up Interface (FMI) [28]. After thorough examination, FMI was selected, a light-weight, open-source, tool-agnostic specification, considered the de facto multi-domain co-simulation standard for automotive applications. FMI defines a master/slave approach, where a central master is responsible for synchronization and data exchange between multiple slaves. Since the standard does not lay down a reference controller implementation, in this work an in-house FMI master was utilized for orchestration (introduced in [6]). On the other hand, FMI slaves, or Functional Mock-up Units (FMUs), encapsulate target tools/models following the light-weight FMI C-API [28]. To clarify the general principles behind FMI, Fig. 1. depicts an abstract example. Herein two model-based design tools (Tool A and Tool B) are considered, assumingly with FMI compliance. In this example two types of models (FMU of type A and B), and three model instances (A→A1, A→A2, B→B1) are created/generated by these tools. After instantiation, the system designer can determine connections between FMUs which are established and managed then by the FMI master. The FMI C-API [28] prescribes FMUs to implement functions for model creation/deletion (e.g., fmi2Instantiate(...)), run-control (e.g., fmi2DoStep(...)) and data exchange (e.g., fmi2Get/Set(...)), among many others, indicated in the figure. The resulting FMUs are bundles that contain the following set of files:

(i) The model implementation in form of source code and/or a pre-compiled shared library.
(ii) A standardized model description XML file for defining its external interface, also exemplified in Fig. 1.
(iii) Further resources (e.g., third-party libraries, documentation, model icon).

Lastly, this work presents a generic method to ensure compliance of domain-specific simulation tools to FMI. The resulting co-simulation system allows coupling arbitrary FMUs to it, thus overcoming the inflexibility of individual, point-to-point connections.

3   The Joint Multi-domain Co-simulation System for Rapid ADAS Prototyping

The selected simulation ecosystems are promising high-performance base technologies for the envisioned full-system simulator. This section provides information on tool adaptations for establishing a fully virtual ADAS rapid prototyping environment. The resulting framework system is described next step by step.

3.1   Generic FMI-Based Tool-Coupling

First, an FMI-based, generic coupling method was designed for the target simulators/models. FMI defines two possible connection options for FMUs: *standalone* or *tool-coupling*. The former FMUs are self-contained, including the model, the simulator and all run-time dependencies. In contrast, tool-coupling FMUs are basic communication adapters, interacting with a simulator that contains the target model. Although standalone FMUs are more straight-forward to implement, research indicates severe problems with multiple instantiation and library co-dependencies [6]. Thus, in this work the tool-coupling technique was favored, as it separates the adapter and the target simulator into isolated processes, which is a more reasonable approach for the envisioned framework system.

First a Generic FMI Tool-Coupling Adapter was designed for this purpose, shown in Fig. 2. For simplicity, the adapter was implemented as a standalone FMU. This way, the FMI master can load the module without run-time dependencies directly into its own host OS process. At instantiation, the adapter

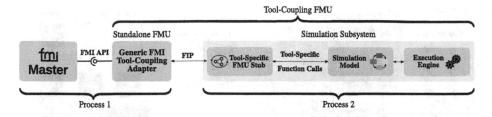

Fig. 2. Generic FMI-based tool-coupling layer (based on [7]).

Start of Frame	Command / Acknowledgment	Comma Separated Arguments	End of Frame
$	5 characters	0 to n	#

FMI Request	FIP Request Packet	Example
Initialize Model	cinit	$cinit#
Request Model Step	cstep(step_size_sec)	$cstep1#
Fetch All Integer Variables	cgtin(n), vr[0], ... vr[n-1]	$cgtin2,9,6#

FMI Response	FIP Response Packet	Example
Acknowledge Model Init. Request	ainit	$ainit#
Acknowledge Model Step Request	astep	$astep#
Return All Integer Variables	dgtin(retstat), val[0], ... val[n-1]	$dgtin0,5,6# (0: fmi2OK)

Fig. 3. Mapping of FMI functions to FIP commands/acknowledgments [7].

Fig. 4. Sequence diagram of FMI and FIP-based communication [7].

opens a shared memory based inter-process communication channel for interacting with a target simulation tool. So that the adapter remains simulator independent and can be reused for arbitrary subsystems, a user-layer command protocol was defined (inspired by [18]), named *FMI Inter-process communication Protocol* (FIP). This implements a remote procedure call mechanism, where FMI API functions are mapped to commands/acknowledgments of FIP, as exemplified in Fig. 3. Herein, first the frame format can be observed, including the delimiters $ and #. Below, a few examples of FMI function to FIP frame mappings are demonstrated for various requests and responses. For instance, the fmi2DoStep(...) API function with $t_{step} = 1$ s translates to the FIP message $cstep1# and later to the acknowledgment $astep#, returned to the FMI master.

On the other side of the interaction, individual, Tool-Specific FMU Stubs are to be designed. These receive the FIP packages and execute the initial FMI request on the target model, as depicted in Fig. 2. To clarify the complete communication process, Fig. 4 shows a sequence diagram. Following up on the previous example, the FMI master invokes again the fmi2DoStep(...) API function with $t_{step} = 1$ s. This request is translated to the FIP command cstep by the Generic FMI Tool-Coupling Adapter and is transmitted to the Tool-Specific FMU Stub.

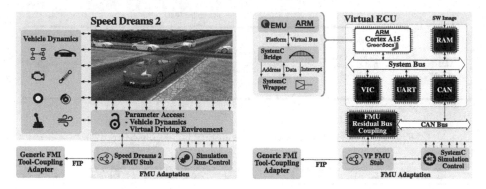

Fig. 5. Block diagram of the adapted Speed Dreams 2 driving simulator (based on [7]).

Fig. 6. Block diagram excerpt of the virtual platform base technology (based on [7]).

The packet is then interpreted, and a tool-specific function call is invoked by the stub, in this meta-code example `model_step(...)`. After the model step is completed, the stub sends a corresponding acknowledgment `astep` to the adapter, which transmits the call return status to the master.

The FIP-based adapter-stub mechanism addresses the **#3** objective of this work (detailed in Sect. 1), providing a generic technique for target tools to comply to FMI. The corresponding framework extensions are presented next.

3.2   Adaptation of Speed Dreams 2

As mentioned previously, the original Speed Dreams 2 racing game was extended within the scope of this work to support regular traffic simulation and ADAS virtual test drives. Firstly, rural tracks were created, and support for two-lane roads, intersections, two-way traffic and buildings was added, as shown in Fig. 5. Moreover, traffic agents were adapted to follow regulations, e.g., comply with speed limits and yield the right of way, which is essential in intersections.

Using the mechanisms detailed in Sect. 3.1, the FMI adaptation of the driving simulator was performed next. As shown in Fig. 5, a tool-specific Speed Dreams 2 FMU Stub was created to process the FIP commands sent by the master. The stub executes control requests via the Simulation Run-Control module, including stepping vehicle dynamics calculations. The stub can also expose parameters of the simulator, required for data exchange with other FMUs. Herein a Parameter Access module handles safe data management for properties of Vehicle Dynamics and the Virtual Driving Environment, as indicated in the figure.

These adaptations address the **#1** and **#3** objectives of this work (Sect. 1). First, the virtual driving environment overcomes the limitation of artificial I/O. Moreover, FMU compliance allows for external connections and control, required for multi-domain co-simulation. These features can be exploited to achieve ADAS modeling beyond the functional level by utilizing a VP, detailed next.

3.3   Automotive Virtual Platform Design

Following the strict requirements discussed in Sect. 2, an automotive-flavor VP was designed to extend the scope of ADAS testing. Shown in Fig. 6, the VP consists of virtual ECUs (vECUs), modeling a modified ARM Versatile board [3]. At the heart of each vECU a high-performance GreenSoCs-based ARM Cortex-A15 CPU model [2] is embedded. This particular CPU model was selected due to the increasing requirement of high-performance ARM architectures in ADAS development, underlined for instance in [23] and [8]. Depicted in Fig. 6, the GreenSoCs simulation model consist of *(i)* the QEMU-based ARM instruction set simulator, *(ii)* a SystemC Bridge, capturing access commands of QEMU's virtual bus, converting them to SystemC transactions/signals (e.g., address, data, interrupt), *(iii)* a SystemC Wrapper, encapsulating the whole package as a SystemC module, providing necessary CPU interfaces via, e.g., TLM sockets.

Further, vECUs contain additional in-house designed device models, e.g., an on-chip memory, a system bus, serial communication modules (UART) and a Vectored Interrupt Controller (VIC), among others. This particular set of virtual devices was chosen so that vECUs can execute full-fledged OSs. Moreover, the platform architecture was designed for scalability by instantiating a configurable number of connected vECUs to create a distributed multi-core system. Hence, each vECU was also equipped with a Controller Area Network (CAN) transceiver for inter-vECU communication over a single CAN-bus, as shown in Fig. 6.

After its construction, the platform was transformed into a tool-coupling FMU (recalling Sect. 3.1). Herein, first a VP FMU Stub was designed to process FIP commands. Shown in Fig. 6, the stub also executes control requests via the SystemC Simulation Control unit, which is responsible for creation/deletion of SystemC modules, as well as run-state management. To expose the internal HW/SW state towards the co-simulation, an FMU Residual Bus Coupling component was designed, acting as a bridge between SystemC and FMI. This module can buffer/update certain user-selected messages via their unique CAN addresses as they are transmitted over the CAN bus. Each of these messages can correspond to particular HW/SW parameters (e.g., SW variables, HW signals). If the FMI master requests reading a parameter, a look-up is performed in the buffer for the matching CAN identifier, and the message is fetched, decoded and interpreted. If the master sends data to the VP, parameters will be embedded into CAN frames as payload by the buffer and then injected to the bus.

In the achieved initial platform version, simulation performance measurements have shown a notable slowdown in multi-core setups, linearly with the number of added CPU models. As this issue contradicted the scalability and speed requirements, a more advanced technique was required alongside the Green-SoCs approach. The idea arose to exploit the inherent parallelism of the VP due to its structure. This resulted in executing each CPU model on a separate host thread and the remaining peripherals of the vECU on another, as they are less performance-critical. The resulting parallel segments run decoupled, ahead of the global simulation time, but are synchronized whenever their own local time reach a pre-defined limit. Platform parallelization achieves major performance gains, reaching execution speeds beyond real-time, as presented later.

The resulting performance-optimized VP addresses the **#2**–**#5** objectives of this work (Sect. 1). It extends the simulation spectrum to the HW/SW system, covering analysis of non-functional properties. Moreover, the FMU adaptation allows for external connections and control, required for multi-domain co-simulation. Lastly, the performance improvements address the speed/accuracy trade-off and the pursuit for near real-time full-system execution.

3.4   The Virtual Platform Software Stack

Afterwards, the software layer was designed for integrating ADAS prototypes as embedded code onto the constructed VP. Initially, the integration can be achieved in form of bare-metal software. For this purpose, base SW components were created, consisting of low-level utilities (e.g., cross-toolchain, linker script, bootloader), a standard C library and a driver layer for the peripheral devices. The bare-metal setup enables early validation of functional ADAS properties, as well as HW/SW design space exploration, partitioning and distribution.

However, safety-critical ADAS applications have far stricter requirements, e.g., hard real-time execution guarantees and HW/SW protection mechanisms. To manage such applications, the automotive industry laid down Real-Time Operating System (RTOS) standards, such as OSEK/VDX [29] and its successor AUTOSAR [4]. Both impose portability of SW components, priority-based multi-tasking, standard communication layers, safe resource management and real-time scheduling, among others. Since AUTOSAR implementations were not available at the point this work was conducted, OSEK/VDX was chosen instead. Herein several variants were examined (e.g., FreeOSEK [17], TOPPERS [37], osCAN [39], among others), and *ERIKA Enterprise* [16] was selected, a comprehensive, open-source implementation with full tool support. ERIKA is especially favored in open-source RTOS-based research activities, since it is developed towards the AUTOSAR specification. Following the guidelines outlined in [15], ERIKA was ported to the designed VP in this work, detailed next.

Porting Erika Enterprise to the Virtual Platform
Regarding the HW setup, the original Erika Enterprise package supports several target architectures, including ARM Cortex M0, M4 and R4 microcontrollers, among many others. In this work, the original ARM hardware-dependent software layer was extended to support the high-end ARM Cortex A15 processor, residing in the developed virtual platform (as detailed in Sect. 3.3).

Firstly, Erika Enterprise supports various scheduling policies, from which the non-preemptive, fixed priority scheduler with immediate priority ceiling [33] protocol was adapted. This allows for elemental RTOS functionality with support for the management of basic tasks for small concurrent systems. Next, mono-stack tasks were required to be implemented, sharing a common stack and initially not using interrupts. Herein, basic RTOS and task related actions can be tested, such as starting the scheduler and activating/terminating tasks, among others. Subsequently, basic and nested interrupt support was added for mono-stack applications, mostly affecting the drivers of the VIC, the CAN transceiver and further devices relying on interrupts. Hereby interrupt and context handling helper functions were adapted (e.g., EE_hal_enableIRQ(...), EE_hal_disableIRQ(...), EE_hal_resumeIRQ(...), EE_hal_suspendIRQ(...)), required by RTOS primitives for task handling. Lastly, inter-task communication was implemented beyond virtual ECUs by integrating the CAN layer for incoming/outgoing task messages.

3.5 The Full Design Automation Flow

After all subsystems were integrated, the joint framework system can be used as follows. Depicted in Fig. 7a, ADAS development and early functional testing begins using Simulink. Once a prototype is mature enough, Simulink's built-in code generator can be invoked to obtain embedded C/C++ code for it. The resulting pieces of code can first be integrated onto the VP as bare-metal SW for early algorithmic testing and HW/SW design space exploration. To support this, the VP can be configured to include any user-defined number of vECUs desired for the current development stage (Fig. 7b). Software integration and validation is supported by the possibility of run-time debugging on the VP, as the GreenSoCs technology allows attaching SW debuggers to virtual CPU models. Furthermore, in more mature development stages, ADAS applications can be integrated as ERIKA Enterprise tasks onto the VP for refining non-functional properties, e.g., execution times and scheduling. For each such design exploration cycle, a whole-system co-simulation can be assembled via the FMI master, loading the tool-coupling FMUs of the virtual platform and the driving simulator (Fig. 7e), among others possible tools/models. In the presented setup, the user can engage test driving in Speed Dreams 2, while the target ADAS is executed on the VP, regulating the behavior of the virtual vehicle. To catch possibly spurious errors, a Driver Behavior Record/Replay FMU was added to the co-simulation (Fig. 7d), thus ensuring exact test repeatability. The most outstanding benefit of

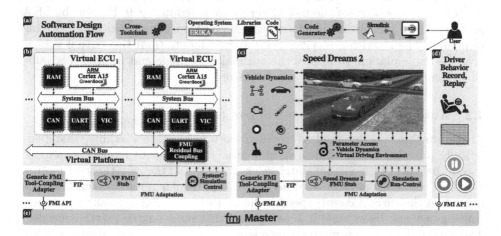

Fig. 7. The joint multi-domain co-simulation system, tool/model connections and design automation flow used for rapid ADAS prototyping (based on [7]).

the presented system in terms of productivity is that it can achieve the complete ADAS exploration cycle (adjustment, code generation/integration, test drive) in a matter of minutes. To highlight its capabilities in more details, two driver assistance applications were prototyped with its support, presented next.

4 Rapid ADAS Prototyping

This section presents the refinement process of ADAS benchmarks. It must be noted that the focus here is not on the designed ADAS, but on the framework system's capability to explore HW/SW properties on various abstraction levels.

4.1 Lane Keep Assistant (LKA)

This application performs a closed-loop steering control of a vehicle, trying to center it in the driving lane. Two operating modes were designed for the LKA: *(a)* automatically keeping the mid-point of the lane *(b)* actively avoiding lane departure, while the driver is still mainly in control. Algorithm 1 depicts a meta-code description of the fully automatic mode. Herein, first the road and lane widths are used to calculate the optimal and current vehicle positions in the driving roadway (lines 2–4). Next, according to the selection of the incoming/ongoing lane, the distance error is calculated (lines 5–9). Afterwards, the steer angle is corrected via the current vehicle-road angle and the segment-relative yaw to compensate the distance error (line 10). The segment-relative yaw is defined as the rotational movement along the axis which is perpendicular to the chassis plane. This parameter is calculated as the angular difference between the x-y plane of the car chassis coordinate system and the x-y plane of the road segment within the world coordinate system. Lastly, the updated steer angle is normalized to the range $\{\sphericalangle_{steer} \in \mathbb{R} \mid -\varPi \leq \sphericalangle_{steer} \leq \varPi\}$ (lines 11–16).

This algorithm was prototyped initially as a bare-metal application and was later refined as an ERIKA Enterprise task. A high-level representation of the interconnection scheme of the test system is depicted in Fig. 9. Herein the LKA is executed on the virtual platform in a closed-loop manner with the driving simulator. The algorithm receives the required inputs from the virtual vehicle over the co-simulation, computes the optimal steer angle and returns this value as user control input to the driving simulator.

4.2 Automatic Transmission Control (ATC)

This algorithm was designed as a closed-loop, finite state machine, that periodically provides a gear control output after evaluating its inputs: the engine speed, the state of the virtual clutch release sensor and the user throttle control. The application supports several use-cases, e.g., regular up and downshift with respect to the current engine speed, vehicle start/stop and overtake assistance, shifting one gear lower once it is recognized that more engine power is needed. The operation of the automatic transmission control is best described via a flow chart, as shown in Fig. 8:

1. From the initial vehicle start condition, the gear is incremented upon changes in the user throttle control input.
2. At every model step the clutch status is evaluated. If the vehicle is in the midst of a transmission, the algorithm enters a wait state until the clutch is released again, allowing for possible changes in gear control.
3. Afterwards, if the engine speed is lower but the user throttle control higher than predefined thresholds, the gear value is decremented so to provide additional engine power, which is essential in, e.g., a vehicle takeover scenario.
4. Lastly, the engine speed is evaluated with respect to certain upper and lower thresholds. If the engine speed remains within these bounds, the algorithm enters a wait state, else an increment/decrement of the gear is requested accordingly. Herein a last check is performed to avoid unwanted switching to neutral gear.

As previously, the ATC was prototyped first as a bare-metal application and later refined as an ERIKA Enterprise task. A high-level representation of the interconnection scheme of the test system is shown in Fig. 10. Herein the ATC is executed on the VP in a closed-loop manner with the driving simulator. The algorithm receives its inputs from the virtual vehicle over the co-simulation, computes the output gear and passes it as a control signal to the driving simulator.

Algorithm 1. LKA steer control [7].

Input: w_{road}: road width [m], w_{lane}: lane width [m], $\sphericalangle_{veh\_abs}$: vehicle-road angle [rad], θ_{rel}: segment-relative yaw [rad], $lane$: ongoing/incoming

Output: $\sphericalangle_{steer}$: steer angle [rad]

```
1  Function step_lane_keep_assist(...):
      // Update vehicle position in lane
2     d_left  ← get_dist_from_left(...)
3     d_right ← get_dist_from_right(...)
4     d_opt   ← w_lane/2
      // Select the target lane
5     if lane == ongoing then
6     |   d_diff ← d_right - d_opt
7     else
8     |   d_diff ← d_opt - d_left
9     end
      // Correct steer angle
10    ⊲_steer ←
         ⊲_veh_abs + θ_rel - d_opt/w_road
      // Normalize ⊲_steer to -Π...Π
11    while ⊲_steer > Π do
12    |   ⊲_steer ← ⊲_steer - 2 * Π
13    end
14    while ⊲_steer < -Π do
15    |   ⊲_steer ← ⊲_steer + 2 * Π
16    end
17 return ⊲_steer
```

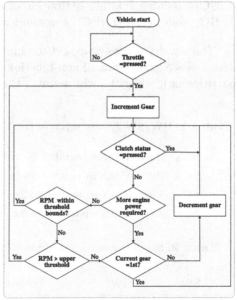

Fig. 8. Flow chart representation of the automatic transmission control (based on [7]).

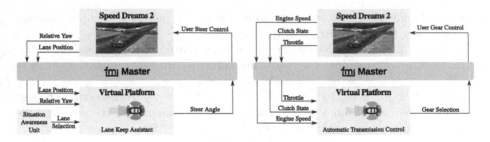

Fig. 9. Closed-loop interconnection scheme of the lane keep assistant system.

Fig. 10. Closed-loop interconnection scheme of the automatic transmission.

4.3   Hardware/Software System Configurations

Both applications were integrated on the virtual platform in the System Configurations (SCs) shown in Table 1. The corresponding transitions in system design stages are presented in Table 2. This particular order was established to continuously explore and refine new HW/SW properties by lowering the design abstraction level as follows:

1. SC_A: functional/algorithmic prototyping and initial software integration
2. SC_B: early timing analysis, RTOS integration, inter-task communication
3. SC_C: refining spatial distribution of applications
4. SC_D: adding inter-vECU communication between distributed tasks

The novelty of the proposed combination of frameworks is to enable such a design space exploration of non-functional traits (e.g., timing behavior, HW/SW partitioning), while stepwise refining the level of system abstraction.

Table 1. HW/SW system setup of the VP used for benchmarking (based on [7]).

SC_A	Both ADAS integrated on 1x virtual ECU as bare-metal software
SC_B	Both ADAS integrated on 1x virtual ECU as ERIKA tasks
SC_C	Two ADAS separated on 2x virtual ECUs as bare-metal software
SC_D	Two ADAS separated on 2x virtual ECUs as ERIKA tasks

Table 2. Stage transitions of hardware/software system design (based on [7]).

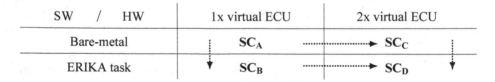

SW / HW	1x virtual ECU	2x virtual ECU
Bare-metal	SC_A	SC_C
ERIKA task	SC_B	SC_D

4.4   Functional and Temporal Analysis

Various co-simulation runs[1] were executed in the whole-system setup depicted in Fig. 7 for ADAS test and refinement. All of these were orchestrated by the FMI master applying a fixed step size of 2 ms on each subsystem.

First, signals of the LKA were captured. Figure 11 depicts the lane position of the test car around the optimum mid-point of 2.5 ms. Shown in Fig. 13, the vehicle's segment-relative yaw ranges from -1.0 to $+1.0$ rad. The resulting steer control is depicted in Fig. 15, where negative values indicate right, positive values left steering. The LKA's reaction in automatic mode can be observed between 1.5-3.5 s in a sharp right, and between 9.5-15 s in a broad left curve. Only minor differences can be observed in both plots between $\mathbf{SC_A}$ vs. $\mathbf{SC_B}$ which is explained by the short execution time of the ADAS. Thus, even as ERIKA Enterprise task, less system events (e.g., interrupts) disrupt its execution. Tests were also executed for $\mathbf{SC_C}$ and $\mathbf{SC_D}$, but as only minor differences were noted (due to CAN messages transmit times), the results are not shown.

More variance was found refining the ATC. First as shown in Fig. 12, a consistent throttle control was applied in all virtual test drive scenarios. Figure 14 depicts the engine speed between 1-5 s while steadily accelerating, and between 5-12 s while alternating the throttle. The resulting gear control is shown in Fig. 16. Herein functional and temporal deviations can be observed. As earlier, the minor timing changes between $\mathbf{SC_A}$ vs. $\mathbf{SC_C}$ and $\mathbf{SC_B}$ vs. $\mathbf{SC_D}$ are caused by CAN message delays induced by distribution. Yet, bare-metal vs. ERIKA Enterprise task implementations $\mathbf{SC_{A,C}}$ vs. $\mathbf{SC_{B,D}}$) show strong variations, causing even extra gear shifts (around 9 s). In $\mathbf{SC_{A,C}}$ the gear control loop is executed more frequently as it is triggered by ad hoc activations of CAN message interrupts. In contrast, the refinements of $\mathbf{SC_{B,D}}$ grant a scheduler-based execution with activations at discrete time stamps. Although such triggers occur less often, the mechanism provides real-time execution guarantees, that $\mathbf{SC_{A,C}}$ lack.

Furthermore, Fig. 18 depicts the captured clutch signal, where an undesired oscillation was observed between 6.5-9.2 s. This test pointed out an algorithmic error, violating the mandatory wait time between gear shifts, found and corrected by attaching a debugger to the vECU. This finding further affirms the advantages of the co-simulation system for ADAS prototyping.

Lastly, ADAS execution times were measured in $\mathbf{SC_B}$. Hereby, tasks were assigned fixed priorities from highest to lowest as follows: ATC, LKA and the idle Background Task (BT). As depicted in Fig. 17, ERIKA Enterprise schedules the tasks with a 1 ms period, according to their priorities. Furthermore, the runtimes of both applications can be observed: around 2 μs for the ATC and 8 μs for the LKA. Herein, the ATC required less time to execute as it was in a wait state, checking only for the expiration of the mandatory stay in gear time. Although no timing violations were detected due to the relatively short application runtimes, the measurements highlighted the potential of the proposed system of frameworks to provide dynamic execution time and schedulability analyses.

---

[1] Simulation host: 6x AMD Phenom II 1100T x86_64, $f_{clk} = 3.3$ GHz, 64K L1D and L1I, 512K L2 and 6144K L3 caches, 12 GB RAM, using Scientific Linux 6.8.

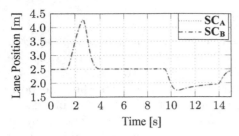

Fig. 11. LKA lane position [7].

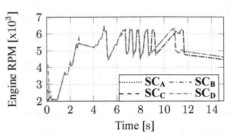

Fig. 12. ATC user throttle input.

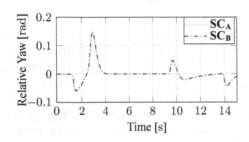

Fig. 13. LKA segment-relative yaw.

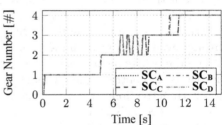

Fig. 14. ATC engine speed [7].

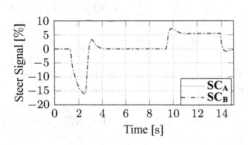

Fig. 15. LKA steer output [7].

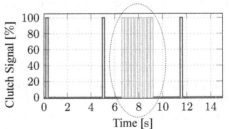

Fig. 16. ATC gear control [7].

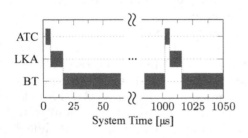

Fig. 17. ERIKA task execution times [7].

Fig. 18. ATC clutch oscillation error [7].

Table 3. Achieved co-simulation speeds in various SCs (based on [7]).

System configuration	SC_A	SC_B	SC_C	SC_D
Average co-simulation execution speed [FPS]	31.7	14.49	19.06	7.63

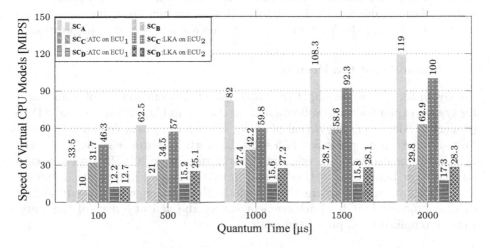

Fig. 19. Execution speeds of the CPU model(s) within the virtual platform, using various quantum settings, measured in various system configurations (based on [7]).

4.5 Co-simulation Performance Evaluation

As anticipated earlier, performance profiling results have shown that the virtual platform is the main simulation bottleneck of the full framework system. For deeper analysis, the number of executed Million Instructions Per Second (MIPS) was captured for all virtual CPU models within the platform, shown in Fig. 19. Since the virtual CPU models were clocked at $f_{clk} = 100$ MIPS, the goal was to reach around 100 MIPS with each of them, theoretically resulting in near real-time execution. To achieve this, the quantum (recalling Sect. 2.) was also increased, with the trade-off of lowering the timing accuracy. Here it must be noted, that even higher quanta did not cause disturbances in RTOS execution. As the results in the figure indicate, bare-metal vs. ERIKA Enterprise based SCs achieve higher performance (SC_A vs. SC_B and SC_C vs. SC_D), since the RTOS induces a large number of extra events (e.g., interrupts) causing simulation overhead. Figure 19 also indicates that multi-vECU setups achieve lower performance than single-vECU ones (SC_C vs. SC_A and SC_D vs. SC_B), since the simulation effort scales linearly with added vECUs but parallel efficiency does not. In SC_C and SC_D it can also be observed that the vECU executing the LKA achieves higher performance than the one running the ATC. This is explained by the relatively simple implementation of the LKA, leading to faster execution of the algorithm's step function and more simulation idle time.

Lastly, the performance of the full system (as shown in Fig. 7) was analyzed, with the VP quantum set to the overall co-simulation step size of 2 ms. The achieved average Frames Per Second (FPS), rendered by the Speed Dreams 2 graphic engine, was chosen as measure, since it reflects the real-time perception of the whole co-simulation system. Table 3 illustrates the achieved results. As the virtual platform dominates the whole co-simulation efficiency, the same trends can be noted as for the VP with regards to the applied system configurations.

4.6 Summary of the Results

Firstly, in Sect. 4.4 we highlight the potentials of the combination of frameworks for system exploration and validation of functional and beyond-functional ADAS properties. Moreover, the virtual platform and whole-system co-simulation performance measurements in Sect. 4.5 show that certain setups (e.g., $SC_{A,C}$) reach near real-time execution speeds. Since frame rates over 20 FPS are considered adequate for human perception in real-time, the results indicate that the co-simulation system can interactively include the developer in the virtual test driving process. This final achievement covers the #5 objective of the work, thus accomplishing all predefined goals.

5   Related Work

Several approaches emerged for simulation-driven ADAS design by joining distinct tools and techniques. For instance, Schneider and Frimberger [32] present an FMI-based co-simulation framework, joining a driving environment with a purely functional ADAS simulator to develop a dynamic headlight adjustment unit. Herein the HW/SW simulation was abstracted away by static test benches, excluding closed-loop ADAS testing and non-functional evaluation.

To bridge this gap, authors of [6] present techniques to interface SystemC-based virtual platforms with FMI. Although the work covers many aspects of hardware exploration and ADAS design automation, the rudimentary vehicle models used for evaluation strongly limit testing capabilities. Furthermore, the virtual platform benchmarking results imply that 1 s of simulation time is executed in only 22.4 s of real-time, making it unfeasible to include the developer in the test driving process.

Wehner and Göhringer [40] present the prototyping process of an adaptive cruise control using a Xilinx Zynq virtual platform [9] and a driving simulator. In contrast to the present work, since multiple platform instantiation is not possible, network-distributed system configurations cannot be created. Authors also recognize that the integrated embedded Linux distribution lacks real-time guarantees, required by safety-critical ADAS. Since simulation performance measurements indicate that 1 s of simulation time is executed in only 5.3 s of real-time, interactive ADAS test driving with the presented setup is strongly limited. Lastly, an ad hoc coupling is used between the subsystems, restraining the scalability of the simulation.

Raffaëlli et al. [30] use a combination of simulation frameworks to validate a lane departure warning and an automatic emergency brake system. In their work a driving simulator is coupled over a test automation server with a fast QEMU-based virtual platform, named Rabbits [20]. Since the platform does not have parallel simulation capabilities, a linear slowdown is expected with each added virtual CPU model. Although performance numbers remain undisclosed in the work, since the platform was used in an octa-core setup, the anticipated scalability gap likely causes a vast simulation efficiency degradation. Thus, although the setup is conceptually similar to the presented co-simulation system in this work, it can not reach the same near real-time performance.

Our proposed framework system combines the benefits of model-based design, driving simulators and virtual platforms to accelerate ADAS prototyping. Herein FMI is used for tool coupling to overcome the inflexibility of ad hoc connections. The main novelty of this work lies in the developed virtual platform, used to explore non-functional traits. In contrast to previous works, the platform implements advanced technologies for accurate and fast simulation. Thus, the overall co-simulation system can reach near real-time execution speeds, allowing to include the developer in ADAS test driving. As to the best knowledge of the authors, these aspects have not yet been addressed by other scientific efforts.

6   Summary and Outlook

This work presented a joint framework set for virtualizing the ADAS prototyping flow via whole-system simulation. Firstly, a generic FMI-based tool-coupling mechanism was implemented for all target tools. Next, the Speed Dreams 2 originally racing game was adapted for ADAS test driving and multi-domain simulation. The focus of the work lies in the design of the high-speed VP, supporting distributed, multi-core vECU configurations and FMI coupling. The capabilities of the VP were extended by porting the ERIKA Enterprise automotive RTOS to it, thus providing real-time guarantees for safety-critical applications. To highlight the advantages of the assembled framework system, an automatic transmission control and a lane keep assistant application was prototyped in various system configurations. Lastly, algorithmic and system-level analyses were presented, alongside simulation performance evaluation.

As future work, fully automatic ADAS code generation and integration is envisioned from within the model-based design tool, without the necessity of potential error prone manual code adaptations. Regarding the RTOS, support for higher OSEK/VDX conformance classes is planned thus extending the capabilities of Erika Enterprise tasks. Herein multi-stack applications and the utilization of more advanced synchronization primitives is envisioned, among others. Moreover, the extension of the OS communication layer and support for multi-core vECUs is planned. Lastly, the creation and evaluation of further ADAS is considered, heading towards a fully simulation-driven development of highly automated driving applications.

References

1. Accelera: SystemC Language Reference Manual. IEEE Std. 1666–2011 (Revision of IEEE Std. 1666–2005), pp. 1–638, January 2012
2. ARM: ARM Cortex-A15 MPCore Technical Reference Manual, July 2012. https://www.arm.com/
3. ARM: Versatile board. http://infocenter.arm.com/help/index.jsp?topic=/com.arm.doc.dsi0034a/index.html. Accessed May 2018
4. AUTOSAR: AUTomotive Open System ARchitecture Operating System Standard v4.1 (2014). https://www.autosar.org/
5. Bellard, F.: QEMU, a fast and portable dynamic translator. In: USENIX Annual Technical Conference. ATEC 2005, pp. 41–41 (2005)
6. Bücs, R.L., et al.: Virtual hardware-in-the-loop co-simulation for multi-domain automotive systems via the functional mock-up interface. In: Forum on Specification and Design Languages (FDL), pp. 1–8, September 2015
7. Bücs, R.L., Lakshman, P., Weinstock, J.H., Walbroel, F., Leupers, R., Ascheid, G.: Fully virtual rapid ADAS prototyping via a joined multi-domain co-simulation ecosystem. In: Proceedings of the 4th International Conference on Vehicle Technology and Intelligent Transport Systems, VEHITS 2018, Funchal, Madeira, Portugal, March 16–18, 2018, pp. 59–69 (2018)
8. Burgio, P., Bertogna, M., Olmedo, I.S., Gai, P., Marongiu, A., Sojka, M.: A software stack for next-generation automotive systems on many-core heterogeneous platforms. In: 2016 Euromicro Conference on Digital System Design (DSD), pp. 55–59, August 2016
9. Cadence: Virtual Platform for Xilinx Zynq-7000 EPP User Guide, April 2012
10. Cardamone, L., Loiacono, D., Lanzi, P.L., Bardelli, A.P.: Searching for the optimal racing line using genetic algorithms. In: IEEE Conference on Computational Intelligence and Games (CIG), pp. 388–394, August 2010
11. Charette, R.N.: This car runs on code. IEEE Spectrum, February 2009. https://spectrum.ieee.org/transportation/systems/this-car-runs-on-code
12. ChiasTek: CosiMate Official Product Website. https://site.cosimate.com/. Accessed May 2018
13. CIVITEC: Pro-SiVIC Official Product Website. http://www.civitec.com/applications/. Accessed May 2018
14. Dahmann, J., Fujimoto, R., Weatherly, R.: The department of defense high level architecture. In: Winter Simulation Conference, pp. 142–149 (1997)
15. Evidence: Porting guide for ERIKA Enterprise (2014). https://erika.tuxfamily.org/wiki/index.php?title=Porting_ERIKA_Enterprise_and_RT-Druid_to_a_new_microcontroller
16. Evidence: ERIKA Enterprise Official Website. http://erika.tuxfamily.org/drupal/. Accessed May 2018
17. FreeOSEK: Official Website. http://opensek.sourceforge.net/. Accessed May 2018
18. GDB: Remote Serial Protocol. https://sourceware.org/gdb/onlinedocs/gdb/Remote-Protocol.html. Accessed May 2018
19. Georgakos, G., Schlichtmann, U., Schneider, R., Chakraborty, S.: Reliability challenges for electric vehicles: from devices to architecture and systems software. In: Design Automation Conference (DAC), pp. 1–9 (2013)
20. Gligor, M., Fournel, N., Pétrot, F.: Using binary translation in event driven simulation for fast and flexible MPSoC simulation. In: IEEE/ACM International Conference Hardware/Software Codesign and System Synthesis (CODES+ISSS), pp. 71–80 (2009)

21. GreenSoCs: Virtual Platforms. https://www.greensocs.com/. Accessed May 2018
22. Huang, J., Tanev, I., Shimohara, K.: Evolving a general electronic stability program
    for car simulated in TORCS. In: IEEE Conference on Computational Intelligence
    and Games (CIG), pp. 446–453, August 2015
23. Hurtado, A.F., Gómez, J.A., Penenory, V.M., Cabezas, I.M., García, F.E.: Proposal
    of a computer vision system to detect and track vehicles in real time using an
    embedded platform enabled with a graphical processing unit. In: 2015 International
    Conference on Mechatronics, Electronics and Automotive Engineering (ICMEAE),
    pp. 76–80, November 2015
24. Imperas: Open Virtual Platforms. http://www.imperas.com/ovpworld. Accessed
    May 2018
25. ISO 26262: Road vehicles - Functional safety. ISO, Geneva, CH (2011)
26. MathWorks: Simulink. https://mathworks.com/help/simulink/. Accessed May
    2018
27. Mechanical Simulation Corporation: carSIM Official Product Website. https://
    www.carsim.com/. Accessed May 2018
28. Modelica Association: Functional Mock-up Interface Standard Official Website.
    http://www.fmi-standard.org/. Accessed May 2018
29. OSEK Group: OSEK/VDX Operating System Standard v2.2.3 (2005). https://
    www.osek-vdx.org/
30. Raffaëlli, L., et al.: Facing ADAS validation complexity with usage oriented testing.
    Computing Research Repository (CoRR) arXiv:1607.07849 (2016). http://arxiv.
    org/abs/1607.07849
31. RoR: Rigs of rods website. https://www.rigsofrods.org/. Accessed May 2018
32. Schneider, S., Frimberger, J.: Significant reduction of validation efforts for dynamic
    light functions with FMI for multi-domain integration and test platforms. In: Inter-
    national Modelica Conference, March 2014
33. Sha, L., Rajkumar, R., Lehoczky, J.P.: Priority inheritance protocols: an approach
    to real-time synchronization. IEEE Trans. Comput. **39**(9), 1175–1185 (1990)
34. Speed Dreams 2 Official Website: www.speed-dreams.org/. Accessed May 2018
35. Synopsys: Virtualizer Official Product Website. https://www.synopsys.com/
    verification/virtual-prototyping/virtualizer.html. Accessed May 2018
36. TIMA: SocLib Project Website. http://www.soclib.fr. Accessed May 2018
37. TOPPERS: Official Website. https://toppers.jp/en/index.html. Accessed May
    2018
38. U.S. Government Department of Transportation - National Highway Traffic Safety
    Administration: SafeCar Website. https://www.safercar.gov. Accessed May 2018
39. Vector: osCAN Official Product Website. https://vector.com/vi_operating_
    systems_en.html. Accessed May 2018
40. Wehner, P., Göhringer, D.: Evaluation of driver assistance systems with a car
    simulator a virtual and a real FPGA platform. In: Design and Architectures for
    Signal and Image Processing (DASIP), pp. 345–346, October 2013
41. Wymann, B., Espié, E., Guionneau, C., Dimitrakakis, C., Coulom, R., Sumner, A.:
    TORCS, the open racing car simulator, v1.3.5 (2013). http://torcs.sourceforge.net/

Static Environment Perception Based on High-Resolution Automotive Radars

Mingkang Li[1,2(✉)], Zhaofei Feng[1], Martin Stolz[1], Martin Kunert[1],
Roman Henze[2], and Ferit Küçükay[2]

[1] Advanced Engineering Sensor Systems, Robert Bosch GmbH,
Daimlerstr. 6, 71229 Leonberg, Germany
{mingkang.li,zhaofei.feng,martin.stolz2,
martin.kunert2}@de.bosch.com
[2] Institute of Automotive Engineering, Technische Universität Braunschweig,
Hans-Sommer-Str. 4, 38106 Brunswick, Germany
{r.henze,f.kuecuekay}@tu-braunschweig.de

Abstract. High-resolution radar sensors have the capability to perceive the surroundings around the vehicle very exactly by detecting thousands of reflection points per measurement cycle. To model the static environment with these detection points, a novel approach of occupancy grid mapping is developed in this paper. The reflection amplitudes of all data points are compensated, normalized, and then converted to a detection probability value that is based on a predefined radar sensor model. According to the movement of the test vehicle, the a posteriori occupancy probability after several measurement cycles is computed to build the occupancy grid map. Thereafter this occupancy grid map is transformed into a binary grid map, where the grid cells, with an obstacle present, are defined as occupied. Through the Connected-Component Labelling algorithm, these occupied grid cells are then clustered and all the outliers with only a few grid cells are eliminated. Then, the boundaries of the clustered, occupied grid cells are recognized by the Moore-Neighbor Tracing algorithm. Based on these boundaries, the free space of an interval-based model is determined by using the Bresenham's line algorithm. The occupancy grid map and the free space detection results elaborated in this paper from the recorded radar measurements show a perfect match with the real road scenarios.

Keywords: Automotive radar sensor · Environmental perception ·
Occupancy grid · Data fusion · Free space detection · Imaging radar

1 Introduction

By taking the advantages of all-weather robustness and a relatively low cost, various applications with the radar sensors are found in the automotive industry, especially in the area of Advanced Driver Assistance Systems (ADAS). For instance, in Adaptive Cruise Control (ACC) system, the radar sensors can detect objects within a wide range. After acquiring the value of object distance, the vehicle can be accelerated or decelerated automatically by the ACC system.

© Springer Nature Switzerland AG 2019
B. Donnellan et al. (Eds.): SMARTGREENS 2018/VEHITS 2018, CCIS 992, pp. 202–226, 2019.
https://doi.org/10.1007/978-3-030-26633-2_10

The development of ADAS towards Highly Automated Driving (HAD) improves continuously the demands on the high-resolution radar sensors. In order to handle complex applications and traffic situations, the radar sensors need a high angular and range resolution to capture enough environment information. In addition, the high-resolution radar is required for the data fusion with the LiDAR or camera sensor on a pixel-level.

The fast chirp linear Frequency-Modulated Continuous-Wave (FMCW) radar system (Chirp Sequence radar) with an antenna array is already proved to be one of the most suitable solutions [1]. Based on the thousands of reflection points detected within one single measurement cycle, this radar system has an ability of environment perception at a high-resolution level.

In the field of environment modelling with high-resolution data, one of the common methods is occupancy grid mapping, which is originally known from probabilistic robotics [2, 3]. In this method, the environment is divided into a pattern of uniform grid cells, after which the detection points are filled into the corresponding grid cells. Instead of the points, the grid cells are tracked over time and hence the measurement noise and uncertainties are eliminated. At the same time, the probability of each grid cell being occupied is computed. This method is sufficient to model the static environment, because the reflection points from the static objects are detected at the same physical location in continuous measurement cycles and thus a stable occupancy grid map is achieved.

Based on the occupancy grid map, the free space zone can be recognized. For the vehicle trajectory planning, the free space shall be estimated as precisely as possible, otherwise a collision with obstacles nearby may occur, especially after an evasive maneuver [4].

The paper is organized as follows: Sect. 2 presents the state of the art in terms of the occupancy grid mapping and free space detection. Section 3 explains the used radar sensor and data preparation tasks like the coordinate system. In Sect. 4, an approach of the occupancy grid mapping with the single front high-resolution radar data is first described. Then, in Sect. 5, the occupancy grid map with multiple, complementarily fused radar sensors is introduced. Based on the occupancy grid map, the algorithms required to detect the free space zone are presented in Sect. 6. Finally, a short summary for this paper with future perspectives is given.

2 Related Work

In this section, the works related to the occupancy grid mapping and free space detection are described.

2.1 Bayes' Theorem

Based on the Bayes' theorem, the new data in the current measurement cycle are combined with the previous data during the mapping of occupancy grid, in order to calculate the *a posteriori probability* over maps given the data: $p(m|R_{1:t}, V_{1:t})$, where m is the grid map, $R_{1:t}$ is the set of sensor measurement data from the time 1 to t, and $V_{1:t}$ the set of the vehicle position data from the time 1 to t.

$$\ell_t = \log \frac{p(m|R_{1:t}, V_{1:t})}{1 - p(m|R_{1:t}, V_{1:t})} \tag{1}$$

The log odds ratio of the a posteriori probability ℓ_t in the Eq. (1) can be computed as following

$$\ell_t = \ell_{t-1} + \log \frac{p(m|R_t, V_t)}{1 - p(m|R_t, V_t)} - \ell_o, \tag{2}$$

where $p(m|R_t, V_t)$ represents the *detection probability* processing the sensor data R_t and vehicle data V_t of the current measurement. The log odds ratio of the detection probability before processing any measurements ℓ_o is typically assumed as 0, since nothing is known about the surrounding environment before the first measurement.

2.2 Occupancy Grid Mapping

The occupancy grid mapping is previously implemented with the LiDAR sensor [5] and the camera sensor [6]. With an advanced forward inverse sensor model, the reflection data from LiDAR sensor are converted to the occupancy probability, which is used as the detection probability in the Bayes' theorem [7]. If the LiDAR sensor detects an object, the grid cell, where the target is located, is recognized as occupied (see Fig. 1). Between the occupied grid cell and LiDAR sensor, the grid cells within a certain radial distance to the LiDAR sensor are labelled as free. The occupancy probability of the grid cells over the distance threshold is computed with a linear function of the distance between the grid cells and the target. The grid cells (grey in Fig. 1) without any measurement information are marked as unknown.

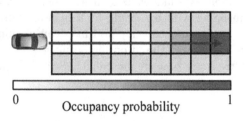

Fig. 1. LiDAR sensor model.

Since the radar sensors can sense objects behind obstacles, a different sensor model is needed for the computation of the occupancy probability. In [8], Degerman et al. extract the Signal-to-noise ratio (SNR) and compute the detection probability together with the Swerling 1 model. Using a static radar, Clarke et al. calculate the occupancy probability as a function of the reflection power, the Fast Fourier Transform (FFT) bin number of the range, as well as the bearing [9]. Werber et al. utilize the information about the Radar Cross Section (RCS) to develop an amplitude-based approach with occupancy grid mapping [10]. Considering the different properties and modulations of the radar sensors, a general radar sensor model can be created by converting the reflection strength of the detection points into the occupancy probability.

Since the previous automotive radar sensors can only provide rather few reflection data mostly on the object-level, the occupancy grid map is often created from multiple measurements in a limited area with the Simultaneous Localization and Mapping (SLAM) algorithm. Combining all the measurements, an occupancy grid map of the whole measured area is built, which helps to locate the vehicle position. The grid map is also used to classify the stored objects on the cell-level [11]. However, this approach is not applicable for the occupancy grid mapping in the scope of real-time measurements.

2.3 Free Space Detection

Based on the occupancy grid map, the free space detection function is already developed in some previous works with the LiDAR and camera sensor.

With the LiDAR sensor model, the free space is defined as a function of the distance between the sensor and the target [12]. The further works focus on the road border recognition with the classification ability in terms of the camera sensor data [13, 14]. Konrad et al. present an approach for road course estimation using a multi-layer laser scanner [15]. Lundquist et al. create a curve fitting method to detect the road boundary on the motorway [16]. Schreier et al. develop a parametric free space map, which describes a B-spline contour of arbitrarily shaped outer free space boundaries around the ego vehicle with additional attributes of the boundary type [17]. In a complex vehicle environment, a large number of the curve parameters have to be estimated.

Due to noise and uncertainty in the radar-specific data, the created occupancy grid map needs to be adapted accordingly before free space detection. A free space model focusing on the area along the future vehicle trajectory shall be developed, because the radar detections can only cover a limited area.

3 Measurement Setup and Data Preparation

A developed high performance radar system is installed in the test vehicle and the measurement data are recorded. The vehicle motion model is simulated with the vehicle dynamic data from the Controller Area Network (CAN) bus. The coordinate systems of the vehicle and the grid map are adapted with each other.

3.1 Radar Sensor

A 77 GHz FMCW experimental high performance radar system is developed and mounted at the front of the vehicle (see Fig. 2). A Chirp Sequence modulation with bandwidth $B = 2.4$ GHz, observation cycle time $T = 50$ ms and a 16 channel receive antenna array is applied.

The measured raw data dimensions are 4096 samples, 1024 ramps and 16 channels. A Field-Programmable Gate Array (FPGA) development board is used to realize the

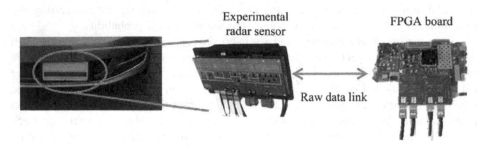

Fig. 2. Experimental radar sensor and FPGA board [18].

signal-processing algorithms. A FFT over the samples is performed to determine the distance information (range) of detection points. For radial velocity detection, a second FFT over the ramps is computed. In these two dimensions, a Chebyshev window is employed. An Ordered Statistics Constant False Alarm Rate (OS-CFAR) algorithm generates a threshold for the target extraction of the calculated two-dimensional range-Doppler spectrum. The targets above the threshold level are processed and their directions (angle of arrival) are calculated with a Deterministic Maximum Likelihood (DML) algorithm.

A velocity threshold is set to select the relevant target points from the static environment. The range and angle of the reflection points in the radar polar coordinate system are converted to $x_{r,i}$ and $y_{r,i}$ in the Cartesian coordinate system. The middle of the vehicle rear axle is defined as the origin point of the coordinate system. The reflection amplitude $A_{r,i}$ of each point is computed with the signal-processing algorithm above. Thus, the information of reflection points R_t at the time t can be represented by

$$R_t = \left[x_{r,i}, y_{r,i}, A_{r,i}, t\right]^T, i \in 1 \ldots N, \tag{3}$$

where N is the number of the reflection points.

3.2   Vehicle Motion Model

Figure 3 shows the vehicle coordinate system defined by ISO 8855:2011. From the CAN-Bus, the vehicle dynamic data like velocity v, acceleration a and turn rate $\dot{\varphi}$ are recorded. The ego vehicle motion is calculated based on the Constant Turn Rate and Acceleration (CTRA) model [19] by

$$\begin{bmatrix} \dot{x} \\ \dot{y} \\ \dot{v} \\ \dot{\varphi} \end{bmatrix} = \begin{bmatrix} v \cdot cos(\varphi) \\ v \cdot sin(\varphi) \\ a \\ \dot{\varphi} \end{bmatrix}. \tag{4}$$

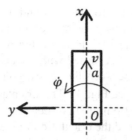

Fig. 3. Vehicle motion model.

By integrating Eq. (4), the ego vehicle position is calculated and presented by

$$V_t = [x_v, y_v, \varphi_v, t]^T. \tag{5}$$

Based on the ego vehicle position, the grid map is tracked.

3.3 Grid Map Coordinate System

Generally, the coordinate system of the occupancy grid map can be defined by two methods:

(1) Ground-fixed coordinate system. The ego vehicle moves in this coordinate system at different points. This method is suitable for the measurement at limited place, like parking lot, otherwise a large grid map is recommended to ensure the ego vehicle is always in the map.

(2) Vehicle-fixed coordinate system. The grid map is shifted and rotated to keep the origin point staying at the middle point of the vehicle rear axle. However, undesirable offsets appear during the shift and rotation. After the movement of the ego vehicle, one single grid cell in the past map may occupy several new grid cells in the shifted and rotated map, which makes the grid map unstable or inaccurate.

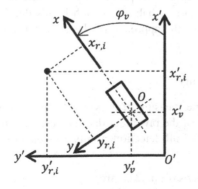

Fig. 4. Grid map coordinate system.

To model and visualize the environment around the vehicle in any places, the grid map coordinate system needs to move with the ego vehicle like in method 2. Meanwhile, some modifications are applied to solve the offset problem. According to the vehicle position, the grid map is just shifted with integer rows and columns in x- and y-direction. The rest differences between the origin point of the grid map and the ego position x'_v and y'_v are retained (see Fig. 4). The orientation of the grid map is fixed by using the ego vehicle direction from the first measurement. During the vehicle motion the grid map is not rotated, instead the orientation of the ego vehicle φ_v is saved. These values are used to update the points in the coordinate system of the grid map. With this method, the grid map is shifted in such a way, that no offset is caused during tracking grid map with the vehicle motion.

The length and width of the whole grid map are adapted with the detection range of the radar sensor. The size of a single grid cell is comparable with the resolution of the radar sensor.

The coordinates of the radar detection points in the coordinate system of the ego vehicle are converted into the grid map coordinate system by

$$\begin{bmatrix} x'_{r,i} \\ y'_{r,i} \end{bmatrix} = \begin{bmatrix} cos\varphi_v & -sin\varphi_v \\ sin\varphi_v & cos\varphi_v \end{bmatrix} \begin{bmatrix} x_{r,i} \\ y_{r,i} \end{bmatrix} + \begin{bmatrix} x'_v \\ y'_v \end{bmatrix}. \tag{6}$$

4 Occupancy Grid Mapping

Depending on the position, the radar reflection points are assigned to the corresponding grid cells. In each time step, the occupancy grid is updated considering the current measured value by the radar sensor and the previous values of the grid. This leads to reduced measurement uncertainties and errors, since the real obstacles are typically detected in continuous measure cycles and mapped in the same grid cells over time.

The reflection strength of every new point is converted into a normalized value. Combining the values of all points in one single cell, the detection probability in the cell is calculated. In each cycle, this probability is computed and combined with each other to gain the a posteriori probability, which builds the final valid occupancy grid map. In the following part, the approach of the detection probability and a posteriori probability is introduced.

4.1 Detection Probability

In Fig. 5, an image of one measurement cycle at a parking spot is shown; its corresponding bird's-eye view of the raw radar data is presented in Fig. 6. In the next parts, the reflection amplitudes of all detection points are converted to the detection probability in each grid cell.

Free-Space Loss Compensation. The free-space loss describes the decrease of the power density during the propagation of electromagnetic waves in free space according to the distance law, without taking additional attenuating factors (e.g. rain or fog) into

Fig. 5. Image of real scenario at a parking spot [20].

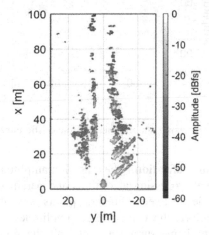

Fig. 6. Bird's-eye view of radar reflection points [20].

account. The reflection amplitude is weakened with the increasing distance to the radar sensor.

In order to make the reflection strength and the converted detection probability of the obstacles independent of the distance, the free-space loss is compensated. The relationship between the reflection amplitude and the radial distance of the points is given in the Eq. (7). The amplitudes of all points are converted to the equivalent value $A_{r,i}^N$ at a reference distance d^N to the radar sensor.

$$A_{r,i}^N = A_{r,i} - 40 log_{10} \left(\frac{d'_{r,i}}{d^N} \right) \tag{7}$$

with $d'_{r,i} = \sqrt{{x'_{r,i}}^2 + {y'_{r,i}}^2}$

Antenna Gain Compensation. The reflection amplitudes of the points are additionally influenced by the angle between the target and the radar sensor, which is related to the antenna gain. The different antenna gain pattern is compensated, to achieve a reflection amplitude that is independent of the angle of arrival. In order to know the relationship between the amplitude and the angle of the reflection point, a corner reflector is placed at the same distance but with different angles to the radar sensor and the reflection amplitudes of the reflector at different angles are measured (see Fig. 7). With this antenna pattern, the amplitudes of all points are converted to an isotropic value that eliminates any angular dependency.

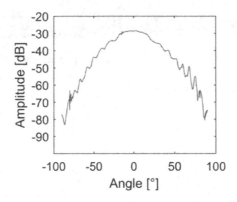

Fig. 7. Antenna gain empirical characteristic curve [20].

Reflection Amplitude Normalization. The reflection amplitude is a relative value and varies with different signal-processing algorithms and parameters. However, the relationship of the amplitudes between different points always presents the relative reflection strength. Therefore, the compensated amplitude is normalized to a value between 0 and 1. For each measurement cycle, all the points are sorted by their amplitudes (see Fig. 8).

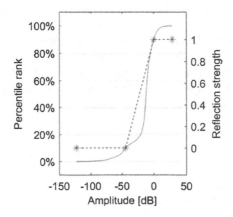

Fig. 8. Distribution and normalization of reflection amplitude [20].

If the maximum amplitude value is set to 1 for the reflection strength and the minimum amplitude value to 0, an unsuitable scale is applied, since some points have an extreme value. Due to this, the 10% maximum value is normalized to 1 and the 10% minimum value to 0. The reflection amplitude between them is converted according to a linear function to the value. Thus, the reflection strength of all points is normalized (see Fig. 9).

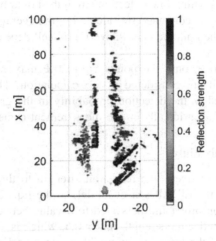

Fig. 9. Normalized reflection amplitude [20].

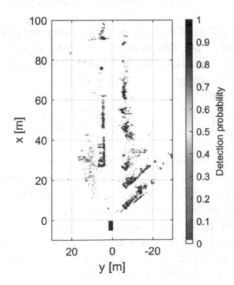

Fig. 10. Detection probability (ego vehicle is near origin point) [20].

Detection Probability in Single Grid Cell. After the compensation and normalization of the reflection amplitude, the points are allocated into the grid cells. Each grid cell can be occupied by several points with different reflection strength. The detection probability in one single grid cell can be calculated with the reflection strength of all points or the point number in this grid cell. In the grid cell, some points with a high reflection strength are detected from one object, while some points with a low reflection strength are reflected from another object nearby because of the antenna side lobes. The influence of those points with a low reflection strength should be ignored; otherwise, a low detection probability is computed by calculating the average reflection strength in one grid cell. Besides, the point number in every grid cell depends strongly on the size of the grid cell.

For the reasons above, only the points with 20% maximum reflection strength values in each grid cell are considered in the calculation. Their average reflection strength value is defined as the detection probability in the grid cell. In Fig. 10, the detection probability of all grid cells in one measurement cycle is depicted.

4.2 A Posteriori Probability

The radar sensor model converts the reflection strength to the detection probability, which is different from the LiDAR sensor model, so the Eq. (2) is modified.

At first, the detection probability is scaled to a value between 0.5 and 1 with the Eq. (8); otherwise, the reflection strength under 0.5, which is also from the obstacles, leads to the reduction of the log odds ratio of the a posteriori probability.

$$p'(m|R_t, V_t) = 0.5 + 0.5 * p(m|R_t, V_t) \tag{8}$$

However, with the scaling of the detection probability, the a posteriori probability is increased every time when the data from the new measurement cycle are calculated. This problem is solved by the degradation factor k. Then, the log odds ratio of the a posteriori probability is computed with the equation

$$\ell_t = k * \ell_{t-1} + log \frac{p'(m|R_t, V_t)}{1 - p'(m|R_t, V_t)}. \tag{9}$$

With the movement of the ego vehicle, the grid cells with the value of occupancy probability are shifted. Thus, each grid cell holds the detection probability based on the radar data in the current cycle and the occupancy probability in the previous cycles. The previous radar data should have less influence on the final occupancy probability than the new data. With the degradation factor k, the log odds ratio of the occupancy probability ℓ_{t-1} is reduced with respect to time. Therefore, in each cycle, the value of occupancy probability in the grid cells is reduced with the degradation factor at first and then increased with the current detection probability.

The log odds ratio ℓ_t in the grid cell is normalized to the value between 0 and 1, which indicates the a posteriori occupancy probability. The maximum and minimum limits are decided with a prognosis method: an object is located in one grid cell and detected with the same detection probability p_{th} in every cycle. After n measurement cycles, the grid cell is assumed to be 100% occupied. The current log odds ratio value is set to be upper limit $\ell_{th,max}$, which is represented by value 1 of the a posteriori probability. $\ell_{th,max}$ can be calculated by

$$\ell_{th,max} = \sum_{i=1}^{n} k^{i-1} * log\frac{P_{th}}{1 - P_{th}}. \tag{10}$$

In the following m cycles, no point with any reflection is detected in this grid cell. The grid cell is assumed to be free again. The current log odds ratio value is defined as the lower limit $\ell_{th,min}$, which is represented by value 0 for the a posteriori probability. $\ell_{th,min}$ can be calculated by

$$\ell_{th,min} = \ell_{th,max} * k^m. \tag{11}$$

The log odds ratio between the upper and lower limits is converted to the value between 0 and 1. In Fig. 11, the change curve of the occupancy probability with the measurement cycle in the prognosis ($p_{th} = 0.9, n = m = 10$) is shown. In the 10th cycle, the occupancy probability reaches the maximum value, then decreases and appears in the 20th cycle at the minimum.

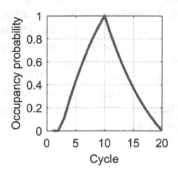

Fig. 11. Change curve of occupancy probability in prognosis [20].

4.3   Results

The a posteriori probability stands for the final occupancy probability in each cycle. In Fig. 12, the occupancy grid map from the measurement at a parking spot is shown, where several trucks and vans are parked (see Fig. 5). In the occupancy grid map, the contours of the trucks are recognized, although they are parked close to each other. The occupancy probability in the area of trucks is almost 1 and the grid cells between them have an occupancy probability of 0. This occupancy grid map represents correctly the static environment.

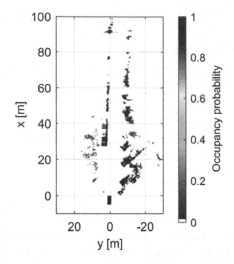

Fig. 12. Occupancy grid map at a parking spot [20].

4.4   Amplitude Grid Mapping

The amplitude grid mapping is another common method to map the grid, which normalizes the maximum value of reflection amplitude over time in every grid cell into the occupancy probability. In Fig. 13, an example of the amplitude grid mapping is shown. In contrast to the occupancy grid mapping, the measurement noise is not filtered and presented in the grid map, since only the maximum value is considered and the duration cycle of the measurement value is ignored. Because of the measurement noise, in some existing free space a high occupancy probability is computed, which disturbs the free space detection. Therefore, the approach mentioned previously in Sects. 4.1 and 4.2 is used in the following parts.

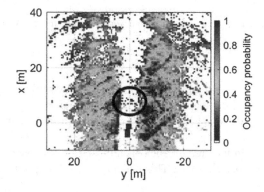

Fig. 13. Example for amplitude grid mapping [20].

5 Occupancy Grid Map Fusion

In order to extend the Field of View (FoV), three high-resolution radars are mounted around the vehicle. After introduction of the radar sensor setup, the occupancy grid mapping processed with the data from all three radars is presented. By using the above-mentioned method, a stable grid map with a large FoV is achieved.

5.1 Sensor Setup

The radar sensor mounted in the center of the front spoiler (represented by FC radar, see Fig. 2) holds an azimuth aperture of approximately ±50°. That means, the most detection points are located in front of the vehicle but the surroundings on both sides cannot be perceived very well. More radar sensors are needed for the extension of sensing areas.

Due to the lack of installation space at the left side of the vehicle, where the wiper fluid reservoir and the exhaust pipe are located, two additional radar sensors are consequently mounted at the front right corner (represented by FR radar) and at the rear right corner (represented by RR radar) of the vehicle, respectively (see Fig. 14). The sensors installation position and orientation are described in the vehicle coordinate system (see Fig. 3), e.g. $(x_{FR}, y_{FR}, \varphi_{FR})$ for the FR radar.

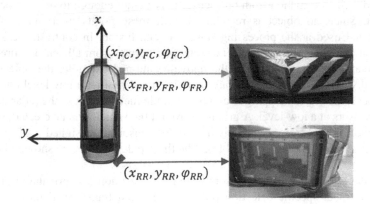

Fig. 14. Three radar sensors mounted around the vehicle (the front center radar is already shown in Fig. 2).

5.2 Data Fusion

The three radar sensors can detect different reflection points in their own FoV, which overlap partly with each other (see Fig. 15). For a simultaneous and synchronized processing and storage of the data from the individual radar sensor, a data fusion between them is required.

Depending on the processing stage at which the fusion is performed, the sensor data fusion can be categorized into low-level and high-level. The data fusion at a high-level

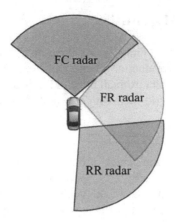

Fig. 15. FoV of three radar sensors.

means that the detections and their information from each radar sensor are first separately preprocessed to an object-level. Then, the objects from different sensors are merged and fused together. A high-level data fusion is time-efficient but some information is lost or ignored undesirably during the preprocessing before data fusion. For example, when an object only reflects few points in the FoV of each sensor, these points and their information from one sensor may be not enough to be preprocessed to an object. Since no object is recognized with these points, their data cannot be delivered and used at the processing stage for data fusion. In contrast, the low-level data fusion combines the raw data (i.e. detection points) from all sensors directly and then generates fused raw data. In the above-mentioned example, the object can be recognized with the fused data that are more informative after a low-level data fusion.

The occupancy grid mapping is a rather suitable method to fuse the radar data from different sensors at a low-level. A grid map around the vehicle can be created, where all the reflection points from each individual radar sensor are assigned. In Fig. 16, the single-shot reflection points detected from the three radar sensors are shown in different colors.

With the knowledge of the sensors installation position and orientation, the locations of the radar-specific detection points can be first transformed into the vehicle coordinate system by Eq. (12) and then into a common grid map coordinate system by Eq. (6). After that, they are assigned to the corresponding grid cells.

$$\begin{bmatrix} x_{r,i} \\ y_{r,i} \end{bmatrix} = \begin{bmatrix} cos\varphi_j & -sin\varphi_j \\ sin\varphi_j & cos\varphi_j \end{bmatrix} \begin{bmatrix} x_{ra,i} \\ y_{ra,i} \end{bmatrix} + \begin{bmatrix} x_j \\ x_j \end{bmatrix}, j \in (FC, FR, RR) \qquad (12)$$

where $x_{ra,i}$ and $y_{ra,i}$ are the coordinates of a detection point in the coordinate system of radar sensor.

By taking the assigned points with a high reflection strength for each single grid cell into account, the detection probability is calculated and the occupancy grid map is built by the methods mentioned previously in Sects. 4.1 and 4.2.

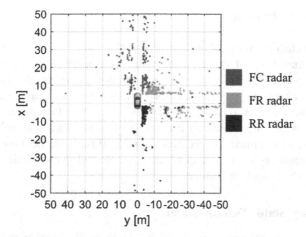

Fig. 16. Detection points from the three radar sensors (instantaneous, single-shot record).

5.3 Results

The occupancy grid map from the measurement in a street with several crossings is shown in Fig. 17. With data fusion between the three radar sensors, the street contours in front and right side of the vehicle are clearly visible in the grid map. The grid cells in the area of roadway have an occupancy probability of 0. The measurement results show that the detection of crossings, roadway boundaries and free space driving zones can be well recognized by using the occupancy grid map with the fused high-resolution radars.

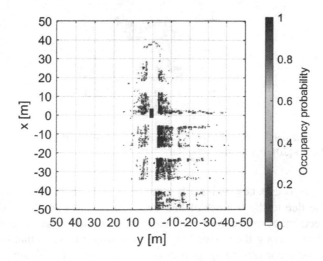

Fig. 17. Occupancy grid map in a street with several crossings.

6 Free Space Detection

The free space detection in the whole area around the vehicle is not achievable, because no data are captured out of the detection range and aperture of the radar sensor or behind some larger obstacles. For the vehicle motion planning, the Field of Interest (FoI) is the area along the possible trajectory. At first, the occupancy status in all grid cells is determined in order to create a binary grid map. With the clustering method, the occupied areas, which are caused by constant and strong reflection points from measurement errors, are defined as free space again. Based on the border recognition algorithm, the boundary of the occupied areas is detected, which realizes a free space detection along the vehicle trajectory.

6.1 Occupancy Status Determination

Before detecting the free space, it should be determined, whether the grid cells are occupied or not. The easiest way is to use a constant threshold of the occupancy probability. The occupancy status of the grid cells is decided, so that the occupancy grid map can be converted to a binary grid map (see Fig. 18).

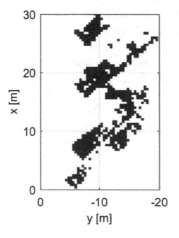

Fig. 18. Binary grid map with a threshold of occupancy probability (red: occupied grid cell, white: free grid cell) [20]. (Color figure online)

However, the occupancy status of some grid cells has a mismatch with the respective value due to the features of the radar sensor and the OS-CFAR algorithm. From one object, many reflection points are detected and assigned to different grid cells. Some points among them have low refection amplitudes, so that the occupancy probability of their corresponding grid cells is close to zero. Those grid cells are detected as free space, which actually belong to the obstacles. Here two methods are developed, in order to recognize the grid cells belonging to the obstacles but with a low occupancy probability as occupied.

(1) The grid cells with an occupancy probability lower than the threshold are considered. The amount of the grid cells in the neighborhood, which have a much higher occupancy probability than the selected grid cell, is calculated (see grid cells N in Fig. 19, image on the left). If this amount is larger than a threshold, the selected grid cell (grid cell C in Fig. 19) is set as occupied. Using this method, the grid cells with a lower occupancy probability in the inside and border area of obstacles are recognized as occupied.

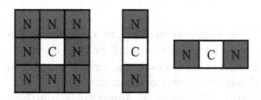

Fig. 19. Neighboring grid cells (C: center grid cell. N: neighboring grid cell).

(2) The grid cells with zero occupancy probability are handled. If the two "sandwiched" grid cells (see grid cells N in Fig. 19, middle and right) have a high occupancy probability and are declared as occupied, the selected grid cell is set to be occupied. Thus, especially the grid cells with zero occupancy probability in the inside area of obstacles are detected as occupied.

Using the methods above, the occupancy status of all grid cells can be determined. An example of the results is shown in Fig. 20.

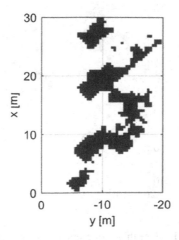

Fig. 20. Processed binary grid map [20].

6.2   Clustering Binary Grid Cells

With the occupancy grid mapping, the random measurement noise is filtered. However, some reflection points are caused by the strong objects nearby or the measurement errors. In the binary grid map, the points usually occupy some areas with small size outside the obstacles, which are named as outliers. Using the threshold of the connected occupied area size, the outliers are filtered.

In order to calculate the size of the connected occupied areas, it is necessary to group the binary grid cells at first. Three popular clustering algorithms are discussed here:

(1)   K-Means [21]. The partitions of the grid cells are divided into a predefined number of clusters in which each grid cell belongs to the cluster with the nearest mean. Since the environment around the vehicle changes all the time, it is not efficient to predefine the number of clusters.

(2)   Density-Based Spatial Clustering of Applications with Noise (DBSCAN) [22]. The grid cells are grouped together and classified into core, border and noise grid cells depending on the number of occupied neighboring grid cells. The noise grid cells here are recognized as outliers. In order to filter the noise grid cells precisely, a relative low distance threshold between the grid cells and a relative high threshold of the grid cell number is selected. However, the calculation time is very long, because it is a quadratic function of the grid cell number in the worst case.

(3)   Connected component labelling (CCL) [23, 24]. The connected occupied grid cells in binary grid map is detected and clustered. It is not necessary to predefine any parameters. Moreover, it takes significantly less computational burden than DBSCAN. For this reason, CCL is chosen as the clustering algorithm here.

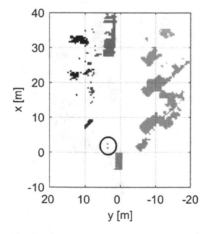

Fig. 21. Clustering with CCL algorithm (different colors represent different clusters) [20]. (Color figure online)

The number of the grid cells in each cluster is calculated. With a number threshold, the outliers are found and the grid cells from the outlines are marked as free again.

This processing step is meaningful, because some outliners are located directly in front of the vehicle, where belongs to the FoI. In Fig. 21, an example of the clustering result with CCL algorithm is demonstrated. The grid cells in the black circle are clustered and then defined as free again.

6.3 Border Recognition

The boundaries of the clustered and occupied binary grid cells are mostly relevant for the free space detection. The Moore-Neighbor Tracing (MNT) algorithm is introduced here to recognize the border of the occupied areas [25]. In Fig. 22, the MNT algorithm is described. Starting from a random occupied grid cell B1, the next occupied neighboring grid cell in the clockwise direction B2 is searched. The iteration loop terminates when the initial grid cell is visited for a second time.

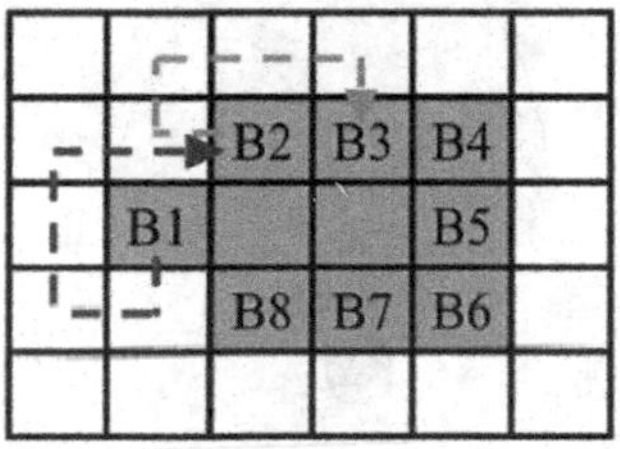

Fig. 22. MNT Algorithm (B: border grid cell).

All reached grid cells are labelled as border grid cells, which helps to detect the free space along the trajectory. In Fig. 23, an example of the border recognition result is shown.

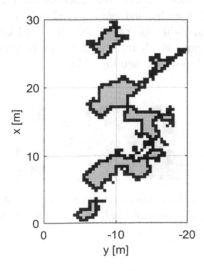

Fig. 23. Border recognition (black: border grid cell, grey: occupied grid cell) [20].

6.4   Interval-Based Free Space Model

The free space along the vehicle trajectory is defined by the narrowest distance between the vehicle future possible position and the border of the occupied areas.

At first, the trajectory of the ego vehicle is calculated with the current dynamic data based on the CTRA model, where the vehicle positions and orientations along the trajectory are computed. It is also possible to calculate the vehicle trajectory with any maneuvers. The vehicle trajectory is defined as baseline and extended with a certain distance considering the orientation at each position to an area, which is similar to a sector and defines the FoI along the trajectory (see Fig. 24).

Fig. 24. FoI and intervals along the trajectory.

Thereafter the FoI is divided into intervals with a certain length along the trajectory. The interval is always perpendicular to the vehicle orientation at each point. The length of one single interval is defined as a function of the vehicle velocity, because a wider free space is needed with increasing velocity.

In order to realize the interval-based free space model, the grid cells, in which the vehicle positions in the FoI are located, are selected to be the baseline grid cells. The grid cells on the left and right side of the baseline grid cells are visited with the Bresenham's line algorithm, which is located in the perpendicular direction to the vehicle orientation at each position (see Fig. 25).

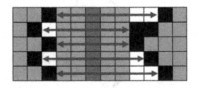

Fig. 25. Free space detection in one interval (blue: baseline grid cell, green: free space grid cell, black: border grid cell, grey: occupied grid cell). (Color figure online)

The occupied grid cell with the smallest distance to each baseline grid cell is searched. Then this distance is defined as the width of the free space interval. The grid cells in the interval, which are closer to the baseline grid cells, are labelled as free space. Similarly, the width of all the intervals can be calculated, so that the free space along the vehicle trajectory is detected.

6.5 Results

In Fig. 26, an example of the free space detection at the parking spot is shown. On the left side in front of the vehicle, more free space exists than on the right side, which means, the evasive trajectory to left is more feasible than right. Furthermore, the parking slots between the trucks are recognized as free space, which helps to generate the parking maneuver.

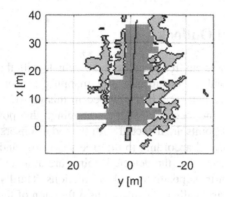

Fig. 26. Example for free space detection [20].

In Figs. 27 and 28, another example on the public road is shown. There are several warning posts at the left side of the road, which are separately detected as obstacles in the map. The distance between the warning posts is recognized as free space.

Fig. 27. Image for measurement on public road [20].

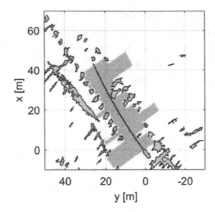

Fig. 28. Free space detection on public road [20].

7 Conclusion and Outlook

In order to model the static environment around a vehicle with the high-resolution radar sensors, an approach with an occupancy grid mapping concept and a thereof determined free driving space detection is developed in this paper.

As input data for the occupancy grid mapping, the positions and reflection amplitudes of the target points are detected with the radar sensors. Firstly, the reflection amplitudes are compensated according to the free-space loss and antenna pattern gain, and then normalized. Secondly, the detected points are assigned to the corresponding grid cells depending on their positions and orientations. Thirdly, the detection probability in the individual grid cells is calculated as a function of the reflection strength of the detection points. Fourthly, the value of the grid cells is degraded during the movement of the ego vehicle and then combined with new measurement data to compute the a posteriori occupancy probability. Finally, an occupancy grid map is created and updated over the course of time. Meanwhile, the occupancy grid map is utilized for the data fusion between three radar sensors.

Thereafter, the occupancy grid map is converted to a binary grid map. In addition, the grid cells in the obstacle areas are labelled as occupied depending on the neighboring grid cells status. In order to eliminate the outliers, the connected occupied grid cells are clustered using the CCL algorithm. Through the MNT algorithm, the border of the clustered, occupied grid cells is recognized. Finally, an interval-based free space driving zone is detected based on the Bresenham's line algorithm. The determined free space and the detected roadside obstacles, as elaborated in this paper, match perfectly with the real world scene in which the car drives.

In future works, it is planned to include the height information of radar detections also in the occupancy grid mapping. This requires, of course, that the high-resolution radar sensor is further developed to be able to estimate both azimuth and elevation angles. Further applications of the occupancy grid map, such as vehicle localization and SLAM, can also be developed.

Acknowledgements. This work has received funding from the European Community's Eighth Framework Program (Horizon2020) under grant agreement no. 634149 for the PROSPECT project and funding from the German Federal Ministry for Economic Affairs and Energy (BMWi) for the iFUSE project. The PROSPECT and iFUSE consortium members express their gratitude for selecting and supporting these two projects.

References

1. Meinl, F., Stolz, M., Kunert, M., Blume, H.: An experimental high performance radar system for highly automated driving. In: IEEE MTT-S International Conference on Microwaves for Intelligent Mobility (ICMIM), Nagoya, pp. 71–74. IEEE (2017). https://doi.org/10.1109/icmim.2017.7918859
2. Moravec, H., Elfes, A.: High resolution maps from wide angle sonar. In: Proceedings of IEEE International Conference on Robotics and Automation, St. Louis, pp. 116–121. IEEE (1985). https://doi.org/10.1109/robot.1985.1087316
3. Elfes, A.: Using occupancy grids for mobile robot perception and navigation. Comput. **22** (6), 46–57 (1989). https://doi.org/10.1109/2.30720
4. Mouhagir, H., Cherfaoui, V., Talj, R., Aioun, F., Guillemard, F.: Using evidential occupancy grid for vehicle trajectory planning under uncertainty with tentacles. In: IEEE 20th International Conference on Intelligent Transportation Systems (ITSC), Yokohama, pp. 1–7. IEEE (2017). https://doi.org/10.1109/itsc.2017.8317808
5. Weiss, T., Schiele, B., Dietmayer, K.: Robust driving path detection in urban and highway scenarios using a laser scanner and online occupancy grids. In: IEEE Intelligent Vehicles Symposium (IV), Istanbul, pp. 184–189. IEEE (2007). https://doi.org/10.1109/ivs.2007.4290112
6. Badino, H., Mester, R., Vaudrey, T., Franke, U., Daimler AG: Stereo-Based free space computation in complex traffic scenarios. In: IEEE Southwest Symposium on Image Analysis and Interpretation (SSIAI), Santa Fe, pp. 189–192. IEEE (2008). https://doi.org/10.1109/ssiai.2008.4512317
7. Nuss, D.: A random finite set approach for dynamic occupancy grid maps. Ph.D. thesis, University of Ulm, Ulm (2017). https://doi.org/10.18725/oparu-4361
8. Degerman, J., Pernstål, T., Alenljung, K.: 3D occupancy grid mapping using statistical radar models. In: IEEE Intelligent Vehicles Symposium (IV), Gothenburg, pp. 902–908. IEEE (2016). https://doi.org/10.1109/ivs.2016.7535495
9. Clarke, B., Worrall, S., Brooker, G., Nebot, E.: Sensor modelling for radar-based occupancy mapping. In: IEEE/RSJ International Conference on Intelligent Robots and Systems (IROS), Vilamoura, pp. 3047–3054. IEEE (2012). https://doi.org/10.1109/iros.2012.6386255
10. Werber, K., et al.: Automotive radar gridmap representations. In: IEEE MTT-S International Conference on Microwaves for Intelligent Mobility (ICMIM), Heidelberg, pp. 1–4. IEEE (2015). https://doi.org/10.1109/icmim.2015.7117922
11. Lombacher, J., Laudt, K., Hahn, M., Dickmann, J., Wöhler, C.: Semantic radar grids. In: IEEE Intelligent Vehicles Symposium (IV), Los Angeles, pp. 1170–1175. IEEE (2017). https://doi.org/10.1109/ivs.2017.7995871
12. Homm, F., Kaempchen, N., Ota, J., Burschka, D.: Efficient occupancy grid computation on the GPU with LiDAR and radar for road boundary detection. In: IEEE Intelligent Vehicles Symposium (IV), San Diego, pp. 1006–1013. IEEE (2010). https://doi.org/10.1109/ivs.2010.5548091

13. Badino, H., Franke, U., Mester, R.: Free space computation using stochastic occupancy grids and dynamic programming. In: International Conference on Computer Vision (ICCV), Workshop on Dynamical Vision, Rio de Janeiro. IEEE (2007)
14. Andrew, B., Isard, M. (eds.): Active Contours: The Application of Techniques From Graphics Vision Control Theory and Statistics to Visual Tracking of Shapes in Motion. Springer, London (1998). https://doi.org/10.1007/978-1-4471-1555-7
15. Konrad, M., Szczot, M., Dietmayer, K.: Road course estimation in occupancy grids. In: IEEE Intelligent Vehicles Symposium (IV), San Diego, pp. 412–417. IEEE (2010). https://doi.org/10.1109/ivs.2010.5548041
16. Lundquist, C., Schön, T.B., Orguner, U.: Estimation of the free space in front of a moving vehicle. In: Proceedings of the SAE World Congress and Exhibition. Detroit, SAE International (2009)
17. Schreier, M., Willert, V., Adamy, J.: Compact representation of dynamic driving environments for ADAS by parametric free space and dynamic object maps. IEEE Trans. Intell. Transp. Syst. **17**(2), 367–384 (2016). https://doi.org/10.1109/TITS.2015.2472965
18. Li, M.: High-Resolution radar based environment perception and maneuver planning. In: CTI Symposium on Automated Driving, Future Mobility and Digitalization (ADFD). Hannover, Euroforum (2017)
19. Stellet, J.E., Straub, F., Schumacher, J., Branz, W., Zöllner, J.M.: Estimating the process noise variance for vehicle motion models. In: IEEE 18th International Conference on Intelligent Transportation Systems (ITSC), Las Palmas, pp. 1512–1519. IEEE (2015). https://doi.org/10.1109/itsc.2015.212
20. Li, M., Feng, Z., Stolz, M., Kunert, M., Henze, R., Küçükay F.: High resolution radar-based occupancy grid mapping and free space detection. In: Proceedings of the 4th International Conference on Vehicle Technology and Intelligent Transport Systems (VEHITS), Funchal, pp. 70–81. SciTePress (2018). https://doi.org/10.5220/0006667300700081
21. Lloyd, S.: Least squares quantization in PCM. IEEE Trans. Inf. Theory **28**(2), 129–137 (1982). https://doi.org/10.1109/TIT.1982.1056489
22. Ester, M., Kriegel, H.P., Sander, J., Xu, X.: A density-based algorithm for discovering clusters in large spatial databases with noise. In: Proceedings of the Second International Conference on Knowledge Discovery and Data Mining, Portland, pp. 226–331. AAAI Press (1996)
23. Rosenfeld, A., Pfaltz, J.L.: Sequential operations in digital picture processing. J. ACM **13**(4), 471–494 (1999). https://doi.org/10.1145/321356.321357
24. He, L., Chao, Y., Suzuki, K.: A run-based two-scan labeling algorithm. IEEE Trans. Image Process. **17**(5), 749–756 (2008). https://doi.org/10.1109/TIP.2008.919369
25. Gonzalez, R.C., Woods, R.E., Eddins, S.L.: Digital Image Processing Using MATLAB. Pearson Prentice Hall, Lexington (2004)

Real-Time Overtaking Vehicle Detection Based on Optical Flow and Convolutional Neural Network

Lu-Ting Wu[1], Van Luan Tran[1], and Huei-Yung Lin[1,2(✉)]

[1] Department of Electrical Engineering, National Chung Cheng University,
168 University Road, Chiayi 621, Taiwan
b10013108@yuntech.edu.tw, tranvanluan07118@gmail.com, lin@ee.ccu.edu.tw
[2] Advanced Institute of Manufacturing with High-Tech Innovation,
National Chung Cheng University, 168 University Road, Chiayi 621, Taiwan

Abstract. For the development of driver assistance systems, overtaking detection plays an important role in commercial vehicle applications. In this paper, we present a real-time overtaking vehicle detection system using a monocular camera mounted in the rear of a vehicle. It aims to assist the drivers or self-driving cars to perform safe lane change operations. In the proposed method, the possible overtaking vehicles are first located based on motion cues. The candidates are then identified using Convolutional Neural Network (CNN) and tracked for behavior analysis in a short period of time. We present an algorithm to solve the issue of repetitive patterns which is commonly appeared in highway driving. A series of experiments are carried out with real scene video sequences recorded by a dashcam. The objective is to detect other vehicles passing by so as to alert the driver and avoid the potential traffic accidents. The performance evaluation has demonstrated the effectiveness of the proposed technique.

Keywords: Overtaking vehicle detection · Optical flow · CNN

1 Introduction

Nowadays, most vehicles move at high speed, particularly on highways. Moving vehicles at high speed creates the convenience of shortening the travel time. However, the danger of potential traffic accidents can be exacerbated by the road users. Thus, the development of driver assistance systems is a necessity in today's safety trend. The driver assistance system will also be a significant part of the fully autonomous vehicles. They are commonly used to improve the traffic safety, efficiency, and keep away from potential traffic accidents. For examples, lane departure warning system (LDWS), forward collision warning system (FCWS), and lane change assistance (LCA) are some typical applications of ADAS. At the present, many high-end vehicles are equipped with ADAS directly from the

© Springer Nature Switzerland AG 2019
B. Donnellan et al. (Eds.): SMARTGREENS 2018/VEHITS 2018, CCIS 992, pp. 227–243, 2019.
https://doi.org/10.1007/978-3-030-26633-2_11

original manufacturer. Some traffic recorders in the after-market such as Mobileye 660 [17] and Papago P3 [20] are also equipped with various ADAS functions [17]. The driving recorder or dashcam not only record the traffic conditions but also assist the driver to acquire the traffic information [5]. The main objective is to provide a safe and comfort driving experience.

There are many kinds of sensor used in advanced driving assistance systems such as radar, lidar, and visual sensor, etc. Among them, the imaging technology using visual sensor has the greatest progress potential in recent years. The visual sensors become cheaper and lighter than ever before. They can provide rich sensing information of the environment and therefore are used to design more functions for driving assistance. Some examples include vehicle identification [14], traffic sign recognition [16,23], forward collision warning [12], parking assistance [7], vehicle speed detection [13], and other applications. In the past few years, image processing speed is also greatly improved because of the use of graphics processor unit (GPU). The progress of this hardware makes the image processing task rapid and more suitable for advanced driving assistance systems.

Overtaking vehicle detection is an integral part of a driver assistance system, which plays an important role in the driving environment [1]. Because of the unsafe situations that are likely to be caused by overtaking, effective side monitoring with rapid detection of vehicles is important. One of the most important applications related to overtaking is blind spot monitoring, where rear-view cameras are often used. Vehicle drivers usually assess the surrounding traffic before changing lanes, and make turns after checking their rear view and side mirrors. However, even for those who follow the standard procedure, the blind-zone of vehicles is still a source of danger and often the cause of serious accidents. The blind-zone of a vehicle can be described as "an area around the vehicle that cannot be seen directly by the driver by looking forwards or by using any of the vehicles standard rear-view mirrors (internal and external) from the normal sitting position" [8]. According to Taiwan Area National Freeway Bureau [18], the main cause of major traffic accidents in the state roads was the result of "improper lane changes" followed by "not paying attentions to the state in front of the vehicle".

In this paper, we propose a real-time system to detect overtaking vehicles based on Lucas-Kanade optical flow algorithm for continuously tracking, and deep convolutional neural network (CNN) to classify, identify the segmented area of vehicles and remove the repetitive patterns. Our system uses a dashcam installed in the rear of the vehicle to detect the blind-zone of the overtaking vehicles. It is able to provide the necessary information for the driver about the situation in advance to avoid the car accident due to an improper turn or lane change. In this work, our experiments contain image sequences acquired from a variety of scenes during day and night. To reduce the cost, a monocular camera is used as the primary sensor. It is also a common approach to analyze the traffic condition using a camera system.

The rest of this paper is organized as follows. Section 2 describes some recent research. Section 3 presents our method for overtaking vehicles detection.

The implementation and experimental results are provided in Sect. 4, followed by the conclusion of this work in Sect. 5.

2 Related Work

In recent years, many general vehicle detection techniques are investigated in the literature and developed for the driver assistance systems. For related work, we mainly survey the vision based approaches for vehicle overtaking and blind-zone detection. The camera system for image acquisition is commonly installed in the front, rear, or sides of the vehicle. For the camera mounted in the front, the overtaking detection is based on the vehicle's motion cues. The advantage of using motion cues is the computation speed. It can still lead to good results even when the vehicle is only partially visible due to occlusion or limited field of view of the camera. Thus, a more complete and continuous trajectory can be obtained. It is, however, easy to be affected by noise and generates erroneous results.

For vehicle overtaking detection, Hultqvistet et al. [9] and Chen et al. [4] proposed efficiency detection algorithms using optical flow. Their approaches have a single camera placed in the front of the vehicle. The proposed solution makes use of optical flow evaluated along lines parallel to the motion of the overtaking vehicles. The optical flow is computed by tracking features along these lines. Based on these features, the position of the overtaking vehicle can also be estimated. As a result, they cannot notify the driver about the occurrence of overtaking in advance. Alonso et al. [2] presented a blind-zone overtaking vehicle detection system using optical flow with the cameras installed below the side-view mirror. Wu et al. [24] proposed an embedded blind-zone security system with a camera mounted below the side-view mirror. First, they detect the low-level features such as shadows, edges and headlights to locate the vehicle, followed by vehicle tracking and behavior analysis. The cameras below the side-view mirror can detect overtaking vehicles better than others in the blind-zone. However, this technique requires a pair of cameras which are installed in per external rear mirror and the functions of the cameras are limited compared to other approaches.

In blind-zone detection, some solutions were proposed with a camera mounted in the rear of the vehicle to detect the overtaking in the blind-zone. It is not only used to inform the driver in advance, but also used by other advanced driving assistance functions. For example, the parking collision avoidance system can use the rear camera to detect the obstacles in the back to avoid collision. Dooley et al. [6] installed a fisheye camera in the rear of the vehicle, and used the AdaBoost classification technique and two wheel detection methods to identify the blind-zone vehicles. The vehicles were then tracked by the optical flow technique. The limitation of the AdaBoost method becomes obvious as vehicles moving toward the image border when coming near from the rear in an over-taking maneuver. Ramirez et al. [21] installed cameras in the front and the rear of the vehicle. They used deformable part model (DPM) [19] to combine optical flow with the mobile information to detect the overtaking vehicles. According to their experimental results, combining these two methods is able to increase the accuracy of the detection compared to the use of only an appearance detector.

3   Proposed Method

In this section, we present our main architecture. It contains (1) pre-processing and segmentation, (2) convolutional neural network, (3) repetitive pattern removal, and (4) tracking and behavior detection, as illustrated in Fig. 1. We use a monocular camera mounted in the rear of a vehicle to detect the overtaking and assist the driver to change lanes. The monocular camera is installed at the height of about 1 m from the ground.

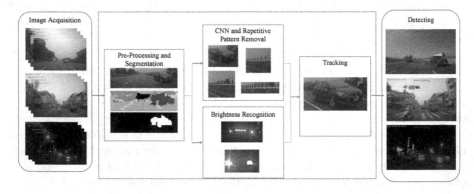

Fig. 1. The system flowchart of the proposed overtaking detection technique. It consists of three basic modules: (1) pre-processing and segmentation, (2) convolutional neural network and repetitive pattern removal, and (3) tracking and behavior detection.

3.1   Pre-processing and Segmentation

In order to increase the operating speed of the system, we usually use only about a half size of the original image by removing unnecessary regions such as the sky, buildings or traffic signs located in the upper part of the image. Thus, the region of interest (ROI) is first defined before performing the image segmentation algorithm. To obtain the motion clues in an image, the settings on the tracking points are very important. Chen *et al.* [4] use Canny edge detection to extract the edges in the image, and then use the optical flow to calculate the edges of the motion clues. Ramirezet *et al.* [21] detect the strong corners, and then use the optical flow to calculate the corners of the motion clues. Although using edges or corners as tracking features can derive more robust results, it may increase the amount of extra computations. Furthermore, it is hard for us to determine the number of tracking feature when the image is complicated, which will also cause the uncertainty of computation time.

To avoid the above problems, we set a fixed number of tracking point in a fixed location. First, we set a tracking point per 10×10 pixels in an ROI. Second, we use the pyramid model of Lucas-Kanade optical flow [15] to calculate the optical flow information of the tracking points. Third, according to the direction and measurement of the tracking output, we divide it into five different categories: (i) road and sky, (ii) land marking, (iii) overtaking vehicle, (iv) object further away, (v) uncertain region.

When a vehicle is moving forward, there will be a large amount of optical flow around the vehicle. However, the image of road and sky is relatively smooth, and the optical flow is small. Therefore, if the optical flow of a feature point is very small, we can assign the point to the road and sky region. If the optical flow in the y-direction is very large and moves to the vanishing point, then the point is assigned to the land marking. The points are considered as a part of the overtaking vehicle if the optical flow in the x-direction is large and moves further away from the vanishing point. Otherwise, if the optical flow in the x-direction is large and moves towards the vanishing point, it indicates that some object is moving further away. These conditions are illustrated in Fig. 2. We use the uncertain region to conclude the situations which do not belong to any of the above criteria.

Here we only use the x-direction of the optical flow to distinguish the overtaking vehicle from the object moving further away, and discard the y-direction

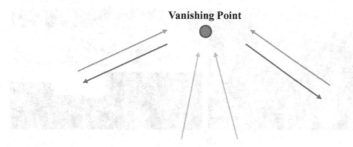

Vanishing Point

Fig. 2. Directional classification diagram. The yellow lines represent the land marking. The blue lines illustrate the objects (vehicles) approaching from the sides. The pink lines illustrate the objects (vehicles) moving further away. (Color figure online)

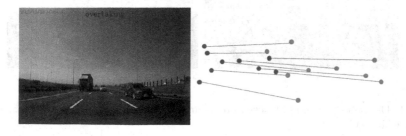

Fig. 3. The optical flow in the x-direction.

of the optical flow. The main reason is that the y-direction of the optical flow in two adjacent frames is very small, and the approaching vehicle will be deformed (see Fig. 3). Thus, it is difficult to use the y-direction optical flow to distinguish the direction of the object motion.

An overtaking vehicles is continually approaching, so the space correlation between two vehicles is used to filter out the noise. We accumulate every tracking point of the approaching object to a grayscale image and binarize it. Then, a 10×10 mask is used to dilate each tracking point, to make a connection between the points, with small connection areas filtered out. An illustration of these rules is shown in Fig. 4(a). The left is the original image, the upper right is the result of a single frame, and the bottom right is the binarized result from multiple frames.

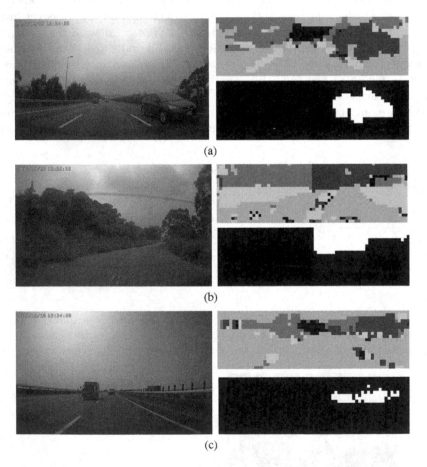

(a)

(b)

(c)

Fig. 4. The accumulation of tracked points and image segmentation used to detect the approaching vehicles.

When a vehicle makes turns or there are repetitive patterns in the image, the segmentation results might not be correct, as illustrated in Figs. 4(b) and (c). In the urban area, there are a variety of curved roads. This makes the vehicle move in a more complicated way, so the optical flow of the rear objects and background will be away from the vanishing point. Another common problem is the repetitive patterns in the images. When a vehicle is in fast motion, another image point close to the original image point might be identified as the original image point. With this continuous appearance, a repetitive pattern will be generated and false targets will be tracked by the optical flow algorithm. Since the repetitive patterns usually appear for a period of time in the same image region, it is difficult to filter out the wrong features using the spatio-temporal correlation of the image pixels. Figure 5 shows some repetitive patterns commonly seen in Taiwan's highway and local road. To deal with this problem, we use convolutional neural network to identify the segmented area and remove the non-vehicle objects to avoid the false segmentation to produce false positives.

3.2 Lucas-Kanade Optical Flow

In the Lukas-Kanade optical flow method [15], we consider the images from the camera change over time, and the image can be treated as a function of time:

Fig. 5. Common repetitive patterns in Taiwan street scenes.

$I(t)$. At time t and the pixel at (x, y), the brightness can be expressed by

$$I(x, y, t)$$

In this way, the image is viewed as a function of position and time. Its range is the brightness of the pixels in the image. Now, we consider a fixed space point whose coordinates at time t, the pixel at (x, y). When the camera is moving, the image coordinates change. We calculate the location of this space point in the image at other times. The pixel brightness value of the same spatial point is fixed in each image. For the pixel at (x, y) at time t, we assume that when $t + dt$ it moves to $(x + dx, y + dy)dt$. Because the brightness does not change, we will have

$$I(x + dx, y + dy, t + dt) = I(x, y, t) \tag{1}$$

The constant brightness is a strong assumption, and very likely it is not true in the actual situation. For example, because of the difference in the material of the object, pixels will have high brightness or shaded parts; Sometimes the camera automatically adjusts the exposure parameters to make the image overall darker or brighter. The assumption of constant brightness at these times is untenable. Therefore, the result of optical flow is not always reliable. However, we hereby believe that this assumption holds.

Applying Taylor expansion on Eq. (1), the optical flow constraint equation can be expressed in the form of

$$I(x + dx, y + dy, t + dt) \approx I(x, y, t) + \frac{\partial I}{\partial x}dx + \frac{\partial I}{\partial y}dy + \frac{\partial I}{\partial t}dt \tag{2}$$

Since we assume that the brightness is constant, the brightness at the next time does not change, and

$$\frac{\partial I}{\partial x}\frac{dx}{dt} + \frac{\partial I}{\partial y}\frac{dy}{dt} = -\frac{\partial I}{\partial t} \tag{3}$$

where dx/dt is the speed of the pixel moving in the x-axis and dy/dt is the speed in the y-axis, which are represented by u and v, respectively. At the same time, $\partial I/\partial x$ is the image gradient in the x-direction, and the other is the gradient in the y-direction, denoted as I_x and I_y, respectively. The change in the brightness of the image with respect to time is recorded as I_t. Thus, Eq. (3) can be written in the matrix form as

$$\begin{bmatrix} I_x & I_y \end{bmatrix} \begin{bmatrix} u \\ v \end{bmatrix} = -I_t \tag{4}$$

One needs to calculate the pixel's motion u and v, but it is a linear equation with two variables. Therefore, additional constraints must be drawn to calculate u, v. In the LK optical flow, it is assumed that the pixels in a certain window have the same motion.

Consider a window of size $w \times w$ with w^2 pixels. Since we assume that the pixels in this window have the same motion, we have a total of w^2 equations:

$$\begin{bmatrix} I_x & I_y \end{bmatrix}_k \begin{bmatrix} u \\ v \end{bmatrix} = -I_{tk}, \qquad k = 1, \ldots, w^2 \tag{5}$$

Denote

$$A = \begin{bmatrix} [I_x, I_y]_1 \\ \vdots \\ [I_x, I_y]_k \end{bmatrix}, b = \begin{bmatrix} [I_{t1}] \\ \vdots \\ [I_{tk}] \end{bmatrix} \tag{6}$$

So the equation is rewritten as

$$A \begin{bmatrix} u \\ v \end{bmatrix} = -b \tag{7}$$

This is an over-determined linear equation about u, v. The traditional solution is to minimize the least squared error, thus

$$\begin{bmatrix} u \\ v \end{bmatrix}^* = -(A^T A)^{-1} A^T b \tag{8}$$

In this way, we can derive the pixel moving speed in the image u, v, where t takes the discrete time. Thus, the position of a certain pixel can be calculated accordingly.

3.3   Convolutional Neural Network

The convolutional neural network architecture used in this work is CaffeNet [3]. It is a replication of the model described in the AlexNet [11] but with some differences. This network was originally designed to classify 1.2 million high-resolution images in the ImageNet LSVRC-2010 contest to 1000 different classes. The neural network, which has 60 million parameters and 650,000 neurons, consists of five convolutional layers, some of which are followed by max-pooling layers, and three fully-connected layers with a final 1000-way softmax. We performed fine-tuning using our data in BVLC CaffeNet model and changed the output to 6 categories.

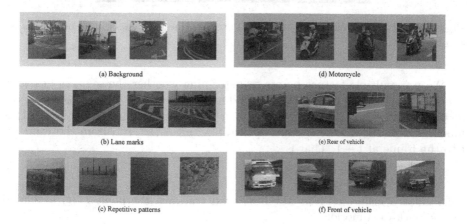

(a) Background

(b) Lane marks

(c) Repetitive patterns

(d) Motorcycle

(e) Rear of vehicle

(f) Front of vehicle

Fig. 6. Some sample images in the training data used in this work.

It contains "front of vehicle", "rear of vehicle", "motorcycle", "repetitive patterns", "background" and "lane markings". Some of the images are shown in Fig. 6. The images are segmented by the algorithm described in Sect. 3.1. The deep learning framework, Caffe [10], is used to train and evaluate the neural network. We added CaffeNet to our system to identify the segmented area and remove the non-vehicle objects.

3.4   Repetitive Pattern Removal

In some situations, wrong segmentation, especially when the algorithm is confused with a vehicle on the opposite lane, the segmentation and CNN identification are erroneous at the same time. This kind of error is due to the feature points of the optical flow tracking on the repetitive pattern, but the CNN recognizes it as the vehicle in the opposite lane. One such example is shown in Fig. 7. To overcome this problem, we consider the case that a moving vehicle is in the opposite lane and the repeated pattern occurs due to the separation poles. As shown in Fig. 8, they make the optical flow disorder, resulting in forward and backward optical flow inconsistency.

Fig. 7. The use of segmentation and CNN at the same time can still be erroneous for repetitive patterns.

We use multiple feature points to determine whether the segmented region contains repetitive patterns. First, "good features to track" is used to detect the feature point $F(t)$ on the frame at time t [22]. Then, its succeeding $F(t + 1)$ is found by referring to the forward optical flow $o_t^+ = (u^+, v^+)$ from the frame at t to the frame at $t + 1$. That is,

$$F(t + 1) = F(t) + o_t^+(F(t))$$

Similarly, generated from the backward tracking, the point $F'(t)$ is related by the backward motion,

$$F'(t) = F'(t + 1) + o_{t+1}^-(F'(t + 1))$$

Fig. 8. An illustration of messy optical flow when repetitive patterns occur.

where $o_{t+1}^{-} = (u^{-}, v^{-})$ is the backward optical flow from the frame at $t + 1$ to the frame at t.

Ideally, if the feature point $F(t)$ does not belong to a repetitive pattern and the optical flow is correctly estimated, then we have

$$F(t) - F'(t) = 0$$

However, from our experience, there are some errors in the real situations, i.e.,

$$F(t) - F'(t) \leq \varepsilon$$

where ε is the error between $F(t)$ and $F'(t)$, and is very small. If most of the feature points on the target are smaller than ε, we will classify this object as a vehicle. Otherwise, it is classified as a repetitive pattern and thus eliminated.

3.5   Tracking and Behavior Detection

After the segmentation using CNN and the repetitive pattern removal, we track the object until it is disappeared in the image or there is no overtaking. Continue the previous step of "repetitive pattern removal" and the detection of feature points, we use Lucas-Kanade optical flow for continuously tracking in order to

- detect the movement of objects for a period of time,
- overcome the shape, size and scale of the object changes as it approaches the camera,
- get the operation speed quickly,
- have a more complete trajectory which can be provided at the edge or part of the field.

A tracking result is shown in Fig. 9.

We expect that CNN is able to identify and remove the repetitive patterns, and have the correct overtaking detection. However, the camera resolution is

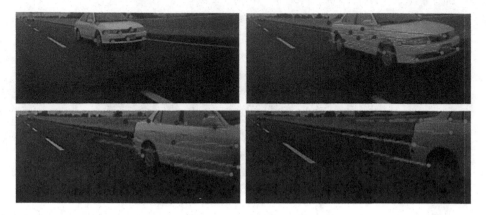

Fig. 9. Overtaking tracking diagram. The red point is the initial position, and the green point is the current position. The blue line is the corresponding line. (Color figure online)

too low, and the image segmentation is not good enough for identification due to some errors. To further reduce the false detection, we assess whether the direction of tracking has continued to stay away from the vanishing point for a period of time to help us effectively remove the wrong detection.

3.6   Night Time

In general, the appearance of the vehicle at night cannot be clearly obtained from the camera because the brightness of the image is too low. The camera usually captures the information of the headlights. If only the brightness is used to grab the headlights, it can be easily disturbed by other background lights. Furthermore, the headlights of the vehicles in the sides do not have the symmetry property, which makes the overtaking detection at night a difficult issue.

We present a method that uses motion cues to combine the brightness information to capture the overtaking vehicles. The steps of overtaking detection at night includes: (1) pre-processing and segmentation, (2) brightness recognition, (3) tracking, and (4) behavior detection. First, we use ROIs to remove

Fig. 10. Overtaking vehicle detection and tracking at night using the headlights.

the image regions which are not important. Second, the headlight areas are segmented when they approach the vehicle by the algorithm described in Sect. 3.1. Figure 10 shows a typical result. Third, the low brightness areas are removed by binarization. Finally, we track the brightness region and analyze its behavior by the method given in Sect. 3.5. If it continues to keep away from the vanishing point, it is considered as the headlights of an overtaking vehicle.

4   Implementation and Experimental Results

To evaluate the performance of our overtaking detection method in the real world scenarios, we use a dashcam to capture the dynamic images. Our dashcam is installed in the rear of the vehicle at about 1 m about ground. The original image size is 1200 × 800, and the sub-image region for process is 600 × 200. We test our algorithms on a PC with ubuntu 16.04 operating system, 4.0 GHz Intel CPU, and NVIDIA GTX 1080 GPU. The execution time is divided into three parts and tabulated in Table 1.

Table 1. The execution time for individual stages of the algorithm.

	Segmentation	CNN	Repetitive pattern removal	Total time
Time	6 ms	3 ms	1 ms	6–10 ms

Table 2. The experimental results and performance evaluation.

Scene	True overtakes	Detected	Missed	False
City traffic	102	102	0	13
Highway	79	79	0	1
At night road	42	37	5	4

There are totally 7,587 images collected in our training data with 6 categories. We segment objects and manually label each image. There are 808 lane markings, 470 motorcycles, 2405 repetitive patterns, and 1301 rear of vehicle, 1385 front of vehicle, and 1218 background. The image sequences are segmented using the algorithm described in Sect. 3.1. Similarly, the validation data of 2770 images are collected from 80-min video sequence and marked manually. The recognition results for each category are tabulated in Table 3.

It is not easy to evaluate the accuracy and efficiency of the real image sequence at the present time. In particular, the algorithms for detecting vehicles by motion cues do not have a good benchmark for performance evaluation. There are totally 50 image sequences collected in our database. It contains 20 highway image sequences, 15 city image sequences and 15 night image sequences. Each image sequence is about two minutes long. If we detect the vehicle before it is

Table 3. The recognition results for each category and the recall.

	BG	LM	MC	RP	FV	RV
Groundtruth	375	252	545	408	480	710
Background (BG)	322	1	2	0	1	11
Land marking (LM)	2	249	0	2	0	0
Motorcycle (MC)	0	0	524	1	0	0
Repetitive pattern (RP)	25	2	0	405	0	3
Front of vehicle (FV)	13	0	16	0	470	34
Rear of vehicle (RV)	13	0	3	0	9	662
Recall	0.858	0.988	0.961	0.992	0.979	0.932

disappeared in the image sequence, the overtaking detection is successful. Otherwise, it is called missed. It is considered as failed if the approaching vehicle is not detected. The evaluation is tabulated in Table 2 and some overtaking vehicle detection result images are shown in Figs. 11, 12 and 13, which are respectively tested in a city traffic, highway, and on a night road in the city traffic.

In our vehicle recognition module, it does not matter if the overtaking is identified or not since a subsequent tracking stage will be performed. However, a false alarm will occur if the vehicle makes turns with another behind. In this case, the other vehicle is too close behind and it is recognized as overtaking as shown in Fig. 14.

Because of the vehicle motion and the dynamic change of the scene, the development of onboard camera systems is not a trivial task in terms of the operation efficiency and result accuracy. The image sequence is constantly blurred due to the rapid movement of the vehicle, which introduces unwanted artifacts when the overtaking vehicles approach the camera. Furthermore, the limited field of

Fig. 11. Results of testing in a city traffic.

Fig. 12. Results of testing on a highway.

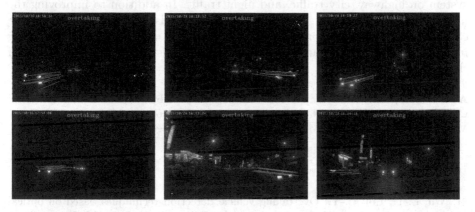

Fig. 13. Results of testing on a night road in the city traffic.

(a)   (b)

Fig. 14. The false alarm might happen if the vehicle makes turns with another behind, that is too close behind.

view of the camera poses additional challenges on vehicle tracking. The vehicle detection is generally more difficult in the urban areas and at night. In the urban areas, the environment is complicated and the vehicles will have various kinds of behavior to respond to. At night, in additional to the complex environment, the image sequences also contain less information due to the illumination condition. In most situations, the feature used for the detection of overtaking vehicles is only the headlights.

5 Conclusions

This paper has proposed a real-time system to detect overtaking and assist in driving lane change based on visual cues from a dashcam. We use the motion cues based on Lucas-Kanade optical flow and combine with CNN to detect the vehicle appearance while removing the repetitive patterns. Compared to the low-order features and weak classifier, our approach is faster and more robust. It is not susceptible to light and complex environments. We successfully tested our system on highway, city traffic, and night traffic. In addition to improving the limitation and shortcomings of the existing methods, the proposed technique can maintain the operation efficiency and provide more complete overtaking information. The performance evaluation has demonstrated the effectiveness of the proposed techniques.

Acknowledgments. The support of this work in part by Create Electronic Optical Co., LTD, Taiwan and the Ministry of Science and Technology of Taiwan under Grant MOST 104-2221-E-194-058-MY2, is gratefully acknowledged.

References

1. Wu, L.-T., Lin, H.-Y.: Overtaking vehicle detection techniques based on optical flow and convolutional neural network. In: Proceedings of the 4th International Conference on Vehicle Technology and Intelligent Transport Systems, pp. 133–140 (2018)
2. Alonso, J.D., Vidal, E.R., Rotter, A., Muhlenberg, M.: Lane-change decision aid system based on motion-driven vehicle tracking. IEEE Trans. Veh. Technol. **57**(5), 2736–2746 (2008)
3. BVLC. https://github.com/BVLC/caffe/tree/master/models. Accessed Oct 2017
4. Chen, Y., Wu, Q.: Moving vehicle detection based on optical flow estimation of edge. In: 2015 11th International Conference on Natural Computation (ICNC), pp. 754–758 (2015)
5. Dai, J.M., Liu, T.A.J., Lin, H.Y.: Road surface detection and recognition for route recommendation. In: 2017 IEEE Intelligent Vehicles Symposium (IV), pp. 121–126 (2017)
6. Dooley, D., McGinley, B., Hughes, C., Kilmartin, L., Jones, E., Glavin, M.: A blind-zone detection method using a rear-mounted fisheye camera with combination of vehicle detection methods. IEEE Trans. Intell. Transp. Syst. **17**(1), 264–278 (2016)
7. Fernandez-Llorca, D., Garcia-Daza, I., Martinez-Hellin, A., Alvarez-Pardo, S., Sotelo, M.A.: Parking assistance system for leaving perpendicular parking lots: experiments in daytime/nighttime conditions. IEEE Intell. Transp. Syst. Mag. **6**(2), 57–68 (2014)

8. Hughes, C., Glavin, M., Jones, E., Denny, P.: Wide-angle camera technology for automotive applications: a review. IET Intell. Transp. Syst. **3**(1), 19–31 (2009)
9. Hultqvist, D., Roll, J., Svensson, F., Dahlin, J., Schn, T.B.: Detecting and positioning overtaking vehicles using 1d optical flow. In: 2014 IEEE Intelligent Vehicles Symposium Proceedings, pp. 861–866 (2014)
10. Jia, Y., et al.: Caffe: convolutional architecture for fast feature embedding. In: Proceedings of the 22nd ACM International Conference on Multimedia, MM 2014, pp. 675–678. ACM, New York (2014)
11. Krizhevsky, A., Sutskever, I., Hinton, G.E.: ImageNet classification with deep convolutional neural networks. In: Proceedings of the 25th International Conference on Neural Information Processing Systems, NIPS 2012, pp. 1097–1105. Curran Associates Inc., USA (2012)
12. Lin, H.Y., Chen, L.Q., Lin, Y.H., Yu, M.S.: Lane departure and front collision warning using a single camera. In: 2012 International Symposium on Intelligent Signal Processing and Communications Systems, pp. 64–69 (2012)
13. Lin, H.-Y., Li, K.-J., Chang, C.-H.: Vehicle speed detection from a single motion blurred image. Image Vision Comput. **26**(10), 1327–1337 (2008)
14. Liu, X., Liu, W., Mei, T., Ma, H.: A deep learning-based approach to progressive vehicle re-identification for urban surveillance. In: Leibe, B., Matas, J., Sebe, N., Welling, M. (eds.) ECCV 2016. LNCS, vol. 9906, pp. 869–884. Springer, Cham (2016). https://doi.org/10.1007/978-3-319-46475-6_53
15. Lucas, B.D., Kanade, T.: An iterative image registration technique with an application to stereo vision. In: Proceedings of the 7th International Joint Conference on Artificial Intelligence, IJ-CAI 1981, vol. 2, pp. 674–679. Morgan Kaufmann Publishers Inc., San Francisco (1981)
16. Luo, H., Yang, Y., Tong, B., Wu, F., Fan, B.: Traffic sign recognition using a multi-task convolutional neural network. IEEE Trans. Intell. Transp. Syst. **99**, 1–12 (2017)
17. Mobileye: Mobileye 660. http://www.mobileye.com/. Accessed Oct 2017
18. MOTC: Taiwan Area National Freeway Bureau. http://www.freeway.gov.tw/. Accessed Oct 2017
19. Pandey, M., Lazebnik, S.: Scene recognition and weakly supervised object localization with deformable part-based models. In: 2011 International Conference on Computer Vision, pp. 1307–1314 (2011)
20. Papago: Papago P3. http://www.papago.com.tw/. Accessed Oct 2017
21. Ramirez, A., Ohn-Bar, E., Trivedi, M.: Integrating motion and appearance for overtaking vehicle detection. In: 2014 IEEE Intelligent Vehicles Symposium Proceedings, pp. 96–101 (2014)
22. Shi, J., Tomasi, C.: Good features to track. In: 1994 Proceedings of IEEE Conference on Computer Vision and Pattern Recognition, pp. 593–600 (1994)
23. Shi, J.-H., Lin, H.-Y.: A vision system for traffic sign detection and recognition. In: 2017 IEEE International Symposium on Industrial Electronics, pp. 1596–1601 (2017)
24. Wu, B.F., Kao, C.C., Li, Y.F., Tsai, M.Y.: A real-time embedded blind spot safety assistance system. Int. J. Veh. Technol. **2012**, 1–15 (2012)

Evaluation of Iterative Calibration of Vehicle Cameras Using Reference Information from Traffic Signs

Alexander Hanel[✉] and Uwe Stilla

Photogrammetry and Remote Sensing, Technical University of Munich,
Arcisstrasse 21, 80333 Munich, Germany
{alexander.hanel,stilla}@tum.de

Abstract. Intrinsic camera parameters can be estimated by camera calibration using multiple images of a priori known reference points on a test field. In particular during driving, vehicle cameras might be exposed to mechanical and thermal effects, leading to a change of these parameters over time and making iterative camera calibration useful to correct for these changes. As on roads no special test fields are available, reference information has to be extracted from road scene images. In this contribution, a method for iterative calibration of a vehicle camera using references on traffic signs is proposed. The references are obtained from the shape of traffic signs detected in road scene images, exploiting that the shape is known a priori. A test with a road scene image sequence acquired during a test drive in a car park equipped with traffic signs shows no decrease in the standard deviation of the parameters iteratively estimated with the proposed method compared to test field calibration.

Keywords: Advanced driver assistance systems · Camera calibration · Self-calibration · Convolutional neural network · Image processing

1 Calibration of Vehicle Cameras

Many advanced driver assistance systems in modern vehicles evaluate information about the surrounding area [1], which is acquired by different types of sensors in a vehicle. Because vehicles typically move forward, the area in front of a vehicle is in particular relevant for advanced driver assistance systems. Front-looking sensors can be grouped according to their operating range, which makes them suitable for different driver assistance functions [2]: (i) Ultrasonic sensors operate in the range of a few meters in front of the vehicle and are typically used for parking assistance systems, (ii) short-range and medium-range radar sensors operate in the range up to approximately 50 m in front of the vehicle [3] and are used for intersection assistance systems, for instance, (iii) cameras and LiDAR sensors operate in the range up to 100 m and are used for pedestrian detection or traffic sign recognition, for example [4] and (iv) long-range radar

© Springer Nature Switzerland AG 2019
B. Donnellan et al. (Eds.): SMARTGREENS 2018/VEHITS 2018, CCIS 992, pp. 244–265, 2019.
https://doi.org/10.1007/978-3-030-26633-2_12

sensors have an operating range up to 250 m and can be used for adaptive cruise control systems, for instance.

Both vehicle cameras and LiDAR sensors can be used to create 3D point clouds of the vehicle surrounding. For the case of cameras, image series of the surrounding are processed by methods like structure from motion (e.g. [5]) or visual SLAM (e.g. [6]) to create 3D point clouds. According to [7], an advantage of using a camera instead of LiDAR systems being typical for the automotive sector, is the higher point density of the resulting point cloud. While 3D point clouds from a LiDAR system are always Euclidean with a metric scale, there are several possibilities for 3D point clouds from a mono camera [8,9]: (i) Point clouds are perspective, if the intrinsic camera parameters are not known, (ii) point clouds are Euclidean with scale ambiguity, if just the intrinsic camera parameters are known and (iii) point clouds are Euclidean with a metric scale, if both intrinsic camera parameters and metric scale information are known. In the last case, it is possible doing metric measurements, for example to get the distance of detected objects in the surrounding area from the vehicle.

Metric scale information can be provided by known reference information, in the case of vehicle cameras by urban structures in the surrounding area, like a known road width [10]. Intrinsic camera parameters can be estimated by camera calibration [11,12]. Intrinsic camera parameters describe the camera model and can cover parameters to describe image distortions, as well. Image distortion parameters can be distinguished according to their effects on images: radial-symmetric distortions [13], tangential distortions [13], distortions caused by affinity and skew of the imaging sensor [14] and distance-dependent distortions (e.g. [15]). In contrast to camera calibration, system calibration covers the estimation of both intrinsic and extrinsic parameters of all components of a measurement system [11]. Both camera calibration (e.g. [16]) and system calibration (e.g. [17]), the latter for example relative to a common vehicle coordinate system (e.g. [18]), are used for automotive applications based on cameras.

Camera calibration is often performed as test field calibration (e.g. [11]) or self-calibration [19], both typically using known 3D object coordinates and corresponding 2D image coordinates of multiple reference points to estimate the intrinsic parameters. Test field calibration relies on reference points on special test fields, while self-calibration relies on reference points on objects being present in the acquired scene anyway. For vehicle cameras, the distinction between static calibration with manufacturer-specific test fields in workshops and dynamic calibration by driving according to pre-defined patterns on public roads is common as well (e.g. [20]). For vehicle cameras observing the surrounding area, both test field calibration and self-calibration are used (e.g. [21–23]). Besides mobile test fields (e.g. [24]), stationary test fields painted on special test roads [22] or provided by workshop equipment (e.g. [25]) can be used. Reference points for self-calibration of vehicle cameras, in particular relevant on public roads, where typically no test fields are available, can be provided along road markings (e.g. [23,26]), for instance. In road scene images (example see Fig. 1) of front-looking vehicle cameras, road markings are typically shown in the lower half of the image, subsequently providing reference points only for the lower half, as well. According to [11], estimated intrinsic camera parameters, especially distortion parameters, are only valid for those image parts showing reference points. For other image parts, the distortion parameters might be invalid and could lead to errors in the metric scale of 3D point clouds and to errors in distance measurements subsequently. In the case of using reference points along road markings, such errors might be caused for the upper half of a road scene image from a front-looking vehicle camera. Further, if markings are not available on a road, no reference points can be provided at all. Complementary objects to road marking being present in road scenes anyway can be traffic signs to provide reference points, which would be typically shown in the upper half of road scene images of front-looking vehicle cameras and subsequently can be used to estimate intrinsic camera parameters valid for the upper half, as well. As the shape and size of traffic signs are standardized in many countries (e.g. in Ireland [27]), this a priori known information can be used to identify unique points on traffic signs, which can be used as reference points.

Fig. 1. Urban road scene image with road markings and traffic signs (bright rectangles) taken with a front-looking vehicle camera.

Special cameras made for advanced driver assistance systems (e.g. [28]) are often available in combination with software for driver assistance functions, and with no or only limited access to the acquired images. Action cameras (e.g. [29]) are a low-price alternative type of cameras providing access to the acquired images; further, their capability to run on battery and the small device size allows flexible placement of such cameras in cars, making them attractive especially for research purposes. Typical wide-angle lenses used by action cameras show larger distortions compared to normal-angle lenses, making camera calibration important for action cameras in particular.

Depending on the demanded accuracy of the estimated intrinsic camera parameters, camera calibration can be done once or iteratively. There might be time-dependent changes of the intrinsic camera parameters, which could make previously estimated parameters invalid and lead to errors in the scale of an Euclidean point cloud subsequently. For instance, auto focus or camera-internal post-processing of images can cause changes of the intrinsic camera parameters, according to [11]. Especially consumer-oriented action cameras have typically fewer settings to let the operator avoid such changes compared to more expensive and larger cameras (e.g. DSLR cameras like the Nikon D5 [30]). In addition to camera-internal aspects, there might be external effects, for example mechanical and thermal ones, with influence on the intrinsic parameters over time [31,32]. Mechanical vibrations while driving or heating of the interior of a vehicle by the sun might lead to a stronger influence of such effects on vehicle cameras compared to cameras operated in other environments. As the aforementioned internal and external effects can change the intrinsic parameters even from image to image, calibration of a vehicle camera might be desirable as often as possible, which makes the use of other reference information, like from traffic signs, in addition to road markings desirable, as well.

In this contribution, a method for iterative estimation of the intrinsic camera parameters using scale reference information extracted from traffic signs is described. According to [33], in particular scale reference information has influence on the intrinsic camera parameters.

Therefore, the main contributions of this paper are methods for

- using scale reference information from traffic signs for camera calibration,
- extracting 2D image coordinates of scale reference information typically from road scene images,
- modelling scale reference information from traffic signs for camera calibration as line segments in 3D object coordinates.

The remainder of this paper is organized as follows: In Sect. 2, the steps to extract scale reference information from from traffic signs shown in road scene images and to perform iterative camera calibration are described. In Sect. 3, the experimental setup and data used to test the proposed method are described. In Sects. 4, 5 and 6, preliminary results and the results of the camera calibration are described and discussed. In Sect. 7 the paper is concluded.

2   Initial and Iterative Camera Calibration

The pipeline (Fig. 2) of the proposed method contains an initial camera calibration step to be performed before using a vehicle camera on public roads to provide initial estimates for the intrinsic camera parameters. Example situations to do initial camera calibration are after a cameras has been mounted in a vehicle or before doing a recording drive with high-quality intrinsic camera parameters required. The pipeline further contains an iterative camera calibration step to be performed when the camera-carrying vehicle is driven on public roads to

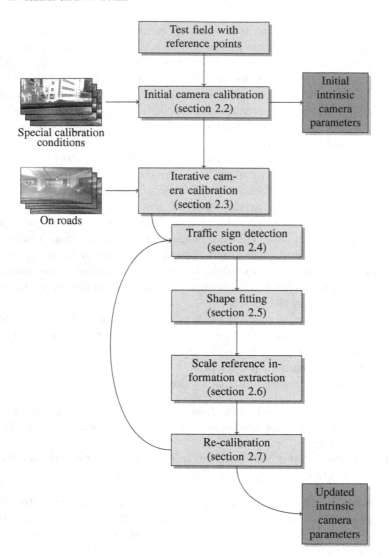

Fig. 2. Pipeline for initial camera calibration in special calibration conditions before driving and iterative camera calibration while driving on public roads.

iteratively estimate updated intrinsic camera parameters. Example situations to do iterative camera calibration are when additional reference information are available or after a fixed time interval.

2.1   Camera Model

Following [34], we propose to use a central-perspective camera model for calibration of wide-angle action cameras, which becomes valid if the camera-internal distortion correction has been applied to images of the camera to be calibrated as pre-processing step. These authors state that the correction can reduce the largest part of image distortions, leading to only small remaining distortions, which can be modelled by a central-perspective camera model. To mention additionally, these authors state that using this correction, it becomes valid to use a planar test field to provide reference points.

The intrinsic camera parameters used in this work are the x-component x_0' and the y-component y_0' of the principal point, the focal length c' and the radial-symmetric distortion parameters A_1, A_2, A_3 according to Brown's model [13]. As [34] have reported difficulties in successfully estimating decentering distortion parameters, only radial-symmetric distortion parameters are further used.

2.2   Initial Camera Calibration

We propose to use test field calibration for initial camera calibration to avoid typical problems of self-calibration leading to strong correlations between estimated orientation parameters, for example due to insufficient rotation of reference points between multiple images or incomplete coverage of the image format by reference points [11]. As initial calibration is intended to be performed in special calibration conditions before driving on public roads, it is possible to use calibration environments with stationary test fields or to place mobile test fields in the field of view of the camera, i.e. in front of a car in the case of a front-looking vehicle camera, both which can't be done while driving on public roads. Scale reference information can be provided by a known length between reference points.

Mobile test fields with reference points for camera calibration provide the flexibility to place it at different distances from the camera, take images with different viewing angles and with different rotations relative to the camera, to avoid the mentioned problems of self-calibration. This becomes important in particular, as the proposed iterative camera calibration process is a combination of test field calibration and self-calibration. From multiple images of the test field, 2D image coordinates of reference points have to be extracted. 3D object coordinates of the reference points have to be known a priori, e.g. estimated by a previous bundle adjustment [35] itself using high-quality reference information. In the later bundle adjustment to obtain initial intrinsic camera parameters, residuals between the extracted image coordiantes of the reference points and the image coordinates projected from the object coordinates using the stepwise estimated intrinsic parameters are minimized.

2.3   Iterative Camera Calibration with Scale Reference Information from Traffic Signs

As example for scale reference information, the proposed method for iterative camera calibration to provide updated intrinsic camera parameters is explained for traffic signs with a circular shape, from which the sign diameter can be used as reference information. The diameter in object coordinates can be obtained e.g. from governmental regulations (e.g. [27]); the diameter in image coordinates can be obtained by the following steps (Fig. 3; described in Sects. 2.4, 2.5, 2.6 and 2.7) applied to road scene images acquired by the camera to be calibrated. The steps described in this section can be repeated for each new road scene image provided by the camera.

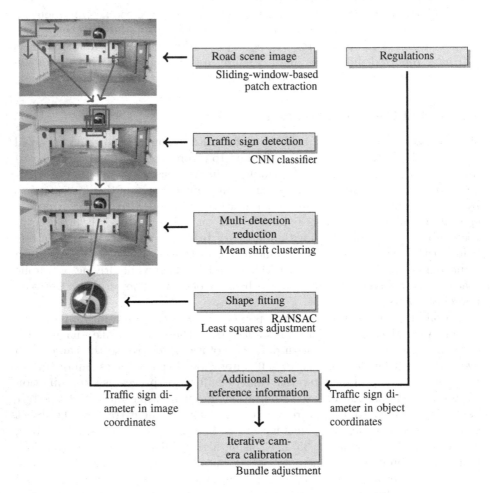

Fig. 3. Processing steps for one iteration of the iterative camera calibration. Input is a road scene image acquired by a vehicle camera, whereof additional scale reference information for camera calibration are extracted. Output are updated estimates for the intrinsic parameters obtained by bundle adjustment. A new iteration of these steps can be performed for each image captured over time when the vehicle is on the road.

In the first step, image patches (example see Fig. 4) are extracted from a road scene image, which is step-wise reduced to smaller geometric resolutions, by a sliding-window approach (Fig. 3, first image from the top). The image patches have fixed geometric and radiometric resolution, matching the input size of the neural network used for traffic sign detection in the following step.

2.4 Traffic Sign Detection with a Convolutional Neural Network

Objective of traffic sign detection is to classify each extracted image patch as either belonging to the class *traffic sign* or to the class *other objects*. The detector uses a neural network (architecture see Fig. 4) to classify an image patch, as several other authors have recently shown high detection performance of neural network-based traffic sign detectors (e.g. [36,37]). The architecture of the network used in this contribution is a modification of the Lenet-5-based [38] network proposed by [36] for traffic sign detection. The convolutional layer and the two max pooling layers are used to extract features from the input image patch and to down-sample them, the following fully-connected layers are used for classification based on these features. Softmax activation is applied to the last layer, the network therefore provides the probabilities for both classes *traffic sign* and *other objects*; image patches are assigned to the class with the higher probability. "ReLu" activation is applied to each layer to achieve non-linear activations. Dropout is applied to the last max-pooling layer during training to avoid overfitting. In post processing, a high threshold for the classification probability is applied to image patches detected as *traffic sign* to remove detections with low probability, assuming that low probability is an indicator for false positive detections. Hereby, the risk of further using image patches not showing traffic signs and subsequently extracting incorrect scale reference information should be reduced.

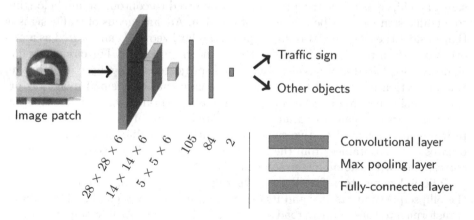

Fig. 4. Architecture of the convolutional neural network for traffic sign detection consisting of a convolutional layer, two max pooling layers and three fully-connected layers. Input is an image patch which is assigned to either the class *traffic sign* or *no traffic sign*.

If a small shift between consecutive image patches is used by the sliding window approach or the resolution of the road scene image is changed only gradually, the same traffic sign can be contained partly or completely in multiple image patches. Consequently, if several of those patches are classified as *traffic sign*, there might be multiple detections for the same real-world traffic sign (Fig. 3, second image from the top), what is supposed to occur typically for a sliding-window-based detector [39].

As the basis for the scale reference information to be extracted are image patches classified as *traffic sign*, there might be duplicate references in the case of multiple detections, which should be avoided. Therefore, mean shift clustering [40] is applied to all traffic sign detections in a road scene image to cluster multiple close detections to a single detection (Fig. 3, third image from the top). The center of the image patch describing a single detection is determined by the center of mass of all image patches in one cluster; its size is calculated by the mean size of those image patches. Hereby it is assumed that the center of mass of the detections in one cluster corresponds to the position of the real-world traffic sign in the image. As advantage of mean shift clustering, it does not require the number of clusters to be defined a priori, making it therefore usable for road scene images showing an unknown number of traffic signs.

2.5   Traffic Sign Shape Extraction

The diameter as scale reference information can be extracted in image coordinates from a geometric primitive fitted to the contour of a traffic sign shown in an image patch (Fig. 3, forth image from the top). Single patches obtained by mean shift clustering are used for this purpose. For the case of circular traffic signs, an ellipse as geometric primitive can be fitted to contour points belonging to a traffic sign to describe the shape of the sign. Advantageous of traffic signs is that besides the sign size, also the shape is standardized and can be used as a priori information to select an appropriate geometric primitive. For circular traffic signs, it is exploited that a real-world circle is projected to an ellipse in an image; this projection is assumed to be valid in the case that only small image distortions remain in a road scene image after having applied distortion-correction using the intrinsic camera parameter estimated by initial camera calibration or previous iterations of iterative camera calibration. The diameter in image coordinates can be obtained from the length of the major ellipse axis, as the length corresponds with the diameter according to [41].

The following steps for shape extraction are used to provide estimates for the ellipse position, its size and its orientation in an image patch, which can be transformed to the complete road scene image afterwards. As first step, the image patch is converted to grayscale and normalized to 8-bit value range to increase the contrast. Second, a binary image (see Fig. 5) is created by applying intensity thresholds to the grayscale image patch; some of the intensity edges remaining in the binary image are assumed to follow the contour of the traffic sign in the image patch. Third, groups of contour points along the edges (balls of different colors in Fig. 5) are extracted from the binary image patch (algorithm from [42]).

Fig. 5. Idealized visualization of a binarized image patch showing a traffic sign (black circle in the center) and a background object (black rectangle). The balls with different colors visualize separate groups of contour points along intensity edges in the binary patch. (Color figure online)

Groups with a small number of points are neglected for further processing, assuming that the traffic sign is covering large parts of the image patch, leading to a large number of points of the group corresponding to the sign contour. Forth, ellipse fitting with RANSAC [43] is used to iteratively select the largest consensus set of contour points, i.e. the contour points closer to the fitted ellipse than a distance threshold; the largest consensus set is assumed to correspond with the contour of the traffic sign in the image patch. The number of RANSAC iterations is chosen to have at least one outlier-free set of contour points used for ellipse fitting with a probability of 99%. The final ellipse parameters are estimated in a least squares adjustment using the largest consensus set.

As the quality of camera calibration relies on the quality of reference information, fitted ellipses with a possibly low quality are removed. Therefore, plausibility checks are applied, e.g. to remove image patches, in which the ellipse is not completely contained in the image patch, which might indicate an incorrect fit therefore; image patches are not considered for further steps, if the residuum from least squares adjustment between the fitted ellipse and contour points exceeds a threshold.

2.6 Extraction of Scale Reference Information from Traffic Sign Shapes

As the traffic sign diameter in image coordinates depends on the distance of the real-world traffic sign from the camera, the distance has to be known to use the diameter for camera calibration. There are several ways to obtain the distance, for example by additional vehicle sensors like a radar sensor or a second camera. When just the camera to be calibrated is available, structure-from-motion or visual SLAM can be used to generate a 3D point cloud of the road scene around the vehicle. The traffic sign can be detected in the point cloud (e.g. [44]) or image rays from the camera projection centre through the fitted shape, both in a common coordinate system with the point cloud, intersected with the point cloud, for instance. In both cases, the point cloud has to be metrically scaled (e.g. using the approach from [10]).

For camera calibration, there are different ways to model scale reference information. One way is to model it as straight line in 3D object coordinates (e.g. implemented by [45]). Both the a priori known reference length of the straight line and the length calculated from 3D object points has to be available therefore. In the case of circular traffic signs, the known sign diameter can be used as reference length. The 3D object points can be calculated from the end points of the major axis of the ellipse, whose length corresponds with the diameter, in image coordinates. Basis therefore are two 3D image rays through the camera origin and the end points; the desired 3D object coordinates are determined by the 3D position of the point along each image ray at the given distance of the sign from the camera.

2.7   Iterative Re-Calibration of the Camera

By iterative re-calibration of the camera, updated intrinsic camera parameter values are estimated by bundle adjustment using the described camera model (see Sect. 2.1). Available additional scale reference information are added as line segments to the set of reference information used already for initial camera calibration.

3   Datasets and Experiments

The neural network is trained and validated with image patches from the GTSRB dataset [46] and the GTSDB dataset [47]. The GTSRB dataset provides image patches showing centered traffic signs (Fig. 6 left) with a border containing background objects around the sign. The image patches show different daylight illumination situations (sunny, shadowy) with an approximately frontal view on the signs. Those around 50,000 image patches are used as samples for the class *traffic sign*. Image patches showing other objects (Fig. 6 right) like buildings, sky or vegetation are extracted at random positions and with random size from road scene images of the GTSDB dataset. Known traffic sign labels for the GTSDB ensure that no traffic signs are contained in these patches. These image patches, around 50,000 as well, are used as samples for the class *other objects*. All samples are resized to have a common geometric resolution, they are randomly shuffled and split into a 80% part for training and a 20% part for validation. Network hyperparameters are: learning rate of 0.001, dropout rate of 0.5, max. 80 training epochs or until there is no remarkable decrease in the cross-entropy loss anymore.

Initial camera calibration is performed with multiple images of a planar test field. The proposed method for iterative camera calibration is tested with an image sequence extracted from a video taken during a five minute test drive through an underground car park. During the first seconds of the drive, there

Fig. 6. Examples for an image patch showing a traffic sign (left) and an image patch showing other objects (right) as used to train and validate the traffic sign detector.

was no movement of the camera, afterwards the camera moved with a velocity lower than 10 km/h. The images of the sequence show the car park from a typical viewing angle of a front-looking vehicle camera (example see Fig. 7). Several traffic signs are available in the car park and are shown in the images as well. The video was recorded with a wide-angle action camera, Garmin VIRB Ultra 30 (technical specifications see Table 1). Following the recommendations from [34] for stable intrinsic camera parameters, the camera-internal distortion correction of the action camera has been activated. The steps for traffic sign detection, shape fitting and scale reference information extraction have been applied to the acquired images, iterative calibration has been performed. For bundle adjustment, the software Aicon 3D Studio [45] was used.

Table 1. Technical specifications [29] of the action camera to be calibrated and video recording settings used to record the test video [48].

Camera	Garmin VIRB Ultra 30
Lens	2.73 mm fix focal length
Geometric resolution	2,688 × 1,512 px
Temporal resolution	30 fps
Settings	ISO 400, focus inf, f/2.6

4   Performance of the Traffic Sign Detector and Shape Fitting Method

On the validation dataset, an overall accuracy of 95.9% can be achieved for the trained traffic sign detector (confusion matrix see Table 2). Note for the interpretation of the overall accuracy that the number of samples for both classes (*traffic sign*, *other objects*) is the same; with this knowledge, the overall accuracy can be seen as that the detector is not assigning all samples to the same class or randomly assigning samples to a class, as in both cases the overall accuracy would be around 50%.

Table 2. Confusion matrix with the two classes *traffic sign* (TS) and *other objects* (OO) for the traffic sign detector applied to the validation dataset [48].

		True class	
		TS	OO
Predicted class	TS	96%	4%
	OO	4%	96%

The rates of false positives (i.e. image patches showing other objects classified as *traffic sign*) and false negatives (i.e. image patches showing traffic signs classified as *other objects*) are both 4%. As the given overall accuracy is based on a classification probability of 50%, an increased probability threshold to decide for traffic signs could help to decrease the number of false positives and to decrease the risk of using incorrect scale references lowering the quality of estimated intrinsic parameters subsequently. Increase of false negatives is to be expected, but is less important, as it does not influence the estimated parameters.

Visual analysis of the detections has shown that applying the trained traffic sign detector to road scene images of the test drive through the underground car park, several real-world trafffic signs are detected multiple times for slightly shifted image patches (Fig. 7).

Fig. 7. Example image of the test drive used to evaluate iterative camera calibration. Multiple image patches classified as traffic sign (visualized by rectangles) around each real-world traffic sign can be reduced to a single image patch by mean-shift clustering (visualized by a dot on a traffic sign). Ellipses are fitted to the contour of traffic signs (visualized by ellipses) to extract reference information for camera calibration from the road scene image [48].

Applied to image patches detected as traffic signs in the test image sequence, a residuum (see Sect. 2.5) of 1 pixel in average can be achieved for the proposed shape fitting method. Visual analysis of fitted shapes without having applied a threshold to the residuum has further shown that larger residuum values occur in particular for image patches with partly occluded traffic signs or for image patches, for which the largest consensus set corresponds with other objects in the image patch, but not with the contour of the traffic sign. A threshold for the residuum value therefore can be seen as suitable to neglect such image patches with potentially wrong shape fits for further processing.

5   Traffic Sign Distribution

As mentioned in the introduction, the distribution of reference points in the image has influence on the validity of estimated intrinsic camera parameters. Figure 8(a) shows for road scene images of the Cityscapes dataset [49] that the

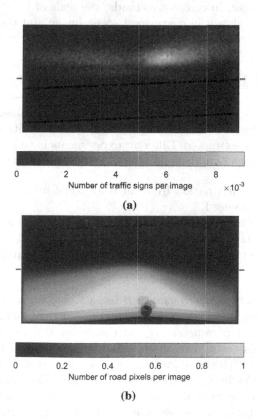

Fig. 8. (a) Distribution of traffic signs in the road scene images of the Cityscapes dataset. Majority of traffic signs are shown in the upper half (above dash indicators on the left and right) of the Cityscapes images acquired with a front-looking vehicle camera. (b) Distribution of road pixels in the road scene images of the Cityscapes dataset.

majority of traffic signs is in the upper half of these road scene images. It further shows that traffic signs are not equally distributed in the upper half and some parts of the upper half show even no traffic signs. Reference points extracted from traffic signs would be missing in these parts of the upper half, therefore. The Cityscapes dataset is used for this visualization, as it provides several thousand road scene images from different European cities in different countries taken with a front-looking vehicle camera. These conditions match with possible application scenarios of the proposed method.

Figure 8(b) shows, for the Cityscapes dataset as well, that roads are typically shown in the lower half of these road scene images. Road markings and reference points extracted thereof will be shown in the lower half of these road scene images, as well. Compared to traffic signs in the upper half, there are less parts in the lower half, in which there are no roads shown at all and therefore no reference points could be extracted.

Note the different scales in Figs. 8(a) and (b), indicating that roads are shown in every road scene image, as expected. Nevertheless, road markings might not be shown in all images. In contrast to roads, the scale of Fig. 8(a) indicates that traffic signs are not shown in every road scene image and the possible number of reference points to extract from will therefore probably be lower.

6   Estimated Intrinsic Camera Parameters

The proposed method allows to estimate the intrinsic camera parameters for those road scene images of the test sequence, for which additional scale reference information could be extracted. Different experiments have been conducted with different combinations of additional scale reference information:

(a) Scale reference information from all road scene images since beginning of the test drive are used.
(b) Scale reference information from the last three images acquired during the test drive, including the current one, are used.
(c) Scale reference information from the current image acquired during the test drive are used.

The outcome of the experiments will be analyzed in the following based on the intrinsic camera parameters focal length, principal point and the radial-symmetric distortion parameter A_1, estimated for the whole image sequence (Fig. 9). Hypothesis tests have shown that by the proposed method only A_1 could be estimated with statistical significance, A_2 and A_3 not.

Common to all estimated parameters are larger value changes between consecutive images in the beginning of the sequence in contrast to smaller value changes for later parts of the sequence. Only for experiment (b), there have occurred larger changes for some of the later images as well, for images 29 and 36 in particular. As the scale reference information used by the different experiments is more similar in the beginning of the image sequence than in the

Table 3. Number of scale references extracted from the road scene images from the test drive. No numbers are given for road scene images, from which no scale reference information could be extracted.

Road scene image number	1	2	3	4	8	9	10	11	12	14	15	16	17	18	22	24	29	36	38	40	43	45
Number of scale references	3	1	2	1	1	2	1		2	2	1	1	1	1	1	1	1	1	1	1	1	1

end (much more references used by experiment (a) than by the others), differences between the experiments can be observed especially for later parts of the sequence. Looking at the larger value changes at the beginning of the sequence, there are several possible explanations: One might be the change from the scale references used for initial calibration and the scale references used for iterative calibration: Distances between reference points on the planar test field and distances on traffic signs, respectively. Another explanation might be incorrect scale references, as visual analysis has shown that some of the first images are blurred, e.g. to a wrong automatic focus setting of the camera, which could influence shape fitting in particular. Another explanation might be the influence of the number of scale references per image (Table 3) on the value changes of estimated parameters. Pearson's correlation coefficient ρ between the number of scale references per image and value changes of focal length shows moderate positive ($0.3 < \rho < 0.5$) linear correlation: $\rho_{(a)} = 37\%, \rho_{(b)} = 35\%, \rho_{(c)} = 30\%$. In general, misdetections or errors in the shape fitting are possible as well, leading to incorrect scale references.

Between estimates for consecutive images, the maximal relative changes (rounded to whole numbers) are 0%, 14%, 2% and 5% over the complete image sequence and over all experiments for focal length, x- and y-component of the principal point and A_1, respectively. It might be worth noting, that the least maximal changes have appeared for the focal length, in contrast to the statement of [33], that scale references influence the focal length in particular and changes of the scale references could therefore let expect stronger changes in the focal length than in other parameters. Comparing the three experiments, the maximal difference is three percentage points, calculated over all parameters; this can be seen as that the value changes are similar for all three experiments. Relative to the values from the initial camera calibration, the maximal changes of the values from iterative calibration are 0%, 24%, 2% and 6% for focal length, principal point and A_1. There is in the maximal case 25% deviation between the three experiments; it is not possible to identify one experiment which shows remarkable larger deviations from the two others. From these numbers, the influence of iterative calibration compared to the initial calibration is strongest for the x-component of the principal point and remarkably less strong for the other three parameters. Hypothesis tests (Z test, significance level 5%) show statistical significance for all value changes between two consecutive images; this applies for all estimated parameters over the complete image sequence and for all experiments. Hypothesis tests show statistically significant changes of the values from initial camera calibration to the values from the first iteration of iterative camera calibration as well.

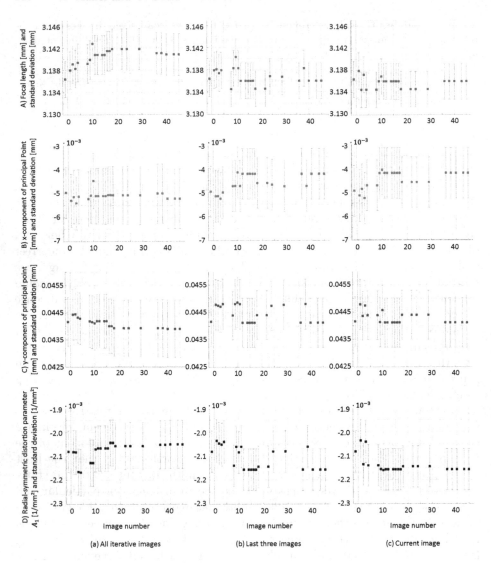

(a) All iterative images   (b) Last three images   (c) Current image

Fig. 9. Intrinsic camera parameters (A) focal length, (B) x-component of principal point, (C) y-component of principal point, (D) radial-symmetric distortion parameter A_1 and their standard deviations (vertical bars) estimated by initial (image number $= -1$) and iterative camera calibration (image number ≥ 1). Estimates are given for three experiments with different combinations of scale reference information: (a) from all road scene images since the beginning of the image sequence, (b) from the last three road scene images, (c) from the current image.

The standard deviations of the parameters show a maximal relative change of 4%, 5%, 3% and 6% over time and all experiments for focal length, x- and y-component of the principal point and A_1, respectively. This might be interpreted that iterative camera calibration with the proposed method does not have a strong influence on the accuracy of the iteratively estimated intrinsic camera parameters. Relative to initial camera calibration, it is remarkable, that there are changes in the standard deviation of around 16% for all parameters for experiment (a); in contrast for experiments (b) and (c) the standard deviations change only around 4% relative to the standard deviations from initial calibration, for all parameters as well. Therefore, it might be concluded that using scale references from very distant iterations, like in experiment (a), can lead to a decrease in the standard deviation of the estimated parameters.

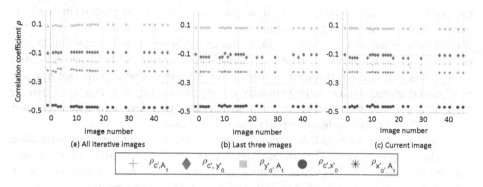

Fig. 10. Correlations between estimated intrinsic camera parameters for all three experiments.

Moderate correlations occur between the focal length and the x-component of the principal point (Fig. 10). Other correlations shown in that figure can be considered as weak ($\rho < 0.3$). Further, that figure shows that the level of correlation between parameter pairs does not change over time, i.e. that parameter pairs with moderate correlations in initial calibration have moderate correlations in iterative calibration and the same for pairs with weak correlation. This observation is seen as notable, because self-calibration, being used for iterative calibration, could have an influence on correlation between pairs of parameters [11]. As the test field from initial calibration, without the scale references, is used for iterative calibration as well, the influence of self-calibration might be damped. Last, it is notable that the largest correlation is between the x-component of the principal point and the focal length, but the x-component values are changing remarkably stronger during the image sequence than the focal length values.

To mention finally, the difference of the estimated focal length values from the focal length given in the technical camera specifications (Table 1) has to be mentioned. One aspect possibly contributing to this difference is that the focal length given in the technical specification is related to the full image sensor, while the test data has been recorded in a *video mode* being capable to record several frames per second. Several frames per second can avoid large differences in the image content between two consecutive images when driving at higher speeds, but at the cost of a lower geometric resolution of the images, as just a part of the image sensor is being used in video mode by the action camera used for the tests.

7 Conclusion

In this paper, a method for iterative calibration of a vehicle camera with scale references extracted from traffic signs in acquired road scene images has been proposed. It has been shown that every few images, a scale reference could be extracted for a test drive of a camera-equipped vehicle through an underground car park with traffic signs. The intrinsic parameter values estimated during iterative camera calibration show larger value changes for the first images of the test drive and smaller changes for later images. The standard deviations of the estimated parameters are at least one decimal power smaller than the estimated values. Regarding the estimation of distortion parameters being valid for a whole road scene image, traffic signs typically shown in the upper image half can be seen as supplementary extension to road marks, typically shown in the lower image half, to extract reference points for calibration.

Possible future work can be a comparison of the parameter values estimated with the proposed method with independently estimated values. These values can be obtained from separate camera calibration performed iteratively with reference points on test fields manually placed in the underground car park.

References

1. Ziebinski, A., Cupek, R., Erdogan, H., Waechter, S.: A survey of ADAS technologies for the future perspective of sensor fusion. In: Nguyen, N.-T., Manolopoulos, Y., Iliadis, L., Trawiński, B. (eds.) ICCCI 2016. LNCS (LNAI), vol. 9876, pp. 135–146. Springer, Cham (2016). https://doi.org/10.1007/978-3-319-45246-3_13
2. Automotive Glazing Academy: ADAS - Automotive Glazing Academy. Website (2018). http://aga.uk.net/wp-content/uploads/2015/11/ADAS.jpg. Accessed 24 May 2018
3. Mende, R., Rohling, H.: New automotive applications for smart radar systems (2002)
4. Geiger, A., Lenz, P., Urtasun, R.: Are we ready for autonomous driving? The KITTI vision benchmark suite. In: Conference on Computer Vision and Pattern Recognition (CVPR) (2012)
5. Fitzgibbon, A.W., Zisserman, A.: Automatic camera recovery for closed or open image sequences. In: Burkhardt, H., Neumann, B. (eds.) ECCV 1998. LNCS, vol. 1406, pp. 311–326. Springer, Heidelberg (1998). https://doi.org/10.1007/BFb0055675
6. Lemaire, T., Berger, C., Jung, I.K., Lacroix, S.: Vision-based slam: stereo and monocular approaches. Int. J. Comput. Vis. **74**, 343 (2007)
7. Uhrig, J., Schneider, N., Schneider, L., Franke, U., Brox, T., Geiger, A.: Sparsity invariant CNNs. In: International Conference on 3D Vision (3DV) 2017 (2017)
8. Heyden, A., Astrom, K.: Euclidean reconstruction from constant intrinsic parameters. In: Proceedings of 13th International Conference on Pattern Recognition, vol. 1, pp. 339–343 (1996)

9. Somanath, G., Rohith, M.V., Kambhamettu, C.: Single camera stereo system using prism and mirrors. In: Bebis, G., et al. (eds.) ISVC 2010. LNCS, vol. 6454, pp. 170–181. Springer, Heidelberg (2010). https://doi.org/10.1007/978-3-642-17274-8_17
10. Hanel, A., et al.: Metric scale calculation for visual mapping algorithms. In: The International Archives of the Photogrammetry, Remote Sensing and Spatial Information Sciences (2018)
11. Luhmann, T., Robson, S., Kyle, S., Harley, I.: Close Range Photogrammetry. Principles, Methods and Applications. Whittles Publishing (2006)
12. Hartley, R., Zisserman, A.: Multiple View Geometry in Computer Vision. Cambridge Books Online. Cambridge University Press, Cambridge (2003)
13. Brown, D.C.: Close-range camera calibration. Photogramm. Eng. **37**, 855–866 (1971)
14. El-Hakim, S.: Real-time image metrology with CCD cameras. Photogramm. Eng. Remote. Sens. **52**, 1757–1766 (1986)
15. Fraser, C.S., Shortis, M.R.: Variation of distortion within the photographic field. Photogramm. Eng. Remote. Sens. **58**, 851–855 (1992)
16. Heng, L., Li, B., Pollefeys, M.: CamOdoCal: automatic intrinsic and extrinsic calibration of a rig with multiple generic cameras and odometry. In: IEEE/RSJ International Conference on Intelligent Robots and Systems (IROS), pp. 1793–1800. IEEE (2013)
17. Friel, M., Savage, D.A., Hughes, C., Ermilios, P.: Online vehicle camera calibration based on road surface texture tracking and geometric properties. Patent (2012)
18. Hanel, A., Stilla, U.: Structure-from-motion for calibration of a vehicle camera system with non-overlapping fields-of-view in an urban environment. Int. Arch. Photogramm. Remote. Sens. Spat. Inf. Sci. **42**, 181–188 (2017)
19. Faugeras, O.D., Luong, Q.-T., Maybank, S.J.: Camera self-calibration: theory and experiments. In: Sandini, G. (ed.) ECCV 1992. LNCS, vol. 588, pp. 321–334. Springer, Heidelberg (1992). https://doi.org/10.1007/3-540-55426-2_37
20. Thatcham Research and ADAS Repair Group: Code of Practice For the Replacement & Refitting of Automotive Glazing for vehicles fitted with screen mounted Advanced Driver Assistance Systems (ADAS) (2016)
21. Broggi, A., Bertozzi, M., Fascioli, A.: Self-calibration of a stereo vision system for automotive applications. In: Proceedings of the 2001 IEEE International Conference on Robotics and Automation, vol. 4, pp. 3698–3703 (2001)
22. Bellino, M., Holzmann, F., Kolski, S., de Meneses, Y.L., Jacot, J.: Calibration of an embedded camera for driver-assistant systems. In: Proceedings of the 2005 IEEE Intelligent Transportation Systems, 2005, pp. 354–359 (2005)
23. Ribeiro, A.A.G.A., Dihl, L.L., Jung, C.R.: Automatic camera calibration for driver assistance systems. In: Proceeedings of 13th International Conference on Systems, Signals and Image Processing, pp. 173–176 (2006)
24. Hanel, A., Hoegner, L., Stilla, U.: Towards the influence of a car windshield on depth calculation with a stereo camera system. Int. Arch. Photogramm. Remote. Sens. Spat. Inf. Sci. **41**, 461–468 (2016)
25. Hella Gutmann Solutions GmbH: CSC-Tool. Operating Instructions (2016)
26. Paula, M.D., Jung, C., Silveira, L.D.: Automatic on-the-fly extrinsic camera calibration of onboard vehicular cameras. Expert. Syst. Appl. Int. J. **41**, 1997–2007 (2014)
27. Department of Transport - Ireland: Traffic Signs Manual (2010)
28. Mobileye Technologies Limited: Mobileye 5 Series — Mobileye. Website (2018). https://www.mobileye.com/en-uk/products/mobileye-5-series/. Accessed 12 June 2018

29. Pemble, C.A.: Garmin VIRB Ultra 30 Technical Specifications. Website (2017). http://www8.garmin.com/automotive/pdfs/VIRB-Ultra30-specs.pdf. Accessed 29 Jan 2017
30. Nikon UK Limited: Nikon D5 Spiegelreflexkamera — Profikamera — Technische Daten. Website (2018). https://www.europe-nikon.com/en_GB/product/digital-cameras/slr/professional/d5#tech_specs. Accessed 12 June 2018
31. Dang, T., Hoffmann, C., Stiller, C.: Continuous stereo self-calibration by camera parameter tracking. IEEE Trans. Image Process. **18**, 1536–1550 (2009)
32. Smith, M.J., Cope, E.: The effects of temperature variation on single-lens-reflex digital camera calibration parameters. In: International Archives of Photogrammetry, Remote Sensing and Spatial Information Science, vol. XXXVIII, pp. 554–559 (2010)
33. Luhmann, T., Robson, S., Kyle, S., Boehm, J.: Close-range Photogrammetry and 3D Imaging. De Gruyter Textbook. De Gruyter, Berlin (2013)
34. Hastedt, H., Ekkel, T., Luhmann, T.: Evaluation of the quality of action cameras with wide-angle lenses in uav photogrammetry. In: International Archives of the Photogrammetry, Remote Sensing and Spatial Information Sciences, vol. XL-1/W4 (2016)
35. Triggs, B., McLauchlan, P.F., Hartley, R.I., Fitzgibbon, A.W.: Bundle adjustment — a modern synthesis. In: Triggs, B., Zisserman, A., Szeliski, R. (eds.) IWVA 1999. LNCS, vol. 1883, pp. 298–372. Springer, Heidelberg (2000). https://doi.org/10.1007/3-540-44480-7_21
36. Wu, Y., Liu, Y., Li, J., Liu, H., Hu, X.: Traffic sign detection based on convolutional neural networks. In: The 2013 International Joint Conference on Neural Networks (IJCNN), pp. 1–7 (2013)
37. Zhu, Z., Liang, D., Zhang, S., Huang, X., Li, B., Hu, S.: Traffic-sign detection and classification in the wild. In: 2016 IEEE Conference on Computer Vision and Pattern Recognition (CVPR), pp. 2110–2118 (2016)
38. Lecun, Y., Bottou, L., Bengio, Y., Haffner, P.: Gradient-based learning applied to document recognition. Proc. IEEE **86**, 2278–2324 (1998)
39. Comaschi, F., Stuijk, S., Basten, T., Corporaal, H.: RASW: a run-time adaptive sliding window to improve Viola-Jones object detection. In: 2013 Seventh International Conference on Distributed Smart Cameras (ICDSC), pp. 1–6 (2013)
40. Fukunaga, K., Hostetler, L.: The estimation of the gradient of a density function, with applications in pattern recognition. IEEE Trans. Inf. Theory **21**, 32–40 (1975)
41. Elder, J.: Determining rotations between disc axis and line of sight. Website (2017). http://web.ncf.ca/aa456/scale/ellipse.html. Accessed 29 Oct 2017
42. Suzuki, S., Abe, K.: Topological structural analysis of digitized binary images by border following. Comput. Vis. Graph. Image Process. **30**, 32–46 (1985)
43. Fischler, M.A., Bolles, R.C.: Random sample consensus: a paradigm for model fitting with applications to image analysis and automated cartography. Commun. ACM **24**, 381–395 (1981)
44. Soilán, M., Riveiro, B., Martínez-Sánchez, J., Arias, P.: Traffic sign detection in MLS acquired point clouds for geometric and image-based semantic inventory. ISPRS J. Photogramm. Remote. Sens. **114**, 92–101 (2016)
45. Schneider, C.T., Boesemann, W., Godding, R.: AICON 3D systems GmbH (2014)
46. Stallkamp, J., Schlipsing, M., Salmen, J., Igel, C.: Man vs. computer: benchmarking machine learning algorithms for traffic sign recognition. Neural Netw. **32**, 323–332 (2012). Selected Papers from IJCNN 2011

47. Houben, S., Stallkamp, J., Salmen, J., Schlipsing, M., Igel, C.: Detection of traffic signs in real-world images: the German traffic sign detection benchmark. In: International Joint Conference on Neural Networks. Number 1288 (2013)
48. Hanel, A., Stilla, U.: Iterative calibration of a vehicle camera using traffic signs detected by a convolutional neural network. In: Proceedings of the 3rd International Conference on Vehicle Technology and Intelligent Transport Systems (2018)
49. Cordts, M., et al.: The cityscapes dataset for semantic urban scene understanding. In: Proceedings of the IEEE Conference on Computer Vision and Pattern Recognition (CVPR) (2016)

Implementation and Investigation
of a Weather- and Jam Density-Tuned
Network Perimeter Controller

Maha Elouni[1,2], Hesham A. Rakha[1,2,3(✉)], and Youssef Bichiou[1]

[1] Center for Sustainable Mobility, Virginia Tech Transportation Institute,
3500 Transportation Research Plaza, Blacksburg, VA 24061, USA
{emaha, hrakha, youssefl}@vt.edu
[2] Bradley Department of Electrical and Computer Engineering, Virginia Tech,
Perry St, Blacksburg, VA 24061, USA
[3] Charles E. Via, Jr. Department of Civil and Environmental Engineering,
Virginia Tech, Patton Hall, Blacksburg, VA 24061, USA

Abstract. This paper implements and evaluates the performance of a network fundamental diagram (NFD) proportional-integral perimeter controller (PC) using base tuned parameters (clear weather conditions and a base jam density of 160 veh/km/lane). The parameters were then re-tuned separately for different weather conditions and jam density values (reflecting different percentage of trucks), resulting in two new control methods: a weather-tuned perimeter controller (WTPC) and a jam density-tuned perimeter controller (JTPC). The WTPC was shown to outperform the no control strategy and the PC for different weather conditions. Specifically, the WTPC decreased the congestion inside the protected network (PN) and improved the overall performance of the full network (FN) by decreasing the average vehicle travel time, decreasing the vehicle total delay, increasing the average vehicle speed and decreasing the average vehicle fuel consumption. Alternatively, the JTPC was shown to perform similar to the PC for jam densities higher than the base-case jam density used in the PC (in our case 160 veh/km/lane). However, the JTPC outperformed the PC for smaller jam densities given that these smaller jam densities result in queues spilling back faster to upstream traffic signals. The results demonstrate the need to tune the controller to the actual jam density especially when the jam density decreases (e.g. trucks are introduced to the network).

Keywords: Network Fundamental Diagram (NFD) ·
Proportional-integral (PI) controller · Gating · Weather · Jam density

1 Introduction

Traffic growth and limited roadway capacity increase congestion, decrease traveler mobility, and increase fuel consumption. Traffic managers employ various control techniques to mitigate the aforementioned problems. One well-known network-wide control strategy is perimeter control (or gating). Perimeter control is based on the Network Fundamental Diagram (NFD) and consists of attempting to maintain the

© Springer Nature Switzerland AG 2019
B. Donnellan et al. (Eds.): SMARTGREENS 2018/VEHITS 2018, CCIS 992, pp. 266–278, 2019.
https://doi.org/10.1007/978-3-030-26633-2_13

accumulation around a set point (which corresponds to the maximum throughput) to avoid network oversaturation or congestion building up (Fig. 1).

Li et al. tested a perimeter control strategy for an oversaturated network using the NFD concept [2]. However, the approach proposed a fixed signal timing method that is not adapted to real-time traffic conditions. Many studies have overcome this issue and achieved real-time perimeter control using techniques such as the standard proportional-integral (PI) controller [3], a robust PI controller [4] and model predictive controller [5]. However, our focus is on the standard PI controller because it is simple and computationally efficient.

Keyvan-Ekbatani et al. described a simple, real-time, feedback-based gating concept that exploits the urban NFD for smooth and efficient traffic control operations [3]. They used a standard PI feedback controller and tested the method in a network in Chania, Greece using the microscopic traffic simulator AIMSUN. Although simple, the method was demonstrated to be very efficient. In consequent works, Keyvan-Ekbatani et al. tried to improve his original controller to make it work when using less loop detectors [6] and when the controlled junctions are further upstream from the protected network by introducing a time delay [7]. They then proposed strategies for queue and delay balancing at the gated links under perimeter control [8].

Goodwin and Pisano introduced some successful methods to change signal timings in response to weather [9]. Their studies revealed that weather-responsive traffic signal timing could improve the system mobility by increasing the average vehicle speed and reducing vehicle delays. Papageorgiou et al. found that variable speed limits decrease the slope of the flow occupancy diagram at under-critical conditions, increase the critical occupancy, and enable higher flows at the same occupancy values in over-critical conditions [10]. These strategies mitigate localized weather impacts on relatively short road segments [11].

Elouni and Rakha implemented a weather-tuned control strategy at a macroscopic level based on the NFD [1]. The NFD gives an aggregated view of the network characteristics, namely: the average network density, flow, and space mean speed. The NFD's physical model was initially proposed by Godfrey [12]. The NFD was observed with dynamic features in a congested urban network in Yokohama [13]. Their analyses and simulations demonstrated that NFDs are curves that can be reproduced for homogeneous conditions in urban networks. They also showed that NFDs are a property of infrastructure and not of demand, which means that the average flow in a network is maximized for the same density value, regardless of the time-varying origin-destination (O-D) tables.

Elouni and Rakha studied the impact of weather on the NFD [14]. They showed that inclement weather affects the critical Total Time Spent (TTS) and maximum Total Traveled Distance (TTD), which are the x and y axes of the NFD, respectively. Figure 8 in Ref. [14] shows that the impact of weather on critical TTS is minimal compared to its impact on maximal TTD. In other words, the weather affects the y-axis of the NFD (or the flow) much more than it affects the x-axis of the NFD (or density). This was confirmed by Rakha et al., who demonstrated that traffic stream jam density is not affected by weather conditions [15].

The weather-tuned perimeter controller (WTPC) represents a perimeter controller (PC) tuned based on weather (which affects the y-axis of the NFD) [1]. In this paper, we

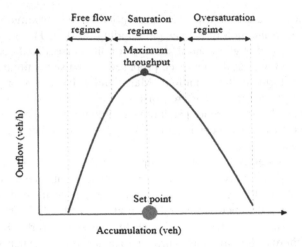

Fig. 1. NFD of a network [1].

are also interested in investigating a PC tuned based on jam density (which affects the *x*-axis of the NFD).

First, we describe the simulated network and the NFD. We then present the PI-PC. Subsequently, a WTPC and jam density-tuned PC (JTPC) are presented. Finally, we present the study conclusions.

2 Network Description and Network Fundamental Diagram

2.1 Network Setup

A modelled network was used to study the impact of the implemented PC strategy on the NFD. For that reason, a protected network (PN) was identified. The PN is the sub-network that needs to be protected from congestion. The PN corresponds to the zone surrounded by the green rectangle in the middle of the network in Fig. 2.

The PN contained 91 links, as shown in Fig. 2. The yellow chevrons in Fig. 2 represent the eight links where gating was applied. The gated links were sufficiently long to accommodate the queues caused by gating without spilling back onto other links. Future work will integrate queue spill-back prevention strategies. All links were one-way, and each link had only one lane.

The full network (FN) comprised 36 signalized intersections running on a fixed-time plan. In Fig. 2, the origins and destinations are represented by blue circles. Loop detectors were placed on each link in the network to collect the needed measurements, and those measurements were collected every cycle (60 s in this study). The traffic demand was loaded for 75 min, with demand increasing during the first 37.5 min and then decreasing during the second 37.5 min, representing realistic demand behavior. To ensure that the network was empty at the end of the simulation, the total simulation time was set to be 176 min (approximately 3 h). A feedback dynamic traffic assignment was activated to reflect realistic driver behavior during congested conditions.

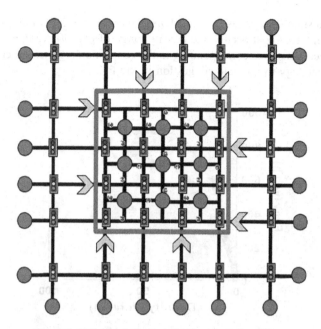

Fig. 2. Grid network modelled in INTEGRATION.

2.2   Derivation of NFD Equations

In this work, the NFD is presented based on the average density and flow calculated from the loop detector measurements:

$$K(k) = \frac{\sum_{z \in Z} K_z(k).L_z}{\sum_{z \in Z} L_z}, \tag{1}$$

where z is the link index; Z is the set of measurement links; $k = 0, 1, 2, \ldots$ is an index reflecting the cycle number; $K_z(k)$ is the measured number of vehicles on link z during cycle k; and L_z is the length of link z. $K_z(k)$ is calculated using Eq. 2:

$$K_z(k) = l_z.k_j.\frac{o_z(k)}{100}, \tag{2}$$

where l_z is the number of lanes on link z; k_j is the jam density; and o_z is the measured time-occupancy (in %) on link z during cycle k.

The flow F is calculated using Eq. (3):

$$F(k) = \frac{\sum_{z \in Z} q_z(k).L_z}{\sum_{z \in Z} L_z} \tag{3}$$

where $q_z(k)$ is the measured flow on link z during cycle k.

Running a simulation in INTEGRATION, we obtain the NFD presented in Fig. 3. The maximum throughput occurs in a density range of [41, 50] veh/km. Note that the NFD has a decreasing area corresponding to the congestion regime, indicating the need for a control strategy to mitigate congestion in the PN.

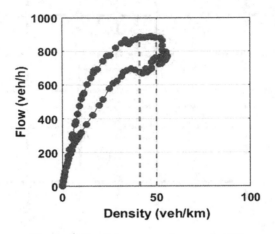

Fig. 3. NFD of the protected network (PN).

3   Implementation of the Perimeter Controller (PC)

3.1   Mathematical Modelling

To avoid congestion inside the PN, a PI-PC is applied based on the NFD. The idea of the PC is to maintain the density K around a set value $\widehat{K}$, which corresponds to the density at the maximum flow. In our case, $\widehat{K} = 48.76$ veh/km, which is within the range of the K values corresponding to the maximum flow $F[41, 50]$.

The system and feedback controller structure is represented in Fig. 4. The process, shown in Eq. 4, is what happens in the PN; its input is q_{in}, which corresponds to the PN's entering flow, and its output is K:

$$\Delta K(k+1) = \mu.\Delta K(k) + \zeta.\Delta q_{in}(k) + \varepsilon(k), \tag{4}$$

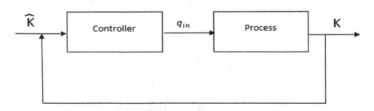

Fig. 4. System and feedback controller structure.

where $\Delta x = x - \bar{x}$, and $\bar{x}$ corresponds to the steady-state variable used in the model linearization. The desired steady state is common in control engineering. In this case, it corresponds to the region where F is maximized. Note that $\bar{K} = \widehat{K}$, and μ and ζ are two model parameters that can be found using a least-squares approximation of the simulated data (q_{in}, K) around the maximum K range.

The controller's inputs are K and $\widehat{K}$, and its output is the ordered flow that should enter the PN. Equation 5 corresponds to the PI feedback regulator equation:

$$q_{in}(k) = q_{in}(k-1) - K_p(K(k) - K(k-1)) + K_I\left(\widehat{K} - K(k)\right), \tag{5}$$

where K_p and K_I are the proportional and integral gains, respectively. These can be found by manual fine-tuning or using control engineering methods.

The controller ordered flow q_{in} is distributed among the gated links. The flow entering the PN from each gated link has to be between two bounds: q_{min} and q_{max}. These bounds can be calculated based on the minimum and maximum green times, respectively.

The controller always works in the background, and the fixed signal timings are set for all signals. Once K is close to the set value $\widehat{K}$ (i.e., 85% of $\widehat{K}$), the controller is activated, and the signal timings are calculated based on the controller ordered flow q_{in}. When K decreases to less than 85% of $\widehat{K}$, the controller is deactivated, and the signals display the fixed timings again.

3.2   Use of Perimeter Controller (PC) for Clear Weather Conditions

Since INTEGRATION is a stochastic micro-simulator, simulations were run for the PC case and the NPC case using ten different random seeds. The parameters used in these simulations were as follows: $\mu = 0.782$, $\zeta = 0.00124$, $K_p = 631$, $K_I = 176$, $\overline{q}_{in} = 4340\,\text{veh/h}$, and $\bar{K} = 48.76\,\text{veh/km}$.

Table 1 shows that the PC improves the FN travel time, total delay, fuel consumption and average speed compared to NPC.

Table 1. Performance metrics of the PC for the FN using the average of ten different seeds.

	NPC	PC	% Improvement
Travel time (s)	575.25	529.25	8.0
Total delay (s)	213.22	188.84	11.43
Fuel (l)	0.40	0.38	3.5
Speed (km/h)	16.90	18.18	7.55

For the performance inside the PN, Fig. 5 clearly shows that the control algorithm decreased the congestion. Note that the decreasing NFD area no longer exists.

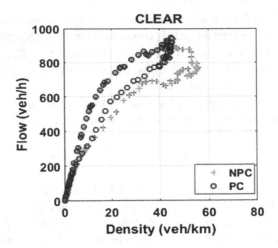

Fig. 5. Comparison of the NFDs for NPC and PC during clear weather conditions.

4 Weather-Tuned Perimeter Control (WTPC)

4.1 Description

Rakha et al. studied the impact of weather on free-flow speed, speed-at-capacity and capacity. They developed weather adjustment factors [WAF in Eq. 6] to compute these three traffic stream parameters based on precipitation intensity i (cm/h) and visibility level v (km) for each of the rain and snow cases [15, 16]:

$$\text{WAF} = a_1 + a_2 i + a_3 i^2 + a_4 v + a_5 v^2 + a_6 iv. \tag{6}$$

In this work, the calibrated model parameters a_1 through a_6 are chosen to be the Twin Cities parameters because it has the highest WAF (Table 1 in [16]). These WAFs are used to adjust the clear condition parameters and reflect the inclement weather effects.

Rakha et al. [16] also modelled vehicle deceleration and acceleration behavior for inclement weather. They provided rolling and friction coefficients for different roadway surface conditions (including wet and snowy surfaces).

To model different weather conditions in INTEGRATION, the set of inputs containing the free-flow speed, speed-at-capacity, capacity, rolling resistance coefficients and coefficient of friction are calculated and given to the software.

The PC uses the same set of parameters for inclement weather as for clear weather conditions: $\mu = 0.782$, $\zeta = 0.00124$, $K_p = 631$, $K_I = 176$, $\overline{q_{in}} = 4340$ veh/h, and $\widehat{K} = 48.76$ veh/km.

However, the WTPC uses a specific set of parameters for each weather condition. For clear weather, it uses the parameters defined above: $\mu = 0.782$, $\zeta = 0.00124$, $K_p = 631$, $K_I = 176$, $\overline{q_{in}} = 4340$ veh/h, and $\widehat{K} = 48.76$ veh/km. The re-tuned parameters obtained for rain conditions are $\mu = 0.588$, $\zeta = 0.00138$, $K_p = 425$, $K_I = 298$, $\overline{q_{in}} = 4300$ veh/h, and $\widehat{K} = 48.76\,\text{veh/km}$. For snow conditions, the parameters are $\mu = 0.775$, $\zeta = 0.000139$, $K_p = 5590$, $K_I = 1620$, $\overline{q_{in}} = 3900\,\text{veh/h}$, and $\widehat{K} = 49\,\text{veh/km}$. These values demonstrate, as would be expected, that the desired controlled flow decreases for rain (4300 veh/h) and further decreases for snow conditions (3900 veh/h).

4.2 Results and Conclusions

Performance Within the PN. The NFD plots of the PN for both rain and snow conditions are presented in Fig. 6. The red, blue, and green curves correspond to the NFDs for the NPC, the PC, and the WTPC, respectively. As the curves show, the values of K for the WTPC case were lower than those for the PC and NPC cases, especially under snow conditions. Thus, the WTPC performed better than the PC in decreasing congestion inside the PN.

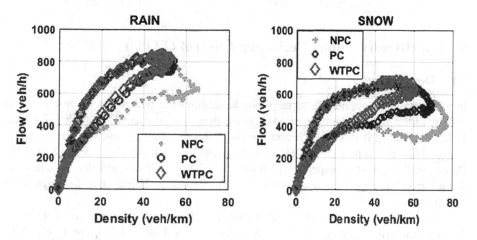

Fig. 6. NFD for rain conditions and snow conditions. (Color figure online)

Performance of the FN. The average speed, total delay, travel time and fuel consumption were calculated for the FN for the rain and snow cases (Table 2). We notice that using the WTPC, the improvements are better than when using the PC, especially for the snow case.

Table 2. Performance metrics on the FN for the NPC, PC and WTPC cases.

Performance metric	Strategy	Rain		Snow	
		Value	Improvement (%)	Value	Improvement (%)
Avg. speed (km/h)	NPC	12.42	-	6.26	-
	PC	14.12	13.70	7.29	16.35
	WTPC	14.19	14.22	8.22	31.26
Total delay (s)	NPC	315.20	-	773.33	-
	PC	257.22	18.39	633.72	18.05
	WTPC	255.73	18.86	537.18	30.53
Travel time (s)	NPC	802.66	-	1615.13	-
	PC	690.36	13.99	1365.81	15.43
	WTPC	686.68	14.50	1201.38	25.61
Fuel (l)	NPC	0.450	-	0.65	-
	PC	0.417	7.05	0.58	9.95
	WTPC	0.416	7.20	0.54	16.68

5   Jam Density-Tuned Perimeter Control (JTPC)

5.1   Description

In this section, we applied the same principle as above but with re-tuning based on jam density rather than weather. We used clear weather with jam densities of 100, 120, 140, 160, 180, and 200 veh/km. The base case is the jam density used in the previous section (i.e., 160 veh/km/lane). These jam densities reflect a truck percentage of 29%, 20%, 7%, 3% and 0%, respectively considering that a truck is equivalent in length to 4.4 passenger car vehicles (the length of a trailer-truck is 21.3 m and the length of a typical car is 4.9 m).

The PC case uses the set of parameters for clear weather and a jam density of 160 veh/km, as above: $\mu = 0.782, \zeta = 0.00124, K_p = 631, K_I = 176, \overline{q_{in}} = 4340$ veh/h, and $\widehat{K} = 48.76$ veh/km. For the re-tuning, the set point $\widehat{K}$ was changed to 12.76, 35, 25, 48.76, 50 and 51 veh/km for jam densities of 100, 120, 140, 160, 180, and 200 veh/km, respectively.

5.2   Results

Performance Inside the PN. Figure 7 presents the NFDs of the PN for each jam density. The jam density of 160 veh/km is not shown in the figure because it is the base case used in the PC (clear weather plotted in Fig. 5), so there is no re-tuning. We then have two groups of jam densities: less than 160 veh/km and higher than 160 veh/km.

Starting with the first group of jam densities, we notice that for the smallest one used (100 veh/km), the PC could not alleviate the congestion inside the PN, and gridlock occurred. However, the JTPC did a very good job at totally avoiding congestion. For

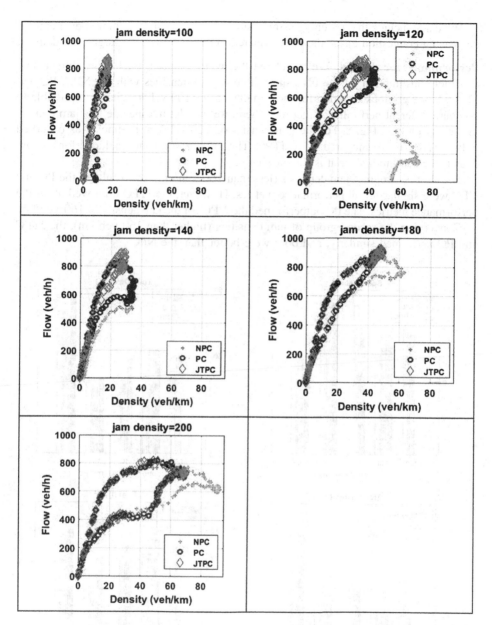

Fig. 7. NFDs of PN for different jam densities.

the jam densities of 120 and 140 veh/km, it is clear from Fig. 5 that the JTPC decreased the congestion better than the PC.

Concerning the second group (jam densities of 180 and 200 veh/km), we notice that the NFDs obtained using the PC and JTPC are very similar, and both decreased the congestion compared to the NPC case.

We can conclude that re-tuning using a smaller jam density was more beneficial for decreasing congestion inside the PN compared to re-tuning using a larger jam density.

Performance for the FN. We calculated the average speed, total delay, travel time and fuel consumption for the FN using different jam densities with the NPC, PC and JTPC. Since gridlock occurred for the jam density of 100 veh/km, it is not possible to compare different performance metrics. Therefore, we did not include this jam density in the bar plots in Fig. 8. For the jam density of 120 veh/km, gridlock was observed only for NP, so we compared PC to JTPC. The JTPC result is not included for the jam density of 160 km/h since it is the base case.

For the first group of jam densities (less than 160 veh/km), the results of the PC and NPC were similar for all performance metrics. However, the JTPC improved all of the performance metrics. The PC outperformed the NPC for the jam density of 160 veh/km.

Concerning the second group of jam densities (higher than 160 veh/km), the JTPC and PC performed similarly, and both were better than the NPC.

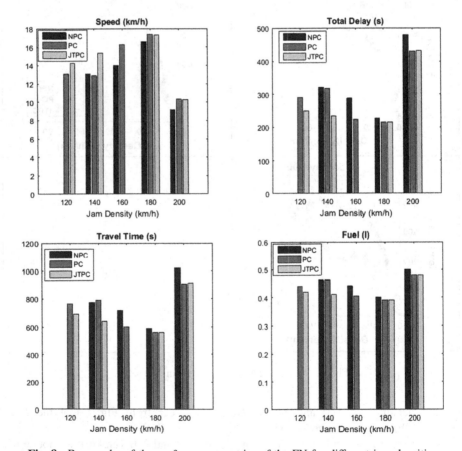

Fig. 8. Bar graphs of the performance metrics of the FN for different jam densities.

6 Conclusions

A perimeter control strategy based on the NFD was implemented in the INTEGRA-
TION micro-simulator. It was originally tuned based on data from clear weather
conditions and a jam density of 160 veh/km/lane. The control strategy was shown to be
efficient for different weather conditions and for all jam densities except the smallest
value (100 veh/km/lane). A WTPC was implemented and shown to outperform the
original PC in decreasing congestion inside the PN and improve the network-wide
performance of the FN. A JTPC was also implemented and tested. The JTPC performed well for jam densities less than the one used in the PC. However, its performance was similar to that of the PC for higher jam densities. Both WTPC and JTPC
performed better than the NPC in decreasing congestion inside the PN and improving
the overall performance of the FN. These results demonstrate the need to tune the PC to
the actual conditions of the network by accounting for weather and truck effects.

Acknowledgements. This effort was funded through the Office of Energy Efficiency and
Renewable Energy (EERE), Vehicle Technologies Office, Energy Efficient Mobility Systems
Program under award number DE-EE0008209.

References

1. Elouni, M., Rakha, H.: Weather-tuned network perimeter control - a network fundamental
   diagram feedback controller approach. In: Conference: 4th International Conference on
   Vehicle Technology and Intelligent Transport Systems (2018)
2. Li, Y., Xu, J., Shen, L.: A perimeter control strategy for oversaturated network preventing
   queue spillback. Procedia-Soc. Behav. Sci. **43**, 418–427 (2012)
3. Keyvan-Ekbatani, M., et al.: Exploiting the fundamental diagram of urban networks for
   feedback-based gating. Transp. Res. Part B Meth. **46**(10), 1393–1403 (2012)
4. Haddad, J., Shraiber, A.: Robust perimeter control design for an urban region. Transp. Res.
   Part B Meth. **68**, 315–332 (2014)
5. Sirmatel, I.I., Geroliminis, N.: Model predictive control of large-scale urban networks via
   perimeter control and route guidance actuation. In: 2016 IEEE 55th Conference on Decision
   and Control (CDC). IEEE (2016)
6. Keyvan-Ekbatani, M., Papageorgiou, M., Papamichail, I.: Feedback gating based on sparse-
   measurement urban network fundamental diagrams. In: Transportation Research Board 92nd
   Annual Meeting (2013)
7. Keyvan-Ekbatani, M., Papageorgiou, M., Knoop, V.L.: Controller design for gating traffic
   control in presence of time-delay in urban road networks. Transp. Res. Procedia **7**, 651–668
   (2015)
8. Keyvan-Ekbatani, M., et al.: Balancing delays and relative queues at the urban network
   periphery under perimeter control (2017)
9. Goodwin, L.C., Pisano, P.A.: Weather-responsive traffic signal control. Inst. Transp. Eng.
   ITE J. **74**(6), 28 (2004)
10. Papageorgiou, M., Kosmatopoulos, E., Papamichail, I.: Effects of variable speed limits on
    motorway traffic flow. Transp. Res. Rec. J. Transp. Res. Board **2047**, 37–48 (2008)
11. Pisano, P., Goodwin, L.: Research needs for weather-responsive traffic management.
    Transp. Res. Rec. J. Transp. Res. Board **1867**, 127–131 (2004)

12. Godfrey, J.: The mechanism of a road network. Traffic Eng. Control **8**(8) (1900)
13. Geroliminis, N., Daganzo, C.F.: Existence of urban-scale macroscopic fundamental diagrams: some experimental findings. Transp. Res. Part B Meth. **42**(9), 759–770 (2008)
14. Elouni, M., Rakha, H.: Impact of inclement weather on the network fundamental diagram (2018)
15. Rakha, H., et al.: Inclement weather impacts on freeway traffic stream behavior. Transp. Res. Rec. J. Transp. Res. Board **2071**, 8–18 (2008)
16. Rakha, H., Arafeh, M., Park, S.: Modeling inclement weather impacts on traffic stream behavior. Int. J. Transp. Sci. Technol. **1**(1), 25–47 (2012)

City-Level Agent-Based Multi-modal Modeling of Transportation Networks: Model Development and Preliminary Testing

Ahmed Elbery[1], Youssef Bichiou[1], Hesham A. Rakha[1,2(✉)], Jianhe Du[1],
Filip Dvorak[3], and Matthew Klenk[3]

[1] Center for Sustainable Mobility, Virginia Tech Transportation Institute,
Blacksburg, VA 24060, USA
{aelbery,ybichiou,hrakha,jdu}@vtti.vt.edu
[2] Charles E. Via, Jr. Department of Civil and Environmental Enginering,
Virginia Tech, Blacksburg, VA 24060, USA
[3] Palo Alto Research Center (PARC), Palo Alto, USA
filip@dvorak.fr, matthew.klenk@parc.com

Abstract. Digital cities have the potential to produce major improvements in the transportation system with the eminent availability of data and the use of advanced modeling techniques. This modeling entails a number of challenges, namely: the network scale that covers large urban multi-modal transportation networks and the trade-off between model scalability and accuracy. This paper introduces a novel simulation framework that efficiently supports large-scale agent-based multimodal transportation system modeling. We call this framework "INTEGRATION Ver. 3.0", or "INTGRAT3" for short. The INTGRAT3 framework utilizes both microscopic and mesoscopic modeling techniques to take advantage of the strengths of each modeling approach. In order to increase the model scalability, decrease the model complexity, and achieve a reasonable simulation speed, the INTGRAT3 framework utilizes parallel simulation through two partitioning techniques: spatial partitioning by separating the network geographically and vertical partitioning by separating the network by transportation mode for odes that interact minimally. The INTGRAT3 framework creates multimodal plans for a portion of the trips (controlled trips) and tracks the traveler's trips on a second-by-second basis across the different modes. We instantiate this framework in a system model of Los Angeles (LA) supporting our study of the impact on transportation decisions over a 6 h period of the morning commute (6am–12pm). The results show that by modifying travel choices of only 5% of the trips, large reductions in traffic congestion (ranging from 3.8 to 17.2% reductions in vehicle delay) are achievable with marginal reductions in vehicle fuel consumption levels (ranging from 1.4 to 3.5%).

Keywords: Modeling large-scale · Multimodal · Agent-based ·
Transportation network · Smart city

© Springer Nature Switzerland AG 2019
B. Donnellan et al. (Eds.): SMARTGREENS 2018/VEHITS 2018, CCIS 992, pp. 279–303, 2019.
https://doi.org/10.1007/978-3-030-26633-2_14

1   Introduction

The performance of transportation systems are critical in improving our quality of life in urban cities. The environmental impact of the transportation sector has major effects on human health [1]. Traffic congestion not only increases fuel consumption and emission levels but also wastes travelers' time. Moreover, the congestion experienced by travelers increases the stress and affects individual social interactions [2]. As a result of all these economic, social, psychological and health impacts, the academic community has devoted significant research efforts to improving transportation system performance. While the majority of these studies use simulation [3–5], there are significant modeling challenges including scaling, calibrating, and validation issues that impact the accuracy of the results.

In this paper, we present a novel agent-based framework for the modeling of large-scale transportation systems. The presented framework supports city-level networks with different modes of transportation (cars, buses, railways, walking, biking, and carpooling). The developed framework utilizes both microscopic and mesoscopic simulation to leverage their respective strengths of accuracy and scalability. The framework spatially partitions the network enabling distinct portions of the region to be micro-simulated in parallel and vertically partitions the network into layers representing loosely interacting modes. In this way, we can utilize the available processing resources either using single or multiple machines. The framework is capable of tracking individual travelers on a second-by-second basis from their origin to their destination across the different transportation modes.

To the best of our knowledge, INTGRAT3 is the first tool that supports an agent-based city-level transportation system, combining both microscopic with mesoscopic simulations, tracking individual travelers and vehicles on a second-by-second basis, and supporting multimodal mobility. We instantiate this framework into a system to study the impact of routing on travel time and fuel consumption in the Greater LA city from 6 am to 12 pm.

The paper first introduces the related literature followed by an overview of the system architecture, components, and the high-level operations. Subsequently, the last two sections demonstrate the case study on the Greater LA network along with sample simulation results.

2   INTGRAT3 Model Versus Previous Models

The benefits of modeling large-scale transportation networks have attracted scholars' attention over the last three decades. Numerous techniques have been developed to model transportation systems. These techniques can be categorized into three basic simulation techniques, namely: macroscopic, mesoscopic and microscopic.

2.1   Traffic Modeling Techniques

Macroscopic modeling techniques compute the average number of vehicles traversing each road segment based on average macroscopic link parameters (traffic stream flow, density and space-mean speed) to model the spatio-temporal evolution of the transportation system. Because of this simplicity, macroscopic models are characterized by high scalability and high simulation speed. However, the high scalability and speed come at the cost of precision and accuracy because the use of aggregated traffic stream parameters result in an inability to capture many transportation phenomena including longitudinal and lateral vehicle movements. These shortcomings mean that the model does not capture vehicle acceleration/deceleration events, which is the predominant factor affecting vehicle fuel consumption and emission levels. In summary, macroscopic models lack the needed accuracy.

On the other extreme, **microscopic** models achieve the highest possible accuracy at the cost of computation and scalability complexity. To achieve the highest accuracy, microscopic models track individual vehicles on a deci-second-by-deci-second basis. Microscopic models can model and capture all the events that happen in the transportation network, as well as model the interactivity between the vehicles on the road as well as between vehicles and control systems such as traffic signals. However, the computation and memory requirements for this level of accuracy limit the scalability and reduce the simulation speed.

Between these two modeling approaches, **mesoscopic** models model individual vehicles where each roadway link is modeled without considering the behavior of the vehicle along the link except for the queueing at the end of the link. These mesoscopic models can estimate a time-varying average for the link parameters based on the traffic density on the link and the queue at the end of the link. By the help of queuing theory, mesoscopic models can compute different travel times for different vehicles on the same link at the same time. Consequently, mesoscopic models are typically more accurate than macroscopic models. However, because mesoscopic models do not model vehicle motion along roadway segments they suffer from the same drawbacks of macroscopic models with the only advantage over macroscopic modeling techniques in that they track individual vehicles.

The authors in [6] compared microscopic and macroscopic modeling approaches for estimating vehicle fuel consumption levels. The comparison showed that the use of macroscopic approaches can result is incorrect routing decisions, which can significantly affect the system-wide performance. Consequently, in our model we attempt to use microscopic modeling for all the critical roadway segments (minor- and major-arterials and highways/freeways). Alternatively, messocopic modeling is only used for local streets where vehicles typically travel at free-flow speeds in order to achieve high scalibility with minimal loss in modeling precision/accuracy.

2.2   State-of-the-Art Modeling of Large-Scale Transportation Systems

In the last three decades, there have been many attempts to build systems that are capable of simulating large-scale transportation systems. For example in 1997, the TRANSIMS simulation tool [7] was developed and used to simulate large urban networks. The research work in [7] used discrete space modeling for the traffic micro-simulation based on the cellular automaton approach [8], where the road is divided into cells (of length 7.5 m) that are either empty or occupied by one car. A simple car following and lane changing algorithms were developed. The use of cellular automaton makes this system computationally fast, however, it cannot accurately capture observed transportation phenomena including car following, lane changing, and gap acceptance behavior and produces abrupt vehicle accelerations (in steps of $7.5\,\mathrm{m/s^2}$). In 2002, TRANSIMS was updated to better include the impact of the congestion on the system performance and was run on a parallel cluster for fifty iterations to achieve better trip planning [9]. TRANSIMS has been used to model the Switzerland network in the morning peak hours using parallel computation [10,11]. Then, in 2012, TRANSIMS was used in [12] to evaluate the performance of the transportation network of the Buffalo-Niagara metropolitan area during significant snow events. However, the authors mentioned that extensive efforts are required to make the simulated network realistic in terms of network configuration, lane connectivity, pocket lane and signal locations. In [13] the same modeler was used to evaluate the impact of dynamic routing on the fuel consumption levels. In summary the use of the cellular automaton model to model vehicle movements produces unrealistic vehicle accelerations, which significantly impacts the fuel consumption and emission estimates.

A hybrid traffic modeler was presented in [14–17] to model large-scale transportation networks. The hybrid modeler simulates different network spatial partitions with different fidelity levels (microscopic or mesoscopic levels), where microscopic simulation was applied to areas of specific interest while simulating a large surrounding network in lesser detail with a mesoscopic model. In this way, it can provide a customized performance and simulation speed.

In 2015, the authors of [4] proposed the Scalable Electro-Mobility Simulation (SEMSim), an architecture for a cloud-based platform, as a proof of concept to use the cloud for simulation of large-scale transportation systems. The authors used this model to simulate the network of Singapore that included approximately 500,000 private owned vehicles. However, the model uses simple vehicle characteristics (e.g., kinematic model) and driving behavior models.

MATSim [18] is a transportation simulation software designed for large-scale scenarios, it adopts a queue-based approach which is computationally efficient. But the queue-based approach lacks the accuracy because the car-following effects are not captured. To increase the computation efficiency, MATSim combines the waiting-queue approach with an event-based approach. However, this event based technique still lacks the accuracy because it does not consider car following, lane-changing and gap acceptance behavior. For example, links do not have to be processed while agents traverse them.

Under the umbrella of modeling large-scale transportation systems, we developed a novel multi-modal agent-based framework, INTGRAT3, that is capable of modeling a city-level system. INTGRAT3 uses the INTEGRATION software [19] as its core system for microscopic simulation and integrates it with other system components, such as a simulation controller that tracks the movement of travelers across different modes and simulation realizations, a route planner and mesoscopic simulator to achieve the required scalability and accuracy levels, a microscopic public transport rail modeler, and a bicycle and pedestrian modeler. These components are integrated together by implementing a set of application programming interfaces (APIs) to enable communication. Similar to TRANSIMS, our framework supports the parallel computation either on single multi-core or even multiple machines. However, the definition of the microscopic simulation in TRANSIMS is limited to the demand side, where each trip is simulated individually as an agent. However, links and the mobility of vehicles on these links are modeled mesoscopically using a parallel queuing approach [20]. These queuing models are inaccurate in estimating the link travel time especially in congested situations such as the LA morning commute. Furthermore, it cannot capture the acceleration/deceleration events of each vehicle that have a significant impact on the vehicle fuel consumption and emission levels. In contrast to TRANSIMS, our framework uses a continuous space model for the micro-simulation, which is the enabler to capture many of the mobility parameters.

Compared to the hybrid traffic modeler presented in [14], the INTGRAT3 system also utilizes microscopic-mesoscopic hybrid modeling. However, in our model, we do not have that spatial separation between the microscopic and mesoscopic simulations. The two simulators are spatially overlapping but assigned different links depending on the level of congestion and importance of those links. In INTGRAT3, links are assigned to the simulator based on their importance and their impact on the network performance. ng desition Compared to the MATSIM [18] model, which is considered the state of the art in simulating large-scale transportation systems, INTGRAT3 is not only an agent-based simulation but also utilizes a hybrid simulation approach. Specifically, it is also capable of microscopically simulating all the transportation aspects including demand, mobility, traffic signals, and road network aspects, as will be described in next Sect. 3. Furthermore this microscopic modeling of the system extends to the modeling of train movements, pedestrians and bicyclists.

3   The INTGRAT3 Model

The INTGRAT3 model redefines the state-of-the-art of modeling and simulation of large-scale transportation systems by introducing a new framework that is capable of modeling large city level transportation systems. To achieve both the required accuracy and scalability, we utilize both the microscopic and mesoscopic modeling techniques.

The microscopic simulation defined in this paper includes all the aspects of simulation that covers demand, mobility, and network modeling. From the demand perspective, our framework can microscopically model each individual traveler and vehicle as an agent in the network that interacts with other travelers/vehicles as well as with traffic signals and control devices. It also provides dynamic demand modeling, that is, traffic demand changes throughout the simulation. From the mobility standpoint, the INTGRAT3 framework tracks every individual vehicle at a time resolution of a deci-second (0.1 s). These features are gained basically from the microscopic nature of the INTEGRATION traffic simulator [19] utilized in the INTGRAT3 model. Based on this time resolution, it captures all the driving events by using validated models for car following, lane changing and gap acceptance behavior modeling. The model also can simulate different stochastic mobility phenomena such as stochasticity in speed calculation, route selection, and driver aggressiveness in acceleration/deceleration events. From the network standpoint, many network topological details such as link control methods (stop sign, yield sign, and traffic signals), lane striping, lane prohibition, and high occupancy vehicles (HOV) lanes are modeled in this framework. To the best of our knowledge, none of the current traffic simulators support all these features for large-scale networks. The INTGRAT3 framework also incorporates other simulators for the modeling of the railway, pedestrian, and biking travel modes in addition to buses and carpooling. However, the details of these simulators are beyond the scope of this thesis.

An important advantage of the INTGRAT3 framework is its ability to track trips on a continuous basis across different modes. Because of the computational cost required for the above-mentioned simulations, the implemented framework uses two partitioning techniques: vertical and spatial. Vertical partitioning combines mesoscopic and microscopic road vehicle simulation along with mode specific simulations for walking, biking, and trains. Spatial partitioning divides the microscopic network into smaller geographic regions. A simulation controller divides each trip into sub-trips to be simulated in different processes and monitors each sub-trip to ensure consistency.

Before describing the model, the following subsection provides some definitions that will be used later in the model description.

3.1 Definitions

Global-network: The global road network includes all the road links in the area of interest. Each link is marked to be in the micro-network, the meso-network, or the train and pedestrian networks.

Meso-network: The meso-network is the connected subset of the links in the global-network that is simulated mesoscopically.

Micro-network: The micro-network is the connected subset of links in the global-network that is simulated microscopically.

Subnetwork: A subnetwork is a spatial partition of the micro-network. Subnetworks are simulated microscopically using INTEGRATION software.

Zones: Nodes that can act as an origin or destination of the traffic. To have a fully connected network, each zone in the micro-network is mapped to a corresponding zone in the meso-network. However, some zones in the meso-network do not exist in the micro-networks.

Interconnection Zones (IZones): Interconnection zones are correspondences between zones in different networks. For example, for the micro-meso network connectivity, the zones exist in both micro and meso networks are IZones.

Trip: A trip is a traveler's planned path from origin zone to destination zone in the global-network. A single trip can go through multiple network layers (multimodal trips) and/or multiple subnetworks. For example, in the trip shown in Fig. 1, a person can drive his/her car on the local road (in meso-network) from his/her home to the main road. Then, he/she continues driving on the main road in the micro-network (where he/she travels through two micro subnetworks). Then he/she parks his/her car and walks (on the pedestrian network layer) to the nearest railway station (rail network) from which he/she takes the train. Then he/she walks again to his/her work.

Trip Local Origin/Destination: Local origin/destination is the origin or destination for the controlled trip in one of the simulator or subnetwork.

Trip Origin/Destination: These are the ultimate origin or destination for each controlled trip on the global network.

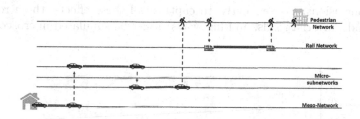

Fig. 1. Multimode trip example [21].

3.2 Vertical Partitioning

In vertical partitioning, each network type (micro and meso road networks, train and subway system network, biking network, and walking network) is represented by a different layer in the system. The connectivity between these layers is managed by the simulation controller. Multimodal trips across all these transportation modes and networks are achieved by the trip planner.

The micro- and the meso-network layers are critical because all vehicles are simulated in these two networks, while the other networks serve other modes of transportation working almost separately with minimum loss of coupling and interaction between them. Because both the micro and meso networks represent portions of the road network, one important question is how to divide the road network into these two layers. The main objectives of combining micro and meso simulations together is a double folded reason: to achieve the highest possible precision and accuracy while maintaining the system scalability. To achieve these two goals (precision/accuracy and scalability), we studied the different road link types and their impact on the system performance. The freeways, the minor and major arterial roads are the most influential roadway segments of the city transportation network compared to the local roads that are typically not highly traveled. These highly traveled roads can significantly affect the network performance because of two reasons. Firstly, the high traffic demand they carry compared to the local roads. Secondly, the traffic condition on the main roads, arterial roads and highways are characterized by their high variability from the uncongested regime through the congested regime compared to travel on the uncongested regime on the local roads, as shown in Fig. 2.

First, at moderate and high traffic demand levels, a vehicle's behavior can affect other vehicles because of the lateral and longitudinal interaction between vehicles. For example, if the leading vehicle decelerates, the following vehicle will have to decelerate to avoid a collision with the lead vehicle. Furthermore, when the headway increases, vehicles can accelerate towards the road free-flow speed. These acceleration/deceleration events have a noticeable impact on the network performance including fuel consumption and emission levels in addition to other measures of effectiveness including travel time, delay, stopped delay and vehicle stops. Using mesoscopic simulation for such links cannot capture all these events, which reduce the system fidelity considerably and has been shown to produce wrong conclusions. Consequently, to capture all these effects, these road links (main roads, arterial roads, and highways) must be simulated microscopically.

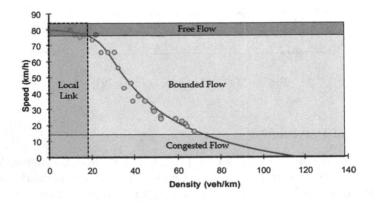

Fig. 2. The speed-density fundamental diagram and the link types.

On the other hand, the local roads that connect the main roads to residential areas are of low importance because of their low traffic demands. However, we cannot totally ignore these local roads, because they contribute to the travel time and fuel consumption of the vehicles. The low traffic demand on the local roads means that vehicles on these roads will be moving, most probably, at the road speed limits with minimal variations as shown in Fig. 2. Consequently, by using the average speed of the vehicles on the local road links to estimate the fuel consumption, emission levels and travel times, the accuracy will not be significantly reduced. Thus these links can be safely simulated mesoscopically with minimum impacts on the modeling precision/accuracy.

Secondly, the temporal traffic flow variation on minor/major arterials and highways/freeways are typically significant. Consequently, to accurately capture these temporal changes, the minor/major arterials and highways/freeways are modeled microscopically. Alternatively, for the local roads the variability in traffic flow is typically limited and are typically uncongested. Thus, the mesoscopic modeling is sufficient for the local roads.

Recognizing these issues, in the INTGRAT3 framework, the minor/major arterials and highways/freeways are simulated microscopically, thus providing the highest possible fidelity for this portion of the network. Alternatively, the local roads are modeled mesoscopically with minimum loss in modeling precision and accuracy.

Consequently, the framework has two vehicular layers: the meso-network and the micro-network layers. In addition, the framework supports layers for other transportation modes such as railway travelers, pedestrians and bicyclists. Figure 3 demonstrates the layering concept. A traveler using more than one transportation mode moves from one network to another, consequently from one simulator to another. These interactions between different simulators are managed by a simulation controller (SC). Simulations notify the SC when a traveler completes a sub-trip at an IZone. The SC finds the next sub-trip for the traveler and sends them to the appropriate simulator. The IZone must exist in the next network to guarantee trip connectivity.

Based on the scale of the area of interest, the micro-network can be divided into a set of subnetworks (spatial partitioning that will be described in the next subsection). Each subnetwork can run on a different processor or machine. In this way, we can utilize the available resources, and increase the simulation speed.

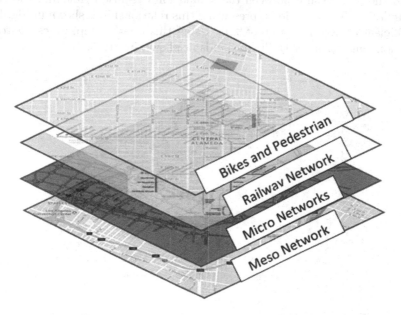

Fig. 3. Partitioning the network into different layers [21].

However, there is a trade-off between the simulation speed and accuracy. The larger the subnetwork size, the slower the simulation speed, but the higher the precision of the simulation results. Within a subnetwork, the simulator models all the impacts between all connected road links (e.g., queue spillbacks from one link to its upstream link, and the interactions between vehicles along a link and across different lanes along a roadway). Selecting the appropriate subnetwork sizes depends on the total network size, the traffic demand level, the available computational resources, and the desired simulation speed.

3.3   Spatial Partitioning

Spatial partitioning divides the road network into subnetworks, such that each subnetwork is simulated on a separate processor. All these processes are managed and connected using the simulation controller. Dividing the global network of interest into a set of subnetworks can significantly increase the simulation speed, because the simulation speed depends on the network size and the number of vehicles in the network. Our analysis for the simulation speed of the INTEGRA-TION software shows that the time to simulate one second can be represented as a square function in the number of vehicles in the network as shown in Figs. 4 and 5.

To get the results in these figures, we first ran the INTEGRATION software on a network with high traffic demands, and we recorded the execution time and the number of vehicles in the network periodically. We then fit a function to find the relationship between the simulation execution time and the vehicle accumulation. The equation representing this relationship is shown in Fig. 4 with a coefficient of determination of 0.95. Using this relationship, we estimated the execution time for lager traffic demands as shown in Fig. 5.

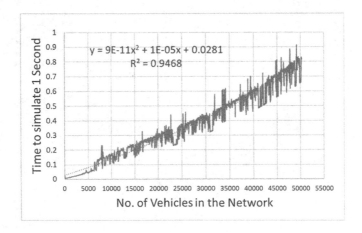

Fig. 4. Simulation time versus number of vehicles in the network.

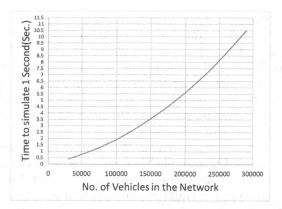

Fig. 5. Expected simulation time versus number of vehicles in the network.

Based on this relationship, in addition to the network information (size and traffic demand levels), we can identify the number of subnetworks needed to achieve the desired simulation speed.

3.4   Traveler Types

In our framework, there are two types of travelers: background and controlled.

Background Travelers: Background travelers create the network traffic conditions in each network, such as congestion levels in the micro-network and meso-networks and vehicle loading on public transit vehicles. In the micro-network, INTEGRATION tracks every individual traveler (both background and controlled). In the other simulators, the travelers of the background traffic are not tracked individually, instead, they are used to estimate the network state (e.g., congestion levels and train loads) in order to accurately calculate the travel time and fuel consumption.

Controlled Travelers: Each controlled traveler represents a person traveling from an origin to a destination at a particular time. The planner creates a multi-modal trip for each controlled traveler and submits it to the simulation controller, which in its turn ensures the traveler traverses the networks in the appropriate simulators. Each controlled trip is tracked on a second-by-second basis in all the transportation modes. Moreover, the controlled trip can be rerouted or replanned, while the person is traveling.

3.5   System Architecture and Components

Figure 6 shows the general architecture of the INTGRAT3 framework. A basic idea is separating the system software components from the hardware components. The communication layer is the enabler to transparently run this system on different infrastructures with minimal configuration changes. The communication layer utilizes the RabbitMQ implementation [22] of the Advanced Message Queuing Protocol (AMQP) [23].

The execution layer of the system consists of two plans: (1) the planning and simulation plan, which is responsible for simulating trips and creating the multimodal routes for the controlled trips and (2) the control plan, which is responsible for controlling and managing the different system components. The framework components are illustrated in Fig. 7.

The input data repository contains all the required input data to be used by the system components. For example, the roadmaps for both the meso-network, micro-network and the subnetworks are stored in this database along with the OD inputs that represent the traffic demand, transit schedules, energy models, and transit loading.

The SC manages the different simulations. When started, each simulation module imports the corresponding input files from the input database then it initializes its environment and starts its internal synchronization procedure that communicates to the SC.

Due to space limitation, we will give a brief overview of the operation for only the basic components including micro-simulator, meso-simulator, planner, and the SC while focusing on additions not reported in previous research.

3.6   INTEGRATION and Micro-Models

Micro-simulation using the INTEGRATION software is key to our framework. INTEGRATION is a discrete-time continuous-space trip-based microscopic traffic simulation and optimization model which is capable of modeling networks with thousands of cars. It is characterized by its accuracy that comes from its microscopic nature and its small-time granularity. INTEGRATION provides 10 traffic assignment/routing options with a full support of five vehicle classes, each class has its own parameters and routing trees.

INTEGRATION Car Following Model. INTEGRATION updates the vehicle speed and location every decisecond based on a user-specified steady-state speed-spacing relationship along with the speed differential between the subject vehicle and the heading vehicle. INTEGRATION uses the variable power vehicle dynamics model to estimate the vehicle's tractive force. Consequently, it implicitly accounts for gear-shifting on vehicle acceleration, which ensures a realistic estimation of the vehicle acceleration. More specifically, the model computes the vehicle's tractive effort, aerodynamic, rolling, and grade-resistance forces, as described in details in the literature [24,25]. In INTEGRATION,

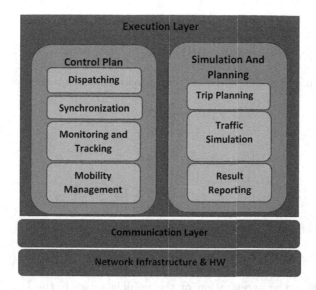

Fig. 6. System architecture [21].

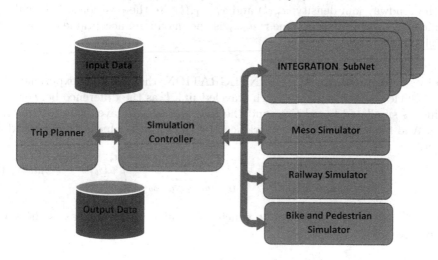

Fig. 7. System components [21].

the car-following model computes the speed $u_n(t + \Delta t)$ of the following vehicle (n) at the new time step $t + \Delta t$ as [19]:

$$u_n(t + \Delta t) = min\left\{ u_n(t) + a_n(t)\Delta t \, , \frac{-c_1 + c_3 u_f + \bar{S}_n(t + \Delta t) - \sqrt{A}}{2c_3}, \right.$$

$$\left. \sqrt{u_{(n-1)}(t + \Delta t)^2 + d_{max}(\bar{S}_n(t + \Delta t) - \frac{1}{k_j})} \right\} \quad (1)$$

where

$$A = \left(c_1 - c_3\, u_f\, \bar{s}_n(t + \Delta t)\right)^2 - 4c_3\left(\bar{s}_n(t + \Delta t)u_f - c_1\, u_f - c_2\right) \qquad (2)$$

and c_1, c_2, and c_3 are the model constants which are computed as:

$$c_1 = \frac{u_f}{k_j\, u_c^2}(2u_c - u_f) \qquad (3)$$

$$c_2 = \frac{u_f}{k_j\, u_c^2}(u_f - u_c)^2 \qquad (4)$$

$$c_3 = \frac{1}{q_c} - \frac{u_f}{k_j\, u_c^2} \qquad (5)$$

and the vehicle $\bar{s}_n(t + \Delta t)$ spacing is computed as:

$$s_n(t + \Delta t) = x_{(n-1)}(t) - x_n(t) + *u_{(n-1)}(t) - u_n(t)\Delta t + 0.5a_{(n-1)}(t + \Delta t)\Delta t^2 \quad (6)$$

Here $a_n(t)$ is the acceleration of the vehicle n; u_f is the free-flow speed of the roadway; u_c is the roadway speed-at-capacity; q_c is the roadway capacity; k_j is the roadway jam density; $x_n(t)$ and $x_{(n-1)}(t)$ are the positions of the subject vehicle the lead vehicle at time t; d_{max} is the maximum acceptable deceleration level (m/s^2).

Delay Computation. Within INTEGRATION, the delay D_n^l experienced by the vehicle n is computed for each traveled link l, as the difference between the vehicle's simulated travel time and the free-flow speed travel time for this link [26]. And the total delay D_n experienced by the subject vehicles is computed as:

$$D_n = \sum_{(l\,\in\,\text{the vehicle path})} D_n^l = \sum_{(l\,\in\,\text{the vehicle path})} \int_{t_0^l}^{t_1^l} (u_f - \frac{u(t)}{u_f})dt \qquad (7)$$

where t_0^l and t_1^l are the times at which the vehicle enters and exits the link l respectively.

Fuel Consumption and Emissions. The INTEGRATION modeler computes a number of measures every decisecond including the fuel consumed, vehicle emissions of carbon dioxide (CO_2), carbon monoxide (CO), hydrocarbons (HC), oxides of nitrogen (NOx), and particulate matter (PM) [19]. The granularity of decisecond computations permits the steady-state fuel consumption rate for each vehicle to be computed each second on the basis of its current instantaneous speed and acceleration level. INTEGRATION computes the fuel consumption and emission levels using the VT-Micro model [27] which was developed as a statistical model from experimentation with numerous polynomial combinations of speed and acceleration levels to construct a dual-regime model, as demonstrated in Eq. 8.

$$F(t) = \begin{cases} exp\left(\sum_{i=1}^{3}\sum_{j=1}^{3}L_{i,j}v^i a^j\right) & if \ a \geqslant 0 \\[2em] exp\left(\sum_{i=1}^{3}\sum_{j=1}^{3}M_{i,j}v^i a^j\right) & if \ a < 0 \end{cases} \qquad (8)$$

where $L_{i,j}$ are model regression coefficients at speed exponent i and acceleration exponent j, $M_{i,j}$ are model regression coefficients at speed exponent i and acceleration exponent j, v is the instantaneous vehicle speed in (km/h), and a is the instantaneous vehicle acceleration (km/h/s) [27].

3.7   Meso-Simulator

Modeling the arterial and highways at INTEGRATION's level of detail was a massive undertaking. To capture behavior the local roads, we introduce a "Meso-Network" that requires less modeling effort. In this network, the individual data of the vehicle (i.e. speed, fuel consumption, etc.), which is resource intensive to compute, is not tracked. A pseudo-macroscopic model is used. In this network each vehicle has an ID and a point in time after which it is expected to exit the current link. All links on the network are treated each as a priority queue based on the time of exit and the First In First Out (FIFO) principle (Fig. 8). At the current stage, we assume the following

1. No overtaking is allowed on the link;
2. A vehicle can only exit the link if there is no vehicle in front blocking;
3. The size of the queue on the link is not limited (i.e. infinite storage capacity);
4. The traffic in the mesoscopic network is composed of 90% background traffic (Traffic A) and 10% controlled traffic (Traffic B);
5. Even though, traffic A and B are on the same network, they do not interact with each other.

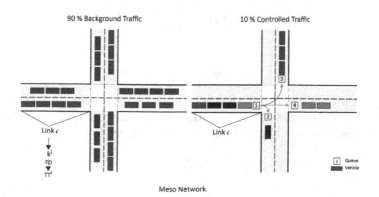

Fig. 8. Meso-Model Intersection representation.

Hypothesis (3) is chosen and currently implemented in order to avoid grid-lock, where the vehicles are stuck in the network and have no possibility of finding an exit way.

$$u = max \left(\frac{1 - C_1 \, k^i + C_3 \, k^i \, u_f - \sqrt{-4C_3 k^i \, (-C_2 k^i + u_f - C_1 k^i u_f) + (-1 + C_2 k^i - C_3 k^i u_f)^2}}{2 \, C_3 \, k^i}, u_c \right) \tag{9}$$

The fundamental diagram plays an important role in determining the time after which a vehicle is expected to exit the current link. Based on the current number of vehicles in the link (i.e. the density k^i of link i), the speed limit (i.e. u_f), speed at capacity (i.e. u_c) and jam density (i.e. k_j), the average speed on the link (i.e. u) is computed (Eq. 9) for the 90% background traffic.

This velocity is considered the average vehicle velocity at link i

$$TT^i = \frac{length \ link \ i}{u} \tag{10}$$

Equation 10 captures the delay caused by the 90% background traffic. It includes queuing and the delay due to traffic lights or stop signs. Since we assume (5) we capture the effect of the 90% on the 10% by accounting for the extra delay generated. The time of exit from the link i for a vehicle of the 10% controlled traffic is given by Eq. 3. It is the sum of the time of exit of the first vehicle ($T^i_{Exit(1)}$) in the queue from link i and the average travel time when considering the 90% uncontrolled traffic (TT^i) and the delay incurred by the vehicle due to the presence of other controlled vehicles in front when there is a traffic light or a stop sign

$$T^i_{Exit} = T^i_{Exit(1)} + TT^i + \begin{cases} t^i_{TL} \\ t^i_s \end{cases} \tag{11}$$

where, t^i_s is the delay associated with the presence of a stop sign on link i and t^i_{TL} is the delay associated with the presence of traffic lights

$$T^i_{TL} = \frac{p - 1}{\mu_{TL}} \tag{12}$$

where,

$$\mu_{TL} = q_c \frac{t_G}{t_Y + t_R + t_G} n \tag{13}$$

where, p is the number of controlled vehicles ahead in the link, t_R is the red time associated with the traffic light, t_Y is the yellow time, t_G is the green time, q_c is the saturation flow rate, and n is the number of lanes in the link.

$$t^i_s = \frac{p - 1}{\mu_s} \tag{14}$$

where, μ_s is the discharge rate associated with a stop sign.

The number of vehicles on a given queue cannot be infinite. Limitation on this number must be implemented, yet the phenomena of grid-lock might happen.

This approach present one main advantage. It has a very low footprint and can be implemented efficiently yet it does not consider the interaction of the queue associated with the 10% controlled traffic and the 90% background uncontrolled traffic. Ultimately, this model will enable a relevant real-time and fast prediction of the state of the network (i.e. congestion, expected delays, etc.) for a short to medium time horizon. This will be fed back to the controller for efficient trip (re)planning and re-routing of the controlled vehicles and could be also used to evaluate pre-defined control plans.

3.8 Planner

Each controlled traveler has an origin, destination, and a travel window. The main task of the planner is the planning of these multimodal routes for the controlled trip. The planner also is responsible for updating or changing these routes whenever needed. During a window that begins 30 min before the earliest possible departure time for the controlled traveler, the planner starts planning the trip by using the up-to-date cost and timing information reported from each individual simulator. It also uses the connectivity information between the different subnetworks and/or layers in order to create the optimal route for the subject trip. The trip can be replanned or rerouted after the trip starts. For example, if the traveler can not catch the train at the scheduled time, or he/she can not board the scheduled bus because the bus is full, the responsible simulator notifies the SC which requests the planner to find an alternative route for the traveler.

In addition to the trip planning, routing is an important function in the system model. In the INTGRAT3 model, there are two routing levels: strategic routing and tactical routing

Strategic Routing. Strategic routing is the high-level routing in the system. When the planner creates a trip, it should create is multimodal route based on the current network state. The objective function in the strategic routing level is to minimize the fuel consumption for each individual controlled trip considering different constraints including the travel time and distance in addition to the traveler preferences. It is easy to realize that using the fuel consumption as the only metric for the strategic routing can result in using the biking and walking only because both of them have zero energy consumption. Thus, the system uses other metrics as constraints when creating routes for the controlled trips. Among these metrics, the planner uses some user preferences such as the transportation mode preferences, the maximum walking distance, and the biking walking distance.

After creating the multimodal trip, the router finds the route for each mode in each network type, including the meso-network and the micro-network, the biking, and walking networks. Subsequently, this plan is sent to the SC to be executed in the network.

Tactical Routing. The different simulators are responsible for simulating the trip in its different modes. The simulators for the micro-network and the meso-network have their own routing engines, which are responsible for routing the vehicles in each individual subnetwork based on its current state. Initially, when the micro-simulator receives a trip from the SC, it initializes the route for this trip based on the route it received from the SC. Then, periodically, it updates this route based on the latest routing information in this subnetwork. Updating the controlled trip route does not change its local destination zone in the current subnetwork.

In the tactical routing level, each simulator uses its local information about the road links in its own network. More specifically, it used the fuel consumption cost for the road links as the metric and applies Dijkstra's algorithm to find the shortest path for the subject trip from its current location to its local destination.

The fuel consumption cost for both micro-network links and miso-network links are periodically updated. In the micro-network, the INTEGRATION software uses the technique described earlier in Sect. 3.6. For the meso-network, the fuel cost for the road links is calculated based on the average speed of the vehicles on each road link. This speed can be computed using the fundamental diagram shown in Fig. 2 by finding the vehicle density of on each road link. Because of the large size of the meso-network, its routing engine uses the A* algorithm [28, 29] instead of Dijkstra's algorithm.

3.9   Simulation Controller

The SC is a core component of the model, which is responsible for:

- Initializing the simulation,
- Synchronizing the different simulators,
- Moving travelers between layers/subnetworks, and
- Tracking the individual controlled trips.

In the initialization process, the SC reads parameters such as the simulation duration and the locations of the input files for each simulation component. Then it reads in the network files, builds the required graphs for the networks, and checks for the appropriate connectivity among the different layers/subnetworks. It also builds a list of all the controlled trips. Then, it starts the different simulators (INTEGRATION, meso-simulator, bike and pedestrian simulator (BPSim), and railway simulator (RailSim)) and waits for all of them to initialize.

When a simulator starts and initializes its own environment, it must send the first synchronization request to the SC and wait for the "simulation start" messages from the SC. When all the simulators are ready, the SC allows them to start the simulation. During the simulation, all the simulators must be synchronized at pre-specified intervals. This period is defined as the maximum synchronization interval, which is a system-wide variable. Its default value is 1 s. After this time interval, the simulator cannot progress the simulation process until permitted by the SC. So, after finishing the maximum synchronization interval, each simulator sends a synchronization request to the SC and waits for a the response from the SC. When the SC identifies that all the simulators reached the same simulation time, it allows them to run the next interval.

During the simulation, the SC receives the state information about each controlled trip or subtrip from each simulator. Consequently, it can track every individual controlled trip in different networks/layers and is responsible for moving the traveler from one subnetwork/layer to another. By doing so, the SC establishes the connectivity between different subnetworks/layers. For example, when a driver finishes his/her subtrip on the meso-network (say, IZone1) and needs to be moved to the micro network, the meso simulator informs the SC to (1) update the trip information (travel time, fuel consumption, and current location); (2) pull the trip information from its database and find the destination of the next sub-trip on the micro subnetwork (say, Z2); and (3) request the corresponding INTEGRATION instance to start a new sub-trip in its network from IZone1 to Z2 and passes the initial route for this sub-trip to INTEGRATION. In this case, INTEGRATION may defer the start time of this vehicle if the link to which the vehicle should enter is at jam density.

4   Case Study: LA Network

We use this system to model the overall city of LA in the morning peak hours. This section describes the network and the simulation results.

4.1   LA Networks

To build the micro-network and meso-network, we used three different data sources: (1) NavTeq is used for generating nodes and links, (2) OpenStreetMap is used for intersection traffic control information, and (3) Google Maps are used for validating road attributes including the number of lanes, one-way streets, speed limits, bus lane locations, etc. The global-network has 62,984 nodes and 181,840 links (Shown in Fig. 9). The LA area is divided into five subnetworks shown in Fig. 9. The walking and biking simulators use the meso-network as input. Our system model includes the largest operator of public rail and buses in LA, LA Metro. LA Metro bus service includes 170 lines, 15,967 bus stops, and 854,693 boardings/day. LA Metro rail service includes 6 passenger rail lines, 93 stations, and 359,861 boardings/day. Station level boarding data were provided by LA metro along with specifications of the vehicle fleet.

4.2   Traffic Calibration

The traffic is created based on real data from Performance Measurement System (PEMS) database. The count and speed data from PEMS database are aggregated and the traffic demand between each Origin-Destination (OD) pair is estimated using the QueensOD [30] software, which utilizes the Maximum Likelihood Least Relative Error (LRE) approach.

We run two levels of traffic calibration; the global demand level and the subnetwork demand level. The global demand calibration is used to compute the traffic demand across the global network during the peak hours (from 7:00 am to 10:00 am). Interested readers can refer to our paper [31] for detailed description of the global traffic demand calibration.

The subnetwork demand level is calibrated to compute the background travelers in each sub-network separately. For the subnetwork demand level, we add one hour (from 6:00 am to 7:00 am) for pre-loading, and two hour (from 10:00 am to 12:00 pm) for clearing the network. The vehicle count in Table 1 is the total traffic on each subnetwork that includes both the controlled and the background traffic.

The global network traffic calibration showed that there were approximately 1,739,665 vehicles trips in the Greater LA Area, from which a 10% random sample was selected uniformly across all OD pairs and was fixed for all experiments. When calibrating the ODs for the micro-networks (subnetwork demand level), it generated a total of 2,951,551 trips as shown in Table 1. The larger number of trips is attributed to the fact that a portion of the global trips pass through

Fig. 9. LA micro-network and selected subnetworks.

multiple subnetworks, and thus are divided into multiple sub-trips across the subnetworks and thus increasing the total number of trips.

In the experiments we also take into account the user acceptance of the planner recommendations. From the 10%, we assume only 50% accept the eco-route plans, resulting in only 5% of the global traffic being controlled. The dividing of the 5% the controlled trips across the sub-networks produced 117,269 controlled sub-trips in the different subnetworks which represents approximately 4% of the total sub-trips.

Table 1. Subnetwork sizes and vehicle counts.

Sub-net	Nodes	Links	Signals	Total vehicles	Controlled vehicles
1	743	1,691	256	515,098	21,823
2	940	2,251	361	610,398	21,586
3	1,625	3,561	459	734,810	29,860
4	741	1,724	237	594,478	23,273
5	647	1,507	203	496,767	20,727
Sum	4,696	10,734	1,516	2,951,551	117,269

5   Simulation Setup and Results

We created the system model to enable assessing potential system-wide effects of individual transportation decisions across the LA region in the morning peak hours. We ran three scenarios for the LA area.

1. **Base Scenario:** In this case all the travelers drive to their destination and make routing decisions based on the network conditions as seen by the system at the departure time, the routes are updated every 5 min. Drivers attempt to minimize their travel time.
2. **Controlled Scenario without Eco-routing:** In this scenario, by enabling the strategic routing, 5% of the total population followed the planner multi-modal route plan recommendations (50% of the 10% controlled trips). These plans were submitted to the different simulators to be executed. Our hypothesis was that the controlled case would produce city-wide energy reductions and reduced network congestion. In the plan execution, each simulator uses its tactical routing to route trips internally in response the local sub-network dynamics. The main simulator here is the micro-simulator, which is configured to use the Time-Dependent Feedback Assignment (SFA) [19] to route all the traffic (background and controlled)
3. **Controlled Scenario with Eco-routing:** this scenario is similar to the previous with the exception that the micro-simulator is configured to use the Subpopulation Feedback-based ECO-routing (SPF-ECO) [32] for the controlled traffic, while the Time-Dependent Feedback Assignment (SFA) [19] is used for the background traffic.

For each case, the total fuel consumption and total delay are computed. We ran each case multiple times (4 to 7 runs) with different seeds, and we used the output to compute the mean and confidence interval.

Looking into the controlled results in more detail, we compared the average fuel consumption per vehicle in both controlled cases for each individual subnetwork as shown in Table 3, which also shows the average total savings. It shows, in both cases, the average fuel consumption for the controlled traffic is lower than that for the background traffic. These results demonstrate that planning routes by utilizing strategic and tactical routing together is better than routing decisions made by the individual travelers (which utilizes tactical routing only).

Table 3 also shows that individual vehicles that were routed using eco-routing saved 17.5% fuel over the standard routing of the background traffic compared to only 8% for those without eco-routing, which shows that eco-routing helps reducing the fuel consumption for the controlled trips. However, it does not improve the system wide fuel consumption significantly given the small percentage of controlled vehicles (5% of the total population).

Table 2 compares the fuel consumption and delay in the controlled case to the base case. It shows that the fuel savings for controlled cases are 2.4% and the delay savings are 9.5% and 10.5% respectively.

Table 2. Fuel consumption and delay.

Measurements	Base	Controlled no ECO		Controlled with ECO	
		Total	Av. saving 95% confidence	Total	Av. saving 95% confidence
Fuel (L)	3,195,637	3,118,768	2.4% 1.2% to 3.5%	3,117,563	2.44% 1.4% to 3.5%
Delay (S)	897,198,320	812,301,524	9.5% 2.1% to 16.8%	802,559,225	10.5% 3.8% to 17.2%

Table 3. Subnetwork sizes and vehicle counts.

Subnet	Controlled no ECO			Controlled with ECO		
	Background	Controlled	Saving%	Background	Controlled	Saving%
1	1.2333	1.1187	9.29	1.2206	1.0063	17.56
2	1.028	0.9495	7.636	0.9963	0.8431	15.4
3	0.9823	0.7981	18.75	0.9819	0.731	25.6
4	0.9603	1.0125	4.62	0.9786	0.8255	15.664
5	1.0926	1.0994	−0.623	1.2608	1.1258	10.7
Total av. saving			8.64			17.55

6   Conclusion

In this paper we utilize parallel computing, interprocess communication and traffic flow theory to propose, develop, and test a novel framework for transportation simulation entitled INTGRAT3. INTGRAT3 is a multimodal large-scale agent-based transportation network modeling system that offers a wide spectrum of applications. The INTGRAT3 system is capable of modeling large urban cities including different transportation modes of travel (driving, biking, walking, riding a bus, riding a train, and carpooling). It can run on different hardware architectures including either single or multiple machines. This system is tested by modeling the Greater LA Area during the morning peak period. The results show that by re-planning 10% of the trips, the performance of the network can be significantly improved in terms of delay (10.5% on average) and marginal savings in fuel consumption (2.44% on average). The results also show that eco-routing can save fuel consumption for the controlled population, however, its system-wide impact is marginal given the low level of market penetration (only 50% of the 10% accept the planner and eco-routing recommendations).

In the future we plan to utilize the system to conduct a sensitivity analysis for different network parameters such as traffic congestion levels and controlled population penetration rates. We also plan to use the system to study the LA transportation system performance in the case of different weather conditions such as heavy rain and special events (e.g. a basketball or baseball game).

An important future work is to improve the system to achieve faster simulation speed. Currently, the average simulation speed is approximately real-time, i.e., every virtual second is simulated in 1 actual seconds. We also plan to improve the mesoscopic traffic simulator to achieve better estimates of energy consumption, delay, and travel time. It is also important to study the complexity of the system by quantifying its simulation speed and memory usage for different demand levels. An advantage of a detailed system model like the one developed in this chapter is that it enables modeling mode changes for different scenarios including traffic incidents, roadway construction, and special events. We intend to explore potential savings that could result from informed decision-making by groups of travelers in these scenarios.

Acknowledgements. This work was funded by the Advanced Research Projects Agency-Energy (ARPA-E) under award number DE-AR0000612.

References

1. Levy, J.I., Buonocore, J.J., von Stackelberg, K.: Evaluation of the public health impacts of traffic congestion: a health risk assessment. Environ. Health **9**, 65 (2010)
2. Boniface, S., Scantlebury, R., Watkins, S., Mindell, J.: Health implications of transport: evidence of effects of transport on social interactions. J. Transp. Health **2**(3), 441–446 (2015)
3. Osorio, C., Selvam, K.K.: Solving large-scale urban transportation problems by combining the use of multiple traffic simulation models. Transp. Res. Procedia **6**, 272–284 (2015)

4. Zehe, D., Knoll, A., Cai, W., Aydt, H.: SEMSim Cloud Service: large-scale urban systems simulation in the cloud. Simul. Model. Pract. Theor. **58**, 157–171 (2015)
5. Zhang, C., Osorio, C., Flötteröd, G.: Efficient calibration techniques for large-scale traffic simulators. Transp. Res. Part B Methodol. **97**, 214–239 (2017)
6. Ahn, K., Rakha, H.: The effects of route choice decisions on vehicle energy consumption and emissions. Transp. Res. Part D Transp. Environ. **13**(3), 151–167 (2008)
7. Nagel, K., Rickert, M., Barrett, C.L.: Large scale traffic simulations. In: Palma, J.M.L.M., Dongarra, J. (eds.) VECPAR 1996. LNCS, vol. 1215, pp. 380–402. Springer, Heidelberg (1997). https://doi.org/10.1007/3-540-62828-2_131
8. White, R., Engelen, G.: Cellular automata and fractal urban form: a cellular modelling approach to the evolution of urban land-use patterns. Environ. Plan. A **25**(8), 1175–1199 (1993)
9. Cetin, N., Nagel, K., Raney, B., Voellmy, A.: Large-scale multi-agent transportation simulations. Comput. Phys. Commun. **147**(1–2), 559–564 (2002)
10. Raney, B., Cetin, N., Völlmy, A., Vrtic, M., Axhausen, K., Nagel, K.: An agent-based microsimulation model of Swiss travel: first results. Netw. Spat. Econ. **3**(1), 23–41 (2003)
11. Balmer, M., Nagel, K., Raney, B.: Large-scale multi-agent simulations for transportation applications. Intell. Transp. Syst. **8**, 205–221 (2004)
12. Zhao, Y., Sadek, A.W.: Large-scale agent-based traffic micro-simulation: experiences with model refinement, calibration, validation and application. Procedia Comput. Sci. **10**, 815–820 (2012)
13. Guo, L., Huang, S., Sadek, A.W.: An evaluation of environmental benefits of time-dependent green routing in the greater Buffalo-Niagara region. J. Intell. Transp. Syst. **17**(1), 18–30 (2013)
14. Burghout, W., Koutsopoulos, H., Andreasson, I.: Hybrid mesoscopic-microscopic traffic simulation. Transp. Res. Rec. J. Transp. Res. Board **1934**, 218–255 (2005)
15. Burghout, W., Wahlstedt, J.: Hybrid traffic simulation with adaptive signal control. Transp. Res. Rec. J. Transp. Res. Board **1999**, 191–197 (2007)
16. Yang, Q., Morgan, D.: Hybrid traffic simulation model. In: Transportation Research Board 85th Annual Meeting, no. 06–2582 (2006)
17. Balakrishna, R., Morgan, D., Slavin, H., Yang, Q.: Large-scale traffic simulation tools for planning and operations management. IFAC Proc. Vol. **42**(15), 117–122 (2009)
18. Balmer, M., Rieser, M., Meister, K., Charypar, D., Lefebvre, N., Nagel, K.: MATSim-T: architecture and simulation times. In: Bazzan, A., Klügl, F. (eds.) Multi-Agent Systems for Traffic and Transportation Engineering, pp. 57–78. IGI Global, Hershey (2009)
19. Rakha, H.A., Ahn, K., Moran, K.: INTEGRATION framework for modeling eco-routing strategies: logic and preliminary results. Int. J. Transp. Sci. Technol. **1**(3), 259–274 (2012)
20. Cetin, N., Nagel, K.: Parallel queue model approach to traffic microsimulations. In: Proceedings of Swiss Transportation Research Conference, STRC 2002 (2002)
21. Elbery, A., Dvorak, F., Du, J., Rakha, H.A., Klenk, M.: Large-scale agent-based multi-modal modeling of transportation networks - system model and preliminary results. In: Proceedings of the 4th International Conference on Vehicle Technology and Intelligent Transport Systems - Volume 1: VEHITS, pp. 103–112. INSTICC, SciTePress (2018)
22. Williams, J., Videla, A.: RabbitMQ in Action: Distributed Messaging for Everyone. Manning Publications, Grand Forks (2012)

23. Fernandes, J.L., Lopes, I.C., Rodrigues, J.J., Ullah, S.: Performance evaluation of RESTful web services and AMQP protocol. In: 2013 Fifth International Conference on Ubiquitous and Future Networks (ICUFN), pp. 810–815, IEEE (2013)
24. Rakha, H., Lucic, I., Demarchi, S.H., Setti, J.R., Aerde, M.V.: Vehicle dynamics model for predicting maximum truck acceleration levels. J. Transp. Eng. **127**(5), 418–425 (2001)
25. Rakha, H., Lucic, I.: Variable power vehicle dynamics model for estimating truck accelerations. J. Transp. Eng. **128**(5), 412–419 (2002)
26. Dion, F., Rakha, H., Kang, Y.-S.: Comparison of delay estimates at under-saturated and over-saturated pre-timed signalized intersections. Transp. Res. Part B Methodol. **38**(2), 99–122 (2004)
27. Rakha, H., Ahn, K., El-Shawarby, I., Jang, S.: Emission model development using in-vehicle on-road emission measurements. In: Annual Meeting of the Transportation Research Board, Washington, DC, vol. 2 (2004)
28. Lerner, J., Wagner, D., Zweig, K.A. (eds.): Algorithmics of Large and Complex Networks: Design, Analysis, and Simulation. Springer, Heidelberg (2009). https://doi.org/10.1007/978-3-642-02094-0
29. Zeng, W., Church, R.L.: Finding shortest paths on real road networks: the case for A*. Int. J. Geogr. Inf. Sci. **23**, 531–543 (2009)
30. Aerde, M., Rakha, H., Paramahamsan, H.: Estimation of origin-destination matrices: relationship between practical and theoretical considerations. Transp. Res. Rec. J. Transp. Res. Board **1831**, 122–130 (2003)
31. Du, J., Rakha, H.A., Elbery, A., Klenk, M.: Microscopic simulation and calibration of a large-scale metropolitan network: issues and proposed solutions. In: Transportation Research Board 96th Annual Meeting, TRB2018 (2018)
32. Ahn, K., Rakha, H.A.: Network-wide impacts of eco-routing strategies: a large-scale case study. Transp. Res. Part D Transp. Environ. **25**, 119–130 (2013)

Distributed Quality of Information-Aware Decision-Making in Vehicular Networks

Tobias Meuser$^{(\boxtimes)}$, Martin Wende, Patrick Lieser, Björn Richerzhagen, and Ralf Steinmetz

Multimedia Communications Lab, Technische Universitaet Darmstadt,
Darmstadt, Germany
`tobias.meuser@kom.tu-darmstadt.de`

Abstract. Advanced Driver Assistance Systems require huge amounts of sensor information to increase driver comfort and safety. As the range of on-board sensors is limited, vehicles exchange information to enhance their view on the environment. However, the exchanged measurements may be outdated or based on inaccurate sensor data, requiring additional processing and reasoning. Thus, the received measurements need to be evaluated to determine the correct value. State-of-the-art decision-making approaches focus on static information and ignore the temporal dynamics of the environment, which is characterized by high change rates in the vehicular scenario. Hence, they lack an optimal balance between adaptability to new information and robustness to false information.

We use a quality of information based weight to rate measurements according to their validity. This aggregation, however, works best if the amount of measurements is high. On barely trafficked roads, in-network caches are volatile. Thus, we utilize server-side cache to increase the performance for those roads. Thus, we combine the advantages of server-side and vehicle-side caches to achieve close-to-optimal results, while keeping hardware requirements of the server low.

In our evaluation, we used a simulation model of the city of Cologne to show the adaptability of our approach to different traffic situations. We show, that our approach increases the quality of other caching and decision-making approaches by up to 13% , while simultaneously decreasing the network load by up to 93%.

Keywords: Decision-making · Distributed · Quality of information · Information Lifetime · Information Accuracy

1 Introduction

Todays Advanced Driver Assistance Systems (ADASs) support the driver to increase comfort and safety [1]. These systems often rely on huge amounts of sensor data, which is gathered by on-board sensors. However, the physical restrictions to those sensors limit the quantity and quality of this data. To support the increasing data demands of ADAS, vehicles exchange information in the form of events.

© Springer Nature Switzerland AG 2019
B. Donnellan et al. (Eds.): SMARTGREENS 2018/VEHITS 2018, CCIS 992, pp. 304–327, 2019.
https://doi.org/10.1007/978-3-030-26633-2_15

Exchanging events induces both additional challenges and possibilities. Using events about the traffic flow provided by other vehicles, a vehicle can increase its route planning and traffic efficiency. Moreover, events about the road state can enhance the comfort of drivers, as the drivers can adapt earlier to arising situations. These events become even more pivotal for autonomous vehicles. The downside of exchanging events is the potential reception and handling of false events. False events occur due to sensor inaccuracy, and as a result of the higher number of messages being received, the number of false events increases likewise.

In a conventional vehicle with a human driver, the validation of information is up to the human driver, who rates information intuitively and makes a decision based on prior knowledge. Unlike, autonomous or partly autonomous vehicles lack human validation and need to make decisions based on contradictory information. As the majority of events is correct, approaches like [2] can be used to determine the correct value. However, these approaches need to be configured and, thus, do not adapt to the dynamic environmental conditions. For example, the traffic situation might be changing more or less frequently depending on the time of the day.

In our previous work [3], we proposed a decision-making process based on an information quality rating method that can cope with ambiguous or contradictory information. Each vehicle execute the decision-making by itself using the events provided to them via push-based communication. However, if a road is barely trafficked, push-based communication is not always sufficient, as the number of vehicles measuring the event is not sufficient.

In this work, we focus on this issue by introducing a trusted server, which is capable of both storing and forwarding of events. While the vehicles are driving along their road, they periodically access the server cache to pull available events using *pull-based* communication. As we expect a monitoring of the vehicles position on the server side to support eCall related functions, this pulling does not induce additional data traffic.

As server resources are expensive, it is important that the available resources are used efficiently. To this end, not all events measured by the vehicles can be stored on the server. In order to improve the performance of our system, we store events at the server that have the biggest impact on the performance. Events with a big impact on the performance are normally events that occur on barely trafficked roads, as edge caching cannot be performed in this case. Events, that cannot be cached at the server will be distributed using *push-based* communication to preserve server resources. Thus, a hybrid strategy combining *push-based* and *pull-based* communication is required.

We evaluate our approach for a traffic jam scenario in the city of Cologne. As an example, Fig. 1 displays one jammed road. The vehicles at the POA can sense the average road speed, while this information is required by the vehicles at the AOI. To this end, the vehicles at the POA transmit the event to a central server, which either preprocesses the event or forwards the raw event dependent on the available resources. In our evaluation, we show that our approach is working properly in complex scenarios and that our approach can utilize even

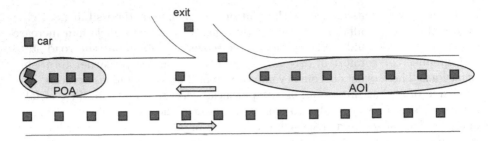

Fig. 1. Jammed/blocked road. The vehicles at the Place of Action (POA) can sense the information and transmit them to the vehicles in the Area of Interest (AOI). Taken from [3].

small server caches to increase the quality of the decision-making. Additionally, the utilization of a server cache decreases the network load significantly.

The remainder of the paper is structured as follows: We discuss existing caching systems and their handling of ambiguous information in Sect. 2. In Sect. 3, we describe the analyzed scenario. After that, we describe our approach presented in [3], the freshness-based majority voting approach for decision-making under ambiguous or contradictory information in Sect. 4. Section 5 describes the utilization of server-side resources to increase the performance of our approach in complex scenarios. Section 6 contains an in-depth evaluation of our approach, comparing its performance against state-of-the-art decision-making processes and our approach from previous work [3]. Finally, we conclude this paper with Sect. 7.

2   Related Work

In this section, we summarize the previous works in the context of this paper. As our approach is based on the quality of the information for decision-making, we first provide an overview of the respective literature. After that, we provide an overview of previous works towards decision-making in distributed systems.

2.1   Quality of Information (QoI) in Distributed Networks

In the literature, Quality of Information (QoI) assessment is a repetitive topic. As one of the first researchers in this field, Wang and Strong [4] surveyed data consumers on essential quality dimensions for information management systems. Based on this work, other researchers adapted the QoI dimensions for their applications like the mobile internet [5] and vehicular networks [2].

In vehicular networks, QoI is pivotal for the evaluation of sensor information [2]. Different quality dimensions have been assessed in the literature: the content quality [3,6], the trust between the vehicles [7] and the spatio-temporal relevance of information [8–11].

Different metrics have been proposed that rate information in the vehicular context. Delot et al. [9,12] estimated the geographical relevance of information in vehicular networks, which they used for hiding irrelevant information from the driver. For enhancing the communication in vehicular networks, we rated the relevance of information in our previous work [11]. To assess the trust in an information, Molina et al. [7,13] researched on evaluating the trust in an information. Compared to that, Meuser et al. [3,6] developed an approach to rate the content quality of information by considering sensor accuracy and the Time to Live (TTL) of information.

The age combined with the TTL is also used as a quality metric in the literature. For the temporal quality, Kuppusamy et al. [10] published an approach called Cluster Based Data Consistency (CBDC). They concentrated on increasing the data consistency and accessibility in clustered Mobile Ad-hoc Networks (MANETs) and assured the freshness of information using a TTL value. After the expiration of the TTL, the information is considered invalid and removed from the cache. While this approach considered a fixed TTL, Fawaz et al. [14] choose the TTL dynamically dependent on the history of changes. With their work, it is possible to estimate the TTL of an information type and, thus, aggregate only recent information to adapt faster to environmental changes.

2.2 Decision-Making

Decision-making approaches are important for vehicular networks, but have already been investigated in the field of Wireless Sensor Networks (WSNs). By utilizing the spatio-temporal relation between events, the decision-making of an entity can be improved [8]. Moreover, different approaches using weighted majority voting have been proposed [15,16]. While most vehicular applications rely on a threshold for the number of messages required to make a decision [2], some approaches utilize the above metrics to improve the quality of the decision.

Hsiao et al. [13] modeled the validation of message based on their quality implicitly. Although their approach focuses on trust, it can be used for inaccurate information likewise. They validated messages of other vehicles using the already received messages and performed an adaptation only if the number of received messages is sufficiently low.

Caballero-Gil et al. [17] performed a probabilistic validation of received data in Vehicular Ad-hoc Networks (VANETs). In their approach, multiple vehicle agreeing on one measurement are signing it to decrease the transmission overhead.

Dietzel et al. [18] proposed a secure data aggregation approach, in which attestation meta-information are used to evaluate the trustworthiness of a message. If a vehicle agrees on an information, it can sign an attestation to express its trust in the value. This attestation can later be used to evaluate the correctness of the information.

In previous work [3], we evaluate the information by performing a weighted majority voting. The weight depends on the information type and considers information-specific properties like accuracy and lifetime. We performed the decision-making on the vehicles, however, the performance drops for barely traf-ficked roads, as storing information at the vehicles is not always sufficient. Often, meta-information about the stored information are kept at static instances to decrease the challenges of mobility [19]. In this work, we will store some informa-tion at a central server to increase the quality of our decision-making. In contrasts to the approaches in the literature, we utilize the existing server resources, while simultaneously storing most information at the vehicles.

3   Scenario Description

In order to exchange events, vehicles utilize multiple different technologies. While the wifi-based 802.11p standard is commonly used for emergency communication, it is not suitable for long-range communication. For long-range communication, the cellular communication is much more suitable. Using the cellular communi-cation, vehicles distribute events to distant vehicles to improve their awareness and decision-making. Events in the vehicular context contain meta-information like the detection time, the detection place and the expected lifetime. That meta-information is essential for other vehicles to rate the information.

In our scenario, we assume that there is complete cellular coverage and a server available for the distribution of events. Each vehicle is equipped with a cellular network connection. Most events are distributed among the affected vehi-cles using push-based communication via the Publish/Subscribe pattern. How-ever, to increase the system performance, the server is capable of storing some events. These events are distributed using pull-based communication, as some events are not suitable for a push-based distribution. In the following section, we explain our event messaging system in more detail.

3.1   Event Messaging System

While driving on the streets, each vehicle perceives its environment and shares the perceived events with interested vehicles. For that, the vehicle publishes the event to a central server, which is responsible for the distribution of the events.

Dependent on the load at the server, this server either stores the event until it is required or distributes it to concerned vehicles. In order to access the stored events from the vehicles, each vehicle provides position updates to the server. If a vehicle is close to an event's location, the server shares the event with that vehicle. However, if the server cannot store an event, the event is forwarded to vehicles in a certain area and cached by those vehicles. By doing this, we decrease the load on the server while simultaneously minimizing the loss of information.

3.2   Scenario Description

In this work, we focus on an example scenario, which is visualized in Fig. 2. It can be divided into 4 different phases. The first phase is the default phase, in which the traffic is flowing as expected.

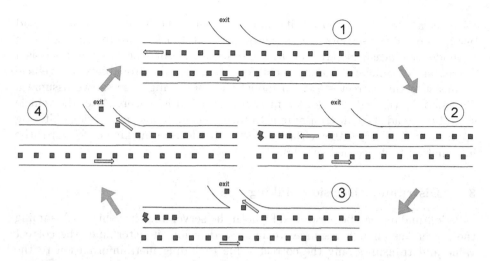

Fig. 2. Visualization of the different road phases. The vehicles require some time to adapt to the environmental changes and adapt their behavior. Taken from [3].

However, due to for example weather conditions, the road starts to get jammed in the second phase. Different to our scenario from previous work [3], a road is not either blocked or not blocked, but the traffic speed is changing constantly. Dependent on the speed of the traffic, a vehicle might want to leave the road to have a more efficient route. However, the vehicles that are able to detour do not have information about the traffic flow after the exit. They receive this information from the server, who forwards or provides information sensed by the vehicles in the jam. Once the vehicles start leaving the road, the third phase starts.

In the third phase, the road is jammed and all vehicles are leaving the road. However, the traffic jam is resolving after some time, while the vehicles still take the exit. This leads to the fourth phase.

In the fourth phase, the vehicles take the exit, although the traffic jam has already resolved. As staying on the road is the fastest route, these vehicles need to be informed about the resolving of the jam and stop exiting the route. Once the drivers start using the road again, the scenario is back in its default state.

3.3   Traffic Jam Modeling

The example scenario uses a traffic jam as an example for a detour reason. To make decisions based on the information type, we need to model the information. We do this using a Hidden Markov Model (HMM) as already used in [6]. With this HMM based on historic data, we can model our traffic jam appropriately. Our model has 15 different states, each state having a width of 10.8 km/h. Thus, the possible average speeds are between 0 km/h and roughly 160 km/h. In the Cologne scenario used in the evaluation, most streets speed limits are between 30 km/h and 70 km/h.

Once a vehicle enters a road, it is able to measure the current state of this road using its on-board sensors. Those sensors are not 100% accurate, thus, we need to model the measuring error of the sensors. The sensor inaccuracy is given as a percentage of which the measurement is correct, i. e., the probability of a vehicle to measure the correct state. To model the measuring process, we assume a Gaussian distributed error for the measurements of the sensors. After the vehicle sensed the road state, it transmits it to the server without any previous filtering operations. The server then either performs the decision-making or forwards the information to concerned vehicles.

3.4 Distributed Decision-Making

Decision-making can be performed by both the server and the vehicles. Assuming the server has enough resources to make a decision, it determines the correct value and transmits only the correct value including meta-information to the vehicles. This process is explained in more detail in Sect. 5.

Every time a vehicle has the chance of a detour, it queries the server for an update and checks the events in its local cache. If there is a road-related information for the road segments after the current and the next exit, the vehicle evaluates the available events. These events might be both already decided and raw events, which are combined by the vehicle to derive the final decision. If the vehicle determines that the road is jammed, it takes the exit.

4   Quality of Information Based Decision-Making

In this section, we describe the decision-making approach proposed in our previous work [3]. Decision-making algorithms are an important enabler for future partly and fully autonomous vehicles. In this work, we focus on the application of jam detection. Like most other information required by vehicular applications, the jam state of the road changes regularly.

While the evaluation of provided information in the current vehicular applications involves humans, this possibility will not be available for future autonomous vehicles. Thus, formalized methods need to be developed to rate the accuracy of an information. Existing approaches from literature do not use the full potential of information, as they do not consider these information-specific properties like accuracy and lifetime. This leads to a lack of either adaptability or robustness, while an optimal balance is desirable.

Missing adaptability leads to a slow adaptation to environmental changes, as the vehicle still considers old information as correct. This misinformation induces costs for the vehicles, which is, e. g., the unnecessary rerouting in case of a traffic jam. Contrary, robustness is very important in the vehicular scenario to be prone to false information. If the robustness is low, the vehicle adapts to information too quickly, leading to frequent decision changes and wrong decisions.

Robustness and adaptability are obviously opposites, if an approach is very robust, it generally lacks adaptability and vice versa. As the requirements on adaptability and robustness are strongly correlated to information-specific properties, we aim to find the optimal balance between adaptability and robustness based on these properties.

In the following, we derive a formula for the costs of both adaptability and robustness. We refer to the costs induced by adaptability as the costs for slow adaptation and to the costs induced by robustness as the costs for fast adaptation. We solve the resulting optimization problem to achieve the lowest possible costs for a certain information type.

4.1   Problem Formulation

For convenience, Table 1 provides an overview of the used variables.

Table 1. Overview of used variables. Taken from [3].

Variable	Description
c_{total}	Total costs of wrong decisions
c_{slow}	Costs of slow adaptation
c_{fast}	Costs of fast adaptation
n	Number of messages for adaptation
n_{opt}	Optimal number of messages for adaptation
p_f	Rate of incorrectly sensed information
p_c	Change probability of the sensed environment per time interval
T	Time to Live (TTL) for the information type
C_{fast}	Costs of an incorrect change of decision per time interval
C_{slow}	Costs of an incorrect keep of decision per time interval
t_i	Age of information i
s_i	State of information i
$f_b(t_i)$	Impact function of information i
$I(s)$	Impact of all information of state s

Our aim is to minimize the costs $c_{total}(n)$, which captures the additional effort of the vehicles caused by wrong information as shown in Eq. 1. n is the optimized variable and states the number of messages after which a vehicle adapts to incoming information. Thus, n states the adaptation speed of the approach and needs to be optimized to achieve the optimal balance between robustness and adaptability.

$$\min c_{total}(n) \tag{1}$$

The total costs $c_{total}(n)$ combine the costs of slow and fast adaptation. As already mentioned before, the costs of slow and fast adaptation are counterparts. The total costs are displayed in Eq. 2.

$$c_{total}(n) = c_{fast}(n) + c_{slow}(n) \tag{2}$$

The costs $c_{fast}(n)$ for a too fast adaptation are induced by a high adaptability. This leads to a high impact of erroneous measurements, which can change the vehicles decision. Thus, for low accuracy measurements, the adaptability is required to be slow, while the robustness is pivotal. The costs $c_{slow}(n)$ for a too slow adaptation are induced by a high robustness. If the real variable value changes, but the vehicle does not adapt to this change, the vehicle makes the wrong decision. For high accuracy information, the decision-making is not required to be robust, but may adapt to incoming information fast.

The costs $c_{fast}(n)$ are calculated in Eq. 3. They consist of the probability for a vehicle receiving a sufficiently high number of wrong information to adapt to them. The vehicle calculates this probability using the false detection rate p_f derived from a HMM. In this work, we utilize the average false detection rate for this purpose. However, not all false decision have the same impact. Thus, the variable C_{fast} captures the average costs that a false adaptation would have. For example, if the false decision would make the vehicle drive into a traffic jam, the costs are lower compared to a vehicle driving into a blocked road.

$$c_{fast}(n) = p_f^n * C_{fast} \tag{3}$$

The costs $c_{slow}(n)$ are shown in Eq. 5. They consider the number of messages n, the probability for a change p_c and the costs of the wrong decision C_{slow}. As long as a vehicle does not receive n messages, it will not adapt to the environmental change. Thus, it will make a the wrong decision. We derive the probability for a change p_c from the rate r of incoming messages per second and the TTL T. Each vehicle measures this rate based on the already received messages, but in the decision-making process, the rate is considered to be constant. We calculate p_c under the assumption that the message is invalid after the TTL T. A message is invalid once the message cannot provide any information about the current state of the variable. Equation 4 shows the value for p_c. $|S|$ describes the number of possible states.

$$p_c = 1 - \sqrt[T]{\left(\frac{1}{|S|}\right)^r} \tag{4}$$

The costs C_{slow} are calculated similarly to the costs C_{fast}, using the additional costs induced by a bad decision.

$$c_{slow}(n) = n * p_c * C_{slow} \tag{5}$$

4.2 Optimization Problem

Our aim is to minimize the costs induced by wrong decisions c_{total}. We find this minimum by deriving the costs $c_{total}(n)$ for our optimization parameter n and set the resulting equation to 0 as shown in Eq. 6. This equation can be transformed to Eq. 7.

$$\frac{\delta}{\delta n} c_{total}(n) = 0 \tag{6}$$

$$p_f^n * \ln(p_f) * C_{fast} + p_c * C_{slow} = 0 \tag{7}$$

Solving Eq. 7 results in the optimal number of messages n_{opt}. If a vehicles adapts to incoming information after n_{opt} messages, the total costs are minimal. Equation 8 shows the optimal value n_{opt}. We require the number n_{opt} to be integral, thus round it.

$$n_{opt} = \left\lfloor \frac{\ln\left(-\dfrac{p_c}{\ln(p_f)} * \dfrac{C_{slow}}{C_{fast}}\right)}{\ln(p_f)} \right\rfloor \tag{8}$$

In order to achieve the minimal costs, our approach needs to adapt to incoming information after n_{opt} messages. An approach from the literature adapts after it receives n_{opt} messages in a row. However, this approach still lacks adaptability, as at least n_{opt} messages in a row are required to adapt to a change of the environment. This assumption is not valid especially for low accuracy information, as the probability to receive n_{opt} correct messages in a row is very small. Thus, the approach cancels the adaptation in most cases, leading to a very poor adaptation to environmental changes. In order to solve this issue, we develop an algorithm that solves this problem in the next chapter.

4.3   Quality of Information-Based Majority Voting

Our freshness-based majority voting approach optimizes the costs for false decisions. In the existing literature, two main approaches are proposed for decision making:

A conventional approach is to decide after a certain amount of information. As already described above, this approach generally lacks adaptability as a certain amount of messages in a row is required for an adaptation. Moreover, the determination of the number of messages is a challenge for this approach and greatly influences its performance.

The other standard approach decides using all information stored in its cache. It considers the information as correct, which is most often stored in the cache. This approach is resilient to incorrect information, but adapts to changes slowly.

Our approach is based on majority voting and combines the advantages of both these approaches. In conventional majority voting, every vote has equal weight. While majority voting is very resilient to incorrect information, it lacks adaptability to environmental changes. We increase the adaptability by introducing a weight for each cache entry in the voting process. The weight the information ensures that the vehicle adapts after an optimal amount n_{opt} of information. Additionally, it depends on the information-specific parameters accuracy and lifetime, which is described in the following:

Given a set of messages M for a particular edge, the vehicle calculates the impact of a message using the age t_i and the state s_i of the messages $i = 1..|M|$ as shown in Eq. 9. M_s is the subset of messages containing messages of the state s.

The function $f_b(t)$ is an impact function, which depends on the information type and the optimization parameter b. The parameter t is the age of the information in the cache.

$$I(s) = \frac{\sum_{i|s=s_i} f_b(t_i)}{\sum_{i=1}^{|M|} f_b(t_i)} \qquad (9)$$

The vehicle chooses the state with the highest impact score $I(s)$. The advantage of our approach is that it adapts faster to environmental changes than conventional majority-voting, as old information are assigned smaller weights. Compared to always adapting to the newest available information, our approach is less prone to false information and can, thus, ensure a higher percentage of correct decisions.

The impact function $f(t)$ weights information in the cache. This function describes the balance between adaptability and robustness. In the next section, we will derive the function $f_b(t)$.

4.4   The Impact Function $f_b(t)$

The impact function $f_b(t)$ depends on information-specific parameters. Those parameters are the expected rate of false information p_f and lifetime, which is considered using the change probability p_c. As described in Sect. 3, we model the road information using a Markov chain. To this end, $f_b(t)$ is a general exponential function with a y-offset as shown in Eq. 10.

$$f_b(t) = a * e^{bt} + d \qquad (10)$$

Based on $f_b(t)$, every possible exponential function can be created using appropriate values for a, b and d. In the following, we will derive the values for the parameters a, b and d using the three requirements of this function.

Impact of New Information. If an measurement is not aged, the weight of this measurement needs to be equal to the expected accuracy of this information. Given the age t the measurement, Eq. 11 must be true.

$$f(0) = a + d = 1 - p_f \qquad (11)$$

Invalidation of Information After the TTL. A vehicle removes information from the cache after the TTL has expired. In order to have a continuous behavior of the cache, the weight of an information needs to be 0 once it is removed. Thus, the impact of the information at the expiration of the TTL equals 0 and Eq. 12 must hold true.

$$f(T) = a * e^{bT} + d = 0 \qquad (12)$$

We can find a family of parametric functions with the parameter b fulfilling both requirements. This function is shown in Eq. 13. To derive the family of functions, Eqs. 11 and 12 replace the values of a and d respectively.

$$f_b(t) = \frac{(1 - p_f) * \left(e^{bt} - e^{bT}\right)}{1 - e^{bT}} \qquad (13)$$

Figure 3 the impact function for different parameters b. If a vehicle is equipped with sensors of low detection accuracy, the impact function needs to stay at its start value for a long time to compensate for the high amount of measurement errors. However, if a vehicle is equipped with sensors of high detection accuracy, the impact function reduces the impact drastically after a short time to utilize the high reliability of the detected information.

To determine the exact value for the parameter b, the third and final requirement to this function is used. For this, we developed a trial-and-error based heuristic to approximate b.

4.5   Approximation of b

In order to chose a value for b, we utilize the optimal amount of messages n_{opt} derived from the optimization problem. We choose b such that a vehicles updates its decision afte rn_{opt} messages, but not after $n_{opt} - 1$ messages. As the messages in the cache contain meta-information about the detection date, we utilize this information to map it to the impact function. For this, we derive the rate of messages r, with which messages arrive at the vehicle. In order to approximate b, we assume a uniform distribution of messages in the cache. This consistent cache is a simplification, as messages do not arrive uniformly. However, we can show in the evaluation that this approximation provides valid estimations for b. We cannot use the actual distribution of the information in the cache, as we will directly predetermine the final result of the decision-making.

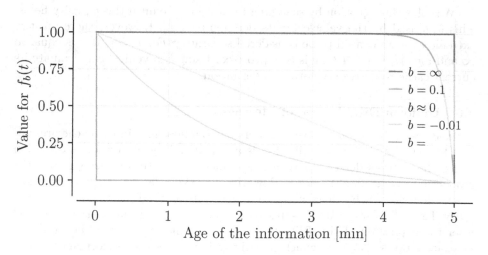

Fig. 3. Visualization of the family of functions for different parameters b.   Taken from [3].

Equation 14 shows the impact $I(s_o)$ for the old state s_o. This state has been active before a change. In our model, the impact $I(s_o)$ can be calculated by assuming that the messages with the ages n_{opt} to the last message T/r are of the old state. The remainder of the cache, i.e. the messages from 0 to n_{opt}, are the messages with the new state.

$$I(s_o) = \sum_{n=n_{opt}+1}^{\lfloor T/r \rfloor} f_b(n * r) \tag{14}$$

In addition to the impact of the old state, Eq. 15 shows the impact $I(s_c)$ of the current state s_c. The change happened at the time $t = n_{opt} * r$, thus, all messages with a age less than this time are of the new state. Thus, we sum the impact of all messages between 0 and n_{opt}

$$I(s_c) = \sum_{n=0}^{n_{opt}} f_b(n * r) \tag{15}$$

As we want to achieve a decision update after n_{opt} messages and no decision update for n smaller than n_{opt}, we need to find a value for b fulfilling this conditions. Due to the behavior of the impact function, a vehicle sticks to its decision if no additional messages are added to the cache. To find the optimal value of b, the impact of the old and the new state need to be similar. Equation 16 shows this equality.

$$\sum_{n=n_{opt}+1}^{\lfloor T/r \rfloor} [f_b(n * r)] = \sum_{n=0}^{n_{opt}} [f_b(n * r)] \tag{16}$$

We solve this equation by searching for a value of b until this equality holds. This b is used by the vehicle for its decision-making. However, there are two extreme cases that need to be considered separately. For $n_{opt} = 0$, b is equal to ∞ and for $n_{opt} + 1 > T/r$, b is equal to $-\infty$. Using b, a vehicle can evaluate its current cache to derive the correct information.

4.6 Uniform Distribution of Messages

For the described approach, we consider that the messages in the cache are uniformly distributed. This distribution is automatically achieved for information which the vehicles detect bypassing, as vehicles are naturally driving over the road segment one after the other. However, if the vehicles get stuck at the information location, each vehicle needs to periodically rebroadcast the measurement every TTL. This approach ensures that no correct information is invalidated after the expiration of the TTL. However, many messages would be produced at exactly the same time, which negatively influences the performance of our approach.

Thus, we add a random factor to the retransmission interval. Instead of retransmitting after the expiration of the TTL, the vehicle performs the retransmission after a random time, which is between 0 and the TTL T. This way, the messages of different timestamps are in the cache, which prevents provides more frequent updates to the vehicles.

5   Distributed Decision-Making in Vehicular Networks

In our previous work [3], the server was a pure forwarding-based server which only distributed information to the vehicles. The vehicles themselves performed the decision-making to reduce the hardware requirements for the server. However, performing the decision-making in a decentralized way also introduces issues. As no server-side cache is available, the server needs to notify all vehicles that can pass the measurement's location during in TTL. For a large TTL, this is barely possible or induces a high load on the network. Thus, the server distributes the measurement only to vehicles in an area of reasonable size. If a road is heavily trafficked, the performance of our approach remains constant as the impact of old messages is rather low. If a road is only slightly trafficked, the performance of our approach diminishes, as the number of messages is the cache is insufficient for a reasonable decision. Additionally, the performance will decrease if the sensor accuracy is very low.

To resolve this issue, we extend our previous work with a server-side cache of limited size. Using this cache, the server is able to store a fraction of the incoming messages. As the server cache is limited, most of the information are forwarded to the vehicles without preprocessing. If server resources are available, the server aggregates measurements before transmitting them to the vehicles. Even for servers with small capacity, this greatly enhances the performance of our system in real-world scenarios as information on barely trafficked roads are distributed efficiently.

5.1   Server-Side Information Management

We combine two dissemination strategies to distribute the information efficiently, the *pull-based* and *push-based* mode. The *pull-based* approach is preferable, as it induces less costs and increases the decision quality of the vehicles. However, the *push-based* approach consumes less server resources and is a backup solution if the server resources are not sufficient. In the following, the two modes are explained in more detail, followed by the strategy to switch between the two modes.

Pull-Based Mode. In *pull-based* mode, the server provides aggregated events only to vehicles which require that event, i. e., to vehicles in direct proximity of the event location. In order to achieve this, the server monitors the location of each vehicle. Once the vehicle is about to enter the road segment previous to the event, the server provides the event to this vehicle.

Compared to our previous approach [3], the server sends aggregated events to save bandwidth and increase the quality of the provided information. This aggregate contains additional meta-information, which are the minimum and maximum timestamp of the measurements and the weights used in the aggregation process.

Push-Based Mode. The *push-based* mode is similar to our approach presented in previous work [3]. If the server distributes an event in this mode, the server purely forwards the event. Using this mode, the server resources are relieved, as no additional data processing or storing is required.

Transition Between Pull- and Push-Based Mode. The server starts in *pull-based* mode for all incoming events, as it outperforms the *push-based* mode if the server resources are sufficient. In most cases, the incoming measurements of the vehicles will overload the server at some point in time. In this case, measurements describing the same value are clustered. The server needs transition to *push-based* mode for some of the clustered measurements, while the remaining clustered measurements remain in *pull-based* mode. Thereby, the load on the server is again reduced and the advantages of the *pull-based* approach are preserved.

Selecting the clustered measurements that should be switched to *push-based* mode influences the performance of the system drastically. To reduce the amount of wrong decisions, the server keeps the clustered measurements that would decrease the system performance the most if switched to *push-based* mode. As already mentioned, measurements on barely trafficked roads perform worst in *push-based* mode. Thus, the clustered measurements with the biggest cluster size are switched to *push-based* mode.

This transition consists of 4 steps, (i) deciding on an aggregate value based on the clustered measurements, (ii) sending the raw values or an aggregate value to concerned vehicles, (iii) removing all clustered values from the cache, and (iv) set the clustered measurements into *push-based* mode. The decision-making process resembles the decision-making process of our previous work [3] and is described in the following.

Meta-Information Preserving Decision-Making. In our previous work [3], the results of the decision-making were not used in further decision-making operations. If the server only sends the raw measurements to the vehicles, no adjustments of our previous work are required. However, it is desirable to aggregate the measurements before caching them at the vehicles. If the server sends such an aggregate to the vehicles, it might be used for further decision-making operations. However, our approach from previous work omits all meta-information it collected in the decision-making process.

Figure 4 displays why meta-information is important for the decision-making process. In Fig. 4a, the decision-making without aggregates is displayed, while Fig. 4b displays the decision-making process with aggregates. The messages in both figures are equal, but the messages at $t = 1$ and $t = 2$ have been aggregated in Fig. 4b. It is expected that the decision-making process makes the same decision for both cases. However, our decision-making will not account for the aggregate without meta-information and, thus, underestimate its weight.

(a) Only raw messages in the decision-making process. Each message can be treated equally.

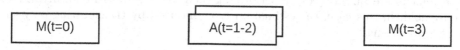

(b) Aggregated messages in the aggregation process. The aggregate messages need to provide additional meta-information to be usable.

Fig. 4. Decision making processes with and without aggregated messages.

In order to use the aggregate in the decision-making process correctly, meta-information about the weights of all states in the decision-making process are pivotal. The number of aggregated measurements is not sufficient, as it neglects inconsistencies in the aggregated measurements. However, even using this meta-information, the usage of aggregated values in the decision-making process only estimates the real result. This inaccuracy is caused by the non-linear aging of the aggregate. Due to the missing age of the measurements involved in the aggregated value, the aging cannot be performed. In order to estimate the weight of the aged aggregate, the aggregate is treated like a normal measurement and aged accordingly. However, aging the aggregate is only estimates the actual aging process, as old measurements, that are part of the aggregate, are not removed from the aggregate after their TTL. This error is minimal if (i) the aggregated measurements have been measured close in time or (ii) the parameter b of the impact function is very small. The decision, if the raw measurements or the aggregate will be distributed to the vehicles is described in the next section.

5.2   Error Estimation of the Aged Aggregate

Given two measurements M_1 and M_2 with their specific ages t_1 and t_2 and $t_1 \leq t_2$. The difference between t_1 and t_2 is Δt. The aggregate A combines those two measurements and has the age $t(A) = \min\left(t(M_1), t(M_2)\right)$. Assuming M_1 and M_2 have measured the same state s_0, the meta-information about the weight of A is shown in Eq. 17. The function $I(M, s)$ is the impact of the state s for the information M.

$$I(A, s) = I(M_1, s) + I(M_2, s) = \begin{cases} f_b(t_1) + f_b(t_2) & \text{if } s = s_0 \\ 0 & \text{else} \end{cases} \qquad (17)$$

As the weights for all states $s \neq s_0$ are 0, those weights are not influenced by the aging. The only weight influenced by the aging is weight for state s_0, which we age according to Eq. 18. By dividing $f_b(t)$ by $1 - p_f$, we ensure that $f_b(0) = 1$, i. e., an information of the age 0 is not aged at all.

$$I(M, s, t) = I(M, s) * \frac{f_b(t)}{1 - p_f} \tag{18}$$

If the server wants to send aggregated measurements to the vehicles, while the vehicles are simultaneously performing their decision-making locally, Eq. 19 must hold. In this case, the estimation error induced by transmitting only the aggregate is small.

$$[f_b(0) + f_b(\Delta t)] * \frac{f_b(t)}{1 - p_f} \approx f_b(t) + f_b(t + \Delta t) \tag{19}$$

This equation can now be simplified to Eq. 20, by considering that $f_b(0) = 1 - p_f$ and using the impact function $f_b(t)$.

$$\frac{\left(e^{b\Delta t} - e^{bT}\right) * \left(e^{bt} - e^{bT}\right)}{1 - e^{bT}} \approx e^{b(t+\Delta t)} - e^{bT} \tag{20}$$

Based on Eq. 20, the server may aggregate measurements before transmitting them if $b * T < \ln(0.1\%)$. The error is even smaller, if Δt is very small, i. e., the measuring timestamps of the two measurements are close to each other. If those requirements are not fulfilled, the server needs to transmit the individual measurements instead of the aggregates.

5.3   Client-Side Information Management

A vehicle needs to prepare itself for both the *push-based* and *pull-based* strategy. For the *push-based* strategy, the vehicle just needs to subscribe to a global topic, to which all events are published. Even if the *push-based* strategy is not active, the vehicles need to subscribe to that topic, as they cannot predict the server-side switch of strategies. For the *pull-based* strategy, the vehicle needs to constantly query location-aware information from the server. As the frequency of the pulls is important for the performance of the system, we only used the coarse location of the vehicles, i. e., the street segment they are driving on. The vehicles subscribes to this street segment and adjacent street segments. We decided on subscribing to these street segments, as the vehicle will receive updates on the road state while driving on those segments. Once a vehicles subscribes to a street segment, the server responds with all available information about this street segment. After the vehicle changes its current street segment, the old subscriptions are removed and the subscription process starts anew.

6   Evaluation

We evaluate the performance of our approach using the event-based Simonstrator framework [20]. The Simonstrator is a network simulator that enables the evaluation of different types of communication (ad-hoc, cellular), and the

Publish/Subscribe (Pub/Sub) paradigm. To enable to evaluation of vehicular scenarios, we integrated Simulation of Urban Mobility (SUMO) [21] into the Simonstrator using the TraCI interface.

For the evaluation of our developed distributed decision-making approach, we simulate multiple traffic jams in the city of Cologne. To simulate the vehicle movement in the city of Cologne, we use the TAPAS Cologne scenario [22], which is one of the largest freely available scenarios for SUMO. In order to keep the simulation speed high, we only use a 2 km × 2 km big area inside the city of Cologne, which is depicted by Fig. 5. In order to simulate a realistic traffic flow, we start our network simulation after 15 min. After that time, number of vehicles in the scenario is realistic. Once the network simulation has started, we force multiple traffic jams at random locations in the scenario. Compared to the scenario in [3], the maximum allowed speed in the jam varies over time. Each vehicle measures the road state as accurate as possible and shares that information with other vehicles using a Pub/Sub system over the cellular network. Due to the changes in speed, the vehicles need to adapt quickly to incoming information, while being able to cope with false information.

Fig. 5. Schematic overview of the road scenario. The colored roads are jammed.

6.1   Simulation Setup

In this evaluation, we compare our distributed decision-making approach (*Distributed*) with a pure Cloud-based approach (*Cloud*) and our approach from previous work (*Edge*) [3]. The *Cloud* approach also has certain storage capacities, but cannot store any more information once this capacity is exceeded. The *Edge* approach does not require any server resources, as it stores all information at the vehicles. Finally, our *Distributed* approach combines the advantages of both approaches, storing information at the server if possible, while forwarding the remaining information to the vehicles.

Metrics. For comparison, we utilize the accuracy of the decision-making process. We define this accuracy as the percentage of vehicles that have derived the correct information using all measurements in their cache. If the vehicle receives only an aggregate value from the server, it considers this value to be correct. Additionally to the accuracy, we use the robustness and the adaptability as metrics. The adaptability captures the ability of an approach to adapt to environmental changes, while the robustness captures its resilience to false information.

Environmental Conditions. We evaluate the performance of our approach for varying environmental conditions. The investigated settings are shown in Table 2, where bold values are the default ones. The sensors in each vehicle measure the average movement speed, which we consider to be Guassian distributed. Each speed measurement has 15 possible states, with each state representing a certain vehicle movement speed. The accuracy of the sensors is also Gaussian distributed. The road jam changes its state with a given rate. In order to investigate on the performance increase of our distributed decision-making strategy, we used different decision-making strategies.

Table 2. Investigated Environmental Setting, bold values are default.

Parameter	Possible values
Average sensor accuracy	**80%**, 90%, 95%, 99%, 100%
Deviation of sensor accuracy	**20%**
Average event change rate	**3 m**
Available server cache [messages]	10, 100, 1000, **10000**
Decision-making strategy	Majority, Newest, **QoI-based**

6.2   Influence of Sensor Accuracy

The sensor accuracy has a big impact on the performance of our approach as shown in Fig. 6a. For all approaches, the quality of the decisions decreases with increasing false detection rate. As the server cache is quite big for this scenario, the *Distributed* and the *Cloud* approach perform equally. The advantages of the *Distributed* approach over the *Cloud* approach are discussed later.

However, the quality of our *Distributed* approach is at up to 11% higher compared to the *Edge* approach, which is due to the higher number of messages that can be used by the decision-making algorithm. While the vehicles receive only a part of the messages in the *Edge* approach, the server collects most information in our *Distributed* approach and caches them persistently.

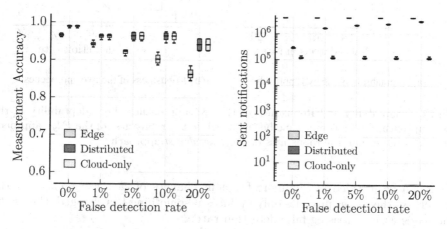

(a) Decision quality captured by the percentage of correctly received information.

(b) Comsumped combile bandwidth for the transmission of the events.

Fig. 6. Overview of the performance of the *Edge* and our *Distributed* approach. Our *Distributed* approach achieves a higher information quality, while simultaneously reducing the consumed mobile bandwidth.

This behavior is also visible in Fig. 7. While the adaptability for both approaches is decreasing roughly by the same percentage as shown in Fig. 7a, the robustness of the *Edge* approach decreases much more than the robustness of the distributed approach as shown in Fig. 7b. This is justified by the higher number of messages available to the decision-making in our *Distributed* approach, which leads to a higher robustness.

Additionally to the higher quality compared to the *Edge* approach, our *Distributed* and the *Cloud* approach consume much less bandwidth as shown in Fig. 6b. The *Cloud* approach consumes even less data then the *Distributed* approach, which is justified by missing backup mechanisms in case of overload. The *pull-based* method of our approach reduces the produced traffic significantly by up to 93% in case of no false detections. However, the produced traffic of our *Distributed* approach is constantly increasing with increasing false detection rate.

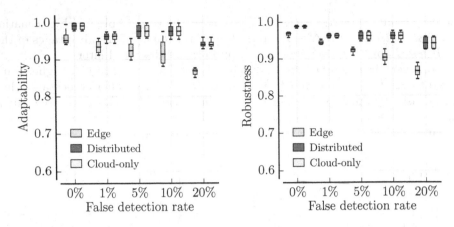

(a) Adaptability of the two approaches.   (b) Robustness of the two approaches.

Fig. 7. Adaptability and Robustness of the two approaches. The adaptability of the two approaches has a comparable behavior, while the robustness of the *Edge* approach decreases more than the robustness of the *Distributed* approach.

This can be justified by the more frequent changes of each cache entry at the server. As the server provides only updates if something has changed, the traffic increases with increasing false detection rate.

6.3   Influence of Server Storage Capacity

Figure 8a displays the achieved decision quality dependent on the size of the cache. In this figure, the *Edge* approach is not included as it is not dependent on the cache size. For a high cache size above 1000 messages, the performance of our *Distributed* approach and *Cloud* approach are equal, as almost no messages need to be removed from the cache. However, for the cache sizes of 10 and 100, our approach significantly outperforms the *Cloud* approach. Even more important, the performance of our approach decreases only slightly with decreasing cache size. This is reasonable as our *Edge* approach already performs well it the amount of messages is high. Our distributed approach only needs to handle the messages on roads, which are barely trafficked. Thus, only few messages from this roads are required to improve the performance of the system.

6.4   Influence of Decision-Making Strategy

Figure 8b displays the influence different decision-making approaches to our *Distributed* approach. As expected, the combination of our QoI-based approach from previous work [3] and our *Distributed* approach outperforms the other approaches. However, an interesting aspect is that the *MAJ* approach outperforms the *QoI* approach for the *Edge* caching. This is due to the lower number

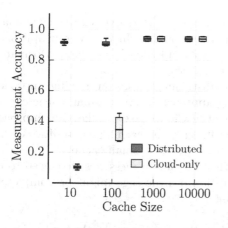

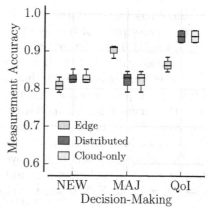

(a) Decision quality captured by the percentage of correctly received information for different cache sizes.

(b) Decision quality captured by the percentage of correctly received information for different decision-making approaches.

Fig. 8. Decision quality of our *Distributed* approach compared to the *Edge* and *Cloud* approach.

of messages in the cache, which naturally increases the adaptability of the *MAJ* approach. As the *MAJ* approach is naturally more robust than the *QoI* approach, it performs slightly better in this specific combination. However, once a sufficient amount of messages is available for decision-making, the combination of the *Distributed* and the *QoI* approach outperform the *MAJ* and the *NEW* approach by 7% and 16% respectively.

7 Conclusion

In this paper, we extended our Quality of Information (QoI)-based decision making process [3]. This decision-making process is based on a weighted majority voting. As the weight is pivotal for the performance of our approach, we developed an optimal impact function considering the information-specific parameters accuracy and lifetime. This impact function is considered optimal, as it balances the negative effects of robustness and reliability dependent on the requirements of the information type.

However, using realistic traces of the city of Cologne, the system performance decreased as our approach is not able to handle barely trafficked roads. As those roads are rarely visited by a vehicle, the number of information to aggregate is very low. Our previous work cached information only at the vehicles, leading to even less information for the decision-making process. This had a negative impact on performance in realistic scenarios.

To resolve this issue, we introduced a central server, which is capable of caching a certain amount of information. Until the server capacities are exceeded, all decision-making is performed by the server. Once the server exceeds its capacities, it executes parts of the decision-making on the vehicles. As our approach performed worst if only few measurements are available, the system performance increased drastically even for small server caches.

In the evaluation, we show that our distributed decision-making approach significantly outperforms the fog-caching approach, even for small cache capacities at the server side. Compared to a pure Cloud-based cache, our approach can increase the system performance by utilizing the caching capabilities of the vehicles, which increases the performance in case of a small cache.

As future work, we aim to improve the selection of messages that need to be cached at a server, including a consideration if a message might be completely obsolete even if the TTL has not expired.

Acknowledgments. The work presented in this paper was partly funded by the LOEWE initiative (Hessen, Germany) within the NICER project and by the German Research Foundation (DFG) as part of projects B1 and C2 within the Collaborative Research Center (CRC) 1053 - MAKI.

References

1. Tigadi, A., Gujanatti, R., Gonchi, A., Klemsscet, B.: Advanced driver assistance systems. IJERGS **4**, 151–158 (2016)
2. Kakkasageri, M., Manvi, S.: Information management in vehicular ad hoc networks: a review. J. Netw. Comput. Appl. **39**, 334–350 (2014)
3. Meuser, T., Wende, M., Lieser, P., Richerzhagen, B., Steinmetz, R.: Adaptive decision making based on temporal information dynamics. In: Proceedings of Vehicle Technology and Intelligent Transport Systems (VEHITS), pp. 91–102. SCITEPRESS (2018)
4. Wang, R.Y., Strong, D.M.: Beyond accuracy: what data quality means to data consumers. J. Manage. Inf. Syst. **12**, 5–33 (1996)
5. Chae, M., Kim, J., Kim, H., Ryu, H.: Information quality for mobile internet services: a theoretical model with empirical validation. Electron. Markets **12**, 38–46 (2002)
6. Meuser, T., Lieser, P., Nguyen, T.A.B., Böhnstedt, D., Steinmetz, R.: Adaptive information aggregation for application-specific demands. In: Proceedings of the 1st BalkanCom (2017)
7. Molina-Gil, J.M., Caballero-Gil, P., Hernández-Goya, C., Caballero-Gil, C.: Data aggregation for information authentication in VANETs. In: 2010 Sixth International Conference on Information Assurance and Security (IAS), pp. 282–287. IEEE (2010)
8. Vuran, M.C., Akan, Ö.B., Akyildiz, I.F.: Spatio-temporal correlation: theory and applications for wireless sensor networks. Comput. Netw. **45**, 245–259 (2004)
9. Delot, T., Cenerario, N., Ilarri, S.: Estimating the relevance of information in inter-vehicle ad hoc networks. In: Ninth International Conference on Mobile Data Management Workshops. MDMW 2008, pp. 151–158. IEEE (2008)
10. Kuppusamy, P., Kalaavathi, B.: Cluster based data consistency for cooperative caching over partitionable mobile adhoc network. Am. J. Appl. Sci. **9**, 1307 (2012)

11. Meuser, T., Richerzhagen, B., Stavrakakis, I., Nguyen, T.A.B., Steinmetz, R.: Relevance-aware information dissemination in vehicular networks. In: Proceedings of IEEE WoWMoM. IEEE (2018)

12. Ilarri, S., Delot, T., Trillo-Lado, R.: A data management perspective on vehicular networks. IEEE Commun. Surv. Tutorials **17**, 2420–2460 (2015)

13. Hsiao, H.C., Studer, A., Dubey, R., Shi, E., Perrig, A.: Efficient and secure threshold-based event validation for VANETs. In: Proceedings of the Fourth ACM Conference on Wireless Network Security, pp. 163–174. ACM (2011)

14. Fawaz, K., Artail, H.: DCIM: distributed cache invalidation method for maintaining cache consistency in wireless mobile networks. IEEE Trans. Mobile Comput. **12**, 680–693 (2013)

15. Xiao, X.Y., Peng, W.C., Hung, C.C., Lee, W.C.: Using sensorranks for in-network detection of faulty readings in wireless sensor networks. In: Proceedings of the 6th ACM International Workshop on Data Engineering for Wireless and Mobile Access, pp. 1–8. ACM (2007)

16. Gao, J.L., Xu, Y.J., Li, X.W.: Weighted-median based distributed fault detection for wireless sensor networks. Ruan Jian Xue Bao (J. Softw.) **18**, 1208–1217 (2007)

17. Caballero-Gil, P., Molina-Gil, J., Caballero-Gil, C.: Data aggregation based on fuzzy logic for VANETs. In: Herrero, Á., Corchado, E. (eds.) CISIS 2011. LNCS, vol. 6694, pp. 33–40. Springer, Heidelberg (2011). https://doi.org/10.1007/978-3-642-21323-6_5

18. Dietzel, S., Schoch, E., Konings, B., Weber, M., Kargl, F.: Resilient secure aggregation for vehicular networks. IEEE Netw. **24**, 26–31 (2010)

19. Lee, U., Magistretti, E., Zhou, B., Gerla, M., Bellavista, P., Corradi, A.: Efficient data harvesting in mobile sensor platforms. In: Fourth Annual IEEE International Conference on Pervasive Computing and Communications Workshops, PerCom Workshops 2006, p. 5. IEEE (2006)

20. Richerzhagen, B., Stingl, D., Rückert, J., Steinmetz, R.: Simonstrator: simulation and prototyping platform for distributed mobile applications. In: Proceedings of the 8th International Conference on Simulation Tools and Techniques. SIMUTools 2015, ICST (Institute for Computer Sciences, Social-Informatics and Telecommunications Engineering), pp. 99–108 (2015)

21. Behrisch, M., Bieker, L., Erdmann, J., Krajzewicz, D.: Sumo-simulation of urban mobility: an overview. In: Proceedings of SIMUL 2011, The Third International Conference on Advances in System Simulation, ThinkMind (2011)

22. Uppoor, S., Trullols-Cruces, O., Fiore, M., Barcelo-Ordinas, J.M.: Generation and analysis of a large-scale urban vehicular mobility dataset. IEEE TMC **13**, 1061–1075 (2014)

Enhanced Cellular Bandwidth Prediction for Highly Automated Driving

Florian Jomrich[1,2]([✉]), Florian Fischer[2], Steffen Knapp[1], Tobias Meuser[2], Björn Richerzhagen[2], and Ralf Steinmetz[2]

[1] Opel Automobile GmbH, 65428 Rüsselsheim, Germany
{florian.jomrich,steffen.knapp}@opel.com
[2] Multimedia Communications Lab (KOM), TU Darmstadt,
64283 Darmstadt, Germany
{florian.jomrich,florian.fischer,tobias.meuser,bjorn.richerzhagen,
ralf.steinmetz}@kom.tu-darmstadt.de

Abstract. Highly automated vehicles will change the future of our personal mobility. To ensure safety and comfort while driving its passengers, the vehicle has to rely on the newest traffic and map updates at any time. Furthermore the passengers want to enjoy infotainment services like video and music streaming during the travel. All these kinds of services require a reliable and fast cellular internet connection. However due to the high speed of the vehicle and the varying deployed cellular infrastructure, the experienced network throughput is constantly changing. To predict those throughput changes and to maintain the overall experienced network quality at a high level, machine learning techniques can be leveraged. In our previous work [1], we first investigated the idea to train machine learning techniques based on specifically localized training data provided by modern day smartphone APIs in a so-called connectivity map to improve their overall performance. From the first promising results obtained in this work, we now further improved the quality of our input feature set in this current work by introducing more precise lower level protocol information to the prediction process. The measurements were obtained from the same real highway driving scenario over a period of three days, in which over 540.000 precise lower layer throughput estimations could be collected. Based on this more accurate data set, we were able to improve the overall prediction accuracy and clearly showcase the performance gains achieved through localized training data in comparison to a general global training data set.

Keywords: Cellular networks · Connectivity map · LTE ·
Throughput prediction · Machine learning · Mobile · Vehicular

1 Introduction

Highly automated driving vehicles will make traveling to desired destinations a more relaxed task in future. The passengers inside the self-driving vehicle won't

Supported by the Opel Automobile GmbH.

have to supervise the surrounding traffic all the time. Instead, they can spend their time on other tasks, e.g. being productive for work or enjoying some info-tainment, while the car drives them to their selected destination. To increase the safety of the passengers and to improve their comfort while driving highly automated, the cars own sensors (like camera, radar, ultra sound and lidar) are further enhanced by a very accurate, so-called high definition street map (HD-Map). This map must be provided with the newest updates regarding the current traffic situation, e.g. traffic jams, car accidents and construction sides. This requires a data exchange between the vehicles and a data processing back end [2,3]. The vehicles provide their own sensor information [4] and receive map updates from the back end, which also receives information from other 3rd party organizations like federal institutions or the police regarding the current traffic situation. In conclusion, it can be stated that to ensure high safety while driving automatically and to realize services that are requested by the passengers in the meanwhile, a strong and reliable internet connection is required. To ensure such functionality, the vehicles must rely upon a robust mobile communication interface. However, due to the mobility of the cars, their experienced connection quality is constantly changing. The cellular network infrastructure is deployed with varying density. The main focus of the providers currently is on covering the cities with the newest available technology for the most revenue from cus-tomers. Highly automated vehicles however also have to rely on a strong cellular infrastructure in between the cities while driving over connecting highways for example. Often only slower and older network technology is deployed in such areas or sometimes there is no connection available at all. To ensure a reliable data connection under these quickly changing conditions, different techniques have been developed over the years. One very popular approach that has been proposed in several research papers [5–8] is the usage of a so-called connec-tivity map. In contrast to the network coverage maps, which are provided by the network operators, these connectivity maps do not rely on mathematical models, which are often not very accurately resembling the real world scenario. Instead, the cars share the information regarding their currently experienced network quality (e.g. signal strength, latency and data throughput) with each other through the data back end in the form of an aggregated map. The map is enhanced by further measurements over time and thereby can provide an accurate historical view on the deployed network infrastructure. Another fre-quently discussed approach to improve the experienced network performance is the prediction of key network parameters [9–11], e.g. the to be expected network throughput, based on the current measurements of network quality indicators experienced by the car. The short term historical data (only a few seconds) pro-cessed by machine learning algorithms then provides a prediction of the near time future network parameters and thus the to be experienced network per-formance. In our previous work [1], we investigated the achievable prediction accuracy of such an approach by only relying on collected sensor data from the API of stock Android smartphones. As expected, the obtained results have not been as high-performing as Related Work, that could rely on much more

timely accurate and diverse data sets, based on detailed lower layer information provided directly from the chipsets of the used devices. However, our work
clearly showed that such a machine learning prediction approach still achieves
reasonable results to be used to improve the experienced network quality. The
possibility to largely deploy our approach and the including higher number of
measuring devices might than outweigh the reduced data collection accuracy.
Furthermore, we investigated the idea to improve the quality of machine learning
prediction by combining both mentioned concepts. Therefore we proposed and
investigated that the learning approach is enhanced through localized training
data provided by the connectivity map. The map thereby provided information
specifically for the cell in which the car currently resides. The obtained results
showed a tendency toward improving the prediction performance, although we
could not clearly state that at that point in time. As the obtained results indicated that the localized prediction approach performed best (in comparison to
the global prediction model), when the achieved prediction accuracy was high,
we wanted to further investigate this phenomenon. Within this extension of our
previous work, we now improved our dataset with additional lower layer features
to investigate the performance of a local training data set with higher measurement accuracy. We thereby achieved the realization of our approach in a cost
efficient manner, as no further hardware or costly software was used. By relying
additionally only on the free and open source software "MobileInsight" [12], we
could rely on smartphone hardware similar to that used in our previous work,
as explained in detail in Sect. 4.

The rest of the paper is structured as follows. First we introduce some technical terms in Sect. 2, which will be used throughout the following Sections, to
simplify the understanding for the reader. In Sect. 3 we give a short overview
about the Related Work [1]. The conceptual extension of our existing approach
is then explained in Sect. 4. In Sect. 5 we introduce the highway scenario in which
we obtained our measurement data. This extended approach is then compared to
our previous work in Sect. 6. We conclude our work and give an outlook regarding
future work in Sect. 7.

2   Background

For better understanding of the following Sections, we first give a short overview
of the technical terms related to modern days cellular LTE networks.

2.1   Carrier Aggregation

In technical terms, the so-called Carrier Aggregation allows the network
providers to "virtually" combine different distinct frequency bands (e.g. 20 MHz
in LTE Band 3 and 20 MHz in LTE Band 20) to one large virtual band (with e.g.
40 MHz bandwidth in total). A smartphone, which is capable of using Carrier
Aggregation, can combine a certain number of different frequencies bands of one
provider (depending on the LTE category of the device), which are available at

one cell tower site or can leverage different bands from neighbouring cell towers as well. This technique allows the phone to be able to tremendously improve its achievable throughput due to the increased available bandwidth.

2.2 Multiple Input Multiple Output - MIMO

By using several transmission and receiving antennas, different data streams can be transmitted from the cell tower to the receiving smartphone on the same frequency. At the smartphone site, the different streams are distinguished between each other through the difference in the received signal strength for the different antennas. This concept is called Multiple Input Multiple Output or short MIMO in telecommunications engineering. It can significantly improve the achievable coding rate of the signal and the overall transmission speed.

2.3 Modulation and Coding Scheme - MCS

The overall achievable data throughput in LTE networks directly correlates with the experienced signal strength at the smartphone site. Based on the received reference signal quality, the smartphone advertises its reception quality through a so-called Channel Quality Indicator (CQI) to the cell tower. Relying on this indicator, the cell tower then selects the proper so-called Modulation and Coding Scheme (MCS) for the specific smartphone to ensure a robust data transmission. Depending on the device category and the currently experienced signal quality, modern day smartphones can use four different modulation methods to transmit their data (QPSK, 16 QAM, 64 QAM and 256 QAM). Correlating with the Modulation different Coding Schemes are selected to ensure error correction and achieve a fast and robust data transmission.

2.4 Resource Blocks and Transport Block Size

A Resource Block is the fundamental, atomic transmission unit for data in the LTE protocol. The available frequency bandwidth (between 1.4 MHz and 20 MHz for one single carrier) therefore correlates with a certain number of Resource Blocks. For example, 10 MHz are equal to 50 Resource Blocks and 20 MHz resemble 100 Resource Blocks. Within its scheduling period of 1 ms, the cell tower distributes those available resource blocks across all its connected devices. In combination with the selected Modulation and Coding Scheme (as described in the previous Sect. 2.3) one Resource Block can transmit a certain amount of data. All allocated Resource Blocks together can transmit a certain amount of data within this period of 1 ms, which is described by the Transport Block Size.

3 Related Work

As already mentioned in our previous work [1], there exist different concepts to improve the experienced network quality while driving. Two of the most popular approaches are namely the connectivity map and the online throughput estimation. Both approaches differ in terms of datasets on which they rely for the prediction and also in terms of the prediction time horizon. The existing papers for those two approaches therefore will be again shortly summarized in the following (see also our previous work for further clarification [1]) together with new Related Work. As a conclusion from our previous work we came up with a new extended concept that improves the achieved prediction accuracy while still maintaining a reasonable effort in terms of hardware and software as explained in Sect. 4.

3.1   Connectivity Map

The fundamental working principle of a connectivity map relies on the collection of information regarding the experienced network quality data from vehicles. The data which is collected by the cars is then shared with each other through a data processing back end, which aggregates the raw sensor data to a network quality statement for each section of the map.

Kamakaris et al. [5] contributed one of the earlier works, which stated the possible benefits, that a connectivity map can provide regarding the experienced network quality of a user. To do this, they investigated the correlation between the Received Signal Strength Indication (RSSI) and the throughput of the WiFi network of their university. In their work they also stated the short average life-time of the possible predictions, which are based on the information provided by the connectivity map. The cause for this phenomenon lies within the dynamic variations of the network quality over time. The reasons therefore are diverse, like the fluctuation of the current network load (due to a changing number of actual users). Furthermore, environmental effects like buildings and weather can also influence the prediction performance. All these influencing factors let the data provided by the connectivity map quickly degrade and suggest an alternative approach for short term predictions as explained in the Sect. 3.2. Within our previous work [1] we proposed a combination of the advantages of the connectivity map and the online throughput estimation by localized training. This concept is further refined in the presented work.

As a work more closely related to an automotive usage scenario, Nagel et al. [6] try to predict the movement of vehicles and their location to establish a robust and well performing ad hoc communication between them. They did not directly investigate the features of a connectivity map, but they propose the sharing of connectivity data between the cars. Therefore they support us in our proposed concept to improve online prediction algorithms regarding the expected network quality with local training data provided by the vehicles to each other.

Two of the more recent works by Kelch et al. [7] and Lu et al. [9] independently from each other investigated the performance of the correlation between the so-called Channel Quality Indicator (CQI) and the achieved throughput value. The CQI is a derived parameter from other signal strength parameters (Reference Signal Received Quality - RSRQ, Reference Signal Received

Power - RSRP and Received Signal Strength Indication - RSSI). The CQI was then mapped into a connectivity map according to the collected global navigation satellite system (GNSS) position when it was measured. Therefore, Kelch and Lu both conducted drive tests within 3G HSDPA cellular networks. Kelch et al. collected their CQI values by using AT-commands on their cellular modem. Lu et al. used the Qualcomm eXtensible Diagnostic Monitor (QXDM), a licensed computer software, that retrieves detailed and time-wise highly accurate cellular protocol information directly from the used Android smartphones. Within the 3G/HSDPA cellular network, the correlation between the CQI and the throughput turned out to be highly correlated as both authors suggested it to be a reliable quality information source to be stored in a connectivity map. In our previous work that solely relied on the stock Android API, the correlation between the CQI and the achieved throughput in LTE networks was not very high, most likely due to the reduced timely accuracy of the Android API (see Sect. 4 for details). Therefore, in this work we increased our timely accuracy to further investigate the correlation between the CQI and our achievable peak throughput values in nowadays LTE networks.

Similar to the previous works, Pögel et al. [8,13] also collected several active and passive cellular network parameters in a vehicular scenario to fit them it into a connectivity map for the further prediction of the to be experienced network quality. Pögel et al. thereby focused on the throughput prediction as well as on the optimisation of a possible handover between consecutive cell towers. In their earlier work [13], Pögel et al. stated that the historic data of a connectivity map should be combined together with recent online estimations as future work to improve the prediction accuracy. This idea however was not further investigated in their more recent work [8]. This also supported us in our proposed and investigated concept within our previous work [1] to introduce localized training data based on the connectivity map into online throughput estimation methods, which rely on machine learning algorithms.

Several related approaches regarding the online throughput estimation are now presented in the following Sect. 3.2.

3.2   Online Throughput Estimation

Yao et al. [14] present one of the earlier approaches to investigate the dependencies between the mobility of a vehicle and its location regarding the experienced throughput. In their work, the authors performed 71 drive tests of about 25 min each within a 3G network. The authors thereby did not investigate the predictability of the throughput, but supported us to investigate the capabilities of localized learning due to the dependencies between location and available throughput in our previous work [1]. The proposed concept therefore is now further investigated within the present work.

Within their work, Xu et al. [15] developed a framework called "PROTEUS", which is one of the earlier approaches regarding instantaneous throughput prediction. They investigated the performance of their framework within 3G networks, but not in the more recent LTE networks. To improve the performance within use cases like VoIP, video conferencing and online gaming PROTEUS relies on regression trees to predict the to be experienced throughput. It therefore solely relies on the previous 20 s of experienced network parameters and does not consider any form of preceding offline training as it is the case in our approach.

In contrast to Xu et al., Liu et al. [16] relied on offline training data gained from previous drive tests performed in 3G networks for prediction. They investigated the prediction of the future 300 s of available network throughput by training with 300 s of historic data. Liu et al. therefore divided the last 300 s of measured network parameters up into 60 unique samples of 5 s each. Although the authors did not take the actual mobility into deeper consideration within their approach, they still stated to have significant differences in the network performance due to different locations. This supported us in our motivation regarding our previous work [1] to identify the possibilities of relying on localized training data. In our opinion, one considerable disadvantage of the approach by Xu et al. might be the significant amount of time (300 s) that was taken into consideration for prediction. This might be a considerable amount of time within the investigated 3G networks. However in modern days LTE networks there might be different periods of time necessary to be considered due to the overall increased speeds of the connection. Smaller amounts of data, like sensor data from the vehicles and map updates for highly automated driving vehicles as described in our previous works [2,17], could therefore be taken into consideration. However this possible disadvantage is already addressed by the work of Yue et al. [18], which we present in the following. In their work, the authors only consider a prediction horizon of 1 s. That also requires only 1 s of historic data with an ongoing active connection.

Jin et al. [10] are one of the firsts to rely on data from 4G/LTE cellular networks to evaluate their throughput prediction algorithm. The authors used ensemble learners for their prediction and relied on the Qualcomm eXtensible Monitor Toolkit (QXDM) to obtain a large set of very precise network parameters. The authors share our opinion stated in our previous work [1] that relying on the QXDM toolkit hinders a current large scale deployment of their approach. As we wanted to investigate the performance of highly accurate localized training data within this further work, we also needed to extend our approach from the stock Android API information to be able to rely on high precision lower layer information. However, as stated in Sect. 4, our approach does not require any further additional costs - whether it is hardware or software licenses in contrast to relying on QXDM.

Margolies et al. [11] presented another approach to obtain the available throughput quality at different places along a track. The authors investigated the influence of so-called "slow-fading" on the obtained channel quality of a 3G network, which is especially experienced by mobile nodes (in our case vehicles) that are moving between different cell towers. Based on this information, they then tried to predict the current road segment in which the car is currently most likely located. Based on this information, a connectivity map is queried to receive the average throughput at this position for further transmission planning.

Ide and Wietfeld et al. [19, 20] presented a concept which they call "predictive Channel-Aware Transmission scheme" (pCAT). Its aim is to identify connectivity hotspots based on Signal To Noise Ratio measurements (SINR) to improve the overall network experience. In their first work [19], the authors propose to combine historic measurement data of a connectivity map together with currently experienced measurements to achieve better planning results. This idea relates to our own concept, however it is not further investigated in their following work [20]. Furthermore the authors also only relied upon the Signal To Noise Ratio measurements (SINR), whereas we are including a much more diverse set of network performance parameters and quality indicators (see Sect. 1 for details) including the availability of Carrier Aggregation, the currently used modulation and coding scheme and the availability of MIMO for separate data streams.

Samba et al. [21] showcase another approach to predict the instantaneous available throughput in currently deployed LTE networks. In their approach the authors therefore rely on Random Forest classification trees. Samba et al. consider more parameters than Ide and Wietfeld et al. in their work (for example the Received Signal Strength Indicator (RSSI) and the Reference Signal Received Quality (RSRQ)). Furthermore, they consider the context of the measuring device, e.g. its current speed and the distance to the celltower to which it is connected. As one of the most recent and state of the art works, we compared our previous work [1] with the results obtained by Samba et al. Thus we also used the same type of machine learning algorithm and the same metrics used for evaluation to achieve comparable results. In order to keep our previous results comparable to our newly obtained results, we will do the same within this work. For further explanation regarding the used algorithms and metrics, see Sect. 4. In their work, Samba et al. rely additionally on a data set provided by a network operator to realize their prediction approach. In our opinion this might severely hinder a large scale deployment as it is unlikely to gain this intellectual property directly from the network provider for his entire network. Their immediate revenue from their customers depends on it and therefore it is not made public in general. Within our work we thus do not use such additional data. Furthermore, the data set, which Samba et al. could obtain, is largely diverse, spanning over 350 different cells totalling in 5700 measurements. In our previous work [1] and this current work, we narrowed the area of measurements down to a compact Section of the German highway A60 (see Sect. 5). This way, we ensured to obtain a significant high amount of data of a smaller number of cells to verify the functionality of our proposed approach regarding local training data.

One even more recent work is performed by Yue et al. [18]. Similar to our work, the authors compare the throughput prediction accuracy of machine learning algorithms trained on data obtained from the currently available (May 2018) stock Android APIs in contrast to data collected from more timely accurate lower layer protocol information. Their approach however is different than the work of Samba et al. [21], upon which we extended our own localized training concept. Instead of trying to achieve an instantaneous throughput prediction based solely on the available passive network quality parameters, Yue et al. have to rely on a period of active data transmission time, as they also take the historical throughput values into consideration as a prediction feature. This way they achieve comparably good results for both datasets (Android and lower layer information). Hence we see herein a great possibility for personal further work to combine their concept with our personal localized training approach. However Yue et al. did not take some lower layer information into consideration, which we consider as crucial for a robust prediction approach even when relying on historic throughput data. This is namely the availability of Carrier Aggregation and the availability of MIMO data transmission, which could have a highly varying impact on the achievable prediction accuracy. In our current work (see Sect. 4) we especially consider those parameters to investigate their impact on the performance of our locally trained instantaneous throughput predictor.

Our extended conceptual approach is now explained in the following Section. For further explanation refer as well to the "Concept" Section of our previous work [1].

4   Concept

The new concept presented in this work relies upon the concepts and tools developed within our previous work [1] and directly builds upon them. Therefore we first explain once again the already existing data collection approach and the used machine learning algorithm, which allowed us to obtain the evaluation results gained in our previous work. We further continued to collect machine learning training data with this old approach in parallel with our new data collection process. This way, we were able to directly compare the obtained results with each other on a common time and location basis. Thus we could put our newly gained results in direct correlation with our previous works evaluation. The details of the base line and the extended tool chain are visualized in Fig. 1. The tool chain used in our previous work is described by black colour and bold arrows. The further extensions of this approach performed in our updated work are marked by blue colour and dashed arrows.

4.1   Base Line Tool Chain

Within our previous work, we wanted to purely rely upon collected network quality measurement data and performance measurements, which could be obtained "right out of the box" from customer hardware and software without the need for any further additional costs or tooling. This way the machine learning throughput prediction process, which relies upon this dataset, would be easily deployable in a large scale scenario. Thus it would be easy to obtain meaningful amounts of training and testing data for future improvements in the prediction accuracy. This especially holds true as we proposed and investigated the feasibility of enabling localized training through the data collection in a geo-referenced connectivity map.

To exemplify this usage scenario, we decided to use present-day Android smartphones (May 2018) as our measurement platform. Using smartphones as measurement units provides several key benefits. First, the phones provide basically the same degree of quality information that is currently provided by the onboard communication units deployed into current production cars. Thus we consider the obtained results a realistic outcome of performance when comparing it with an actual large scale deployment. Second, they are rather inexpensive compared to other hardware and software solutions and furthermore their APIs are easily accessible to retrieve the required network quality data.

To realize our base line tool chain, we developed an Android application that is able to retrieve all available parameters (status of May 2018) relevant to the description of the currently experienced network quality (see Table 1(a) for reference). To experience the currently available peak bandwidth of the network, the application transmits a reasonably high amount of data (as described by Fig. 1 in our previous work [1]) in the upload direction to a well provisioned measurement server at our institute. This server further replies back to the client application on the smartphone with a package of testing data in the downlink direction. For the data transmission in the upload and the download direction, we relied upon the UDP protocol. By using the UDP protocol we could ensure that our measurement results were not influenced by protocol specific behaviour like slow start and congestion control as it is the case for TCP. While these two measurements are executed, all API-obtainable network quality parameters like the currently experienced Reference Signal Received Power (RSRP) or the Reference Signal Received Quality (RSRQ) are collected in parallel (see Table 1). The received measurement results are then concatenated with their respective network quality parameters together and form a so-called single measurement object. This object is then uploaded to the measurement server and persisted in a PostgreSQL database for further evaluation through our machine learning algorithm. A new measurement event is then executed right after the upload of the latest measurement object is finished.

4.2   Extended Tool Chain

To now further investigate the performance gain of localized training data compared to non location specific global training, we needed to extend our previous work to achieve a higher timely accuracy of the obtained measurements. Furthermore we wanted to improve the available feature set for better throughput prediction. The information regarding the availability of Carrier Aggregation or MIMO is not provided by the currently available Android APIs (May 2018) for example. To obtain such values, it was necessary to verify if the local training data could provide a significant improvement in the obtainable training results, as supposed from the results obtained from our previous work [1]. However we still wanted to keep our approach low cost and rather easily deployable. We did not want to spend more money on hardware or licenses, as it would have been required for Qualcomms eXtensible Monitor Software (QXDM). The software requires an additional PC to be connected to the smartphone and further licensing costs. We wanted to have a rather easily deployable hardware setup. Therefore we saw a great opportunity in the availability of the so-called MobileInsight Android application provided through the work of Li et al. [12]. MobileInsight provides nearly the exact same features and timely accuracy of the lower LTE layers as the QXDM toolkit, as it uses the same Qualcomm debug port on the chipset of the smartphone to obtain and decode its data. Thus we were able to quickly and easily obtain additional features for our machine learning approach, which are comparable to the data used in the Related Work. This includes the availability of Carrier Aggregation and MIMO data transmission, as well as the currently used modulation and coding scheme of the LTE network. For the full list of used features, see Sect. 4.4 and the Table 1. The MobileInsight software is free and open source, therefore we were able to easily integrate its provided data into our own measurement application. We therefore relied on the so-called Android Broadcast service, which was provided by the MobileInsight application. It enabled us to transfer the decoded lower layer network quality parameters from MobileInsight directly to our own smartphone application. This additional feature set is then also persisted in the PostgreSQL database for further investigation. The only requirement that MobileInsight has to be operational is that the smartphone on which it shall be executed, is rooted. We are well aware of the fact that this requirement might hinder a large scale deployment as already stated in our previous work [1]. However in contrast to other tool sets, which enable the same network quality features to be collected (e.g. used by Samba et al. [21] or Yue et al. [18]), we consider our approach a rather easily deployable and cost efficient way to obtain the data for further scientific research and to investigate the possibilities in it that can be unlocked through more advanced devices in the future.

4.3   Used Measuring Devices

In contrast to our previous work where we used Nexus 5 and Samsung Galaxy S7 smartphones, the measurement results shown within this work have been obtained by measuring with three Nexus 5X smartphones in parallel, while driving, one for each of the available providers in Germany. The reason lies in our requirement to use MobileInsight to obtain additional data from the LTE protocol stack. Our initial tests with the Nexus 5 smartphone and the Samsung Galaxy S7 smartphone showed that those devices do not provide the full feature set of lower level information through messages, as it was the case for the Nexus 5X. Although they both posses Qualcomm chipsets, which is a requirement by MobileInsight to be able to decode the lower layer information. Especially information regarding the current availability of Carrier Aggregation and the availability of MIMO were not obtainable by using those devices. One possible reason therefore could be the different chipsets, which are used within the different smartphones. This is probably one of the reasons why the Nexus 5 and Samsung Galaxy S7 are not included in the list of supported devices on

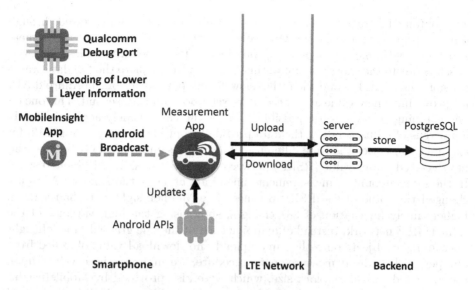

Fig. 1. Extension of our already existing measurement application (black, bold lines) with MobileInsight information (blue, dashed line). Both components are coupled through the Android Broadcast mechanism. (Color figure online)

the website of MobileInsight[1], whereas the Nexus 5X is. This shortcoming could probably be addressed in future releases of MobileInsight as a part of future work.

The Nexus 5X is a smartphone of LTE device category 6. It is able to use 2-way Carrier Aggregation and 2×2 MIMO thus can achieve download speeds of up to 300 MBit/s, if the network provides the necessary resources. Similar to the Nexus 5 used in the previous work, the Nexus 5X did not provide the Channel Quality Indicator (CQI) directly through the Android API (as the Samsung Galaxy S7 did). We could only obtain it directly from the Qualcomm chipset using the decoded information provided by MobileInsight. Thus we had to adapt our available feature set regarding this device specific condition, as explained in the following Section and illustrated by Table 1.

4.4   Used Features for Machine Learning

To make our newly obtained prediction results comparable to our previous work [1] and the Related Work of Samba et al. [21,22], we continued using the Random Forest regression algorithm, as it has already proven itself suitable for this kind of supervised machine learning task. The newly collected data set was therefore divided up into a training set of 70% and a testing set of 30%, as done in our previous work. The used feature sets for the machine learning process, which

---

[1] http://www.mobileinsight.net/.

were obtained from the Android API and MobileInsight, are expressed through Table 1. By using the Android API, we were able to concatenate our active measurements with one set of passively obtained network quality values. This was possible due to the short amount of time required to complete the full data transmission (less than 1 s) and the rather slow timely periodicity of the Android API for providing a new value at a speed of as well about one per second. This one on one mapping however is not possible with the increased timely accuracy of only a few tens of milliseconds of the data provided from MobileInsight. Figure 2, for example, illustrates the time difference of the provisioning of the Reference Signal Received Power value (RSRP) between the Android API and MobileInsight. In the same amount of measurement time of about 11 s - the Android API only changed the value of the RSRP 6 times. The MobileInsight data had a much higher timely fluctuation of 281 changes, showcasing the high variance of the cellular LTE network. Instead of mapping each of the fine grained MobileInsight measurement objects onto the same upload and download value obtained from our personal Android measurement procedure, we mapped those values upon the allocated transport block size, which were also provided by MobileInsight. As described in the background Sect. 2, we were able to calculate the actual obtained throughput in the time period of one MobileInsight measuring periodicity (e.g. only a few milliseconds) by dividing the value of the transport block size currently assigned to the phone by the length of time. The achieved transport block size thereby is granted by the current cell tower to the smartphone based on the combination of two values. One is the amount of allocated resource blocks, which the cell tower schedules every millisecond anew to all the currently active users in the cell. The other one is the currently used Modulation and Coding Scheme (MCS) of the smartphone itself. Both values together result in the achievable transport block size, which can than be transformed into the achievable throughput value in the sort time period of the MobileInsight measurement. This way we were able to create a one on one mapping between passive network quality parameters and achieved throughput values for the data collected by MobileInsight as well. However we did not use the number of available resource blocks and gained transport block size as additional features for our machine learning, as they are directly correlated to the throughput value. Furthermore they also would not be able to be obtained in an instantaneous way, but would rather require the initial transmission of some data. We wanted our approach to avoid this, as our obtained results had to be compared to the work of Samba et al. [21], where the authors as well obtained their results through instantaneous throughput prediction. Therefore, no data had to be transmitted. We still see the possible future improvements that might lie in the usage of historic transport block size values similar to the approach presented by Yue et al. [18]. Therefore we consider this as possible future work, as described in Sect. 7.

To keep our obtained results comparable to our previous work and the work of Samba et al. [21], we assumed the same R^2 performance metrics for the comparison of our newly obtained feature vectors with the old predictors. The formula for the R^2 metric is defined as stated in Formula 1, where $\bar{y}$ is the average of all considered throughput measurements, y_i is the current throughput estimation and is $\hat{y}_i$ the predicted throughput value.

$$R^2 = 1 - \frac{\sum_{i=1}^{n}(\hat{y}_i - y_i)^2}{\sum_{i=1}^{n}(\bar{y} - y_i)^2} \tag{1}$$

It can be stated, that the higher the value of R^2, the better the prediction algorithm works. The best possible value in theory is 1, in which case the predicted values are always the same as the measured values. A value below 0 is rather poor, as it means that the decision to select always the average of all obtained measurements values would have been in sum closer to the actual measured throughput values than the sum of all predicted values.

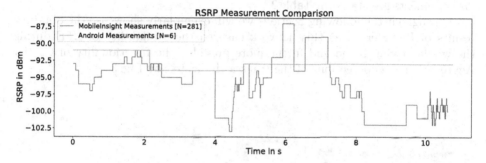

Fig. 2. Comparison between the measurement accuracy of the Reference Signal Received Power (RSRP) between the stock Android API and MobileInsight. Clearly visible is the highly increased timely resolution of MobileInsight in contrast to the Android API.

Table 1. Machine learning features provided by the baseline approach (a) and the extended approach (b, c) using Nexus 5X smartphones.

(a) Machine learning features provided by the Android APIs for Upload and Download direction

RSRP, RSSI, RSRQ, Longitude, Latitude, Speed of the vehicle, TimingAdvance

(b) Machine learning features provided by MobileInsight for the Download direction

RSRP, RSSI, RSRQ, Longitude, Latitude, Speed of the vehicle
CQI, Carrier Aggregation availability, Modulation and Coding Scheme, MIMO

(c) Machine learning features provided by Mobile-Insight for the Upload direction

RSRP, RSSI, RSRQ, Longitude, Latitude, Speed of the vehicle
CQI, Modulation and Coding Scheme

5   Scenario Description

To achieve comparable results between our previous work and our newly obtained results, we selected the same driving test site to perform our measurements of the available LTE networks from the three German cellular providers (in the following stated as A, B and C). All tests have been conducted on the same Section of the German highway A60 (see Fig. 3) over a period of three days to achieve a significant high amount of measurements while connected to each LTE cell along the track (this is exemplary shown for Provider A in Fig. 3(a)). In our previous work we already obtained data from Provider A and B, which can be now compared with the present work. Similar to our previous works data set, this new additional data set with enhanced detailed features and timely accuracy will also be made publicly available on GitHub[2]. The exact numbers of obtained measurements are stated in Table 2.

Throughout the following Sections we will exemplarly showcase the obtained results of Provider A, as this network ensured the availability of LTE during the whole driving range and furthermore provided the functionality of Carrier Aggregation at two Sections of the track as indicated by Fig. 3.

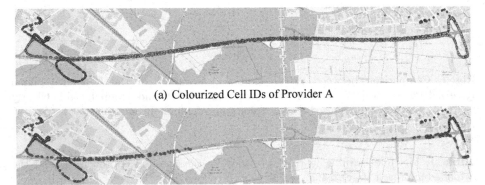

(a) Colourized Cell IDs of Provider A

(b) Measurements with available Carrier Aggregation of Provider A

Fig. 3. Visualisation of the 5 km long Section of the German highway A60 near Rüsselsheim where our measurement drives have been performed. ©OpenStreetMap contributors.

Table 2. Amount of additional measurement data that has been collected for the extended evaluation.

(a) Collected Android Data Points

Provider	A	B	C
Download	8369	8571	6027
Upload	8367	8566	6002
Overall	16736	17137	12029

(b) Collected MobileInsight Data Points

Provider	A	B	C
Download	100920	105377	50506
Upload	149166	89847	46653
Overall	250086	195224	97159

---

[2] https://github.com/florianjomrich/cellularLTEMeasurementsHighwayA60.

6   Evaluation

As mentioned in the previous Sect. 5, we will now showcase our obtained evaluation results using Provider A as an example. Provider A is the most interesting one, as we were able to obtain data, that was measured while Carrier Aggregation was available. However the obtained results of the other two providers are comparable. Thus we are able to generalize our statements for all three providers as described in the following.

6.1   Initial Evaluation

In the style of our previous work [1] we again investigated the distribution of all obtained throughput measurement values in the uplink and the downlink direction for all three providers. This time, we did this once for the obtained Android throughput measurements and once for the calculated throughput values based on the achieved transport block size provided by MobileInsight. The results for provider A are shown in Fig. 4.

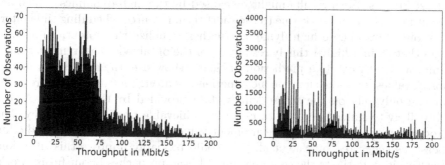

(a) Android Download Measurements - Provider A

(b) MobileInsight Download Resource Allocation / Measurements - Provider A

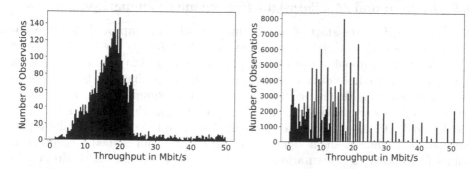

(c) Android Upload Measurements - Provider A

(d) MobileInsight Upload Resource Allocation / Measurements - Provider A

Fig. 4. Histograms of the distribution of throughput measurements obtained from Android and MobileInsight.

To our satisfaction the obtained distributions of the histograms for Android data are quite similar in the upload direction compared to the results of our previous work. The sharp drop of achieved upload measurements at about 25 MBit/s is clearly visible in both data sets. Thus we can state that our measuring approach is producing similar results over a longer period of time. For the newly obtained Android download data set, the decline of the histogram plot is not so linear any more compared to our previous work. This might be due to a smaller set of Android measurements within our new dataset, which possibly did not cover the linear transition as well. Another reason might be changes in the network infrastructure or differences in the used LTE chipset within the Nexus 5X, as the smartphone was able to achieve significantly higher values of throughput ranging in the area of about 125 to 200 MBit/s as compared to an achieved peak bandwidth between 120 to 140 MBit/s for the Nexus 5 and the Samsung Galaxy S7 within our previous work [1].

In contrast to the distribution of the Android upload and download values, the achieved throughput values based on the data provided by MobileInsight look quite differently. The distribution of those values is much more diverse. In the download direction there are three major peaks visible at about 20, 75 and 125 MBit/s. Both results might be caused by the high dynamics, which are present in the LTE network, due to the short term resource scheduling time interval of only 1 ms. These high dynamics further visualize the potential improvements that lie in a higher timely resolution of the obtained measurement results to improve the throughput prediction. It clearly showcases the high timely fluctuation of values, that the smartphone experiences throughout its trip. A predictor that can only rely on the coarse timely data provided by the Android API is highly likely to suffer from it in terms of its achievable prediction accuracy. The introduction of the historical measurement values as features into the prediction process, as suggested by Yue et al. [18], could probably improve this situation. Thus we will investigate the combination of both approaches in our future work.

6.2 Android and MobileInsight Performance Comparison

As we assumed at the start of our extended work, the improved timely accuracy of MobileInsight leads to a much better performance of the Random Forest algorithm in the throughput prediction process compared to the same algorithm relying only on Android data. The obtained performance increase between those two datasets is visualized in Fig. 6 for all obtained measurements. It clearly showcases the quick saturation of the Random Forest algorithm, which is based on the Android API data. The same algorithm based on the data of MobileInsight, however, only showed slight signs of saturation at about 20.000 measurement points (compared to a saturation at about 2000 points for the Android API based learner) and might even improve further its accuracy with more obtained measurements as training data. To our further satisfaction we were now able to achieve comparable performance values of the R^2 metric with regards to the work of Samba et al. [21]. The range of the R^2 value mostly varied between 0.8 and 0.9 depending on whether we were predicting the upload or the download direction, based on all our measurement data as seen in Fig. 6. Samba et al. achieved R^2 values of up to 0.85. To obtain those results however the authors also relied on data, that was directly provided to them by the cooperating network providers back end. As we see this as a significant disadvantage regarding a possible future deployment, we are glad that our approach could achieve similar performance values without having to rely on such data. The overall performance of the Random Forest algorithm, and thus the obtained R^2 values, however varied between the different cells in our measuring scenario as described in the following Sect. 6.3. This further supported us in the assumption that localized training data should further improve the obtainable performance results as described in the following (Fig. 5).

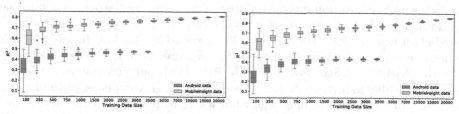

(a) Download throughput prediction perfor- (b) Upload throughput prediction performance
mance comparison   comparison

Fig. 5. Performance comparison between Android and MobileInsight.

6.3 Localized vs Globalized Training Based on MobilInsight Data

The main motivation for this presented extended work came from the evaluation results obtained from our previous work regarding the comparison between specific, localized training data and a general global training data set. The localized training data set thereby was specifically generated for each measured cell individually from its measurement objects. The global training data set, which was used as a comparison, then could contain training data from all the other cells but not the specific one. The results, which we were able to obtain in our previous work suggested that especially under conditions where the prediction process is working well, the localized training data could improve the overall performance of our predictors. This motivated us to extend the used feature set for throughput prediction within this current work regarding the timely accuracy and the available features (as stated in Table 1) to improve the overall prediction performance (as shown in Sect. 6.2).

To deepen our performance investigation regarding the benefits of localized training data, we then prepared datasets as described for the four most frequently measured cells (in the following named accordingly A–D) within our new extended dataset. Then, we executed the training and testing procedure of the Random Forest algorithm. The localized training data consisted only of measurements obtained from the one specific cell, whereas the globalized training data consisted out of a set of measurements, which was selected from all other cells, but not the specific one. The obtained results are separated into the Uplink and the Downlink direction, as MobileInsight provided different sets of available prediction features as shown in Table 1.

As the largest contribution of this work we can state that all the obtained results from our new dataset demonstrate that localized training data significantly outperforms general globalized training data in the prediction accuracy. All investigated cells show this training behaviour in the uplink as well as in the downlink direction. The assumptions made in our previous work [1] thus could be further verified with our new improved prediction model. This behaviour is already visible when using only 1500 measurement points or sometimes even less depending on the specifically investigated cell. Also it can be stated that the overall prediction performance clearly varies between the cells, which further justifies the usage of location specific training data to improve the overall obtainable performance. Most of interest for us is the change of the relevance of the used prediction features for the different cells as stated by Table 3. In our previous work one of the most important prediction features for our trained model was the Received Signal Strength Power (RSRP). With our new obtained features set we were able to investigate that this relevance highly depends on the specific cell that the machine learning algorithm wants to predict. To the best of our knowledge, we are the first to deeply investigate this correlation as for example the work of Samba et al. [21] and Yue et al. [18] as two of the most recent works did not consider Carrier Aggregation as a feature. When the Random Forest algorithm tries to predict the throughput in the downlink direction based on the dataset, which consist out of all four major cells (All), the correlation between the RSRP and the throughput is now the worst correlation factor as shown in Table 3. The correlation between the throughput and the availability of Carrier Aggregation is the most important parameter for the complete set. This correlation however no longer holds true when investigating the specific cells (A–D) individually. The influence of the Carrier Aggregation feature was the highest for the cells C and D, where we also obtained the most measured points with the Carrier Aggregation being available. For the cells A and B instead we only measured a few points with Carrier Aggregation enabled. Thus the prediction in those cases does not rely very much on the feature. In conclusion, the Carrier Aggregation features prediction performance highly depends on its availability and thus on the actual location of the vehicle, where it has measured the dataset. As further expected the RSRP value of the cells A and B had a higher correlation value with the measured throughput than for the cells C and D. The overall prediction performance however cannot be justified by one of these two single parameters, as the overall prediction performance can be high or low with or without the Carrier Aggregation feature being relevant as indicated by the obtained results of cell B and cell C for the downlink direction. Although the current stock Android does not provide the information whether or not Carrier Aggregation is available, it might be possible to still include this feature by mentioning all of the available surrounding cells, which are visible to Android, while the measurement was performed. By this way it might be possible to also identify certain positions where Carrier Aggregation is available. Therefore we will

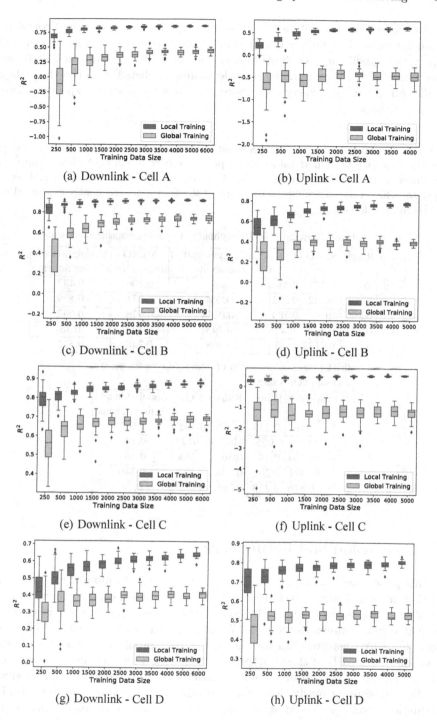

(a) Downlink - Cell A

(b) Uplink - Cell A

(c) Downlink - Cell B

(d) Uplink - Cell B

(e) Downlink - Cell C

(f) Uplink - Cell C

(g) Downlink - Cell D

(h) Uplink - Cell D

Fig. 6. Performance comparison between cell specific training data and global/non specific training data.

further investigate the details of the parameters and their individual correlation in our future work to hopefully enhance the prediction performance of our easily deployable baseline approach even more. In summary, we still can clearly state that localized training data can provide significant benefits to the through-put prediction process compared to a more general - non location specific - global training data set.

Table 3. Results obtained for the correlation between the achieved throughput and the other passive measured values using pearsons correlation coefficient. The values are showcased for both transmission directions for all the measured cells together and for data, which was only obtained from one of the four most frequently measured cells (A–D) in our dataset.

(a) Download - Correlation of Throughput with passive measurement values

Cells	RSRP	RSRQ	CQI	Carrier Aggregation availability	MIMO availability	Modulation and Coding Scheme
All	-0.012	0.187	0.446	0.6	0.406	0.483
A	0.59	0.342	0.662	-0.00514	0.521	0.599
B	0.804	0.31	0.789	-0.0084	0.526	0.682
C	0.473	0.123	0.42	0.743	0.379	0.46
D	0.279	-0.0177	0.35	0.368	0.248	0.385

(b) Upload - Correlation of Throughput with passive measurement values

Cells	RSRP	RSRQ	RSSI	CQI	Modulation and Coding Scheme
All	0.61	0.245	0.576	0.635	0.662
A	0.108	0.0651	0.0877	0.0124	0.294
B	0.564	0.441	0.507	0.584	0.469
C	0.471	0.202	0.446	0.372	0.346
D	0.846	0.223	0.766	0.731	0.76

7   Conclusion and Futurework

In this paper, we investigate the performance gains of online throughput estimation machine learning techniques when reyling on a specific localized training data set. We therefore extend the base line approach, which we developed and evaluated in our previous work [1]. Within this former approach we only relied upon measured feature data for the throughput prediction that was obtained from the stock APIs of the smartphone itself. This way we wanted to ensure an easy distribution realisation of our approach based on hardware that is similar to the hardware currently deployed in production vehicles. From our obtained evaluation results we could show that the prediction performance can be best enhanced through localized training data, when the overall prediction performance is already high. Due to the decreased timely accuracy of the API provided values however, we were not able to improve the prediction performance further with the old collected data set. Within this new and extended work we now introduce a newly improved features set regarding the timely accuracy and the available features. By introducing further and more accurate features we were able to verify that the preprocessing of training data, regarding its localization for each specific cell results in an increased prediction performance as shown in Sect. 6. Further we could show that the overall prediction throughput performance of the used Random Forest Algorithm fluctuates from cell to cell. Thus we consider as a future work the deeper investigation of the relevance of individual parameters for each cell to provide a perfectly trained machine learning algorithm for the individual throughput prediction.

References

1. Jomrich, F., Herzberger, A., Tobias, M., Björn, R., Steinmetz, R., Wille, C.: Cellular bandwidth prediction for highly automated driving evaluation of machine learning approaches based on real-world data. In: Proceedings of 4th International Conference on Vehicle Technology and Intelligent Transport Systems (VEHITS), Vehits 2018, Madera, Portugal, SCITEPRESS, pp. 121–132 (2018)
2. Jomrich, F., Sharma, A., Rückelt, T., Burgstahler, D., Böhnstedt, D.: Dynamic map update protocol for highly automated driving vehicles. In: Gusikhin, O., Helfert, M., Pascoal, A. (eds.) Proceedings of the 3rd International Conference on Vehicle Technology and Intelligent Transport Systems (VEHITS 2017), vol. 3, pp. 68–78. SCITEPRESS - Science and Technology Publications, Lda. (2017). Full Paper
3. Lee, J., et al.: LTE-advanced in 3 GPP rel -13/14: an evolution toward 5G. IEEE Commun. Mag. **54**, 36–42 (2016)
4. Here: Vehicle sensor data cloud ingestion interface specification (2015)
5. Kamakaris, T., Nickerson, J.: Connectivity maps: measurements and applications, p. 307. IEEE (2005)
6. Nagel, R., Morscher, S.: Connectivity prediction in mobile vehicular environments backed by digital maps. INTECH Open Access Publisher (2011)
7. Kelch, L., Pogel, T., Wolf, L., Sasse, A.: CQI maps for optimized data distribution. In: 2013 IEEE 78th Vehicular Technology Conference (VTC Fall), pp. 1–5. IEEE (2013)
8. Pögel, T., Wolf, L.: Optimization of vehicular applications and communication properties with connectivity maps. In: 2015 IEEE 40th Local Computer Networks Conference Workshops (LCN Workshops), pp. 870–877. IEEE (2015)
9. Lu, F., Du, H., Jain, A., Voelker, G.M., Snoeren, A.C., Terzis, A.: CQIC: revisiting cross-layer congestion control for cellular networks, pp. 45–50. ACM Press (2015)
10. Jin, R.: Enhancing upper-level performance from below: performance measurement and optimization in LTE networks (2015)
11. Margolies, R., et al.: Exploiting mobility in proportional fair cellular scheduling: measurements and algorithms. IEEE/ACM Trans. Netw. **24**, 355–367 (2016)
12. Li, Y., Peng, C., Yuan, Z., Li, J., Deng, H., Wang, T.: MobileInsight: extracting and analyzing cellular network information on smartphones. In: Proceedings of the 22nd Annual International Conference on Mobile Computing and Networking, MobiCom 2016, pp. 202–215. ACM, New York (2016)

13. Pögel, T., Wolf, L.: Prediction of 3G network characteristics for adaptive vehicular connectivity maps (poster). In: 2012 IEEE Vehicular Networking Conference (VNC), pp. 121–128. IEEE (2012)
14. Yao, J., Kanhere, S.S., Hassan, M.: An empirical study of bandwidth predictability in mobile computing. In: Proceedings of the Third ACM International Workshop on Wireless Network Testbeds, Experimental Evaluation and Characterization, pp. 11–18. ACM (2008)
15. Xu, Q., Mehrotra, S., Mao, Z., Li, J.: PROTEUS: network performance forecast for real-time, interactive mobile applications. In: Proceeding of the 11th Annual International Conference on Mobile Systems, Applications, and Services, pp. 347–360. ACM (2013)
16. Liu, Y., Lee, J.Y.: An empirical study of throughput prediction in mobile data networks. In: 2015 IEEE Global Communications Conference (GLOBECOM), pp. 1–6. IEEE (2015)
17. Jomrich, F., Grau, M., Meuser, T., Nguyen, T.A.B., Böhnstedt, D., Steinmetz, R.: ICCOMQS intelligent measuring framework to ensure reliable communication for highly automated vehicles. In: Proceedings of 2017 IEEE Vehicular Networking Conference (VNC). SCITEPRESS – Science and Technology Publications, Lda. (2017)
18. Yue, C., Jin, R., Suh, K., Qin, Y., Wang, B., Wei, W.: LinkForecast: cellular link bandwidth prediction in LTE networks. IEEE Trans. Mob. Comput. **17**, 1582–1594 (2017)
19. Wietfeld, C., Ide, C., Dusza, B.: Resource efficient mobile communications for crowd-sensing, pp, 1–6. ACM Press (2014)
20. Ide, C., Nick, M., Kaulbars, D., Wietfeld, C.: Forecasting cellular connectivity for cyber-physical systems: a machine learning approach. Machine Learning for Cyber Physical Systems. TA, pp. 15–22. Springer, Heidelberg (2016). https://doi.org/10.1007/978-3-662-48838-6_3
21. Samba, A., Busnel, Y., Blanc, A., Dooze, P., Simon, G.: Instantaneous throughput prediction in cellular networks: which information is needed? In: 2017 IFIP/IEEE International Symposium on Integrated Network Management (IM). IEEE (2017)
22. Samba, A., Busnel, Y., Blanc, A., Dooze, P., Simon, G.: Throughput prediction in cellular networks: experiments and preliminary results. In: CoRes 2016 (2016)

A Probabilistic Travel Time Modeling Approach Based on Spatiotemporal Speed Variations

Mohammed Elhenawy[1], Abdallah A. Hassan[2],
and Hesham A. Rakha[2,3,4(✉)]

[1] Centre for Accident Research and Road Safety,
University of Technology at the Queensland, Queensland, Australia
elhenawy@vt.edu
[2] Bradley Department of Electrical and Computer Engineering,
Electrical and Computer Engineering, MC 0111, 1185 Perry St.,
Blacksburg 24061, VA, USA
{abdallah, hrakha}@vt.edu
[3] Charles E. via, Jr. Department of Civil and Environmental Engineering,
Blacksburg, VA 24061, USA
[4] Center for Sustainable Mobility, Virginia Tech Transportation Institute,
Blacksburg, VA 24061, USA

Abstract. The rapid development and deployment of Intelligent Transportation Systems (ITSs) require the development of data driven algorithms. Travel time modeling is an integral component of travel and transportation management and travel demand management functions. Travel time has a massive impact on driver's route choice behavior and the assessment of the transportation system performance. In this paper, a mixture of linear regression is proposed to model travel times. The mixture of linear regression models has three advantages. First, it provides better model fitting compared to simple linear regression. Second, the proposed model can capture the bi-modal nature of travel time distributions and link it to the uncongested and congested traffic regimes. Third, the means of the bi-modal distributions are modeled as functions of the input predictors. This last advantage allows for the quantitative evaluation of the probability of each travel time state as well as the uncertainty associated with each state at any time of the day given the values of the predictors at that time. The proposed model is applied to archived data along a 74.4-mile freeway stretch of I-66 eastbound to connect I-81 and Washington D.C. The experimental results show the ability of the model to capture the stochastic nature of the travel time and gives good travel time predictions.

Keywords: Travel time modelling · Travel time reliability ·
Mixture of linear regressions

© Springer Nature Switzerland AG 2019
B. Donnellan et al. (Eds.): SMARTGREENS 2018/VEHITS 2018, CCIS 992, pp. 351–366, 2019.
https://doi.org/10.1007/978-3-030-26633-2_17

1 Introduction

Minimizing drivers' travel times from their origins to their destinations is a major Intelligent Transportation Systems (ITSs) objective. However, it is also extremely challenging due to the dynamic nature of traffic flow, which is, in most cases, highly unpredictable. One straightforward strategy involves directing vehicles or guiding drivers to follow routes that avoid congested paths. A critical step for this route planning or guidance to be effective is the ability to accurately predict travel times of different alternative routes from source to destination.

In addition, travel time represents an important performance measure for traffic system evaluation. It is easily understood by drivers and operators of traffic management systems, and can be viewed as a simple summary of a traffic system's complex behavior. In order for an ITS to accurately predict the travel time, it must have the following capabilities, each of which comes with associated difficulties:

1. Sensing and acquiring the current state of the transportation network of interest where a number of data values need to be detected and collected, including traffic conditions and parameters at different parts of the network, whether some roads are currently congested, current weather conditions, time of day, whether there is an incident on any road in the network, etc. Gathering such data on every road and intersection with the quality that allows accurate forecasting of travel time between two points in the network may be fairly expensive.
2. Storing a long history of traffic parameters for the transportation network of interest to support future prediction of travel times. This historical dataset may be large and difficult to use and manage.
3. Feeding the current state of the network along with its traffic history to some type of model that predicts travel time if a trip will start from some point and end in another in the network at some specific time. Designing such a model is challenging, as is finding a set of current or historical parameters with real prediction power. The most useful model may be road dependent, and even for a single road, it has been shown that different models may describe the traffic behavior more accurately at different traffic conditions. For instance, one model may be more useful when the road is congested, while another model may be more accurate when vehicles are flowing freely, etc.

In short, accurate traffic time prediction is challenging due to the high cost of sensing and collecting enough useful current and historical traffic data. Even when such data is available, it is still difficult to determine which type of model best describes the traffic behavior, and which traffic parameters should be fed to the model for the best predictions. Moreover, the best course of action may be to use two or more models and switch between them depending on current traffic conditions. This option adds a new challenge, as it is necessary to decide which model from the set of models will be used for some specific input data, or whether different models will be used for prediction with some weight applied to each output prediction to reach a final travel time prediction.

In this paper, a new method for travel time prediction is proposed. This method uses a mixture of linear regressions motivated by the fact that travel time distribution is not unimodal, since two modes or regimes of traffic can exist—one at congestion state, and the other at free-flow state. We show how the proposed model is very flexible and gives slightly different accuracy when we model the travel time or the log of the travel time using two different set of predictors. The First set of predictors are the selected elements from the spatiotemporal speed matrix based on their estimated importance using random forest. Then these set of speeds will be the input predictors to the statistical model. The second set of predictors are the instantaneous travel time and the average of the historical travel time. The proposed model is built and tested using probe data provided by INRIX and supplemented with traditional road sensor data as well as mobile devices and other sources. The dataset was collected from a freeway stretch of I-66 eastbound connecting I-81 and Washington, D.C. The traffic on this stretch is often extremely heavy, which makes travel time prediction more challenging, but also makes the data more valuable and helps create a more realistic model.

2 Related Work

Various methods and algorithms have been proposed in the literature for travel time prediction. These methods can roughly be classified into two main categories: statistical-based data-driven methods and simulation-based methods. This section focuses on the statistical-based methods since the proposed solution in this paper falls under this class of methods, and because more research in the literature uses statistical methods.

Several researchers fit different regression models to predict travel time. A typical approach is to fit a multiple linear regression (MLR) model using explanatory variables representing instantaneous traffic state and historical traffic data, as, for example, [1, 2]. The model proposed in [1] was even able to use a single linear regression (SLR) to successfully provide acceptable travel time predictions. Some researchers developed hybrid methods where a regression model was used in conjunction with other advanced statistical methods. For example, [3] used regression with statistical tree methods. Another approach [4] proposed an SLR model using bus travel time to predict automobile travel time.

Regression models are generally powerful in predicting travel time for short-term prediction, whereas long-term predictions are less accurate. Regression models are also reported to be more suitable for use in free-flow rather than congested traffic, and fail to accurately predict when incidents have occurred [5].

The idea of using a mixture models for different traffic regimes has also previously been explored [6]. The model developed in this paper attempts to overcome the drawbacks of previous work that used mixture models of two or three components to model travel time reliability, which suffer from the following limitations:

1. The mean of each component is not modeled as a function of the available predictors.
2. The proportion variable is fixed at each time slot, which limits the model's flexibility.

3. Information provided given the time slot of the day is the probability of each component (fixed) and the 90th percentile.

Another class of statistical-based methods in literature uses time series models for travel time prediction, using, for example, auto-regressive prediction models [7–9], multivariate time series models [10], and the auto-regressive integrated moving average (ARIMA) technique [11]. Similar to regression models, time series models are more suitable for free-flow traffic than for congested traffic, may fail with unusual incidents, and are more accurate for short-term predictions [5].

Another common technique used for travel time prediction is the use of artificial neural networks. A feed-forward neural network is used in [12] to predict journey time. Later, more advanced neural network techniques were used to model and predict travel time [13–19]. Accurate predictions were achieved for most proposed models; for example, in [20] the prediction error was only 4%.

3 Methods

The definitions of historical, instantaneous and ground truth travel times are introduced in this section. In addition, we present a brief introduction of the powerful modelling technique used in this paper. Expectation-maximization (EM) is used to fit the mixture of linear regression models to the historical data.

3.1 Travel Time Ground Truth Calculation

The calculation of the travel time ground truth is based on trajectory construction and the known speed through the trajectory's cells. A simple example of travel time ground truth calculation based on trajectory construction is demonstrated in Fig. 1. In this example, the roadway is divided into four sections using segments of length Δx and a time interval of Δt. We assumed that the speed is homogenous within each cell. The average speed of the red-dotted cell (i = 2, n = 3) in the figure is $u(x2, t3)$. Consequently, the trajectory slope represents the speed in each cell. Once the vehicle enters a new cell, the trajectory within this cell can be drawn as the straight blue line in Fig. 1 using the cell speed as the slope. Finally, the ground truth travel time can be calculated when the trip reaches the downstream boundary of the last freeway section. It should be noted that the ground truth travel times were computed using the same dataset and used as the response (y).

3.2 Instantaneous Travel Time

The instantaneous method is very simple where it assumes the segment speed does not change during the entire trip time. The travel time using the instantaneous approach is shown in Eq. (1).

$$\text{instantaneous travel time} = \sum_{i=1}^{h} \frac{L_i}{v_i^{t0}} \tag{1}$$

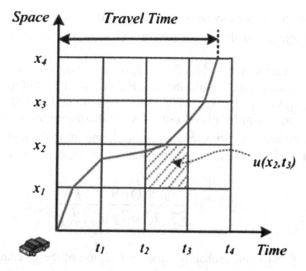

Fig. 1. Illustration of travel time ground truth calculation.

Where

    L_i is the length of segment i

    v_i^{t0} is the speed at segment i at the departure time t0

    h is the total number of segments.

3.3 Historical Average Method

If the spatiotemporal speed matrices are known for several previous months, then the ground truth travel time at each time interval for each day can be calculated. The historical average at any time of day D is calculated using Eq. (2).

$$\text{average historical travel time} = \sum_{i=1}^{Z_{D_i}} \frac{\text{GTTT}_{D_i}^{t0}}{Z_{D_i}} \forall D_i = \text{Saturday}, \ldots, \text{Friday} \qquad (2)$$

Where $\text{GTTT}_{D_i}^{t0}$ is the ground truth travel time at departure time $t0$ at historical day D_i and Z_{D_i} is number of days included in the average.

3.4 Mixture of Linear Regressions

A mixture of linear regressions was studied carefully [21, 22]. It can be used to model travel time under different traffic regimes. The mixture of linear regression can be written as:

$$f(y|X) = \sum_{j=1}^{m} \frac{\lambda_j}{\sigma_j \sqrt{2\pi}} e^{-\frac{\left(y - x^T \beta_j\right)^2}{2\sigma_j^2}} \qquad (3)$$

where y_i is the response corresponding to a vector p of predictors; x_i^T, β_j is the vector of regression coefficients for the jth component and λ_j is mixing probability of the jth component.

The model parameters $\psi = \{\beta_1, \beta_2, \ldots, \beta_m \sigma_1^2, \sigma_2^2, \ldots \sigma_m^2, \lambda_1, \lambda_2, \ldots, \lambda_m\}$. can be estimated by maximizing the log-likelihood of Eq. (1) given a set of response predictor pairs $(y_1, x_1), (y_2, x_2), \ldots, (y_n, x_n)$ using an EM algorithm. The EM algorithm iteratively finds the maximum likelihood estimates by alternating the E-step and M-step. Let $\psi^{(k)}$ be the parameters' estimates after the kth iteration. In the E-step, the posterior probability of the ith observation from component j is computed using Eq. (4).

$$w_{ij}^{(k+1)} = \frac{\lambda_j^{(k)} \phi_j \left(y_i | x_i, \psi^{(k)}\right)}{\sum_{j=1}^{m} \lambda_j^{(k)} \phi_j \left(y_i | x_i, \psi^{(k)}\right)} \tag{4}$$

where $\phi_j \left(y_i | x_i, \psi^{(k)}\right)$ is the probability density function of the jth component.

In the M-step, the new parameters' estimates $\psi^{(k+1)}$ that maximize the log-likelihood function in Eq. (3) are calculated using Eqs. (5–7)

$$\lambda_j^{(k+1)} = \frac{\sum_{i=1}^{n} w_{ij}^{(k+1)}}{n} \tag{5}$$

$$\widehat{\beta}_j^{(k+1)} = (X^T W_j X)^{-1} X^T W_j \tag{6}$$

where X is the predictors' matrix with n rows and $(p+1)$ columns, Y is the corresponding $n \times 1$ response vector, and W is an $n \times n$ diagonal matrix which has $w_{ij}^{(k+1)}$ on its diagonal.

$$\hat{\sigma}_j^{2(k+1)} = \frac{\sum_{i=1}^{n} w_{ij}^{(k+1)} (y_i - x_i^T \widehat{\beta}_j^{(k+1)})^2}{\sum_{i=1}^{n} w_{ij}^{(k+1)}} \tag{7}$$

The E-step and M-step are alternated repeatedly until the change in the incomplete log-likelihood is arbitrarily small as shown in Eq. (8).

$$\left| \prod_{i=1}^{n} \sum_{j=1}^{m} \lambda_j^{(k+1)} \phi_j \left(y_i | x_i, \psi^{(k+1)}\right) - \prod_{i=1}^{n} \sum_{j=1}^{m} \lambda_j^{(k)} \phi_j \left(y_i | x_i, \psi^{(k)}\right) \right| < \xi \tag{8}$$

where ξ is a small number.

4 The Predictors' Sets

In this section, we describe the two approaches used to from the predictors' sets. In the first approach, the random forest machine-learning algorithm (RF) is used to select a subset of important predictors for travel time modelling. Where the second approach incorporate information from the past by using the historical travel time and summarize the current speeds within a window starting right before the departure time t_0 using the instantaneous travel time.

4.1 The First Set of Predictors

The I-66 stretch of the freeway section used for this research consists of 64 segments. The dataset comprises the spatiotemporal speed matrices for every day in 2013. The default approach for modelling and predicting travel time was to take all the speeds within a window starting right before the departure time t_0 and covering L past time slots back to time $t_0 - L$. Setting L = 30 min for example, the number of predictors will be 64 * 6 at 5 min time aggregation. In order to reduce the dimensions of the predictors' vector, RF is used to select the most important predictors for the travel time model. Steps to select the most important predictors are as follows [23]:

1. For each month, build an RF consisting of 100 trees and find the out-of-bag samples that are not used in the training for each tree.
2. Find the mean square error $MSE_{outofbag}$ of the RF using the out-of-bag samples.
3. Randomly permute the value for each predictor x_i among the out-of-bag samples and calculate the mean square error $MSE_{outofbag}^{permutedx_i}$ of the RF.
4. Finally, rank the predictors in descending order based on the $\frac{1}{12} \sum_{month=1}^{12} \left(MSE_{outofbag}^{permutedx_i} - MSE_{outofbag} \right)$ and choose the top m ranked predictors.

The higher the predictor's rank in step 4, the more important that predictor. The ranking result shows that, most of the important predictors are speeds of recent segments ($t_0 - 5$). In addition to speed predictors chosen by RF, the historical average travel time at t_0 given the day of the week is added as a predictor.

4.2 The Second Set of Predictors

The other set of predictors are the instantaneous travel time and the average of historical travel time. For example, if we are interested in the travel time reliability at $t0$ on day D, the predictor vector will be the instantaneous travel time at the times $\{t0 - 45, t0 - 40, \ldots, t0 - 5\}$ and the average of the historical travel times on days D at times $\{t0, t0 + 5, \ldots, t0 + 45\}$. Figure 2 shows the average of the historical travel time for each day of the weak. There are two peaks of the travel time during morning and evening hours. The height of the peaks is different from one day to another especially between weekdays and weekends.

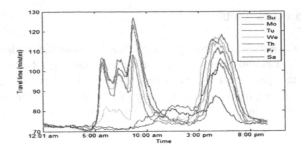

Fig. 2. The average of historical travel time for each day of the week.

5   Data Description

The freeway stretch of I-66 eastbound connecting I-81 and Washington, D.C. was selected as the test site for this study. High traffic volumes are usually observed during morning and afternoon peak hours on I-66 heading towards Washington, D.C., making it an excellent environment to test travel time models.

The traffic data was provided by INRIX, which mainly collects probe data by GPS-equipped vehicles, supplemented with traditional road sensor data, along with mobile devices and other sources [24]. The probe data covers 64 freeway segments with a total length of 74.4 miles. The average segment length is 1.16 miles, and the length of each segment is unevenly divided in the raw data from 0.1 to 8.22 miles. Figure 3 shows the study site and deployment of roadway segments. The raw data provides average speed for each roadway segment and was collected at 1-m intervals.

Fig. 3. The study site on I-66 eastbound. (source: Google Maps) [25].

We sorted the raw data was the roadway direction according to each TMC station's geographic information (e.g., towards eastbound of I-66). Data was examined to check any overlapping or inconsistent stations along the route. Afterward, speed data was aggregated by time intervals (5 min in this study) to reduce noise and smooth measurement errors. This way, the raw data was aggregated to the form of the daily data matrix along spatial and temporal intervals. Data was missing in the developed data matrix, so data input methods were conducted to estimate the missing data using values of neighboring cells. Finally, the daily spatiotemporal traffic state matrix was generated to model travel time.

6 Experimental Analysis

The experimental work is divided into two subsections. The first subsection is travel time modeling using a mixture of two linear regressions with fixed proportions (λ_1, λ_2). In this subsection, we will model the travel time and the log of the travel time using the first set and second set of predictors respectively. Consequently, we will show that log-normal model is better than the normal model. The second subsection describes the travel time reliability modelling approach, where we modified the proposed model to allow the proportions to vary as a function of the predictors. The modified model computes the probabilities of encountering free-flow and congested conditions together with the expected and 90-percentile travel times for each regime.

6.1 Modeling Travel Time Using a Mixture of Linear Regressions with Fixed Proportions

The purpose of this section is to experimentally compare the lognormal model and normal model. Each model used a different set of predictor. In other words, the log-normal model will explain the response vector $log(Y)$ using the corresponding predictors matrix X_2, where Y is the ground truth travel time and X_2 is the second set of predictors. Where the normal model will explain the response vector Y using the corresponding predictors matrix X_1. For the sake of completeness, we also compare each model with the corresponding one component linear regression model, which assumes the travel time distribution is uni-modal distribution. To show that, the parameters of the proposed models are estimated using the EM algorithm. Then, two measures are used to compare the models. The Mean Absolute Percentage Error (MAPE) and the Mean Absolute Error (MAE) are used to quantify the errors of both models with respect to the ground truth. MAPE is the average absolute percentage change between the predicted $\widehat{y_1^j}$ and the true values y_i^j. MAE is the absolute difference between the predicted and the true values.

$$\text{MAPE} = \frac{100}{\text{I} \times \text{J}} \sum_{j=1}^{J} \sum_{i=1}^{I} \frac{\left| y_i^j - \widehat{y_1^j} \right|}{y_i^j} \tag{9}$$

$$\text{MAE} = \frac{1}{\text{I} \times \text{J}} \sum_{j=1}^{J} \sum_{i=1}^{I} \left| y_i^j - \widehat{y_1^j} \right| \tag{10}$$

Here, J is the total number of days in the testing dataset; I is the total number of time intervals in a single day; and y and ŷ denote the ground truth and the predicted value, respectively, of the travel time for the time interval on the day. The lower the value of these error measures, the better the model.

Table 1 shows values for the MAE and MAPE for normal models using a different number of top-ranked predictors. As shown in Table 1, for all models that are built using a different number of predictors, the models built using the proposed mixture of regressions are better than the linear regression models with smaller MAE and MAPE.

Table 1. Comparison between one and two components normal models using the first set of predictors [25].

p	MAE		MAPE	
	m = 1	m = 2	m = 1	m = 2
6	6.57	5.22	7.19	5.69
11	6.39	5.10	6.99	5.63
16	6.36	5.05	6.96	5.57
21	6.32	5.04	6.89	5.56
26	6.31	5.06	6.90	5.59
31	6.32	5.09	6.90	5.64
36	6.30	5.08	6.88	5.62
41	6.30	5.13	6.88	5.69
46	6.29	5.12	6.87	5.68
51	6.23	5.13	6.80	5.70
56	6.24	5.12	6.82	5.69
61	6.18	5.16	6.77	5.74
66	6.18	5.16	6.76	5.74
71	6.20	5.15	6.79	5.73
76	6.19	5.15	6.78	5.73
81	6.20	5.16	6.79	5.74
86	6.18	5.19	6.78	5.78
91	6.19	5.21	6.79	5.80
96	6.19	5.22	6.79	5.80

Table 2 shows values for the MAE and MAPE for lognormal models using the second set of predictors. Table 2 confirms that two component models are better than one-component models. Moreover, it shows that the lognormal models and the second set of predictors are better than the normal models and the first set of predictors (Table 3).

Different number of predictors are shown in Tables 1 and **2**. We tried different number of predictor in order to find the simplest and most accurate model. As shown in the above tables the improvement in the accuracy of the models in terms of MAE and MAPE is not significant. In real time running, we prefer simple models. So that, for the normal model and lognormal model the models which has 16 and 11 predictors respectively are chosen.

Table 2. Comparison between one and two components lognormal models using the second set of predictors.

p	MAE		MAPE	
	m = 1	m = 2	m = 1	m = 2
3	5.04	4.28	5.46	4.58
5	5.04	4.28	5.45	4.58
7	5.03	4.28	5.45	4.58
9	5.03	4.28	5.45	4.58
11	5.03	4.27	5.45	4.57
13	5.03	4.28	5.45	4.58
15	5.03	4.26	5.45	4.56
17	5.03	4.26	5.45	4.56
19	5.03	4.25	5.46	4.56

Table 3. The EM parameters' estimates for a mixture of linear regression assuming normal distribution [25]*.

	1st component	2nd component
intercept	79.4354	96.5943
$x_{29,t0-1}$	−0.0153	−0.0148
$x_{2,t0-1}$	−0.0903	−0.0250
$x_{28,t0-1}$	−0.0668	0.0061
$x_{18,t0-1}$	−0.0912	−0.0519
$x_{27,t0-1}$	0.0187	−0.0449
$x_{40,t0-1}$	−0.2107	−0.1107
$x_{25,t0-1}$	−0.0652	−0.0603
$x_{14,t0-1}$	−0.0245	−0.0136
$x_{29,t0-2}$	−0.0106	−0.0224
$x_{1,t0-1}$	−0.0745	−0.0150
$x_{39,t0-1}$	−0.0174	−0.0331
$x_{21,t0-1}$	−0.0203	−0.0252
$x_{24,t0-1}$	−0.0742	−0.0239
$x_{19,t0-1}$	0.0075	−0.0078
$x_{30,t0-1}$	−0.1269	−0.0558
$x_{13,t0-1}$	0.6767	0.0834
σ_j^2	11.8066	1.7746
λ_j	0.4466	0.5534

*(In this table x_(seg#, time) is the speed at certain segment and time)

Based on the above experimental results we conclude that using the lognormal model is more accurate and simpler in terms of number of predictors than using normal model. So that we can choose the mixture of two linear regression with 11 predictors and use it for the next set of experiments.

Table 4. The EM parameters' estimates for a mixture of linear regression assuming lognormal distribution.

	1st component	2nd component
intercept	3.4875	3.9663
$x^{ins}_{(to-25)}$	−0.0003	−0.0001
$x^{ins}_{(to-20)}$	−0.0002	0.0001
$x^{ins}_{(to-15)}$	0.0001	−0.0001
$x^{ins}_{(to-10)}$	0.0000	0.0000
$x^{ins}_{(to-5)}$	0.0020	0.0026
$x^{his}_{(to)}$	0.0017	−0.0002
$x^{his}_{(to+5)}$	0.0036	0.0010
$x^{his}_{(to+10)}$	0.0028	0.0012
$x^{ins}_{(to+15)}$	0.0013	−0.0008
$x^{his}_{(to+20)}$	−0.0022	0.0011
$x^{ins}_{(to+25)}$	0.0028	−0.0003
σ^2_j	0.1008	0.0222
λ_j	0.4655	0.5345

6.2 Travel Time Reliability

Travel time reliability is the form of information that we can convey to traveler using the travel time model. Using the proposed model, we can provide the traveler what are the probabilities of congestion and free flow. Moreover, the expected and 90% percentile travel time for each regime can be provided. In order to get good estimates for the above quantities, the proportions should be a function of the predictor which means it varies depending on the values of the predictors. Revisiting the EM algorithm, it estimates the posterior probabilities w_{ij} and the model parameters ψ and returns only ψ at convergence and does not use w_{ij}. As shown in Eq. (4), the returned λ_j is an average of the posterior probabilities w_{ij}. In the two component models, if we modeled w_{ij} using logistic regression at the convergence of the EM, this means that λ_j becomes a function of the predictors as well as the components' means. The final w_{ij} obtained while fitting the model described in Table 4 are used to build a logistic regression. This logistic regression models the probability of predictor vector being drawn from component number two. Then using simple algebra manipulation, we got the coefficient of the logistic model for λ_2 which are shown in Table 5. Now, the new model is exactly the model in Table 4 but with variable λ_2 and λ_1.

Table 5. The estimated coefficient for the logistic model for λ_2.

Predictors	Coefficient
intercept	−12.1702
$x^{ins}_{(to-10)}$	−0.0046
$x^{ins}_{(to-5)}$	0.0354
$x^{his}_{(to)}$	0.0890
$x^{his}_{(to+15)}$	0.0476
$x^{his}_{(to+20)}$	−0.1015
$x^{his}_{(to+25)}$	0.0718

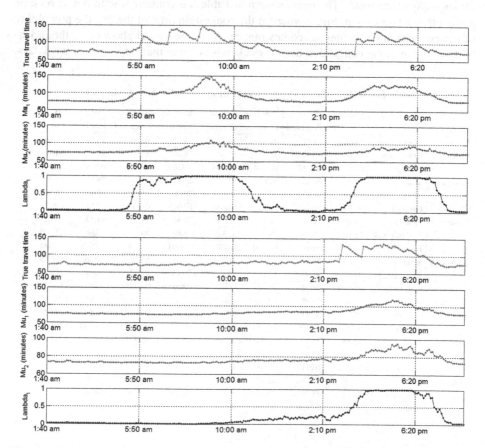

Fig. 4. The ground truth travel time (red curve), the mean of each component of the proposed model (blue curves), and the λ_1 which is the congestion probability for two different days. The upper panel is weekday and the bottom panel is a weekend day (Color figure online).

We tested the proposed model by visually inspect the ground truth travel time for each day and the mean of each component as well as the λ_1, which is the probability of congestion in the fitted model. We visually check if the value of λ_1 is large at the time when the ground truth becomes large. As shown in Fig. 4 for weekday (top panel), there are two peaks at morning and evening and at the same time the values of λ_1 approach one which means the probability of congestion is high. The bottom panel shows a weekend where this no morning congestion but there is an evening congestion and λ_1 has only high values at the evening peak.

In order to better test the proposed model, we calculate the mean, 90% percentile, and probabilities of congestion and free flow for each predictor vector in each day of May 2013. Then based on the curves in Fig. 2, we divided the day into four time interval and calculated the mean of the above quantities within each time interval given for each day of the weak. The result shown in Table 6 is consistent with the travel time pattern that we observe in Fig. 2 where at the congestion time of the day the probability of the congestion component becomes higher. Also, the model shows that the probability of the morning congestion during weekends is lower than its values at weekdays.

Table 6. Testing the model for travel time reliability using May 2013.

		1:40 am – 4:55 am		5:00 am – 10:00 am		10:05 am – 3:00 pm		3:05 am – 7:00 pm	
		Free-flow	Congested	Free-flow	Congested	Free-flow	Congested	Free-flow	Congested
Sunday	Mean	73.05	75.17	73.15	74.73	75.82	80.76	76.24	82.90
	90% percentile	75.16	85.54	75.27	85.04	78.05	91.94	78.46	94.44
	Probability	0.9853	0.0147	0.9864	0.0136	0.8769	0.1231	0.7993	0.2007
Monday	Mean	73.00	74.62	82.07	95.92	75.71	77.99	78.85	91.50
	90% percentile	75.10	84.92	84.76	109.61	78.00	88.81	81.23	104.69
	Probability	0.9876	0.0124	0.3014	0.6986	0.9014	0.0986	0.4528	0.5472
Tuesday	Mean	73.05	74.83	86.19	107.37	76.15	79.69	81.13	98.82
	90% percentile	75.16	85.16	89.02	123.02	78.46	90.81	83.60	113.27
	Probability	0.9859	0.0141	0.1140	0.8860	0.8604	0.1396	0.2819	0.7181
Wednesday	Mean	73.06	74.58	83.52	102.16	76.85	80.26	84.26	105.49
	90% percentile	75.17	84.87	86.16	117.00	79.13	91.42	86.91	120.88
	Probability	0.9874	0.0126	0.1823	0.8177	0.8525	0.1475	0.1676	0.8324
Thursday	Mean	73.02	74.58	84.54	106.41	77.61	82.37	85.91	112.97
	90% percentile	75.13	84.87	87.24	121.97	79.95	93.93	88.59	129.16
	Probability	0.9874	0.0126	0.1352	0.8648	0.7630	0.2370	0.0709	0.9291
Friday	Mean	72.88	74.37	76.93	85.48	75.78	80.43	85.92	111.09
	90% percentile	74.98	84.64	79.24	97.69	78.02	91.62	88.57	127.15
	Probability	0.9888	0.0112	0.6883	0.3117	0.8689	0.1311	0.0733	0.9267
Saturday	Mean	73.00	74.78	73.03	75.00	75.89	82.75	80.59	97.49
	90% percentile	75.11	85.09	75.14	85.36	78.11	94.19	83.04	111.24
	Probability	0.9870	0.0130	0.9837	0.0163	0.8343	0.1657	0.2593	0.7407

7 Conclusions

In this paper, we proposed a travel time model based on mixture of linear regressions. We compared two models using two different predictor sets. The first model assumes the distribution of each component in the mixture follows the normal distribution.

The second model uses the log-normal distribution instead of the normal distribution. The experimental results show that the model that uses the log-normal distribution and the historical and instantaneous travel time predictors is better than the other model. The proposed model can capture the stochastic nature of the travel time. The two-component model assigns one component to the uncongested regime and the other component to the congested regime. The means of the components are a function of various input predictors. The proposed model can be used to provide travel time reliability information at any time-of-the-day for any day-of-the-week if the predictor vector is available. The experimental results show promising performance of the proposed algorithm.

The current model does not consider the weather condition, assumes no incidents, or work zones; however this model has the ability to easily integrate these factors if the historical data includes these variables. Our future work will focus on extending, the proposed model to include these factors and study their effect on the travel time distribution.

References

1. Rice, J., van Zwet, E.: A simple and effective method for predicting travel times on freeways. IEEE Trans. Intell. Transp. Syst. **5**(3), 200–207 (2004)
2. Zhang, X., Rice, J.A.: Short-term travel time prediction. Transp. Res. Part C **11**(3–4), 187–210 (2003)
3. Kwon, J., Coifman, B., Bickel, P.: Day-to-day travel-time trends and travel-time pre- diction from loop-detector data. Transp. Res. Record: J. Transp. Res. Board **1717**(1), 120–129 (2000)
4. Chakroborty, P., Kikuchi, S.: Using bus travel time data to estimate travel times on urban corridors. Transp. Res. Record: J. Transp. Res. Board **1870**(1), 18–25 (2004)
5. Guin, A., Laval, J., Chilukuri, B.R.: Freeway Travel-time Estimation and Forecasting (2013)
6. Guo, F., Li, Q., Rakha, H.: Multistate travel time reliability models with skewed component distributions. Transp. Res. Record.: J. Transp. Res Board. **2315**(1), 47–53 (2012)
7. Oda, T.: An algorithm for prediction of travel time using vehicle sensor data. In: Third International Conference on Road Traffic Control (1990)
8. Iwasaki, M., Shirao, K.: A short term prediction of traffic fluctuations using pseudo-traffic patterns. In: The Third World Congress on Intelligent Transport Systems, Orlando, Florida (1996)
9. D'Angelo, M., Al-Deek, H., Wang, M.: Travel-time prediction for freeway corridors. Transp. Res. Rec.: J. Transp. Res. Board **1676**(1), 184–191 (1999)
10. Al-Deek, H.M., D'Angelo, M.P., Wang, M.C., Travel time prediction with non-linear time series. In: Fifth International Conference on Applications of Advanced Technologies in Transportation Engineering, Newport Beach, California (1998)
11. Williams, B., Hoel, L.: Modeling and forecasting vehicular traffic flow as a seasonal ARIMA process: theoretical basis and empirical results. J. Transp. Eng. **129**(6), 664–672 (2003)
12. Cherrett, T.J., Bell, H.A., McDonald, M.A.: The use of SCOOT type single loop detectors to measure speed, journey time and queue status on non SCOOT controlled links, In: Proceedings of the Eighth International Conference on Road Traffic Monitoring and Control (1996)

13. Rilett, L., Park, D.: Direct forecasting of freeway corridor travel times using spectral basis neural networks. Transp. Res. Rec. J. Transp. Res. Board. **1752**(1), 140–147 (2001)
14. Matsui, H.F.M.: Travel time prediction for freeway traffic information by neural network driven fuzzy reasoning. In: Himanen, V., Nijkamp, P., Reggiani, A. (eds.) Neural Networks in Transport Applications. CRC Prss, Boca Raton (1998)
15. You, J., Kim, T.J.: Development and evaluation of a hybrid travel time forecasting model. Transp. Res. Part C **8**(1–6), 231–256 (2000)
16. Guiyan, J., Ruoqi, Z.: Travel time prediction for urban arterial road. In: Proceedings of Intelligent Transportation Systems. IEEE (2003)
17. Guiyan, J., Ruoqi, Z.: Travel-time prediction for urban arterial road: a case on China. In: Proceedings of the IEEE International Vehicle Electronics Conference, IVEC 2001 (2001)
18. Wei, C.-H., Lin, S.-C., Lee, Y.: Empirical validation of freeway bus travel time forecasting. Transp. Planning. J. **32**, 651–679 (2003)
19. Kisgyorgy, L., Rilett, L.R.: Travel time prediction by advanced neural network. Periodica Polytech., Chem. Eng. **46**, 15–32 (2002)
20. Kisgyörgy, L., Rilett, L.R.: Travel time prediction by advanced neural network. Civ. Eng. **46**(1), 15–32 (2002)
21. De Veaux, R.D.: Mixtures of linear regressions. Comput. Stat. Data Anal. **8**(3), 227–245 (1989)
22. Faria, S., Soromenho, G.: Fitting mixtures of linear regressions. J. Stat. Comput. Simul. **80**(2), 201–225 (2009)
23. Breiman, L.: Random forests. Mach. Learn. **45**(1), 5–32 (2001)
24. INRIX 2012. http://www.inrix.com/trafficinformation.asp
25. Elhenawy, M., Hassan, A.A., Rakha, H.A.: Travel time modeling using spatiotemporal speed variation and a mixture of linear regressions. In: 4th International Conference on Vehicle Technology and Intelligent Transport Systems (VEHITS), Funchal, Madeira-Portugal (2018)

Survey of Passengers' Origin-Destination in Public Transportation Networks Using Wi-Fi

João Ribeiro[1,3], André Zúquete[2,3,4(✉)], and Susana Sargento[2,3]

[1] University of Aveiro, 3810-193 Aveiro, Portugal
[2] Department of Electronics, Telecommunications and Informatics,
University of Aveiro, 3810-193 Aveiro, Portugal
andre.zuquete@ua.pt
[3] Instituto de Telecomunicações, University of Aveiro, 3810-193 Aveiro, Portugal
[4] Institute of Electronics and Informatics Engineering of Aveiro,
University of Aveiro, 3810-193 Aveiro, Portugal

Abstract. The knowledge of Origin-Destination (OD) locations of passengers using public transports is an important instrument to improve the service provided. In this paper, we describe a system that uses the passengers' devices with an enabled Wi-Fi interface to track them along a transportation trip in order to infer OD information. The system does not require the cooperation of passengers other than having a device with an enabled Wi-Fi interface. The tracking system preserves the privacy of passengers, since no centrally stored raw data has any device-specific information. We deployed a prototype of the system in a bus of Porto's public transportation network, which along several months collected 165161 passengers' OD locations. A posterior analysis of the data gathered revealed the presence of false positives, which required the enforcement of filtering procedures in order to get values that are more reasonable for extracting relevant OD information. A comparison of bus occupancy loads of several weekdays during rush hours allowed us to find some patterns, which are an evidence of the correctness of the OD information extracted.

Keywords: Origin-Destination locations · Vehicle occupancy load · 802.11 · Wi-Fi · Public transportation

1 Introduction

To better understand the necessities of passengers it is crucial for the providers of transportation services to have access to data regarding the use of their services, typically represented as Origin-Destination (OD) matrices [1]. In some systems part of this data can be easily acquired (by the purchase of tickets, for example), however in most cases, particularly in transports that do not control when people leave them, it is difficult to accurately know how passengers actually exploit the service.

© Springer Nature Switzerland AG 2019
B. Donnellan et al. (Eds.): SMARTGREENS 2018/VEHITS 2018, CCIS 992, pp. 367–388, 2019.
https://doi.org/10.1007/978-3-030-26633-2_18

Transportation systems tend nowadays to use tokens that can be used to purchase several services. For example, Radio Frequency Identification (RFID) cards can be used to purchase several trips to different locations. The wide variety of possible destinations requires the system to generalize the services, such as grouping possible origin and destinations by area. This poses a problem, since users will always use their card on entering a transportation vehicle, in order to pay for the trip, but they usually do not need to use it on exit (except in some rare cases), making therefore difficult to accurately know where they left the vehicle. This is particularly relevant on public bus transportation systems, which are required to provide a wide variety of possible origins and destinations.

This work attempts to solve this issue by proposing a system that is able to provide accurate OD matrices by indirectly gathering the routes used by bus passengers using a nowadays popular communication technology, Wi-Fi. This paper describes with greater detail the system that was first presented by Ribeiro et al. [2].

1.1   Contribution

The system that we developed collects all kinds of Wi-Fi communications, in all channels, that occur in the vicinity of a bus. It uses the MAC (Medium Access Control) addresses of Wi-FI communications to identify potential passengers. Each collected communication is first analyzed, in order to evaluate its suitability, and suitable samples are recorded together with the time and location of their collection. Traveling paths are formed by two collected samples, one where the device first appeared, the other where the device was listen for the last time. The collected paths are then uploaded to a central repository, upon a proper anonymization. Therefore, no tracing of people is possible using the data stored in the central repository.

Since radio waves cross the boundaries of the transportation vehicle, our system is prone to false positives, i.e., it may consider people out of the vehicle of interest as its passengers. Consequently, we developed several strategies for filtering them out. One of them was to stop the collection process whenever the bus speed is below a given threshold (because otherwise it would enable people outside the bus to be listen for a long time). The other strategy consisted in filtering the collected paths in order to discard those too short in time or distance (which could yield sporadic proximities of cars and buses). Still, we have no means to prevent a person with more than one Wi-Fi enabled device to be counted as more than one.

Our system is also prone to false negatives, since we cannot count people not carrying a Wi-Fi enabled device. While most people carry a mobile phone nowadays, not everybody have their Wi-Fi interface active when travelling, mainly because they can save battery if not expecting to be able to use Wi-Fi networks. Such false negatives affect the precision of occupancy levels, since a vehicle may have more passengers than the ones that are detected. However, they have a lower impact on the gathering of OD matrices, since they reduce the population of the matrices but do not interfere with the detected paths.

The system also includes a strategy, Fake Network Advertisement (FNA), which was meant to force the discovery of otherwise undetectable devices (i.e., devices with an enabled Wi-Fi interface but not sending any frames). In the real deployment scenario it proved to work, but its benefits are small (about 2% more devices were discovered because of FNA).

A prototype of the collecting system was developed, using a RaspberryPi and an external Global Positioning System (GPS) sensor. The collector was deployed on a Porto city bus for several months. From the collected data, and upon their post processing for removing false positives, we could find some similar occupancy levels on some week days, which enables us to conclude that the results obtained are probably legitimate, i.e. in average they yield a percentage of the exact population traveling in the bus.

After the publication of our initial work [2] we got RFID-based ticket validation logs for the bus and period of interest. Such data was meant to establish a ground truth for further asserting the quality of our observations. Unfortunately, such data contains false negatives, since a possibly significant amount of passengers were not counted by the RFID-based ticketing system (they payed for paper tickets in the bus itself, and no detailed logs exist for such activity). Therefore, the combined analysis of our data, that contains false positives and negatives, with the ticketing data, which contains false negatives, is still work in progress.

2 Related Work

In this section we identify other contributions that attempted to use equal or similar communication means, such as Wi-Fi and Bluetooth, respectively, to track passengers on transportation vehicles.

Abedi et al. [3] performed a study to evaluate Wi-Fi and Bluetooth WLAN (Wireless Local Area Network) technologies as a way of detecting devices used by people. The authors performed studies regarding discovery time and popularity of use. Wi-Fi surpassed Bluetooth on both metrics, registering an average discovery time of 1.4 s, while Bluetooth registered 10.6 s. On the popularity test, Wi-Fi was responsible for 92% of the total amount of devices detected by both WLAN technologies.

Musa and Eriksson [4] used similar concepts to track devices inside moving vehicles. Their approach included interesting techniques to increase the amount of data received. These techniques are mostly aimed at increasing the rate of frames received from devices as opposed to our objective, increasing the amount of devices detected. A variation of one of those techniques, Popular SSID AP Emulation, is the FNA implemented in our system. While they implemented their with a fully functional Access Point (AP), our system only emitted beacon frames to tease otherwise silent devices.

Kostakos et al. [5] proposed a solution to obtain the OD matrix by using Bluetooth technology. This solution could accurately determine a user's origin and destination on a trip. However, the percentage of detected passengers was low, approximately 9.7% passengers were detected. The authors state that the low amount of passengers detected is due to the fact that a passenger is required to have a device with Bluetooth active and set to discoverable mode, which according to [6] only 7.5% of individuals do.

Bullock et al. [7] deployed a tracking system at the new Indianapolis international Airport to measure passenger transit times between security checkpoints. This work is also based on Bluetooth, and it also exhibited a low success rate: only 5% to 6.8% of individuals were detected.

Shlayan et al. [8] proposed a system using Bluetooth and Wi-Fi technology in order to estimate the OD matrices and wait-times. The authors performed 2 pilot tests of the system in New York, one at the Atlantic Avenue Subway Station (aimed at subway systems) and another at the Port Authority Transit Facility (aimed at pedestrian flows). The approach chosen by the authors was different than ours: they relied on positioning Bluetooth and Wi-Fi sensors in stations, and not in transportation vehicles as in our system. Similarly to [5], the results show a small amount of devices detected by Bluetooth: less than 4% of all detected devices in 2 separate tests. Therefore, they concluded that Wi-Fi is a far more viable alternative.

This particular study only considered network probing requests in Wi-Fi (which can limit the sample size of obtained results) and encryption was necessary to anonymize the records (due to the nature of the implemented system architecture). On the contrary, we used all kinds of Wi-Fi communications to infer the presence of a personal device and our records are not encrypted, since they are fully anonymized once they leave the collecting device.

Finally, Abedi [3], Schauer [9], Yuan [10] and Chilipirea et al. [11] used Bluetooth or Wi-Fi for monitoring crowds, but they were concerned with counting people moving in open areas, and not with people traveling inside a transportation vehicle.

3   Proposed Solution

The proposed system architecture aims to create a client-server system in which the client is a Data Collector system responsible for collecting data regarding the presence of passengers in a public transportation vehicle, along with its own geographic position history to facilitate data analysis. The Data Collector is also responsible for relaying this information to a central Server. The Server is responsible for processing, storing, exporting and presenting such data (see Fig. 1).

The Data Collector is formed by three major modules:

Capture Module – It implements the capture process, being responsible for capturing frames and generating passenger route records using this information;

Control Module – It is responsible for assessing the status of the vehicle where the Data Collector is deployed, and controlling accordingly the execution of the Capture module. It is also responsible for sending collected data to a Server;

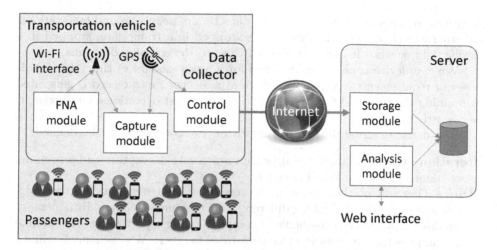

Fig. 1. Architecture of the proposed system.

FNA Module – It is responsible for advertising fake networks, in order to detect otherwise silent devices.

The server is formed by two major modules:

Storage Module – It implements the reception of data gathered by several Data Collectors and its storage in a persistent repository;

Analysis Module – It implements a data analysis interface, in order to extract relevant information and conclusions from the collected data.

3.1   Capture Algorithm

The proposed solution is centered on a capture algorithm, implemented by the Capture module, that is able to detect devices with 802.11 Wi-Fi capabilities and use that information, along with GPS information, to produce passengers' route records.

The algorithm relies on detecting devices with an enabled Wi-Fi interface by capturing frames in all of the available Wi-Fi channels (by sequentially hopping through them all) and identifying them by MAC address (either source or destination addresses). Devices' detection is coupled with a timestamp, which allows the algorithm to estimate when a device has entered and left the bus (first and last detections, respectively).

This detection algorithm is complemented by another one, implemented by the Control module, which is also able to suspend the capture of frames to prevent the detection of devices outside the bus. The capture process is suspended during situations in which we is likely to detect an high amount of devices outside of the bus (e.g. when the bus speed is below a set threshold). With this strategy, we are able to avoid a massive detection of people around bus stations, or otherwise close to the bus when it is stopped in a traffic jam, stopped in a traffic light or when it moves at a speed close to the one of pedestrians.

When a device is no longer detected for a given amount of time, if it fulfills a set of requirements (see Sect. 3.2) then a passenger route record is generated containing the time and GPS position of first and last detections. Otherwise, it is discarded.

In order to describe the capture algorithm two concepts must be defined:

Iteration – One iteration of the algorithm represents the capture and processing of frames in a single Wi-Fi channel;

Run – One run of the algorithm represents several iterations of the algorithm being performed (along different Wi-Fi channels) followed by a memory update. A run can be classified as a complete run or a partial run. A complete run implies that an iteration was performed for every Wi-Fi channel, while a partial run implies that one or more iterations were performed (this happens when a stop order is received). If a stop order is received midway through an iteration, it is completed, but no further iterations will be performed on the current run.

The algorithm uses the following set of tables:

Candidates – This table stores device records that have not yet been deemed to have left the bus (ongoing routes);

Exclusion – This table stores records that represent WLAN networks (and their advertising AP) recently collected. The records in this table are only valid for a limited period of time.

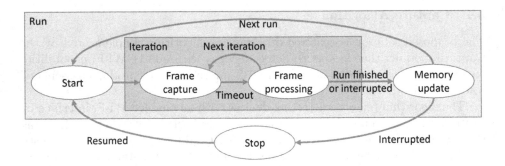

Fig. 2. Finite state machine of the frame capture algorithm.

The capture algorithm was designed as a finite state machine, as represented by Fig. 2, with the following relevant states:

Frame Capture – The Capture module captures frames in a particular Wi-Fi channel for a given fixed period (the iteration period);

Frame Processing – The frames collected in the previous stage are classified as originating from a station (personal device) or AP. By default, all frames are assumed to be from stations, except for frames that are exclusively send by APs (e.g. beacons, probe responses, etc.). Depending on the classification, the MAC address and other relevant information (timestamp and location, for stations) are stored on temporary tables;

Memory Update: The temporary tables populated during the previous stage are used to update the Candidates and Exclusion tables. The Exclusion table is enriched with the new APs detected, while the Candidates table is enriched with all new detected devices that are not already referred in the Exclusion table (thus, they are likely to be stations). The Candidates table is then used to classify devices as inside or outside of the bus.

3.2   Record Validation Algorithm

During the Memory update stage we execute an algorithm to validate each candidate record, in order to conclude if its device has left the bus. Upon such decision, the algorithm also decides if the record is not a potential false positive, in which case it should be discarded. If not, which means it is worth keeping it, the MAC address of its device is removed for protecting the privacy of the device's owner and the record is queued to be uploaded to the Server for being stored (see Fig. 3).

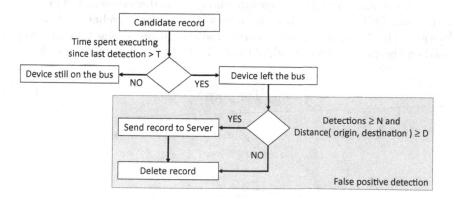

Fig. 3. Flowchart of the record validation algorithm, using a threshold time T for deciding whether or not a device has left the bus, a threshold distance D between the first and the last detection locations and the threshold N for the number of detections of the device.

The validation decision is based on the elapsed time since the last detection of a device. However, we cannot use directly the real elapsed time. In fact, if the detection process is halted for some time due to the slow traveling speed of the bus (e.g. while in a traffic jam), a device could wrongly be considered to have left the bus. In such case, single passengers' paths could be decomposed in many, smaller paths (possibly disjoint) just because of the interference of the bus speed on the collection algorithm. To solve this problem, we use a corrected real time, which is the real time subtracted by an amount equal to the sum of all intervals during which the Capture module remained stopped. Or, on another perspective, the corrected real time is total execution time of the Capture module.

To rule out false positives, the validation algorithm is also based on the likelihood of the record being genuine or relevant for transportation planning. A short traveling distance for a device is a relevant hint for considering the device has being a false positive, i.e., a device that is outside the bus. Furthermore, short traveling distances are usually not critical for transportation planning, since they represent a use of the bus that can easily be replaced by a walk (except if considering disabled or otherwise impaired people). Therefore, the validation algorithm measures the linear distance between the two locations of the record, the one where it was first created and the one where it was updated for the last time, and deletes it if the distance is below a given threshold.

Finally, the validation algorithm discards all records that contain an amount of detections below a given threshold. A natural minimum for this threshold is 2, because we cannot establish a path with a single point. We could not find any reasonable scenarios for using thresholds higher than 2.

3.3   Control Module

The capture algorithm supports suspension in order to disable the capture of frames in situations in which a relevant share of the devices detected are outside of the bus. This happens when the bus is stopped or traveling at low speeds; therefore, the Control module controls the execution of the Capture module based on the bus' current speed, obtained by GPS, as depicted in Fig. 4.

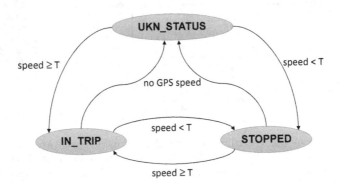

Fig. 4. Finite state machine of the Control module, that controls the execution of the Capture module.

Whenever the Control module enters the IN_TRIP state, the Capture module is signaled to execute. When the remaining states are entered, that module's execution is suspended.

3.4   Fake Network Advertisement (FNA) Module

Passive devices are those that do not pro-actively search for known networks (i.e., for networks preset in the themselves). Because of such behavior, remain silent until listening for the advertisement of those networks.

FNA defines a strategy developed to capture frames from passive devices. This strategy consists on advertising a set of popular Wi-Fi networks, since users tend to have these networks' configurations saved in their devices.

Therefore, a passive device which stays silent, but has previously been associated to those networks, will tend to send a probe request or authentication request to them when they are advertised and result in being detected by the collector, which otherwise would not happen. Upon the reception of the probe request or authentication request, the collector will not respond to the device.

Table 1 displays the Service Set Identifier (SSID) of some of the networks that can be advertised using FNA, representing popular WiFi networks in Portugal.

Table 1. SSID of popular Wi-Fi networks in Portugal that can be used for FNA.

Domestic	Transportation	Other
FON_ZON_FREE_INTERNET	STCP Free WiFi	eduroam
NOS_WIFI_FON	FON ZON Free	guest-eduroam
MEO-WiFi	CP IAB	eduroam-guest
MEO-WiFi-Premium	VINCI Airports	guest-ULisboa
Cabovisao WiFi		
Go Wi-Fi Free & Fast		

This strategy cannot interfere with legitimate APs advertising those networks, therefore a fake network advertisement is only performed if there is no record of an AP advertising the same network in the Exclusion table.

The FNA module advertises these networks in parallel with the execution of the capture algorithm; the networks are advertised using the same interface used to capture frames. This increases the chances to detect passive devices, while slightly decreasing the total time devoted to capturing frames.

This FNA module is also responsible for the maintenance of the records in the Exclusion table. This mainly consists on deleting records that have surpassed a given lifetime threshold.

In order to implement the FNA, it is required to use an 802.11 Wi-Fi adapter that is capable of sending frames while in monitor mode (the one that needs to be used for capturing all frames transmitted in a single channel).

4   Implementation

4.1   Data Collector

We developed a prototype Data Collector using a RaspberryPi Model b+, a GPS receiver, a power converter and a couple of Wi-Fi USB dongles. One of the Wi-Fi interfaces will be used to capture 802.11 frames and the other will be used to connect to some nearby AP, responsible for providing Internet connectivity, in order to send the data to the server.

In our deployment of the Data Collector we used an STCP bus. All STCP buses are equipped with an AP that provides free Internet access to bus passengers through the Veniam's network; therefore, we used this AP for reaching our Server. The Veniam's AP uses a captive portal paradigm for logging in. Since the Data Collector system runs without human supervision, we built some shell scripts for dealing with the HTTP-based authentication in Veniam's Captive Portal.

In order to create a Data Collector that encapsulates all of the requirements and modules described, we developed a concurrent system in which the several required activities cooperate. A simplified version of the Data Collector's software architecture is displayed in Fig. 5. The ovals represent modules that operate concurrently, each with an execution thread. The solid rectangles represent record tables which are accessed by multiple modules and require multiple exclusive access properties in order to maintain data consistency. The dashed rectangles represent tables of records only accessed by one module, which therefore do not require synchronized accesses.

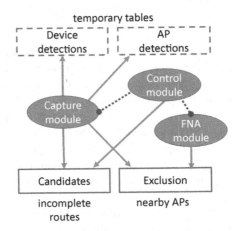

Fig. 5. Simplified Data Collector software architecture. Rectangles represent record tables and ovals represent action threads executed by modules. The arrows represent read or write operations of the threads in tables, while dotted lines represent control actions.

Not represented in Fig. 5, but still present in the system, is the availability of the current GPS position for all of the entities of the system.

The Control module possesses another thread to send the data collected to the Server. This thread moves records that are ready to be sent from the Candidates table to a transmission buffer, which is flushed to the server upon reaching a minimum set of records on it.

In our Data Collector we defined the time interval for the capture of 802.11 frames as 1 s, which, in most cases, is enough to capture beacons from nearby APs and traffic from active station devices.

Our implementation of the record validation algorithm uses the values displayed in Table 2.

Table 2. Parameters used in the record validation algorithm.

Parameter	Value set
T (minimum travel time)	600 s (10 min)
N (minimum number of detections)	2 detections
D (minimum travel distance)	100 m

Our implementation also uses a lifetime of 5 min for the records in the Exclusion table.

The Data Collector also generates, and uploads to the Server, a stream of waypoints, which are of tuples formed by a GPS location and a timestamp. These waypoints are collected each 15 s and help to contextualise the trip being performed by the vehicle where it is installed. As we will see in Sect. 4.4, these waypoints are fundamental for extracting valid information from the collected passengers' records.

4.2 Server

Our system relies on a central Server to store the data collected. The raw data from Data Collectors is received by a TCP/IP server daemon (the Storage module) and then stored in a *postgresql* database, as displayed in Fig. 6.

The Server's Analysis module is the system's component that capitalizes on the raw data generated by Data Collectors, using different heuristics and filtering processes in order to produce useful information. The module was implemented as a Web server, using Django and Apache, and several complementary scripts. The scripts produce auxiliary information extracted from the raw data, such as all the identified bus trips.

4.3 Web Interface

The Web interface presents several views relatively to the raw data gathered and the information produced by scripts. We have views that present the raw data

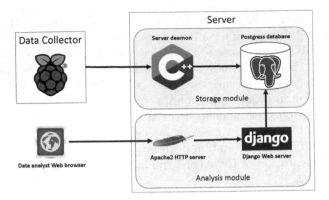

Fig. 6. Server implementation technological overview.

in the appropriate context (e.g. bus waypoints in a map) and other views that present high-level information extracted from the raw data (e.g. OD matrices and bus occupancy charts).

One of the functions of the Web interface is to present a bus trip on a map in a given period of time (see Fig. 7). The trip is a polyline displayed on a street map, which endpoints have the GPS coordinates of the subset of waypoints produced by the Data Collector during the selected period.

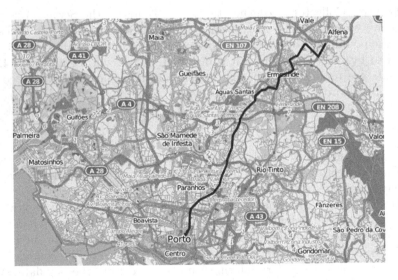

Fig. 7. Example of a bus trip, along line 701, displayed on the Server's Web interface.

Another function of the Web interface is to present raw OD vectors over a map (see Fig. 8). These vectors are not one per detected passenger, but the set of OD choices of passengers that entered and left the vehicle during a selected period. For computing the vectors we first adjust the real OD coordinates to a grid (using a 10 m squared grid) and the intensity of the OD vector reflects the number of passengers with the same OD locations.

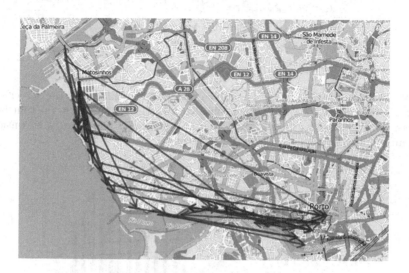

Fig. 8. OD vectors observed during a given period. The color intensity reflects the number of passengers with the same OD locations. The geographical coordinates of the raw OD data were adjusted to a 10 m squared grid for allowing the aggregation of passengers.

Another function of the Web interface is to presented a graphical representation of the bus occupancy load in a given defined period of time. The occupancy load for a time instant is calculated by adding the amount of routes with an origin time before such instant and a destination time posterior to such instant.

The interface has the capability to show different kinds of graphics relatively to bus occupancy loads. One type shows both a curve using all collected records (raw readings) and another curve using a subset of those records that were considered as correct after some filtering (see next section), as displayed in Fig. 9. This allows data analysts to assert the impact of their processing choices in the information outcome.

Another type shows a bus occupancy load, for a given set of parameters for filtering false positives, of a particular bus trip (see Fig. 10).

Finally, another function of the Web interface is to present OD matrices. These matrices can be produced for a single bus trip or for many trips along a time period. In Fig. 11 we present an example of a OD matrix obtained for a single trip.

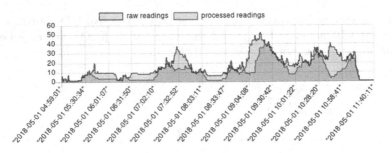

Fig. 9. Bus occupancy load chart for a given time period displayed on the Server's Web interface. The curve with higher values considers all collected records in the time period (raw readings); the other curve only considers a subset of them that was considered valid after a filtering process (processed readings).

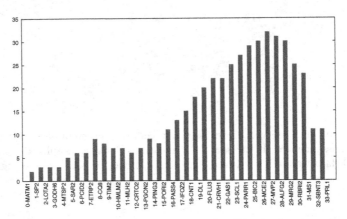

Fig. 10. Example of a bus occupancy load chart of a single trip displayed on the Server's Web interface (borrowed from [2]). This particular one is for the bus line 500 between Matosinhos to Praça da Liberdade.

4.4 Analysis Procedures

In this section we will describe the actions taken by the Analysis module in order to extract useful information from the raw data collected by Data Collectors installed in buses.

Our goal was to produce an OD matrix each time a bus performs a trip along the full length of a bus line. These matrices can then be manipulated using simple algebra to fit the bus network planners' requirements. The construction of those matrices is responsibility of the Analysis module, using the raw data provided by Data Collectors and stored by the Server's Storage Module (see Fig. 1).

The Data Collector that we have implemented has no contextual notion of bus lines. Namely, it does not now if it is travelling along a bus line or any other path, it does not know which bus stops exist and where they are. Part of this information could be easily provided by the bus driver, but in our case

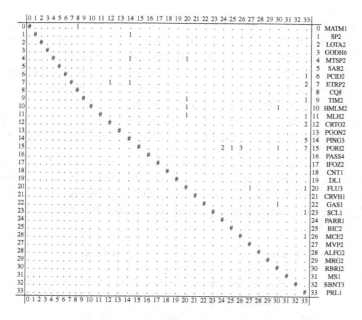

Fig. 11. Example of an OD matrix for a single bus trip. This particular one is for the bus line 500 between Matosinhos and Praça da Liberdade.

we used an unattended device. Therefore, to be able to generate bus passengers' OD matrices for each and every bus trip, we must use a strategy to convert the geographical coordinates of the passengers' data collected to a finite coordinate system: a bus trip along a line and its stops. This is a multi-step process that is performed over the collected data, and it may be modified at any time for improving the quality of the extracted information.

The first step consists is the identification of the bus trip that each detected passenger should be bound to. A bus trip is a tuple formed by tree values: a bus line number, the direction (from A to B or from B to A) and the initial and final timestamps. We used the periodical waypoints of the collecting device and a extra tool [12] to extract its bus trips.

Along with the identification of each bus trip in terms of time, we also find a single timestamp for each bus stop along that trip. Using a list of GPS coordinates of all the bus stops along the bus line, we find the closest waypoint to each bus stop and use its timestamp as the bus stop timestamp. This will latter be used to extract passengers' OD information.

The second step consists on binding each detected passenger to each identified bus trip. In most cases this process is straightforward: for each passenger datum, we look for a trip that started before the first detection of the passenger and ended after the last detection of the passenger. However, some abnormal cases may occur and we had to deal with them.

Abnormal cases occur when passengers' data does not fit into any of the trips. Two cases may occur (see Fig. 12):

- They were detected before the start of a bus trip and stopped being detected before the end of that trip. This can happen when we have a bus stop that is simultaneously the start of a line in one direction and the end of the same line in the other direction. In such cases, a passenger waiting in the bus stop may be detected before the end the previous trip of the bus.
- They were detected during a bus trip but only stopped being detected after the end of that trip. This can happen when a bus, starting a new trip, detects a former passenger that happens to be nearby, possibly in another bus station.

In both cases the passengers' data need to be corrected, which goes as follows. We measure the difference of each passenger timestamps to the beginning and end of two possible bus trips. The timestamp yielding the lower difference is then corrected to take the start or end time of the correct bus trip.

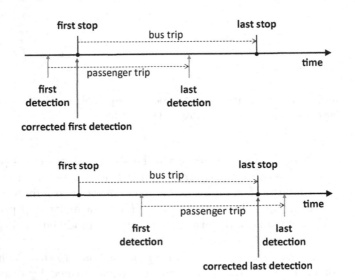

Fig. 12. Correction of passengers' timestamps when not completely fitting into identified bus trips.

The third step consists on binding passengers' geographical locations to actual bus stops. Since we know, from the first step, the code name and the timestamp of each stop on a bus trip, once knowing the bus trips performed by the passengers we can find out the stops where they enter and left the bus. And, once knowing those stops, we can compute the OD matrix for each bus trip.

The discovery of the OD locations uses a straightforward minimum distance approach. Given the set of stops of the line the passenger traveled along, their timestamp is compared with the initial and final timestamps collected for the passenger. The origin bus stop is the closest one, but smaller or equal, than the timestamp of the passenger's first detection. On the contrary, the destination bus

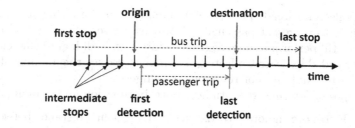

Fig. 13. Computation of OD bus stops from the timestamps where a traveller was first and last detected and the timestamps computed for each stop along a bus trip.

stop is the closest one, but higher or equal, than the timestamp of the passenger's last detection (see Fig. 13).

At the end of this process we have identified all bus trips, we have mapped all detected passengers to a particular bus trip and we have identified their OD values. By adding all OD values in a single matrix we can compute the OD matrix for a particular bus trip or for a bus line.

Once knowing all this information, we can as well compute the occupancy of a bus between stops. Considering a bus trip and all its passengers, the occupancy between stops A and B is given by the number of passengers with an origin before or equal to A and a destination after or equal to B.

5 Results Obtained in a Real Deployment

The Data Collector was deployed on a bus of the STCP (Porto's Public Transport Service[1]) public bus transportation network. A total of 71356 passenger routes were collected in the time period between June 22, 2017 and October 28, 2017. From the collected data we verified that probably not all of its records represented devices inside the bus (at times the bus occupancy load was way above the maximum load capacity), so filtering was applied.

5.1 Raw Data Filtering

After a previous analysis of the data collected, we verified that in some instants an absurd amount of individuals were detected in the bus, mostly likely representing devices outside the bus. This is due to the capture algorithm's inability to differentiate devices inside the bus and outside the bus with complete certainty. The capture algorithm just assumes that if a device is detected long enough while some distance has been traveled, then the device is inside the bus.

As a speculation, we can say that as the amount of distance between origin and destination and time spent on the bus increases for a given device, the chances that the device represents an actual bus passenger bus increases. Therefore, by using higher filtering thresholds than the ones used by the Data Collectors we are able

---

[1] http://www.stcp.pt/.

Data Collectors already perform a minimal filtering for ruling out devices that are not likely to represent passengers. However, those rules may no be enough, and we can still perform a more aggressive filtering, high higher thresholds, over the data provided by Data Collectors, in order to reduce the amount of detected devices that probably do not represent passengers.

Two types of filtering were studied, both in isolation and combined:

Distance Filtering: ignore records with a straight line distance between origin and destination below D;

Time Filtering: ignore records with a time difference between origin and destination below T.

Table 3 represents the impact that some selected filter values have on the total amount of passenger's routes obtained.

Table 3. Effect of filters on the amount of passengers' routes obtained.

Time (seconds)	Distance (meters)			
	0	1000	2000	3000
0	165161 (100.0%)	53721 (32.5%)	34805 (21.1%)	24955 (15.1%)
300	68259 (41.3%)	46589 (28.2%)	34537 (20.9%)	24940 (15.1%)
600	42601 (25.8%)	31189 (18.9%)	28014 (17%)	23614 (14.3%)
900	27942 (16.9%)	21550 (13%)	19739 (12%)	18147 (11%)

We can observe a significant decrease in the total amount of passengers' routes detected when a filter of 1000 m and 300 s is applied. This indicates that there is a high amount of detected devices that were outside the bus. These are mostly detected during short periods of time and have a small distance between origin and destination points.

The usage of this technique can also result in discarding some devices that were inside the bus, but we considered that those records do not have much relevance to the information we want to acquire. A passenger that uses a bus to travel less than 1000 m can possibly cover that distance by foot if necessary. In any case, the information still exists if it is considered to be valid, we just provide the means to selectively discard it in different views.

Note that the values in Table 3 can also be used to have information regarding the amount of time that passenger spend in the bus, and the amount of distance passenger will use the bus for their needs.

We decided to use a 1000 m distance filter along with a 300 s time filter to filter out devices outside of the bus to generate OD matrices. This can result in the exclusion of some legitimate records, however records with values lesser than the ones considered will not have a big impact on the bus network's planning.

Different daily profiles were identified, and the amount of passengers in a day varied between 72 and 4431 passengers. These records have allowed us to successfully generate many OD matrices, such as the one presented in Fig. 11.

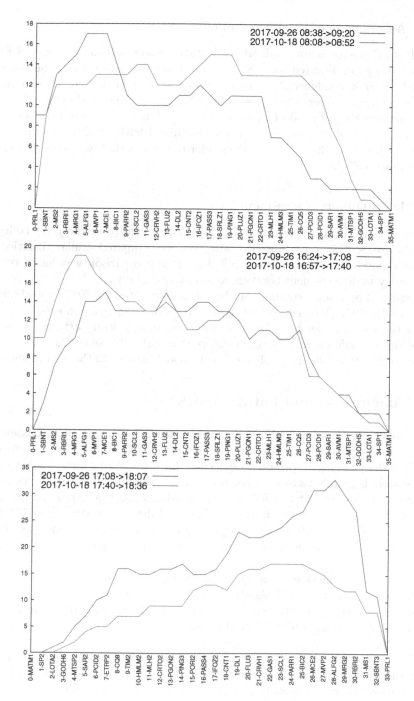

Fig. 14. Comparison of bus occupancy loads by route segment on line 500, obtained for the exact same route, for a similar hour (during rush hours) in two week days, Tuesday and Wednesday (borrowed from [2]).

5.2   Assessment of the FNA Impact

Our Data Collector is able to distinguish stations detected only because of FNA, because they are detected when using exclusively frames to get in contact with our fake beacon producer. This information was kept in the records sent to the Server, so we can assert the relevance of FNA using the stored records.

Analyzing the data collected, we determined that the FNA strategy is responsible for 2.25% of all passengers' routes obtained without filtering and 0.65% using the previous filters. These values refer to devices that were detected exclusively due to FNA.

5.3   Data Quality Assessment

In the absence of a ground truth, to assess the quality of the data collected and the correctness of the posterior analysis, we compared similar situations in different days, but for the same week day. This comparison was based on bus occupancy by line segment between consecutive stations.

Figure 14 represents comparisons between September 26, 2017 (Tuesday) and October 18, 2017 (Wednesday) for similar periods during rush hours.

In these graphs we can observe similar occupancy load patterns in similar situations on different week days of different months. These similarities provide some credibility to the data collected by this system and to the overall solution.

6   Conclusions and Future Work

This paper presented a Wi-Fi based system that is able to collect passengers' routes in public transportation vehicles, namely on buses. The system only requires the passengers' personal devices to have the Wi-Fi interface activated. The system is mainly passive, in the sense that it does not interfere with existing communications, except in the case of the fake network advertisements (FNA strategy), deployed for detecting otherwise silent devices. Nevertheless, the FNA strategy does not introduce any disruption on existing communications, since the fake networks are not announced when there is a real one in the vicinity of the Data Collector.

The system conceived was fully implemented and deployed in a real bus for collecting real data. The Analysis module, together with its Web interface, allowed us to perform multiple analysis of the raw data provided by our deployed Data Collector, in order to validate the its correctness, and produce useful output information.

The obtained results showed a higher number of passengers in the bus than the real ones. This indicated that devices outside the bus were still being detected, which resulted on the need to research additional filtering strategies to be applied to the stored data.

The data collected was filtered and contextualized in order to generate OD matrices. The analysis on the generated OD matrices allowed us to assess the plausibility of the solution and to identify some behaviors and typical passenger routes, which can then be used to improve the service offered by the bus network.

As a side effect of the system, once having OD matrices we can easily compute bus occupancy loads between consecutive stops. Note, however, that such information cannot be computed in real-time, since we do not detect immediately when a passenger leaves the transportation vehicle: this is accomplished only after a period where the respective device is not detected. Nevertheless, given the period the we have used (10 min, see Table 2), we can still detect abnormal occupancy loads with a small delay, which may allow network supervisors to react upon.

Considering the overall results, we observed that Wi-Fi is a promising prospect regarding OD matrix estimation, a powerful resource for public bus networking planning. There is, however, a potential problem that may be created by future privacy enhancements deployed on mobile phones. In fact, some devices already change their MAC address from time to time to avoid being tracked, and this strategy is likely to increase in the future. Fortunately, due to the nature of the Wi-Fi communication model, such MAC address modifications should not take place once a device is connected to a network (because it implies a noticeable disconnection and reconnection). Therefore, the presence of appealing (free) Wi-Fi hotspots on transportation vehicles may reduce the impact of this privacy-enhancing strategy in our tracking system.

For future work we plan to validate the obtained data with ticketing records in buses, in order to assess the relationship between our occupancy loads and the number of passengers' entries on buses. Furthermore, we plan to integrate Data Collectors with information systems that already exist on transportation vehicles. In a bus network such integration would allow us to know, in advance, when the vehicle is in fact being used to transport passengers, the exact instants when it started and stop a trip, and the bus line and direction.

Acknowledgements. This work was supported in part by National Funds through FCT - Fundação para a Ciência e a Tecnologia under the project UID/EEA/50008/2013, in part by the IT Internal Project SmartCityMules and in part by the CMU-Portugal Program through S2MovingCity: Sensing and Serving a Moving City under Grant CMUP-ERI/TIC/0010/2014.

References

1. Ashok, K., Ben-Akiva, M.E.: Dynamic origin-destination matrix estimation and prediction for real- time traffic management systems. In: 12th International Symposium on the Theory of Traffic Flow and Transportation, Berkeley, California, USA (1993)
2. Ribeiro, J., Zúquete, A., Sargento, S.: Survey of public transport routes with Wi-Fi. In: Proceedings of the 4th International Conference on Vehicle Technology and Intelligent Transport Systems (VEHITS 2018), Santa Cruz, Madeira Island, Portugal (2018)

3. Abedi, N., Bhaskar, A., Chung, E.: Bluetooth and Wi-Fi MAC address based crowd data collection and monitoring: benefits, challenges and enhancement. In: 36th Australasian Transport Research Forum (ATRF), Brisbane, Australia (2013)

4. Musa, A.B.M., Eriksson, J.: Tracking unmodified smartphones using Wi-Fi monitors. In: Proceedings of the 10th ACM Conference on Embedded Network Sensor Systems (SenSys 2012), Toronto, Canada, pp. 281–294 (2012)

5. Kostakos, V., Camacho, T., Mantero, C.: Wireless detection of end-to-end passenger trips on public transport buses. In: 13th International IEEE Conference on Intelligent Transportation Systems (ITSC2010), Funchal, Madeira Island, Portugal, pp. 1795–1800 (2010)

6. O'Neill, E., et al.: Instrumenting the city: developing methods for observing and understanding the digital cityscape. In: Dourish, P., Friday, A. (eds.) UbiComp 2006. LNCS, vol. 4206, pp. 315–332. Springer, Heidelberg (2006). https://doi.org/10.1007/11853565_19

7. Bullock, D., Haseman, R., Wasson, J., Spitler, R.: Automated measurement of wait times at airport security: deployment at Indianapolis international airport, Indiana. Transp. Res. Rec.: J. Transp. Res. Board **2177**, 60–68 (2010)

8. Shlayan, N., Kurkcu, A., Ozbay, K.: Exploring pedestrian Bluetooth and WiFi detection at public transportation terminals. In: IEEE 19th International Conference on Intelligent Transportation Systems (ITSC), Rio de Janeiro, Brazil, pp. 229–234 (2016)

9. Schauer, L., Werner, M., Marcus, P.: Estimating crowd densities and pedestrian flows using wi-fi and bluetooth. In: Proceedings of the 11th International Conference on Mobile and Ubiquitous Systems: Computing, Networking and Services, London, United Kingdom, pp. 171–177 (2014)

10. Yuan, Y.: Crowd monitoring using mobile phones. In: Sixth International Conference on Intelligent Human-Machine Systems and Cybernetics (IHMSC 2014), Hangzhou, China, pp. 261–264 (2014)

11. Chilipirea, C., Petre, A.C., Dobre, C., van Steen, M.: Presumably simple: monitoring crowds using WiFi. In: 17th IEEE International Conference on Mobile Data Management (MDM), Porto, Portugal, pp. 220–225 (2016)

12. Ricardo, L., Sargento, S., Oliveira, I.C.: An information system for bus travelling and performance evaluation. In: Proceedings of the 4th International Conference on Vehicle Technology and Intelligent Transport Systems (VEHITS 2018), Santa Cruz, Madeira Island, Portugal (2018)

Author Index

Printed in the United States
By Bookmasters